DEFEATING LEE

DEFEATING LEE

A HISTORY OF THE SECOND CORPS
♣ ARMY OF THE POTOMAC ♣

LAWRENCE A. KREISER, JR.

INDIANA UNIVERSITY PRESS

Bloomington & Indianapolis

This book is a publication of

Indiana University Press
601 North Morton Street
Bloomington, Indiana 47404-3797 USA

First paperback edition 2012
© 2011 by Lawrence A. Kreiser
All rights reserved

Manufactured in the United States of
America

ISBN 978-0-253-00617-2

Book Club Edition

To my grandparents,
William and Vera Eichenberg and Lawrence and Ann Kreiser

CONTENTS

PREFACE

The study of the Union war effort is increasingly filled by unit histories. Books on armies, brigades, and regiments abound, many of them well written and researched.[1] Missing, however, are histories of army corps. No study of an army corps has been published since six written by Union veterans well over one century ago.[2] The oversight is all the more surprising given that many modern-day scholars consider corps as the building blocks of Civil War armies. Corps consisted of two to four divisions and numbered, at any given time, between 10,000 and 30,000 men. Forming the largest organizational divisions within individual Union armies, corps served as the primary means for field commanders to maneuver and fight their forces.

The Union had created nearly forty-five corps by the end of the Civil War, but none achieved the distinction of the Second Corps.[3] Only soldiers in the Second Corps served throughout the war in the Army of the Potomac, the premier Union military force in the eastern theater. The men always seemed to be where the action was the hottest, from storming the Bloody Lane at Antietam on September 17, 1862, to repulsing Pickett's Charge at Gettysburg on July 3, 1863; from capturing the Bloody Angle at Spotsylvania on May 12, 1864, to cutting off the Confederate retreat at Appomattox on April 7, 1865. The Second Corps was also larger than any other Union corps, and by the last year of the war comprised one-quarter of the manpower in the Army of the Potomac.

The illustrious record of the Second Corps came at a high cost. Of the 100,000 men who served during the war, 40,000 were killed, wounded, or captured. These were the highest numerical losses of any

Federal corps. "The Second Corps was prominent by reason of its longer and continuous service, larger organization, hardest fighting, and greatest number of casualties," William Fox, a nineteenth-century authority on the fighting quality of Civil War units, noted. "Within its ranks was the regiment which sustained the greatest numerical loss during its term of service; while of the one hundred regiments in the Union army which lost the most men in battle, thirty-five of them belonged to the Second Corps." The reputation of the soldiers of the Second Corps as hard and skilled fighters endures, with historians ranking the Second Corps as one of the "elite fighting units" of the Union army.[4]

Despite an illustrious record, the Second Corps has found recounting only by Francis Walker. A staff officer throughout much of the war, Walker relied upon his memory and the recollections of his fellow veterans to construct a narrative history, published in 1887. Walker sometimes gave way to his personal involvement with the Second Corps, and bogged down in minute details when defending his former command against some perceived battlefield slight. Walker also assumes his readers are interested only in the war years, and so ends his story in 1865. Yet, simply by writing the history of the Second Corps, Walker offers distinct insight into the Union war effort.

Corps histories are so rare for several reasons. Army corps were large groupings of men, and the level of detail regarding their daily existence is nearly overwhelming. Even Walker was at times driven to distraction by the minutiae. He pleaded that "among so many thousands of separate statements regarding names, numbers, dates, order of events, juxtaposition of troops, direction of movements, etc.," he was certain that he had made some mistakes. He offered that, if so, he had tried his best. Besides the daunting level of detail, corps histories are almost unheard-of because they too easily become tied up in the story of the Union army. Where the army ends and the corps begins becomes almost indistinguishable in describing the outcome of a particular battle or campaign. Even William Fox blurred the lines in summarizing the career of the Second Corps. "The history of the Second Corps," he declared, "was identical with that of the Army of the Potomac."[5]

Rather than simply update Walker, or write a history of the Army of the Potomac by another name, my book takes an analytical approach to the Second Corps. That soldiers of the Second Corps fought from ideological commitment to the Union is the first argument made. These men were not the most likely to become among the most redoubtable fighters in the Union army. Many soldiers of the Second Corps came from Democratic homes and ethnic communities, and they gave little support to the expansion of Federal war aims to include emancipation. Combined with suffering the highest casualty rates in the Union army, soldiers of the Second Corps might quickly have become skittish about seeing the war through. Yet the men reenlisted in large numbers during the winter of 1863–64. That fall, they voted for Abraham Lincoln and the continuation of the war in overwhelming numbers. The commitment displayed by soldiers of the Second Corps adds depth to arguments made by James McPherson and Earl Hess, among others, on the morale of Civil War soldiers. McPherson and Hess have convincingly put to rest earlier arguments that soldiers fought only for their comrades in the ranks, or from misplaced ideals. Rather, soldiers sacrificed much to preserve the ideals and liberties of the American Union for themselves and their families.[6]

The next argument made is that the Second Corps reflected well on the creation of military force by the Union. High-ranking commanders of the Second Corps showed a deft touch in balancing unit cohesion and manpower demands. The Second Corps did not always triumph on the battlefield. But the men fought ferociously far more often than not, allowing the Union to ultimately win the war. This is in contrast to the poor marks that historians often assign to the mobilization of the Union army, when they broach the topic at all. Fred Shannon's work on the organization and administration of the Union army, published in 1928, is still a standard reference in the field, speaking volumes to the lack of scholarly notice.[7]

That soldiers developed a strong sense of pride in the Second Corps is the last argument made. Identity came through hard fighting. Soldiers even came to claim that the vaunted Confederate Army of Northern Virginia feared facing the Second Corps on the battlefield. The men attempted to maintain their hard-won legacy as the war progressed. They often fell into squabbling, sometimes stridently, over battlefield laurels with other members of the Army of the Potomac, and even other members of the Second Corps. Many of these arguments raged well into the postwar era. Corps identity developed more slowly throughout the rest of the Army of the Potomac. The reasons are several, but mainly centered around poor battlefield reputation and political intrigue among high-ranking officers.

My study quickly had to grapple with whether the Second Corps is a sample providing insight into the rest of the Union army or a subject with its own distinct history. The Second Corps is in many ways a sample because, like much of the rest of the Federal army, its soldiers were white, and they were overwhelmingly volunteers. Soldiers also came from every major region of the Union and from nearly every state. In more ways, however, the Second Corps is a subject. Soldiers were cognizant that they were part of an elite group, as expressed by their battle cry, "Clubs are Trump!" A reference by soldiers to the trefoil-shaped badge that they wore, the cry also expressed pride in their battlefield prowess; they were the "trumps," or the best cards, in the deck of the Army of the Potomac.

The history of the Second Corps had four chronological phases. The first phase, explored in chapters 1 and 2, saw the organization of the Second Corps and its first experience of combat during the Peninsula and Maryland Campaigns in the summer and fall of 1862. The second phase, analyzed in chapters 3 and 4, witnessed the rise of the Second Corps to the height of its battlefield success, culminating in the repulse of Pickett's Charge during the Gettysburg Campaign in the summer of 1863. The third phase, analyzed over the next three chapters, involved nearly continuous fighting and rebuilding, from the Overland Campaign in the spring of 1864 to the effective end of the war at Appomattox Court House in the spring of 1865. The last phase, explored in chapter 8, saw veterans attempt to remember their wartime accomplishments and sacrifices. The process occurred most actively through the death of Francis Walker in 1897, thirty-five years after the creation of the Second Corps.

Near the end of the Civil War, Major General Winfield Scott Hancock, the longest-serving commander of the Second Corps and one of the most respected officers in the Union army, assured his men that their battlefield sacrifices would not be forgotten. "The gallant bearing of the intrepid officers and men of the Second Corps on the bloodiest fields of the war," Hancock proudly declared, "[has] won for them an imperishable renown and the grateful admiration of their countrymen. The story of the Second Corps will live in history, and to its officers and men will be ascribed the honor of having served their country with fidelity and courage."[8] Hancock was wrong. Although the formidable reputation of the Second Corps receives mention in studies of the Union war effort, much of its history and accomplishments has suffered neglect. By analyzing the contributions made by soldiers of the Second Corps to defeating General Robert E. Lee and his Army of Northern Virginia, this study seeks to make good on Hancock's promise.

ACKNOWLEDGMENTS

The writing of this book has brought many pleasures, but none as great as the opportunity to thank the many individuals who have helped to bring the project to completion. My colleagues at Stillman College, especially the members of the "Domed Stadium Committee"—R. L. Guffin, Mary Jane Krotzer, and Mark McCormick—have provided much encouragement. I am particularly grateful to Dabney Gray for his humor and willingness to listen. At Indiana University Press, Robert Sloan and Sarah Wyatt Swanson have guided me through the publication process. They have taken a great amount of time to answer my many questions and to keep the project on schedule. Carol Kennedy has greatly improved the manuscript through her copyediting. The many "this is confusing" and "check the spelling" queries strewn across the pages forced me to tighten the writing and saved me from numerous embarrassing mistakes.

Lawrence Kohl championed this book from its beginnings many years ago as a dissertation at the University of Alabama. Professor Kohl always set the bar high. He encouraged me soon after I had entered the graduate program to think about publishing my work. The thought seemed daunting. But Professor Kohl taught me—as well as his other graduate students—how to research and write. The task was not always easy, and burned through many of his differently colored editing pens. His belief in this project never wavered, even when mine sometimes did. More important, Professor Kohl taught me how to be a mentor. He always took my questions seriously, and generously gave me much of his time. Professor Kohl encouraged and inspired and, when necessary, prodded. I only hope that I might pass on to my students some of the many lessons learned.

George Rable read through the manuscript many times, and provided invaluable advice to improve the focus. His comment that I should "recast" this and that paragraph and sentence made the text much more readable. I marvel that Professor Rable so readily gave of his time while maintaining his remarkable pace of scholarship. As a fellow Cleveland Browns fan, Professor Rable sometimes told me that editing chapters on the Second Corps beat listening to the football games. That might be so, at least over the past several seasons, but I appreciate the expertise that he provided. I also thank Howard Jones, Richard Megraw, and Harold Selesky, who read through early versions of the manuscript.

The depth of knowledge and willingness to help of the staff at different repositories struck me often while I conducted research. At the United States Army Military History Institute, Richard Sommers supplied a steady stream of manuscripts, including many that I otherwise might have overlooked. His command of the material, and the Civil War in general, is remarkable. Donald Pfanz generously allowed me access to the treasure trove of materials located at the Fredericksburg and Spotsylvania National Military Park. He also took time from his busy days to talk with me about the Second Corps and its campaigns. Chris Calkins at the Petersburg National Military Park pulled a range of documents for me. He also shared his extensive knowledge on the "dark days" of the Second Corps outside Petersburg during the summer of 1864. Ted Alexander at Antietam National Military Park and the staff at Gettysburg National Military Park graciously allowed me access to a wide range of material when I was on a sometimes too-tight schedule.

The love and support of my parents, Joan and Larry Kreiser, has always been unflagging. Recognizing that, as a child, I had an interest in the Civil War, they went out of their way to take me and my siblings—Catherine, Christopher, and Patrick—on family trips to many of the battlefields. I would be lucky to even come close to emulating their example with my family. My wife's parents, Pat and Ray Browne, always provided encouragement. Ray passed away during the fall of 2009, but he would be delighted, and very proud, that this book finally has gone to print.

My wife, Alicia, means everything to me. Sharing a life with some-one else is easy when the times are good. But Alicia has encouraged me and stood by me when the times were hard. More than anyone else, her faith in me has seen this work through. My daughters, Julia Rae and Anna Catherine, were not even yet born when I began my research on the Second Corps. They have been, and always will be, two of the greatest joys of my life.

ABBREVIATIONS

AAS   American Antiquarian Society, Worcester, Massachusetts

ANMP   Antietam National Military Park, Maryland

B&L   Robert Underwood Johnson and Clarence Clough Buel, eds., *Battles and Leaders of the Civil War,* 4 vols. (New York: Castle Books, 1956)

BPL   Boston Public Library

BRU   Brown University, John Hay Library, Special Collections, Providence, Rhode Island

BU   Boston University, Special Collections, Mugar Memorial Library, Massachusetts

CCW   *Report of the Joint Committee on the Conduct of the War,* 4 vols. (Wilmington, N.C.: Broadfoot, 1998)

CHS   Connecticut Historical Society, Hartford

CL   University of Michigan, William L. Clements Library, Ann Arbor

CWMC   Civil War Miscellaneous Collection

CWTI   *Civil War Times Illustrated* Collection

Duke   Duke University, William R. Perkins Library, Durham, North Carolina

Emory   Emory University, Special Collections, Robert W. Woodruff Library, Atlanta, Georgia

FSNMP   Fredericksburg and Spotsylvania National Military Park, Fredericksburg, Virginia

GNMP   Gettysburg National Military Park, Pennsylvania

IU   Indiana University, Lilly Library, Bloomington

IHS   Indiana Historical Society, Indianapolis

ISL   Indiana State Library, Indianapolis

LC   Library of Congress, Manuscripts Division, Washington, D.C.

MHS   Massachusetts Historical Society, Boston

MNHS   Minnesota Historical Society, St. Paul

NA   National Archives, Washington, D.C.

NC   Navarro College, Pearce Collections, Corsicana, Texas

NHSL   New Hampshire State Library, Concord

NYHS   New-York Historical Society, New York

NYPL   New York Public Library, New York

NYSLA   New York State Library and Archives, Albany

OHS   Ohio Historical Society, Columbus

O.R.   U.S. War Department, *The War of the Rebellion: A Compilation of the Official Records of the Union and Confederate Armies,* 128 vols. (Washington, D.C.: Government Printing Office, 1880–1901). All references are to series I, unless otherwise indicated.

PHMC   Pennsylvania Historical and Museum Commission, Harrisburg

PHS   Pennsylvania Historical Society, Philadelphia

RG   Record Group

RU   Rutgers University, Special Collections, Archibald S. Alexander Library, New Brunswick, New Jersey

TSLA   Tennessee State Library and Archives, Nashville

USAMHI   United States Army Military History Institute, Carlisle Barracks, Pennsylvania

WRHS   Western Reserve Historical Society, Cleveland, Ohio

DEFEATING LEE

THE ORGANIZATION OF
THE SECOND CORPS

The Second Corps officially came into existence on March 8, 1862, when President Lincoln ordered the creation of the first four Union army corps. Yet the history of the Second Corps dates back to the Confederate bombardment of Fort Sumter on April 12, 1861. Over the intervening eleven months, the Union high command debated when to create army corps, how they should be organized, and who should command them. All the while, the soldiers who first served in the Second Corps received their introduction into military life and discussed why they fought. The events that occurred across the Union in 1861 and early 1862 had a significant influence on the Second Corps, and any analysis of its history most properly begins with them.

CREATING THE SECOND CORPS

Major General George McClellan remembered seeing only an armed rabble when he arrived in late July 1861 to take command of the Union forces stationed in and around Washington, D.C. The Union army had suffered a near-rout around Bull Run, Virginia, only a few days earlier, after going into battle for the first time. The results still told when McClellan arrived. Stragglers skulked through the streets of Washington, while their officers found shelter in nearby barrooms. Soldiers who had enlisted for three-month terms of service in the spring, as long as many northerners expected the fighting to last at the time, began to stream home. Everything appeared in disarray. An exasperated

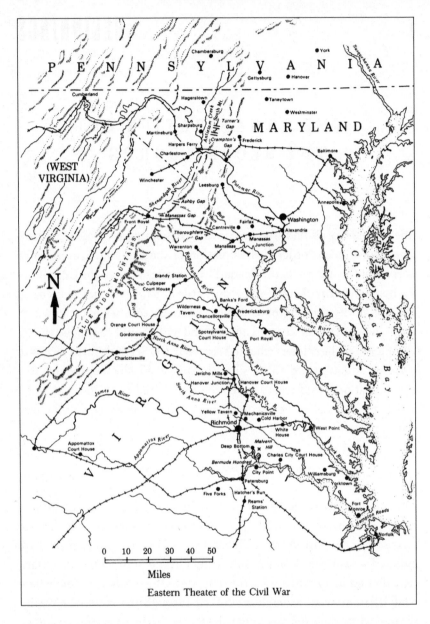

Eastern Theater of the Civil War

The Eastern Theater, 1861–65. Over these grounds, the Second Corps lost more men than any other comparable Union command. Reprinted from David Jordan, *Winfield Scott Hancock: A Soldier's Life*, 41.

McClellan later claimed that he had no army to command, "only a mere collection of regiments cowering on the banks of the Potomac."[1]

McClellan certainly believed himself capable of bringing order from confusion. McClellan was vain and, often, petulant. But he had reason to express pride in his professional accomplishments. Graduating second in his class from West Point in 1846, McClellan had served with distinction as an engineer in the Mexican War. He traveled to Europe in 1855, as part of a commission appointed by the War Department to study military organization and development there. McClellan resigned from the army two years later, to accept a job as chief engineer of the Illinois Central Railroad. Success also came quickly in the civilian world, and by 1861 McClellan served as president of the Ohio and Mississippi Railroad. With the start of the Civil War, McClellan received appointment as the second-ranking officer in the Union army. Assigned to protect the strongly pro-Union residents of western Virginia, McClellan won battlefield victories at Rich Mountain and Corrick's Ford. The two battles marked some of the few Union military successes to date and won McClellan praise across the Union as a "young Napoleon."[2]

The laurels continued outside Washington, where, displaying superb organizational and administrative skills, McClellan built the newly named Army of the Potomac from the ground up. Regiments enlisted for two- and three-year terms of service arrived daily. Regiments fielded ten companies, each with an authorized strength of one hundred officers and enlisted men. McClellan grouped three to four regiments into brigades, a tactical formation most recently employed by Americans during the Mexican War. McClellan brigaded together regiments as they arrived in Washington, a practice with some drawbacks. The battlefield experience varied widely between brigades. Some brigades fielded regiments that all had participated in the Bull Run Campaign. In other brigades, the regiments had only recently arrived in Washington. Soldiers in these units had yet to experience life in the field, let alone the sounds and sights of battle. The payoff to the quick organization of brigades came with the army soon ready to take the field. This was no small consideration to McClellan, who feared that a quick Confederate strike northward might capture Washington. The worry exaggerated Confederate offensive capacities at the time, but McClellan correctly recognized the disaster that such a blow would deal the Union war effort.[3]

Grouping brigades into divisions was the next organizational task to occupy McClellan. He determined assignments by the geographic proximity of brigades in camp to create as little disruption to his deployments as possible. The three brigades that served in Brigadier General Charles Stone's division—and that later fought in the Second Corps—all were stationed along the upper Potomac River when brought together in early October. Stone's command numbered about 11,140 men as created, nearly as large as the American army that had captured Mexico City in 1847. The numbers of men in Stone's division were similar to the other divisions created by McClellan, an indication of the magnitude of the Union war effort in the East. The ten divisions assembled by the late fall of 1861 ranged from the largest (Brigadier General Nathaniel Banks's) at 14,882 men to the smallest (Brigadier General Joseph Hooker's) at 8,342 men.[4]

McClellan began to think about organizing his divisions into army corps by the late summer. First created in the early 1800s by the French emperor Napoleon Bonaparte, army corps had dramatically altered the conduct of war in Europe. Armies to that time had attempted to maneuver massive numbers of men and equipment, sometimes nearing 200,000 soldiers and hundreds of guns, as a single unit. Seeking a war-winning advantage, Napoleon grouped his infantry, cavalry, and artillery into corps that numbered between 20,000 and 40,000 men. These forces maneuvered independently of one another, greatly increasing the French army's operational mobility. Napoleon boasted that, with good leadership, one of his corps "could go anywhere." Napoleon brought his corps back together when battle loomed, thereby gaining the twin benefits of concentration of force and tactical maneuverability. The corps system helped the French to win smashing victories over the Austrians and Russians at Austerlitz in 1805, the Prussians at Jena in 1806, and the Russians again the next year at Friedland. The defeated European powers quickly learned the lesson. Between 1809 and 1815, the Allied nations organized their armies into corps. Campaigns now emphasized material and endurance, rather than decisive battle. By the Battle of Waterloo and the end of the Napoleonic Wars, the use of corps had helped European armies evolve into modern fighting forces.[5]

McClellan recognized the benefit of organizing corps within the Army of the Potomac. He was in uncharted territory, because no previous American army had been large enough to warrant their creation. Not everyone recognized the need for army corps, even as the Union forces swelled in strength. General Winfield Scott, the general in chief of the Union army and the chief military advisor to President Lincoln, argued that the Army of the Potomac need only take the field organized into brigades. Scott was not someone to discount lightly. A veteran of every American war since 1812, Scott had achieved national fame for his bravery and leadership in the Mexican War. McClellan could not see it. Privately he grumbled that Scott "understands nothing, appreciates nothing, and is ever in my way."[6] In meetings with Scott, McClellan correctly pointed out that fighting forces "all the world over" were organized into armies, corps, and divisions. McClellan hardly helped his cause, however, by reminding Scott that the Mexican War was "a very small affair" by comparison to the Civil War. Scott remained unconvinced, perhaps not surprisingly in the face of a perceived professional attack.[7]

The split with Scott became increasingly acrimonious, fueled largely by McClellan. Believing that two generals was one too many to command the Union army, McClellan was determined to come out on top. Here he found unlikely political allies. McClellan was a conservative Democrat, and he fought primarily to preserve the Union. Radical Republicans in Congress, however, called for a no-holds barred struggle to smash the South and destroy slavery. Many Radical congressmen believed Scott too old and feeble to lead a war of conquest. McClellan captured their support by publicly offering that the Army of the Potomac should march quickly and "crush the rebellion at one blow."[8] McClellan could afford such boasts because, at the moment, the military decision making was Scott's. But the Radicals believed that in McClellan they had found their man. Under mounting pressure from Radical leaders, Lincoln allowed Scott to retire for health reasons in late October. McClellan now carried a dual job, as both commander-in-chief of the Union army and commander of the Army of the Potomac. When Lincoln worried whether the burdens and responsibilities of leadership might be too great for any one man, McClellan replied otherwise. "I can do it all," he guaranteed.[9]

The pressures of command cowed many Civil War generals, but none, arguably, as much as McClellan. With Scott gone, McClellan had his way clear to organize army corps, but now he cautioned delay. He maintained that the best time to introduce corps was after the army had gone into battle; only then would he know who among his top generals were "best fitted to exercise these important commands."[10] The argument held some validity, but the problem was that McClellan gave no indication of when he might take the army into a campaign. As commander-in-chief, McClellan imagined swarms of Confederates in northern Virginia. And not only were these conjured-up Confederate battalions present in large number, they were, in McClellan's mind, preparing to launch a full-scale attack on Washington. Boasts of a swift campaign to end the war in Union victory disappeared with the fall leaves.[11]

The delay in organizing army corps doomed McClellan with the Radicals. The congressmen saw nothing good in the failure to organize the army's divisions into higher formations. The Radicals feared that McClellan might use the lack of corps as an excuse to continue to delay launching a campaign to capture Richmond. Or, perhaps worse from their perspective, McClellan might advance the army into the field still organized into divisions. Away from Washington and any Radical influence, McClellan might consult only with subordinate officers sympathetic to his political viewpoints. Democratic generals would wage the war according to their political philosophies, as well as reap any of the martial glories.[12]

The Radicals attempted to regain the upper hand in their standoff with McClellan by creating the Joint Committee on the Conduct of the War in December 1861. Members of the Joint Committee had the authority to investigate any aspect of the Union war effort, and they quickly took up the question of whether the Army of the Potomac should be organized into corps. The one-sided debate featured a procession of star-studded witnesses. Brigadier General Irvin McDowell, the commander of the Union forces at the Battle of Bull Run and a former instructor of tactics at West Point, argued that corps needed to be created before the army could launch a war-winning offensive. Each corps should number up to 30,000 men, and once in the field, they should maneuver parallel to one another. That way, if one corps suffered attack, "there would be one on each side to come to its assistance." Brigadier General Silas Casey, who had recently penned a manual on infantry tactics widely read throughout the Union army, agreed. Casey instructed that all of the "great generals" since Napoleon had found army corps necessary to effectively operate "large bodies of men in the field." The only resistance continued to come from McClellan. The general reminded members of the Joint Committee that appointing officers to command army corps was a tricky business. These men "could not be stowed away in a pigeon-hole" if they proved incompetent. Best for the Union cause to wait and see, rather than guess and be wrong.[13]

President Lincoln ultimately ordered the creation of army corps and broke the deadlock. He did so in part for military reasons. Secretary of War Edwin Stanton and members of the Joint Committee repeatedly pressed upon Lincoln the point that the creation of corps was vital to winning the war. Otherwise the Union army "would not be efficient."[14] Stanton's argument in favor of army corps likely carried special weight with the president. Stanton had taken over the office from the corrupt Simon Cameron in January. A brilliant administrator, Stanton was also a Democrat. That he agreed with the Radical Republicans about the necessity of creating army corps kept the matter in a military light. This is not to say that politics did not come into play. Lincoln, too, feared the specter of a Democratic clique dominating the high command of the army. Lincoln avoided the possibility by appointing McDowell to the First Corps, Brigadier General Edwin Sumner to the Second Corps, Brigadier General Samuel Heintzelman to the Third Corps, and Brigadier General Erasmus Keyes to the Fourth Corps. The four generals were the senior-most division commanders in the army, as well as Republicans. If need be, the new corps commanders might serve as a counterbalance to the political intrigues of McClellan.[15]

Lincoln has received some present-day criticism for his decision to advance the army's senior-ranking division commanders to corps command. Doing so "cursed" the army for much of its early career with "hidebound" officers.[16] And, in truth, none of the four initial Union corps commanders went on to win an independent command. Yet it is hard to see what Lincoln might have done otherwise. Advancing generals based on battlefield talent would have been tricky, because few battles had yet been fought. Additionally, Lincoln wanted generals who were, if not openly supportive of his Republican administration, at least politically neutral. Bumping forward younger officers would only have opened Lincoln to charges of political favoritism. Going with the senior-ranking generals was the easiest option, and filled the otherwise vacant leadership positions.[17]

For an officer generally not widely remembered today, Edwin Sumner provoked strong response from his contemporaries when he assumed command of the Second Corps. No one would deny that Sumner had perhaps the greatest range of military experience of any high-ranking officer by the late winter of 1862. Born in Boston in 1797, Sumner had joined the army as a second lieutenant in 1819. He had served continuously over the next forty-three years, including fighting Indians and Mexicans while serving in the 1st Cavalry. The wear and tear had taken its toll. By the outbreak of the Civil War, fellow Union officers claimed that Sumner was increasingly short-tempered. McClellan thought worse. The army commander publicly praised his top-ranking subordinate as "an ideal soldier." In private, however, McClellan was scathing. Sumner was a "fool," barely fit to command a regiment, let alone an army corps.[18]

McClellan seemingly had a point. Other observers in the Army of the Potomac believed Sumner was in over his head as commander of the Second Corps.[19] In fairness, however, Sumner was the best of the four newly appointed officers. The career of Irvin McDowell was on the wane when he assumed command of the First Corps, after the disastrous Union defeat at Bull Run. McDowell held command in the East only through the end of the summer, when he received transfer to a succession of backwater departments. In the Third Corps, Samuel Heintzelman had compiled nearly as many years in the regular army as Sumner. Heintzelman was a thorough soldier. Subordinates whispered, however, that he lacked dash and, worse, imagination. Erasmus Keyes, the Fourth Corps commander, owed his seniority in rank to his prewar friendship with Winfield Scott. Keyes was more widely known throughout the army in 1861 and early 1862 for his vocal support of the Republican Party than for his leadership skills. McDowell, Heintzelman, and

Edwin Sumner. The oldest of the four Union corps commanders appointed by Lincoln during early 1862, Sumner brought with him considerable prewar military experience and an aggressive battlefield spirit. Library of Congress.

Keyes all were brave. But none possessed the charisma to inspire the men, and no contemporaries considered their subsequent departures a great loss to the army.

A more legitimate criticism of Sumner was that he simply was too elderly to exercise a field command. By the winter of 1862, Sumner was sixty-four years old. The next oldest corps commander was General Heintzelman, at only fifty-four years of age. Sumner had gained fame in the prewar army as "Old Bull" for his physical vitality and vigor.[20] The change by 1862 was startling. Sumner sometimes seemed languid, and took longer to catch his breath. Compounding the decline in energy, Sumner was thrown from his horse while riding across a field that winter. The Union general had remounted and continued to ride, to the cheers of onlookers. But in the fall Sumner had badly bruised his lungs and shoulder. He had not yet recovered, making an open question how well he might confront the physical and mental challenges that would come once the army entered into active operations.[21]

Gray hair notwithstanding, Sumner made an attractive choice for high command for reasons beyond his prewar military experience. In a war that would require at least some Union offensive action to win, Sumner was undeniably aggressive. Lincoln gained firsthand insight into Sumner's all-or-nothing mentality in mid-February 1861, when traveling as president-elect from Springfield, Illinois, to Washington, D.C. Rumors swirled that southern sympathizers planned to kill Lincoln while he switched trains in Baltimore. Most of the assembled entourage, including Allan Pinkerton, the head of the Pinkerton National Detective Agency, urged Lincoln to wait until well after nightfall to enter the city. Sumner, who led the military escort, was one of the few dissenting voices. The former cavalry officer declared the suggested delay "a d____d piece of cowardice." Instead, Sumner recommended that regular army soldiers clear a path through Baltimore, by force if necessary. Lincoln ultimately chose caution, passing through the city during the dead of night. He later regretted the decision because of the aspersions of cowardice cast upon him by much of the northern press. Although never mentioning the episode during the winter of 1862, Lincoln likely remembered Sumner's good judgment when appointing officers to corps command.[22]

Also making Sumner a strong choice for corps command was his belief that volunteers, with training, made good wartime soldiers. Like many other Civil War generals, Sumner had seen citizen-soldiers in action during the Mexican War. Unlike all but a handful of his colleagues, Sumner also had inspected professional armies raised through conscription while on a tour of Europe in late 1854. Upon returning, Sumner had been asked by Secretary of War Jefferson Davis to compare the two methods of recruiting troops. Sumner acknowledged that, during peacetime, when routine dominated, "soldiers raised by conscription are superior to those raised by volunteer enlistment." He made the important qualification, however, that during wartime, "when good men enter the service for patriotism or from a spirit of adventure, they are superior."[23] The attitude was important, because volunteers made up the vast bulk of the Union army.

Going beyond the appointment of corps commanders, Lincoln ordered that each of the Union corps field three divisions. This equally divided the army's now twelve divisions and made for, at least on paper, about 30,000 soldiers in each corps. Showing sound military insight, Lincoln instructed that each corps commander receive his former division—now known as the First Division.[24]

How McClellan determined the remaining two divisions for each army corps is open to speculation, as he made the assignments without official explanation. Francis Walker, in his *History of the Second Army Corps,* argues that McClellan chose the Second and Third Divisions through "casual selection." Walker's claim appears plausible on the surface because none of Sumner's three divisions had contiguous encampments in the winter of 1861–62.[25] The haphazard approach would, however, be out of character for McClellan, who was too able an organizer to do things on a whim. In assigning the Second Division to the Second Corps, McClellan likely was trying to reestablish a prewar connection between Sumner and Brigadier General John Sedgwick. Sumner and Sedgwick had served together as field officers in the 1st Cavalry before the war.[26] McClellan, like Lincoln, presumably recognized the benefits of putting together officers who were already familiar with one another.

McClellan's personal feelings toward Sumner may have colored the assignment of Brigadier General Louis Blenker's Third Division to the Second Corps. Lincoln informed McClellan in late February that he might transfer Blenker's division from the Army of the Potomac to the Department of the Mountains, in western Virginia.[27] When the transfer occurred one month later, Sumner's command was reduced to two divisions, the smallest in the army. The turn of events might have been more than happenstance. By assigning the Second Corps a division with a dubious future in the Army of the Potomac, McClellan may have been attempting to limit the opportunities of his next in command. More likely, McClellan believed that Sumner's advanced age left him out of touch with current military thinking. Whatever the reason, either jealousy or dislike, or both, McClellan stuck Sumner with the only division transferred from the army during the winter of 1862.

Israel Richardson brought a strong reputation as one of Sumner's two remaining division commanders. Richardson had gained abundant military experience after graduating from West Point in 1841. The Vermont native had served in the Seminole War and the Mexican War before settling down in the mid-1850s to farm outside Pontiac, Michigan. Richardson helped to raise the 2nd Michigan at the outbreak of the Civil War, and became the unit's colonel. He commanded a Union brigade during the First Bull Run Campaign, winning promotion to brigadier general for his solid performance.[28] Richardson achieved an ease among his men that quickly won their respect. The general made little display of his rank and often was nearly indistinguishable in dress from an enlisted man. "I am told that this is a characteristic of the western officers," one private wrote, "and would that more of them would come amongst us and bring their manners with them." In addition to being levelheaded and unassuming, Richardson led by example. When soldiers of one brigade hesitated before crossing a stream while on maneuvers near Washington in the winter of 1862, Richardson plunged into the icy water. He called for the men to follow, which they did at a rush. On another occasion, Richardson shared his supplies with soldiers who were without. Word of such incidents spread, earning Richardson praise for making "his men believe that he was one of them."[29]

John Sedgwick also looked after the welfare of the men in his division, but he never achieved the same level of rapport. Sedgwick, like Richardson, had graduated from West Point, but in 1837. Sedgwick saw service in the Mexican War and, after, along the western frontier. He was considering leaving the army by early 1861, only to have the outbreak of the Civil War delay his plans. Sedgwick returned East and, in the late summer, received promotion to brigadier general. His declining enthusiasm for military life may have been obvious to the men. One disgruntled soldier claimed, "Our first impressions of Sedgwick were not happy. I have heard that a smile occasionally invaded his scrubby beard, but I never saw one there."[30] Moreover, Sedgwick was replacing the popular Charles Stone as commander of the Second Division. Stone had suffered arrest and imprisonment by Federal officials following the Union defeat at Ball's Bluff in late October, on thinly based charges of treason. Sedgwick realized that replacing a fellow officer under controversial circumstances was anything but easy. The knowledge was sometimes nearly overwhelming. In a moment of self-doubt, Sedgwick worried that the whole job of division command was "above my capacity."[31] If Sedgwick seemed brooding and introspective, it was because circumstances more than desire had thrust him into the spotlight of high command.

The brigade commanders of the Second Corps were exceptionally well qualified given the selection criteria of the day. Above all, secretaries of war Cameron and, later, Stanton wanted men with prior military experience. As a result, throughout the Union army, about two out of every three high-ranking officers (major generals and brigadier generals) had served either in the regular army or during the Mexican War or, in many cases, both.[32] The stock of past military experience was even higher in the Second Corps. Four officers had graduated from West Point (Brigadier General William French, 1837; Brigadier General Napoleon Dana, 1842; Brigadier General William Burns, 1847; and Brigadier General Oliver O. Howard, 1854), and the three who took their degrees in time had served in Mexico. Also fighting during the Mexican War was Brigadier General Willis Gorman, a civilian who had raised and led a volunteer regiment. The only exception to these patterns was Brigadier General Thomas Meagher, the commander of the Irish Brigade. Yet Meagher was not completely without military experience. In the spring of 1861, he had helped to raise a company of the 69th New York State Militia. Meagher had commanded the men during the fighting at First Bull Run, winning praise for his battlefield gallantry.[33]

Cameron and Stanton also wanted officers with previous managerial experience, given that they now had several thousand men under their charge. Four brigade commanders of the Second Corps came from a business background, two in the military and two in civilian life. By comparison, only about one of four officers throughout the rest of the Union army could claim as much. Burns had served in the 1850s as a staff officer in the commissary of subsistence. Howard had taught mathematics and worked as an ordnance officer at West Point during these same years. Among the brigade officers coming from a civilian business background, Dana had left the army in 1855 and worked as a banker in St. Paul, Minnesota. More distinguished, at least professionally, Gorman had been elected to Congress from Indiana in 1849. After serving four years, Gorman had received an appointment as governor of the Minnesota Territory from President Franklin Pierce. Taken all together, the managerial skills possessed by most of the brigade officers of the Second Corps did not necessarily guarantee success on the battlefield. The experiences did, however, give each officer at least some preparation for coordinating the activities of their staffs and dealing with their many logistical and administrative demands.[34]

McClellan assigned artillery and cavalry units to each of his four corps, an attempt to emulate the combined arms capabilities that had enabled Napoleon to achieve such stunning military successes in Europe. The results never came up to the expectations, at least during the early war years. McClellan attached an artillery brigade to each division, with four batteries fielding a total of twenty-four guns. The pieces ranged in type, but the most common were smoothbore Napoleons and rifled Parrotts. The Napoleon was deadly at close quarters, firing canister rounds loaded with grape shot. The Parrott served better at longer range, throwing its projectiles on a straight trajectory. Recognizing the learning curve required to man any type of gun, McClellan assigned one battery of regular artillery to each brigade.[35]

Four batteries fielded an impressive number of guns, but the artillery brigades never achieved a concentrated weight of fire to blast holes through the enemy's lines. In a glaring oversight, the highest-ranking battery commander, usually a colonel, served as the corps artillery chief. The lack of rank for the artillery chief was at the insistence of the War Department. Union military officials in Washington argued that because artillery batteries mustered only a relatively small number of men, their commanding officers should not receive rank higher than a colonelcy. The practical result was that infantry generals had battlefield authority over any artillery within sight, regardless of their experience, or lack thereof. The artillery would go into a spring campaign to serve as infantry support, rather than as a potentially decisive battlefield weapon.[36]

How to deploy the cavalry proved even more problematic. McClellan originally intended to assign a brigade of cavalry to each corps. These troopers would serve as scouts when the army was in the field. When a battle started, the horse soldiers might exploit any successes won by their foot-bound comrades. A paucity of cavalry regiments thwarted these plans, to McClellan's frustration. He later grumbled that his cavalry force "was never as large as it ought to have been." Rather than concentrate his few available cavalry units into their own formations, as in the Confederate army, McClellan assigned a regiment to each corps. In doing so, he reduced the initial role of the cavalry to little more than observer status.[37]

Hopes for combined arms operations received a final blow when McClellan gave Sumner and the other corps commanders little staff support. McClellan initially had pushed for swarms of staff members to accompany each corps, including a brigadier general to serve as an adjutant general. He backed down when meeting opposition from Winfield Scott, and never again picked up the point. McClellan may have underestimated the demands that directing relatively large numbers of troops placed on his corps commanders. But McClellan had seen professional armies at war during his tour of Europe in the mid-1850s, where he had witnessed some of the last days of the Crimean War. More likely, McClellan was simply too busy attempting to plan for a spring campaign. Rounding up staff officers slipped to secondary importance amid the numerous last-minute tasks necessary for the army to take the field. When the army did open a new campaign in mid-March, the Second Corps listed only a handful of aides for Sumner, primarily to serve as couriers.[38]

Whether combined arms operations were possible should not detract from the significant Union accomplishment in creating army corps. The presence of the First Corps, Second Corps, Third Corps, and Fourth Corps by the late winter of 1862 gave McClellan a far more streamlined control over his forces than otherwise would have been possible. That the Army of the Potomac pushed to the very gates of the Confederate capital at Richmond that spring and summer, as will be

discussed, is a testament to the powerful military organization that it
had become.

SERVING IN THE SECOND CORPS

For all the attention that the Union high command poured into whether and how to create army corps, few soldiers paid much attention. The
formation of the Second Corps received only passing mention in soldiers' writings, if any at all. Since army corps were new organizational
creations in the American military, they had little historical resonance
with soldiers. Geographic distance only compounded the lack of emotional connection. Richardson's division was encamped just outside
Washington, while Sedgwick's division was encamped along the upper
Potomac, several miles to the west. Soldiers of the two divisions of the
Second Corps would not even see one another until the army first went
into battle that spring.[39]

Soldiers instead most closely identified with their regiments and
brigades, reflecting the American method of raising troops in time of
national need through the mid-nineteenth century. The regular army
numbered only 16,000 officers and enlisted men in 1860, one of the
smallest land forces in the Western world. The War Department made
the decision to keep the regular army intact soon after the outbreak of
the Civil War, as it had in all past conflicts. The thought was that the
regular units would provide a trained nucleus to build the larger, if hastily mobilized, American army. This soon proved impossible in the Civil
War, given the scale of the conflict. But the recruitment process worked
the same as in past wars, with state and local officials taking up the slack
in raising regiments and companies. The citizen-soldiers who volunteered went to war with men from their same village, neighborhood, and
city. The connection between those in the military and those at home
remained strong throughout the fighting. The sense of their regiment
as an extension of their home community allowed Civil War soldiers
to endure an enormous amount of bloodshed and physical hardship.[40]

Yet, by virtue of the regiments assigned to it, the Second Corps
acquired several distinct differences from the rest of the Union army.
Soldiers of the Second Corps came from across the Union, but those

Table 1. Area of Recruitment and Manpower of the Sixteen Urban Regiments of the Second Corps, by Region, 1861

Regiment (by Region)	Primary City of Recruitment	Secondary City or County of Recruitment	Date of Muster	Number of Men at Muster
Middle Atlantic				
42nd New York	New York City	None	June 22–28	1,019
52nd New York	New York City	None	August 3–November 5	1,000
57th New York	New York City	Dutchess and Kings Counties	August 12–November 19	751
61st New York	Albany	Madison County	September–November	770
63rd New York	New York City	Albany, N.Y., and Boston, Mass.	September–November	1,000
66th New York	New York City	None	November 4	900
69th New York	New York City	Buffalo, N.Y., and Chicago, Ill.	September 17–November 17	745
82nd New York	New York City	None	May 26–June 17	832
88th New York	New York City	Brooklyn, N.Y.	September–December	800
69th Penn.	Philadelphia	None	August 19	952
71st Penn.	Philadelphia	New York City	May 16	1,100
72nd Penn.	Philadelphia	None	August 10	1,485
81st Penn.	Philadelphia	Carbon and Luzerne Counties	August–October	900
106th Penn.	Philadelphia	Bradford, Lycoming, and Montgomery Counties	August–September	1,020
New England				
19th Mass.	Boston	Essex, Middlesex, and Suffolk Counties	August 28	1,050
20th Mass.	Boston	Nantucket, Mass.; and Norfolk and Suffolk Counties	July 29–August 29	750

Note: All sixteen regiments mustered for three-year terms of service.

Sources: The areas of recruitment and date of muster of each regiment are taken from corresponding regimental histories and rosters, as well as Dyer, *A Compendium of the War of the Rebellion*, vol. 3. The manpower strength of each regiment is taken from sources cited in the text.

from New York, Philadelphia, and Boston were the most numerous (see table 1).[41] The urban cast was not unique to the Second Corps. Soldiers in the Army of the Potomac came primarily from the Northeast, the most heavily urbanized region of the nation by 1860.[42] The Excelsior Brigade of the Union Third Corps is a notable example, with five regiments raised in New York City during the spring of 1861.

Where the heavy urban presence did set the Second Corps apart was in giving it a decidedly ethnic flavor. Ethnic regiments fielded a majority of foreign-born and first-generation soldiers.[43] The 52nd New York was German, one of twelve German regiments eventually raised in New York. The 63rd New York, 69th New York, 88th New York, and 69th Pennsylvania were Irish. The four Irish regiments represented a staggering one-fifth of the Irish regiments raised in the Union. In early 1862, no other Union corps fielded as many ethnic regiments as the Second Corps.[44]

Thomas Francis Meagher was one of the Union's most successful ethnic recruiters, helping to raise the three regiments of the Irish Brigade in New York City during the summer and fall of 1861. Born in Ireland in 1823, Meagher developed a colorful personality. He took part in an uprising in 1848 that unsuccessfully sought independence for his homeland. The British government sentenced Meagher to death for his role in the rebellion, but commuted the punishment to life exile in Tasmania. Meagher eluded the fate in 1852 and escaped by sea to New York City. By the outbreak of the Civil War, Meagher had won acclaim within the Irish-American community for his work practicing law and editing an ethnic newspaper. Meagher added to his fame by serving as a captain in the Irish-American 69th New York State Militia, a three-months regiment that fought at the Battle of Bull Run on July 21, 1861. Meagher portrayed the Civil War as an opportunity for his fellow Irish in America to gain the military experience necessary to one day launch a new war of liberation for their homeland. "Today it is for the American Republic we fight," Meagher tantalizingly promised at one recruiting rally, "to-morrow it will be for Ireland."[45] Meagher also emphasized that Irish Americans owed the United States loyalty for providing shelter from English persecution overseas. The appeals reached beyond the Irish wards of New York City. Men volunteered from as far away as

Buffalo and Pittsburgh to fight in the Irish Brigade, an unusually wide range of recruitment.[46]

Soldiers of the Irish Brigade and the other ethnic soldiers of the Second Corps attempted to maintain their distinct identity. German soldiers in the 52nd New York referred to their regiment as the "Sigel Rifles." The reference was to Franz Sigel, a nationally known German exile turned antebellum politician and Civil War general.[47] Soldiers of the Irish 69th Pennsylvania adopted the same numerical designation as the 69th New York State Militia had borne into battle at First Bull Run. The green flags carried by the four Irish regiments of the Second Corps were the most visible symbol of ethnic pride. The banners depicted an Irish harp over a wreath of shamrocks, and were the only ones of their kind in the Union army. Meagher reminded his men that the flag clearly marked the Irish regiments in camp and on the battlefield. The very conspicuousness should steel the resolve of the Irish soldiers to "die if necessary, but never surrender."[48]

In addition to a strong ethnic flavor, the heavy urban presence gave the Second Corps many other regiments with distinctive backgrounds. City populations had increased to where men with compatible interests formed entire regiments. Members of the Tammany Society, a well-oiled Democratic political machine in New York City by the 1850s, banded together to raise the 42nd New York. Capping the achievement, Grand Sachem William Kennedy, the leader of the Tammany Society for 1861, won command of the regiment.[49] In Philadelphia, supporters of Edward Baker, a Republican senator and close friend of President Lincoln, joined the 71st Pennsylvania. Not to be outdone were the city's volunteer firefighters. Boasting that they were "patriotic, intelligent and brave," they worked together to raise the 72nd Pennsylvania.[50] The two Pennsylvania regiments received brigade assignment in the fall with the 69th Pennsylvania and the 106th Pennsylvania. The result was the Philadelphia Brigade, the only brigade in the Union army named after the home city of most of its soldiers.[51]

Diverse backgrounds characterized soldiers recruited in the countryside (see table 2). Members of the 64th New York, a prewar militia unit, came from dizzying range of jobs and occupations. The list included men "from the varied professions, also the mechanic, the artisan, the tradesman, and tiller of the soil." Ethnic diversity characterized soldiers of the 1st Minnesota. Men from England, Ireland, and France served in the regiment alongside soldiers from Spain, Italy, and Russia. In one company alone, forty-eight men traced their family lineage to central and northern Europe. The 5th New Hampshire had its share of foreign-born soldiers. Nearly one hundred men came from either Canada or England and Ireland, in about equal parts.[52] Political diversity characterized soldiers of the 15th Massachusetts, to the seeming surprise of all. Democrats and Republicans who previously had squared off bitterly during the presidential election of 1860 now mingled together freely at recruiting rallies held in Worcester County. For the first time in recent memory, Worcester was a "unit on a great political subject." Political unity spurred cooperation among different religious faiths in nearby Clinton, Massachusetts. Soldiers found their wives, daughters, and sweethearts sewing extra flannel shirts for them at a Baptist church and an Eastern Orthodox church. One soldier proudly remembered that every scrap of flannel in the town soon was stitched and ready to wear.[53]

Chance for political cooperation was more rare throughout the rest of the Second Corps, because the majority of soldiers were Democrats. The political leanings of the men became well known to their comrades, earning the Second Corps a reputation as, in the words of one field officer, the "Democratic Corps" of the Union army. By contrast, most other Federal soldiers either supported the Republican Party or came from households that supported the Republican Party.[54] Soldiers coming from New York and Philadelphia contributed to the political flavor of the Second Corps. The two cities were strongholds of the Democratic Party by mid-nineteenth century. Most recently, residents of both communities had given strong support to Stephen Douglas in his failed bid to capture the White House.[55] Irish-American soldiers from New York and Philadelphia were especially staunch Democrats. Irish immigrants feared that their economic livelihood would be threatened should the abolitionist wing of the Republican Party achieve its goal of liberating the slaves.[56] Soldiers of the 20th Massachusetts had strong leanings toward the Democratic Party, even though the Republican Party dominated their home state by mid-century. The men were outspoken in their criticism of Lincoln and his policies. The politicking did not go over well

Table 2. Area of Recruitment and Manpower of the Seven Rural Regiments of the Second Corps, by Region, 1861

Regiment (by Region)	Area of Recruitment	Counties of Recruitment	Date of Muster	Number of Men at Muster
Middle Atlantic				
34th New York	Upstate New York	Herkimer	June 15*	786
64th New York	Upstate New York	Allegany, Cattaraugus, and Tompkins	December 10	849
53rd Penn.	Eastern Penn.	Juniata, Luzerne, Montgomery, Northumberland, Potter, and Westmoreland	November 7	940
Midwest				
7th Mich.	Southeastern Mich.	Lapeer, Monroe, Tuscola, and Oakland	August 22	854
1st Minn.	Southeastern Minn.	Dakota, Goodhue, Hennepin, Ramsey, Rice, Wabasha, Washington, and Winona	April 29**	950
New England				
15th Mass.	Central Mass.	Worcester	July 12	1,011
5th New Hamp.	Northern and Central New Hamp.	Carroll, Coos, Grafton, and Merrimack	October 26	1,010

Notes:
*The 34th New York mustered for a two-year term of service, while the remaining six regiments mustered for three-year terms of service.
**Soldiers of the 1st Minnesota mustered for three months on April 29 and for three years on May 10. The War Department later dated the start of their three-year term to April 29.
Sources: The counties of recruitment and date of muster of each regiment are taken from corresponding regimental histories and rosters, as well as Dyer, *A Compendium of the War of the Rebellion,* vol. 3. The manpower strength of each regiment is taken from sources cited in the text.

throughout the rest of the Union army, where the Bay Staters earned reprobation as the "Copperhead" regiment.[57]

Coming from largely Democratic political backgrounds, soldiers of the Second Corps fought primarily to preserve the Union. The men recognized that the United States likely would continue even if the Confederacy established itself as an independent political entity. Yet they believed that the freedoms guaranteed white Americans by a republican form of government would suffer a fatal blow. The awareness prompted soldiers to declare that they were fighting to protect "our great and free government" and the "best government that ever was instituted." If they died in the effort, they did so "in the heart of my great country's defense." Captain Casper Crowninshield was a twenty-three-year-old student at Harvard when the war broke out. He quickly dropped his books to volunteer, arguing that the triumph of the federal government would demonstrate to foreign observers that the American Republic was a viable form of nationhood. He would not feel worthy of enjoying the benefits of citizenship if unwilling to fight for them in time of need. Jonathan Stowe, a farm laborer from Massachusetts, was equally zealous. He declared that southerners who took up arms against a freely elected government were not only "my country's enemy," but "base traitors to humanity and the world."[58]

Many soldiers looked to the American past and future for inspiration. Volunteers from Red Wing, Minnesota, drew inspiration from the Declaration of Independence. They pledged "our lives, our fortunes and our sacred honor" to defend the "Government to which we justly owe our allegiance." Private Herbert Willand recognized that military life was full of dangers and privations, but he never regretted that he had enlisted. That was a hard commitment for Willand to make because his wife, ill and at home, wanted him back. "If it is my fate to fall by bullet or otherwise," Willand consoled, "I shall have given only that which thousands have given before me." Private George Beidelman, a former printer's apprentice from Philadelphia, believed that Union soldiers were defending not only their own liberties, but those of their children. This was because the present contest transcended the "North against the South; it is government against anarchy, law against disorder, and truth and justice against falsehood and intolerance."[59]

Talk about freedom and liberty did not extend to African Americans enslaved in the South. It is unclear whether the sentiment made soldiers of the Second Corps distinct from the rest of the Union army. A recent and well-received study suggests that Union soldiers voiced more support for emancipation in 1861 than previously acknowledged in the scholarship.[60] If so, these men were few and far between in the Second Corps. Private Edward Bassett of the 1st Minnesota was one of the few men who mentioned the institution of slavery and the prosecution of the war in the same breath. Peace would come only when slavery came to an end. Recognizing that the Confederacy never would voluntarily relinquish its source of labor, Bassett grimly warned, "There is no alternative but to fight."[61] Although certainly debatable, Bassett might have based his comments as much on pragmatic assessment as humanitarian spirit.

Fighting for the Union rather than emancipation, soldiers still had no trouble confidently predicting God on their side. Across the way, Confederate soldiers shared the belief with equal fervor.[62] Soldiers of the Second Corps had good reason to make the connection between God and Union, having gone to war with sermons full of "Patrick Henry oratory" ringing in their ears. Private Gorham Coffin of the 19th Massachusetts recognized the formidable military task that the Union had in subduing the Confederacy, with its thousands of miles of territory. Still, northern arms would triumph because "God is on the side of the right, and right will in the end prevail." Lieutenant Cornelius Moore of the 57th New York also believed the Union might have difficult days ahead. The Confederates were full of confidence after their triumph at Bull Run that summer. The military tide soon would turn, because "God has strong arms on the side of the right." Leaving nothing to chance, Moore asked his family to pray to God to "protect the cause in which your brother is engaged."[63]

Sense of duty bolstered belief in the righteousness of the Union cause. Volunteering in time of national need simply seemed the right thing to do. Soldiers believed that a "solemn sense of duty" pledged them to fight under the national flag "of which we hope to be ever proud." Some men, however, wondered whether duty to country superseded duty to family. Martin Sigman thought it did not, and he continued to work on the family farm in upstate New York. Sigman discovered an interest in military life only in the autumn of 1861, when his father declared that he would enlist if his son did not. Louis Chapin found himself conflicted whether to serve or stay home. Like many sons from time beginning, Chapin turned the question over to his mother. She took no pause before answering that, in times of "great extremity," need of country took precedence over need of family. Chapin took the advice and enlisted in the 34th New York. Other men saw little point to debate, arguing that duty to nation encompassed duty to family. Samuel Sexton, a regimental surgeon, received a scolding from his wife that "claims of family are above that of country." Sexton chidingly responded, "This is not correct. We owe our duty to our country next to our God."[64]

Some volunteers enlisted for more immediate reason. Economic downturn had hit the North hard in the late 1850s, and at least some men found powerful draw in the prospect of monthly pay and new clothes.[65] Benjamin Chase volunteered instead from a sense of adventure. Chase found himself hard struck by wanderlust after working on the family farm in New Hampshire. He volunteered to "see a little of the world" rather than "stay at home and do nothing." More than a few men likely enlisted with their heads muddled by drink. One recruiting officer found ample numbers of thirsty volunteers in saloons around Philadelphia. Lost in the haze was "how many drinks of bad whiskey" he had forced down. This was not to be held against him, because the drink had been partaken "in the service of my country."[66]

As soldiers discussed why they fought, they underwent drill and discipline that helped to distinguish their experience to at least some degree from the rest of the army. All Union soldiers found the bulk of their day consumed by drill during the winter of 1861–62, but Sumner was relentless. Drawing on his prewar observation that volunteers needed training to make good wartime soldiers, Sumner had the men "drilling violently" from sun up to sun down. A fatigued lieutenant colonel held some hope for respite by late December, because "Genl. Sumner says he shall not be so strict when we become better drilled." Two months later, a private in the 5th New Hampshire still groused about "very severe drilling, the men now think that a soldiers life is not very pleasant." Soldiers soon recognized the payoff for their time and fatigue was increased proficiency in drill. This was important in itself, but also because strong showings on the parade ground swelled soldiers' pride. The men boasted that it was now "easy" for them "to perform the most intricate movements" and that they "should give good account of themselves in a fight."[67]

Sumner also tightened discipline over the winter encampment. Again, all soldiers found their officers less tolerant of infractions as a spring campaign approached. But Sumner, as on the drill field, seemed almost everywhere in camp. Some men considered Sumner something of a martinet, enforcing regulations for the sake of it. Sumner held himself to the same standards, thereby winning more soldiers' respect. In a notable example, Sumner insisted that all officers avoid sleeping in civilian houses. This might have caused grumbling, especially on cold winter nights, except that Sumner also slept outdoors. The result of Sumner's leadership by example was that the Second Corps had reached a high state of unit discipline by late March. Few soldiers were in the guardhouse, an indication that regimental and company officers had affairs well in hand.[68] By comparison, soldiers in at least two other divisions received reprimand from high-ranking officers for their poor behavior while in camp.[69]

Several regiments in General Stone's former division (now Sedgwick's) received an opportunity to put their training and discipline to the test in the fall of 1861. Soldiers in the 15th Massachusetts, 20th Massachusetts, 42nd New York, and 71st Pennsylvania participated in a Union attempt to occupy the Confederate-held town of Leesburg, Virginia. The Union soldiers bumped into a well-positioned Confederate defense after climbing to the top of Ball's Bluff, a 100-foot-high bank overlooking the Potomac River. After a confused swirl of fighting, Colonel Edward Baker, the overall Union commander, was killed.[70] Any remaining fight quickly went out of Baker's men. Survivors later described the retreat down Ball's Bluff as "wild, disorderly" and a "stampede." They found no relief at the water's edge. Some soldiers desperate to escape the unrelenting Confederate fire overloaded the few boats underway back across the Potomac. Other men threw away equipment, stripped off uniforms, and attempted to swim to safety. By the end of the fighting, the Federals had suffered nearly 1,000 casualties. The great majority of men either were captured by the Confederates or drowned in the Potomac River.[71]

Although a lopsided defeat, the fighting at Ball's Bluff helped to build a unit pride that later served the Second Corps well. Many soldiers believed that they had fought hard against overwhelming numbers. Sergeant Walter Eames of the 15th Massachusetts had fought in the thick of the action while helping to hold the Union right flank. "Eight hours and a quarter we stood before a terrific fire from greatly superior numbers," Sergeant Eames proudly recounted. "The woods were swarming with the fellows." A private in the 71st Pennsylvania thought the Confederates had enjoyed a six-to-one advantage. Given the disparity, "our men fought like tigers." Still, survivors recognized that they had suffered a battlefield defeat. Lieutenant Henry Abbott admitted that he and the other soldiers of the 20th Massachusetts had been "badly licked." That was galling enough. But should the war end and the regiment never get an opportunity to redeem itself, "it would be outrageous."[72] Like Abbott, many other survivors of the battle at Ball's Bluff would go into the spring eager for a chance to redeem their unit's reputation.

Drill and discipline and, for some, the experience of battle remained tolerable because holidays and mail varied the daily routine. Thanksgiving and Christmas won highest place in soldiers' regard, because the holidays often meant a change in diet. Many soldiers feasted upon turkey for Thanksgiving and oyster stew for Christmas.[73] Equally pleasing, the celebrations provided time for socializing and playing games. Officers enjoyed mingling with female visitors from Washington and Baltimore in a log ballroom constructed for Thanksgiving. Enlisted men gathered for athletic contests, such as wrestling, foot racing, and jumping, to mark Christmas morning. Cash awards made participants all the more enthusiastic, with the winner receiving four dollars and the runner-up receiving two dollars. George Washington's birthday ran a surprisingly close third to Thanksgiving and Christmas in soldiers' affections. The holiday likely assumed greater importance in war than in peace because it reminded soldiers that they were fighting to preserve the nation's Revolutionary heritage. Officers made clear the connection by reading to their assembled men Washington's farewell address. Perhaps just as inspiring to soldiers, they listened to band music, cheered the flag, and enjoyed the day off from drill.[74]

Letters and newspapers from home were every bit as welcome by soldiers as holiday celebrations, but for different reasons. Letters from home brought soldiers tangible proof that family and friends remembered them. A Massachusetts sergeant believed that soldiers valued letters from home above any other material possession. This caused some amusement, because the "cry of 'the mail' will cause the boys to move a little more quickly than anything else perhaps excepting bullets." A New York captain nearly broke down in tears after receiving a letter from his family. The updates passed along were nothing out of the ordinary, but that was enough. "You don't know, you cannot know, how such favors are appreciated by me here."[75]

While letters brought reassurance from home, newspapers brought news of the larger Union war effort. The headlines read very well during early 1862. Men excitedly discussed the capture of Roanoke Island and other sites along the North Carolina sounds by Union amphibious forces led by Brigadier General Ambrose Burnside. Soldiers also eagerly read news from the West, where Brigadier General Ulysses Grant led the Union capture of Confederate strongholds Forts Henry and Donelson on the Tennessee and Cumberland Rivers. Yet amid word of Union victories seemingly everywhere else but northern Virginia, some men feared that the war might pass them by. Lieutenant Thomas Livermore and his comrades in the 5th New Hampshire were proud of the "deeds of our Western comrades." They worried, however, "lest the work should all be finished without us."[76]

Spirits were high in the Second Corps all the same. In the late winter, McClellan maneuvered Sedgwick's division to occupy Harpers Ferry, and Sumner's division to occupy Manassas Junction. The Federal advance had helped to force the Confederate army in northern Virginia to retreat behind the Rappahannock River, forty miles to the south. Soldiers were delighted at the turn of events. The Confederate retreat meant that the "backbone of the rebellion is broken," and that the "Rebels are about used up in Virginia." Private Arnold Daines found himself caught up in the excitement. He closed a letter to his wife by declaring that, by early summer at the latest, the war would be over and he would be at home.[77]

THE PENINSULA AND
MARYLAND CAMPAIGNS

Soon after assembling the army into corps, McClellan moved his forces to Fort Monroe. A Union-controlled stronghold on the Virginia Peninsula, Fort Monroe served as the starting point for a Federal offensive to capture Richmond. McClellan planned to push his 89,000 men inland (westward) the roughly fifty miles to the Confederate capital. Supply lines secured by the Union navy along the bordering York and James Rivers would facilitate the Federal offensive. If all went well, Richmond would fall by midsummer from either siege or climactic battle.[1] That hopeful outlook, however, was lost for the moment on Sumner's men. The ships were crowded and the seas were rough, leaving soldiers foul-tempered and seasick. The only entertainment came at the very end of the several-day voyage, when the gathering Federal fleet hove into view. The lights marking each ship appeared "as thick as stars on a clear night" and made a "sight not soon forgotten."[2]

FIGHTING FOR RICHMOND

Union forces struck out from Fort Monroe in early April, only to make slow progress. McClellan settled the army into a three-week siege outside Yorktown, believing the 15,000 Confederate defenders to be present in far greater numbers than that.[3] When the Confederates abandoned the historic town and retreated back toward Richmond in early May, Sumner's men were euphoric. Believing that the Confederates had only so much space to trade, they gloated that the "Rebs are getting in a tight place" and "Richmond will be ours." Soldiers believed ultimate

Union victory all the nearer after reaching the Chickahominy River in late May. The sluggishly flowing river formed the last natural defensive barrier before reaching Richmond, only a few miles distant. The Federals could force a "final battle" before Richmond, or they could follow another Confederate retreat. The latter might delay the end of the war by some weeks, if not months. Major Joseph Dimock explained to his wife that she should not get "down hearted" if the Confederates temporarily prolonged the fighting by abandoning Richmond. He might not be home by the Fourth of July, but certainly by Christmas.[4]

The politics of command came into play before a final Union push began, when all of the Army of the Potomac but for the Second Corps underwent a major restructuring. McClellan used two divisions recently received from the defense of Washington to create the Fifth Corps and Sixth Corps in mid-May. To fill the two new command openings, McClellan appointed Brigadier General Fitz John Porter and Brigadier General William Franklin. McClellan had favorites in Porter and Franklin, who were both close confidants and good Democrats. McClellan simultaneously reduced the influence of Heintzelman and Keyes within the Federal high command by transferring one division from each of their commands to Porter and Franklin. This was less of an issue for Sumner, since the Second Corps already had lost a third division that winter.[5] The only dark cloud for Sumner's men was found in the deployment of the army. McClellan pushed the Third Corps and Fourth Corps south across the Chickahominy, and placed the Second Corps in the center of the remaining Union forces. Noting the presence of Federal troops to the front and to either side, soldiers worried that they would play little role in the capture of Richmond.[6]

Sounds of battle coming from across the Chickahominy River interrupted the reveries enjoyed by Sumner's men. Confederate General Joseph Johnston had launched a counterattack on the early afternoon of May 31, with most of his now 56,000 soldiers. Johnston hoped to crush the Union forces already across the rain-swollen Chickahominy River before help arrived. He was close by later in the day, with a series of Confederate attacks pushing back and threatening to overwhelm the Union defensive lines.[7]

Sedgwick's men crossing the Grapevine Bridge at Fair Oaks on May 31, 1862. Soldiers later claimed that their timely arrival played a major role in the Union's triumph during the two-day battle. Reprinted from *Battles and Leaders of the Civil War,* vol. 2, 246.

Coming to the aid of the embattled Union forces proved no easy task, and here Sumner experienced his finest moment of the war. Sumner had alertly readied his men to march when he first had heard sounds of battle, saving valuable time when the order came from McClellan. The previous night's storm had washed away all but the Grapevine Bridge, to the front of Sedgwick's men. A nearby engineering officer warned Sumner not to attempt to cross the structure, lest it collapse from the muddy currents already overlapping the causeway. Sumner was in no mood to argue, determined to reach the sound of the guns. The infantry crossed with water swirling around their knees, while the artillery creaked along "hub-deep" in the water. After several anxious moments, the men and one battery of guns made it across the river.[8]

Infantry and artillery soldiers pushed toward the Union right at Fair Oaks Station, about three miles distant. A new Confederate assault was looming, and Union Brigadier General Darius Couch was uncertain whether his already badly battered division could hold. The arrival of

Sedgwick's division in the early evening turned the momentum. With the reinforcements, a relieved Couch believed "that God was with us and victory ours."[9] Soldiers of the Second Corps repulsed the subsequent Confederate attack, as well as another launched the next morning. Conceding Union resistance more formidable than expected, the Confederates abandoned their offensive and retreated back toward Richmond during the afternoon of June 1.[10]

Soldiers of the Second Corps had fought well in their first major engagement, in part because of the emphasis on training and discipline the past winter. The men generally were in the thick of the action on both days of the battle. The noise was near-deafening, with Confederate artillery and musket fire echoing "like the incessant pounding in some great steam-boiler shop." Union and Confederate lines of battle often were only yards away in the wooded terrain, and "oh how fast the bullets did fly." Amid the chaos, training took over. Sergeant Charles Fuller of the 61st New York was one of many men who fell back almost instinctively into the routine of drill. Soon after coming under Confederate fire, Fuller, to his later amazement, felt a sense of invulnerability wash through him. The death of one man to his front and another man to his right produced no feeling of horror or anxiety. "I seemed to regard it as the to-be-expected thing," Fuller marveled, "and . . . I loaded and fired my gun from behind their dead bodies as unconcerned as though it had been in a sham battle."[11]

But drill could hardly replicate the chaos of battle, and, more important, Sumner's men fought well because of their devotion to unit and comrade. Like many other Union soldiers, they preferred to risk maiming and death rather than let down their families at home and their friends in the ranks.[12] Captain Henry Lyons of the 34th New York went into battle on the evening of May 31. The bullets whistled "like hail," convincing Lyons that he and other members of his company survived only "by a miracle." Despite the heavy fire, every Union soldier "stood firm." Lyons was sure that had they been able to witness the scene, "it would have done the heart of the Citizens of Old Steuben good." Private Herbert Willand of the 5th New Hampshire survived equally brutal combat the next morning. The Confederate line of battle was so close that Willand and his comrades could hear the rebel commands.

The ensuing musketry fire "was fearful." Soldiers began to fall killed and wounded, including the private on Willand's immediate right. The whole experience was terrifying. The Confederates fell back after several more minutes of fighting, prompting Willand to boast, "we did the regiment proud."[13]

That the Second Corps inflicted and endured significant battlefield punishment at Fair Oaks was not to be taken for granted. Not all of Sumner's men fought well. Some soldiers ran, while others remained in the ranks only through threat of physical coercion.[14] These individual actions pale by comparison to the almost complete collapse of Brigadier General Silas Casey's Fourth Corps division. Casey's men came under the initial Confederate attack on May 31, while holding the Union left around Seven Pines. After several minutes of fighting, the division disintegrated. Survivors streamed toward the perceived safety of the rear, some without even firing a shot. Fugitives crowded the roads so thickly that onrushing Union reinforcements had to force their way through by point of bayonet. The division rallied over the next several days. That mattered little to General Heintzelman, in command of the Union forces south of the Chickahominy. He fumed that Casey's men "did not fight well" and should not be relied upon in the future under any circumstances.[15]

Despite the nearness of the Union victory at Fair Oaks, soldiers of the Second Corps knew they had fought well. The pride received some nurturing from Sumner and his top lieutenants. Sumner declared that over the two-day battle, the Second Corps had suffered Confederate attacks in "great force" and "great fury." Under the onslaughts, "no troops ever behaved better." Richardson boasted that the "general conduct" of soldiers in his division "was all that could be asked." As a reward, Richardson authorized soldiers to inscribe their colors with "the words 'Fair Oaks.'" McClellan also recognized that the Second Corps had fought hard. A private in the First Division later recalled that "Genl. McClellan said the musketry was the most severe that he had ever heard and that our stubborn valor had done the work, meaning the 2nd Corps."[16]

Equally important, morale climbed because Sumner's men believed that they had made the chief contribution to the Union victory. They had been the only sizable Union reinforcements to reach the battlefield, and their efforts and sacrifices had rescued triumph from seeming disaster. "We were not a minute too soon," a surgeon in the Second Division reminded, "and had we been half an hour later the whole army would probably have been driven back and cut up." Private Warren Osgood of the 15th Massachusetts boasted that after marching "through swamps and mud we arrived on the ground just in time to save the day, and a second Bull Run." Sumner's men likely would have been delighted had they known that Confederate General Joseph Johnston echoed their sentiments. Johnston later admitted that he felt his emotions plummet when Sedgwick's soldiers arrived at Fair Oaks. Had the Confederate attack begun even one hour earlier, when Couch's men stood alone, the right of the Federal lines "would have been destroyed."[17]

Soldiers throughout the rest of the army had less to boast about. The men were pleased that the Union offensive toward Richmond would continue. But there were few expressions of unit pride. Franklin's and Porter's men had not been engaged, and crossed over the Chickahominy only in the aftermath of the battle. Soldiers in the Fourth Corps were under a dark cloud, following the dismal showing of Casey's division. Only worsening the mood, Keyes all but abandoned the men when he asked for a transfer from the Army of the Potomac several weeks later. In the Third Corps, soldiers took to squabbling over their otherwise solid showing at Fair Oaks. Matters became so heated that Heintzelman took to publicly quarreling with his two division commanders, hardly contributing to a sense of unit cohesion.[18]

Soldiers had other reason to be happy in early June beyond the victory at Fair Oaks, with the army welcoming reinforcements. The Second Corps received the 2nd Delaware, 29th Massachusetts, and 7th New York. Sumner attempted to keep a relatively equal distribution of manpower by assigning the new regiments to the First Division, the most bloodied in the recent fighting. The reinforcements raised the Second Corps to 17,180 men. Overall, the Army of the Potomac jumped to just under 115,000 men.[19]

This was the first reinforcement of the Second Corps, and Sumner turned in a mixed performance. Sumner followed a similar practice to the other Union corps commanders in distributing new regiments to individual brigades. Otherwise, Sumner paid little attention to what regiment went where. The lack of oversight sent soldiers of the 29th Massachusetts to face the skeptical stares of their new comrades in the Irish Brigade. The newcomers were from the cream of New England society, with many members tracing their family roots back to the *Mayflower*. The odd combination between Massachusetts blue bloods and Irish immigrants might have disrupted the brigade's otherwise strong ethnic identity, but showing his adeptness as a politician, General Meagher, the brigade commander, successfully appealed to the pride of each group. "As sons of Pilgrims and Puritans, and natives of the fair land he was glad to call his adopted country," Meagher later extolled soldiers of the 29th Massachusetts, "they had shown themselves worthy of their honorable ancestry and high heritage." Meagher also reminded the new men that although good, they were only the "equals of any other in the Brigade."[20]

While infantry reinforcements arrived, McClellan concentrated the army's firepower by creating an artillery reserve in each corps. McClellan issued the order on June 2, so it is unclear how much the near-run victory at Fair Oaks influenced his thinking. The artillery reserve in the Second Corps fielded two batteries, with one battery drawn from each of the First and Second divisions.[21] Sumner had direct command over the guns, but this was not an issue that had troubled the Second Corps at Fair Oaks. Sumner had helped to position Lieutenant Edmund Kirby's Battery I, 1st United States, the only Second Corps artillery that had made it into action on May 31. Sumner had posted the battery well, helping to anchor the right of Sedgwick's lines. The Union gunners had fired nearly 350 rounds in helping to break the Confederate attack. Sumner later praised Kirby and his men for their "extraordinary rapidity and accuracy" of fire. The Confederate attackers on the receiving end agreed, describing the storm of Union shot and shell as some of the "deadliest" of the war.[22]

The newly strengthened Second Corps and the rest of the Army of the Potomac prepared to besiege Richmond in mid-June, making daily life into an ordeal. Death and illness were ever present. The Second Corps held the center of the Union siege lines, with only tens of yards sometimes separating the opposing entrenchments. Any man who moved from behind the cover of a tree or rifle pit risked drawing Confederate fire.[23] Soldiers found little escape in the rear lines, where disease was a more relentless killer. The Second Corps suffered before Richmond its highest rate of illness, primarily from outbreak of scurvy. Soldiers had consumed few fruits and vegetables since the start of the campaign. The results of the poor diet now became apparent, with soldiers suffering from open sores, bleeding gums, and other telltale signs of scurvy.[24] Surface water polluted by unburied bodies and dead animals from the Fair Oaks battlefield struck down men nearly as fast. Many soldiers recognized the need to collect rain water and purify surface water by adding dollops of commissary whiskey.[25] The measures failed to prevent various stomach ailments that included, in the words of one soldier, "congestion of various abdominal organs." Captain Samuel Hoffman believed that such preventative measures were ineffective anyway, because the very air was poisonous around Fair Oaks. He grimly recorded that "half of the boys are sick for it smells so where there is so many dead."[26]

Attention turned to other matters on the afternoon and evening of June 26, when the roar of battle came to Sumner's men from the Union right flank. The Union Fifth Corps had suffered attack at Mechanicsville from Confederate General Robert E. Lee and his newly named Army of Northern Virginia.[27] Through official report and camp scuttlebutt, soldiers of the Second Corps believed that the Union forces had smashed the attacking Confederates and won a great victory. Joy turned to frustration the next morning when soldiers learned that the Fifth Corps had barely held its own. "We were much disgusted after our 'jubilation' of last night," Lieutenant Augustus Ayling admitted by hard light of day, "and there is a feeling in the regiment that the next time [we] cheer for a victory, it will be a 'sure one.'"[28] Spirits turned even more sour when Sumner's men received word that the Fifth Corps had collapsed under a new Confederate attack at Gaines' Mill on June 27. Outlook became especially dark among soldiers of French's and Meagher's brigades that McClellan had sent to reinforce the buckling Union lines. The men arrived too late in the day to participate in the battle, but they saw firsthand the wreckage of the defeat. "Everything seemed to be in the greatest confusion," one disheartened private wrote.[29]

Discouragement turned to nervousness over the very survival of the army when orders came on June 28 for soldiers of the Second Corps to retreat toward the James River. Otherwise, McClellan feared that the Confederates would cut the army's supply lines to the York River. McClellan ordered the Second Corps, Third Corps, and Sixth Corps to form the rear guard, to enable the Fourth Corps and Fifth Corps to escape first from the battered Union right. Sumner's men took news of the retreat hard because the decline of Federal fortunes before Richmond had occurred so quickly. From hoping to capture Richmond only days earlier, soldiers of the Second Corps found themselves mired in defeat without ever having fired a shot.[30]

Unit cohesion again played an important role in soldiers' battlefield motivations when the Second Corps reached Savage's Station on the late afternoon of June 29. Sumner's men had reached the small railroad hamlet after retreating several miles east from the former Union lines around Richmond. They were in a dangerous spot, because soldiers of the Union Third Corps, supposedly massed on their left flank, withdrew without notice. Whether the retreat was authorized became a source of recrimination between Sumner and Heintzelman during the following days. In the meantime, several Confederate regiments rolled through the gap. Fortunately for the Union, command muddles on the Confederate side had reduced the assaulting force to only a fraction of the overwhelming strength hoped for by General Lee. Still, the Confederate assault caught the Second Corps almost completely by surprise. Sumner deployed into battle whatever regiments happened to be in sight, a stopgap measure at best.[31]

Officers and enlisted men of the 1st Minnesota were among those who rushed to meet the oncoming Confederate attackers, only to find themselves unsupported and outflanked. The Minnesotans began to waver as they took fire from the front and sides. Sensing the crisis at hand, Lieutenant Colonel Stephen Miller, standing just behind the men, called out "Minnesota, stand firm!" The effect was electric. "'Minnesota' was the magic word that encouraged us to stand firm," Private Richard Wright later proudly declared, "and face that terrible storm of bullets that swept our line." The men rallied, allowing two other regiments from their brigade to arrive and help blunt the Confederate attack.[32] Minutes later, the Confederates broke through another section of the patchwork Union lines. Sumner ordered soldiers of the Irish Brigade into the gap. The men responded with Celtic yells that, in the words of one observer, "might have drowned the musketry." The Irish soldiers breasted heavy artillery and musket fire before driving off the Confederate attackers and capturing two of their artillery pieces. "It was a splendid sight," a watching soldier described of the charge, "to see them with the American, Irish, and state flag at [their] head ... with Meagher leading them on."[33]

Taking much of the glow from the Union triumph at Savage's Station, Sumner turned uncharacteristically stubborn. He balked at leaving a "victorious field," and roused himself to action only late in the night when threatened with arrest by McClellan. The men paid the price, finding themselves bone-weary and marching into inky darkness. One marcher declared, "I was never so sleepy in my life. I know I was sleeping some of the time while I was marching and I heard other men say they did also."[34] There was little time for rest when soldiers crossed through White Oak swamp, several miles south of Savage's Station, at dawn on June 30. Exhausted soldiers had to endure scorching temperatures as they marched to support Brigadier General John McCall's division, under heavy Confederate attack at Glendale. Sumner's men arrived just in time to help stabilize the Union defensive lines until darkness forced an end to the fighting.[35]

Sumner's stubbornness at Savage's Station had forced the men to stay awake for nearly all of the past twenty-four hours and, now on the night of June 30, rest was no more coming. The Second Corps and the rest of the rear guard again pulled back, this time to join the main army stationed several miles to the south and east at Malvern Hill on the James River. Soldiers had only a short time to find their comrades wounded during the fighting at Glendale before moving out. The scene was ghoulish. Soldiers stumbled across the battlefield carrying torches and shouting for their friends. Occasionally they met with a response; more often they met with silence. All too frequently, the badly wounded had to be left behind. Spirits plummeted as soldiers had to part with their hard-fighting comrades.[36] Adding to the gloom, the Second Corps, less badly battered at Glendale than either the Third Corps or the Sixth Corps, was the last to leave the field. Water and food were in short supply on the march, while stragglers from the rest of the rear guard were plentiful. Many of these soldiers attempted to latch onto the last columns of Union blue. "These unfaithful men were a sore trial to our more faithful officers and men," a dismayed private wrote. "They were panicky to the last degree, and, like so many timid children, ran along beside our column, nearly crowding our men out of the ranks."[37]

When the main Union lines on Malvern Hill came into view in the early daylight hours of July 1, the draining effects of the march from Glendale made soldiers of the Second Corps largely unfit for duty. The rest of the rear guard certainly was tired. But, retreating from Glendale prior to the Second Corps, these men had "arrived in good time at the [James] river." A soldier in the Irish Brigade recalled that many of his comrades rushed immediately to the James River "to lap up the water." Other men, too tired to take another step, threw themselves upon the ground to rest.[38] Adding to the poor fighting condition of the Second Corps, straggling on the march from Glendale had left noticeable holes in the ranks. Many soldiers had gone missing or suffered capture after having fallen out from the retreating Union columns. The bedraggled and depleted appearance of the Second Corps did not escape the eye of McClellan. Except for a few regiments, the Second Corps remained in reserve when the rest of the army repulsed several Confederate attacks launched later in the day.[39]

Soldiers of the Second Corps and the rest of the Army of the Potomac retreated another eight miles to Harrison's Landing following the fighting at Malvern Hill. Here they glared at their Confederate counterparts in the Army of Northern Virginia for much of the rest of the summer. During the quiet, McClellan reinforced his army with nine regiments. The Fourth Corps, the smallest since the fighting at Fair Oaks, received the largest influx, with a brigade of four regiments transferred from the Shenandoah Valley. The Second Corps received only the 59th New York, raised in New York City before serving in the defenses of Washington. A more prized addition in manpower and combat experience came in mid-July, with the arrival of Brigadier General Nathan Kimball's brigade of three regiments. Although new to the Virginia Peninsula, Kimball's three regiments had served together in western Virginia in the fall of 1861 and in the Shenandoah Valley the following spring and summer. With the four newly arrived regiments,

Sumner's command numbered 16,950 men. These numbers made the Second Corps the second-strongest in the Army of the Potomac, behind the Fifth Corps and its 21,075 men.[40]

Personal considerations may have influenced McClellan's generous reinforcement of the Second Corps with Kimball's brigade. The westerners initially had received assignment to Franklin's Sixth Corps, which had suffered among the heaviest casualties of the army during the Seven Days Battles.[41] In an odd reversal of fortune, however, Franklin's stock soon fell with McClellan, while Sumner's rose. The switch began during a July 8 visit by President Lincoln to Harrison's Landing, where he discussed the future of the army with McClellan's corps commanders. The president polled the five generals about whether the army should withdraw to Washington, as he favored, or remain on the Virginia Peninsula, as McClellan favored. Sumner, Porter, and Heintzelman all sided with McClellan, believing that a retreat would hurt the morale of the troops. McClellan was not present, but he likely learned the opinions voiced by his subordinates. Although McClellan never said so, he may have transferred Kimball's men to reward Sumner for his support or, as the case may be, to punish Franklin for his opposition.[42]

Whatever McClellan's reason for sending Kimball's men to the Second Corps, their arrival presented Sumner with the awkward problem of how to integrate them. Both Richardson's and Sedgwick's divisions already had three brigades, and no division throughout the rest of the army had four. In the most likely solution, Sumner could have broken the brigade apart and distributed its regiments where needed. But doing so would have destroyed the history of the unit, built on several earlier battlefields. Most notably, soldiers of the brigade had fought at the Battle of Kernstown on March 23, 1862, the only Union victory yet over the vaunted Confederate General Thomas "Stonewall" Jackson.[43]

Sumner opted to keep Kimball's brigade intact, a decision that benefited the Second Corps over the long run. Labeling the command as an "independent brigade," Sumner held Kimball's men outside the organizational control of either of his two division officers. The arrangement was unique to the army, but Sumner knew that it would not last long. Earlier in the summer, President Lincoln had called upon the Union states for an additional 300,000 volunteers. The Army of the Potomac would receive many of these men in their own regiments as reinforcements, and Sumner likely viewed Kimball's veterans as the nucleus of a new division. By keeping the brigade independent, Sumner had practically forced the issue. A third division clearly needed creation, as well as the extra muscle that went along with it.

Soldiers of the Second Corps were of mixed opinion regarding the direction of the Union war effort as they welcomed reinforcements at Harrison's Landing. Private Samuel Maguire believed the Union advance and retreat along the Virginia Peninsula a success, even if it failed to take Richmond. "It is hardly right to call this falling back any thing less than a victory," Maguire argued, "as we have whipped them at every encounter." Lieutenant Edgar Newcomb was less sure. He wondered whether the Union "change of base" to the James River "is strategy or defeat. Time will show."[44] The Union war outside the Virginia Peninsula appeared equally murky between prospects of victory and defeat. Many soldiers excitedly discussed President Lincoln's call for 300,000 more volunteers that summer. The additional manpower would give the Union strength to bring the war to a quick and victorious conclusion. Other soldiers believed that the need for more troops all too clearly indicated that the Union had a more serious job on hand to subdue the rebellion than previously thought. One especially pessimistic private complained that "they have called for 3 hundred thousand more troops and that don't look as though the war is going to end for a year certain."[45]

Morale remained high despite the uncertainties about the Union war effort, because Sumner's men again recognized that they had fought well. They alone had arguably saved the Army of the Potomac from potentially devastating defeats at Fair Oaks, Glendale, and, to a lesser extent, Savage's Station. Regimental pride swelled. Lieutenant Colonel Francis Barlow bragged that soldiers of the 61st New York had shattered several Confederate attacks upon their lines. Lieutenant Henry Ropes claimed that the 20th Massachusetts was among the first Union regiments into battle at Fair Oaks and the last to leave the field at Glendale. Through all the hard fighting in between, the men have "done splendid, everyone says so." Captain Richard Turner was not to be outdone. He claimed that throughout the campaign the Irish Brigade had "fought bravely and won glory."[46]

For other soldiers, pride extended to the entire Second Corps. Soldiers still most closely identified with their regiments and brigades. But that some men already were discussing the battlefield record of the Second Corps indicates a burgeoning sense of loyalty. Major George Batchelder of the 19th Massachusetts drew pride from the larger accomplishments of the Second Corps. His regiment had served well, but did not win any especial distinction. The latter might not be said about the Second Corps. "Sumner's Corps was represented in every battle which has occurred," Batchelder glowed, ". . . and I think no one will say that they have not done their share." Lieutenant Josiah Favill, a brigade staff officer, drew pride from the spit and polish emphasized by Sumner since taking command of the Second Corps. Favill made a point of watching a review parade held in late July by the Fifth Corps. Other reviews were held around the same time, but Porter's corps was the only one that fielded regular army soldiers. Favill judged the old army troops well drilled and well disciplined. Still, Sumner's men "carry themselves more soldierly." This was not to say that "we have no poor regiments, because we have; but they are very few in number."[47]

Spirits throughout the rest of the army were not nearly as high as those enjoyed by the Second Corps. Dissatisfaction was rife in the Third Corps over the failure of the Federal offensive. Several high-ranking officers whispered loudly about the perceived bungling of the campaign by McClellan. Brigadier General Philip Kearny, one of the hardest fighters in the Union army, was even more negative. Kearny grumbled that Heintzelman and McClellan were in collusion to deny him a promotion. Support for the claim was almost nonexistent, but the accusation poisoned an already dispirited atmosphere. The Fourth Corps was upon harder luck, unable to shake the rout of Casey's division at Fair Oaks. McClellan effectively disbanded the command later in the summer, ordering one division to permanently garrison Yorktown. In the Fifth Corps, soldiers had fought well in holding the Union defensive lines at Malvern Hill. Porter's men had their pride tempered, however, by the collapse at Gaines' Mill that had precipitated the Union retreat from Richmond.[48] The same uncertainty between battlefield victory and

defeat characterized the Sixth Corps. After barely holding off the Confederate assaults at Glendale, Franklin's men had promptly abandoned
the field.

The unit pride of the Second Corps was important because camp life
at Harrison's Landing was grueling. The heat drew the most complaints.
A Massachusetts soldier claimed that the weather "is so hot I can't hardly breath." An Indiana soldier was more blunt. His diary entries for
four days in August read, "hot; hotter; hot as hell; hotter than hell."[49]
Monotonous and sometimes foul-tasting food elicited nearly as many
gripes. Men quickly had their fill of hardtack, salt pork, beans, and rice.
Occasionally wormy bread and rancid meat only hastened the desire for
a changed menu. After passing on a particularly nasty meal, one soldier
huffed, "Should like to see a whole brigade of commissaries hung."[50]
Swarms of flies, snakes, and other buzzing and slithering creatures kept
soldiers awake and wary. Those who managed to find sleep often awoke
itching, victims of the lice with which Sergeant Charles Fuller admitted
"we were all well stocked."[51]

Camp discipline slipped amid the difficult living conditions, with
deadly results. Soldiers spent day after day seeking shade and passing
time. Private George Beidelman reported that everywhere he looked
men were sitting "around in the dirt like old shoes." The listlessness
hampered sanitation efforts, and many regimental camps became overrun by dirt and filth. Divisional inspectors who eventually came around
were appalled. They reported finding unwanted foodstuffs rotting in the
open, woods stinking of latrine use, and garbage piling uncollected.[52]
Medical officers quickly took action to improve living conditions, but
the changes came too late for many men struck down by disease. Numbers of men complaining of high fever and nauseous stomachs skyrock-
eted by midsummer. Some of the ill recovered; others did not. A captain
reported that in late July he witnessed "burial now everyday, sometimes
3 or 4." Another soldier declared that the "'Dead March' could be heard
almost every hour of the day."[53]

The end to the Peninsula Campaign came in late July, when Lincoln
ordered McClellan to withdraw the army via water to northern Virginia.
Lincoln wanted the Army of the Potomac to unite with Major General
John Pope's Army of Virginia for a new offensive toward Richmond.

Despite Lincoln's reasoning, Sumner's men strongly disliked the march to Fort Monroe. Lack of rain made the roads dusty, and soldiers found dirt filling their shoes and covering their clothes. One soldier dirty from head to toe guessed, "It will take us about a week to get clean after our march."[54] Dirt and grime were temporary. What really galled Sumner's men was the recognition that the Army of the Potomac was leaving the Virginia Peninsula in defeat. That the Second Corps and the rest of the army marched past the scene of their earlier triumph at Yorktown only reinforced the gloom. Private William Stone remembered marching victoriously through Yorktown earlier in the campaign, "when we were confident in our ability to take Richmond." Back in Yorktown but headed in the opposite direction three months later, "we were in a different mood, occasioned . . . by the abandonment of the Peninsula Campaign and our retreat from Richmond."[55] In late August, soldiers of the Second Corps boarded transports for the trip back to northern Virginia.

STORMING BLOODY LANE

Sumner's men barely had time to shake the dust of the Virginia Peninsula from their shoes before again preparing to take the field. Soldiers heard the boom of artillery while in their encampments outside Alexandria on the morning of August 30. The sounds came from Manassas Junction and the old Bull Run battlefield, where Union General John Pope and his Army of Virginia had blundered into the Confederate Army of Northern Virginia. Veterans recognized that they might soon be called upon to join the battle, an awareness that caused more frustration than anxiety. Many of the men had believed camp rumors that the Second Corps, at least, was going to stay in Alexandria for several weeks to recuperate from the strains of the Peninsula Campaign. The hope faded quickly after soldiers received the midmorning command to fall in. "Instead of fresh bread," a crestfallen private observed, "we again got old crackers, a small piece of salt pork, a little ground coffee—and orders to march!"[56]

The Second Corps marched to Fairfax Court House, and into one of the more controversial moments of the campaign, on August 30. Sumner's men had halted only an easy tramp away from the now raging fighting at Bull Run. McClellan earlier had deployed two divisions of the Third Corps and one division of the Fifth Corps to aid the beleaguered Army of Virginia. The Union general refused to commit the Second Corps and the nearby Sixth Corps to the fighting, however, claiming that the men were in no "condition to move and fight a battle—it would be a sacrifice to send them out now." The decision later engendered much ill will, because some critics charged that McClellan wanted Pope, whom he considered a braggart and intensely disliked, to fail. Even Lincoln conceded that McClellan's failure to commit more reinforcements to Pope was "unpardonable."[57] McClellan's claim, however, had some merit. Soldiers of the Second Corps wrote of feeling "pretty well used up" and being "thinly clad" in their uniforms upon reaching Fairfax. At least these men stayed in the ranks. Many of their comrades had fallen out from fatigue and exposure. The 20th Massachusetts fielded just one hundred men upon reaching Fairfax, while the 61st New York lined up but five more men. The 4th Ohio was robust only by comparison, with three hundred men.[58]

The few men who managed to stay in the ranks watched Pope's defeated army streaming back through Fairfax Court House later that evening, a sight not easily forgotten. Sergeant John Adams remembered "everything in confusion" as wounded soldiers and horse-drawn ambulances and wagons hurried past. Hard on their heels came Confederate prisoners captured during the fighting. Far from defeated, the captives boasted that their liberation day would soon be at hand when the Confederate army captured Washington. At last came the unwounded but dispirited survivors of Pope's command. This encounter was the most painful for Sumner's men. "Everybody," one soldier sadly wrote, "inquired why the Second Corps had not come up in time to save the fortunes of the battle."[59] The Second Corps soon joined in the Federal retreat back to the outskirts of Washington, dimming spirits further. Soldiers gloomily noted that the Union cause appeared as far from victory as at any other point. A Massachusetts private captured the doubts of many of his comrades when he plaintively asked in early September, "Will another year find us no farther in our work of crushing the rebellion?"[60]

Sumner's men did not have long to sit and ponder the situation, because the pace of the war in the East quickened rapidly in the late autumn. On September 4, Lee moved the Army of Northern Virginia, numbering about 50,000 men, across the Potomac River and into Maryland. Lee hoped to score a battlefield victory on northern soil that would precipitate European recognition of the Confederacy, if not win the war outright.[61] The day after the Confederate invasion, Lincoln placed McClellan back in command of the Army of the Potomac as well as the remnants of the Army of Virginia. The president also gave his subordinate the daunting task of organizing the Federal forces into both a field army to pursue the Confederates and a garrison force to protect Washington. Working quickly, McClellan completed the shuffling of his forces on September 6. To attempt to bring Lee to bay, McClellan selected from the Army of the Potomac the Second Corps and the Sixth Corps, as well as the division of the Fifth Corps not engaged during the Second Bull Run Campaign. From the Army of Virginia, McClellan selected the recently renumbered First Corps and Twelfth Corps, as well as the Ninth Corps, which had fought independently of Pope's army at Second Bull Run. All told, McClellan took into the field 87,000 soldiers. He left behind another 72,500 men to guard Washington or, if need be, to reinforce the main army.[62]

The Second Corps was one of the few units of the original Army of the Potomac to gain a place in the Federal pursuit of Lee for two reasons. Manpower strength was the first reason. The slow-footed and tired had caught up on the retreat from Fairfax Court House to Washington, and the Second Corps now numbered 16,858 men. By contrast, McClellan considered soldiers of the Third Corps so badly mauled during the recent fighting around Manassas Junction that they needed several weeks to rest before they could again take the field. A proven battlefield record was the other reason why the Second Corps was in the field and helping to pursue Lee. Soldiers of the Second Corps had fought as well as any in the Union army by the autumn of 1862. Again by contrast, McClellan, as previously mentioned, had effectively disbanded the Fourth Corps. The command still existed on paper until the following summer, but its career with the Army of the Potomac had reached an end.[63]

While closing in on Lee in western Maryland, the Second Corps and the rest of the Army of the Potomac received reinforcements. The Fifth Corps and the Ninth Corps received the greatest boost in manpower, each receiving a new division by September 16. McClellan also distributed newly arriving brigades and regiments throughout the army. The Second Corps received Brigadier General Max Weber's brigade of three regiments (the 1stDelaware, 5th Maryland, and 4th New York) that previously had served on garrison duty in Suffolk, Virginia. Additionally, the Second Corps received four regiments (the 14th Connecticut, 108th New York, 130th Pennsylvania, and 132nd Pennsylvania) that had been raised that summer and were coming straight from their state training camps. The 4th New York had a two-year term of service, like a handful of other New York regiments accepted into Federal service at the outbreak of hostilities. The 130th Pennsylvania and 132nd Pennsylvania had only nine-month terms of service, a result of Secretary of War Stanton's acceptance of so-called militia soldiers to temporarily boost Union ranks.[64]

These reinforcements proved a mixed blessing for the Second Corps. The newcomers boosted the manpower under Sumner's command to 18,815 present for duty. The numbers were the highest reached in the Second Corps since the previous winter.[65] The newly arriving soldiers brought more than just their muskets, adding a new sense of dash to otherwise bedraggled-looking veterans. Colonel Richard Oakford described seeing survivors of the Peninsula Campaign march by the encampment of the 132nd Pennsylvania. "It was one of the saddest sights I ever saw," he admitted. "Poor weary, worn men. Almost used up." Private William Reed of the 127th Pennsylvania was more contemptuous after seeing Sumner's men. "Grand army indeed, a rough looking set," Reed scoffed. Detracting from numbers and spirit, the new soldiers added little experience to the Second Corps. The worst-off were soldiers raised that summer, who received constant torment from veterans. Soldiers in the 14th Connecticut reached the front to jeers of "'Hulloa children! Poor boys, dark blue pants, soft bread three times a week, three hundred miles from home and ain't got but one mother apiece.'" Green soldiers of the 132nd Pennsylvania received no better reception. They had their camp supplies raided by veterans, who all the while mocked, "'Did our 'Ma's know we were out?' 'Get off those purty duds.' 'Oh, you blue cherub!'"[66]

Sumner integrated the new regiments by organizing the Third Division on September 10.[67] This was a logical step, since the Second Corps otherwise listed two divisions and one independent brigade (Kimball's). Sumner organized the 14th Connecticut, 108th New York, and 130th Pennsylvania into their own brigade and sent the 132nd Pennsylvania to bolster the ranks of Kimball's brigade. The decision to concentrate the four regiments raised in 1862 carried risk, because each was at or near its full manpower strength of 1,000 soldiers. The result was that the largest division in the Second Corps, at 6,830 men, had very little battlefield experience. Other options existed to integrate the newly raised regiments. Sumner could have distributed these units throughout the First Division and Second Division, his most experienced commands. Generals Porter and Franklin of the Fifth Corps and Sixth Corps set the example when they distributed green regiments that they received during the Maryland Campaign into their battle-tested divisions.[68] Doling out the new regiments individually might have better dispersed them throughout the Second Corps, but doing so would have disrupted the hard-won cohesion of Richardson's and Sedgwick's brigades. With battle looming, Sumner was emphasizing experience over manpower.

An unintended consequence of assigning the new units to the Third Division was that it concentrated together almost all of the short-term regiments serving in the Second Corps. The War Department had accepted regiments enlisted for both two-year and nine-month terms of service without much heed to a longer war. Sumner gave no recorded insight into how long he thought the struggle might last. Presumably he, like many other high-ranking Union officers, believed that the current maneuvering in Maryland might end the war in a Federal triumph. When this did not turn out to be the case, the departure of the short-timers early the next summer made fewer gaps in the organizational charts of the Second Corps than the rest of the Union army.

Sumner appointed Brigadier General William French to command the Third Division. French, a West Point graduate (1837) and Mexican War veteran, was one of the five remaining original brigade commanders of the Second Corps. French's stock, already high because of his prewar experiences, had risen during the Peninsula Campaign. French had led the largest brigade in the Second Corps (six regiments) through the Seven Days Battles.[69]

Despite impressive qualifications and experiences, French made a poor division commander. In a bad misstep, he lost the respect of his volunteer soldiers by making elaborate displays of his rank. French "never makes his appearance without being dressed up in the greatest style," one private disapprovingly remarked, "and it was very seldom that he ever spoke to a private." Equally damaging to his reputation, French reportedly drank to excess. In an army full of hard-drinking officers, nips from the bottle were not unusual. But French had trouble limiting his drinks to days when the army was safely idle. The Third Division commander reportedly drank amid the pressures of a campaign. The rumors started as early as the Army of the Potomac's retreat down the Virginia Peninsula. A soldier in the 64th New York commented that French was too busy to fight at Savage's Station because he was "trying to save the surplus whiskey from falling into Rebel hands." The innuendo continued into the Maryland Campaign. Private David Rice of the 108th New York described seeing French yelling and shouting and otherwise behaving erratically one day on the march. Referring to French, Rice wrote in disgust, "the old cuss was about three sheets in the wind."[70]

McClellan had closed upon Lee by September 16, when both generals began to marshal their armies around Sharpsburg and Antietam Creek. McClellan hoped to fight and win the decisive battle of the war in western Maryland. To achieve this end, he maneuvered his forces to hit the flanks of Lee's army, anchored along Antietam Creek, at dawn. McClellan positioned the Second Corps in reserve on the Union right, where the hours passed slowly. The crash of artillery fire filled the late afternoon and made, according to one soldier, "a devilish music such as I never heard before." When quiet did come with the onset of night, many men found their sleep troubled by thoughts of the morning.[71] Bleary-eyed at dawn, soldiers heard sound of heavy artillery and musketry fire as the attack of the Union First Corps and Twelfth Corps against the Confederate left flank in the West Woods met heavy resistance. Sumner's men munched their breakfast and drank their coffee while listening to the fighting rage, knowing that they soon would receive orders to reinforce the Union assault. Admitted one soldier with butterflies in his stomach, the knowledge of impending battle "gave one a feeling very difficult to describe." Private James Maycock took no chances as the sounds of battle increased, vowing from that moment forward to "live closer to the Lord."[72]

The suspense ended in midmorning, when soldiers of Sedgwick's and French's divisions received orders to move against the Confederate left flank. Sumner inexplicably lost contact with French's trailing division, dangerously weakening any upcoming Union attack. After reaching the front lines, Sumner almost immediately pushed Sedgwick's men forward toward the West Woods. In doing so, he ignored advice for caution from Union officers on the scene. The Confederates, although severely bloodied in the morning's fighting, were lurking somewhere to the front. Yet the battlefield situation reinforced a sense of urgency. Sumner believed that the choice was between attack or retreat. Should he order a retreat, McClellan's entire battle plan might collapse. This was not much of a choice for Sumner, and, caught up in the moment, he pressed forward with Sedgwick's men.[73]

With some reason for continuing the earlier Union attack, Sumner made several surprisingly poor battlefield decisions. Sumner advanced Sedgwick's division in a tightly bunched column of brigades, the better to smash any head-on Confederate resistance. The formation was completely vulnerable, however, to fire from any other direction. This might have been less of a worry had Sumner acted like a corps commander, rather than galloping into action with Sedgwick's men. Sumner had lined up no artillery support for the Union advance, even though he had the Second Corps artillery reserve at his disposal. And by advancing himself into action, Sumner removed himself from coordinating the actions of any supporting units.[74]

The questionable decisions might have turned into needless second-guessing had not Sumner moved his men into an ambush. Confederate soldiers, hidden among rock outcroppings and swells that ran roughly perpendicular to the West Woods, suddenly opened fire into the advancing Union columns. The artillery and musket fire was as unrelenting as it was unexpected, creating a crush of battle unlike anything before experienced by soldiers of the Second Corps. Veterans of Fair Oaks and the Seven Days found that they could describe the horror of the chaos and death now around them only through metaphors with the more familiar. A Massachusetts captain declared that his men fell "like grass before the scythe." A New York lieutenant described Union soldiers dropping around him "like dead flies on a frosty morning." Noise and smoke only added to the confusion. Enlisted men struggled to hear commands given by their officers among roar of battle that was near-deafening. Soldiers not stunned by the noise had trouble even seeing their Confederate attackers, who became, according to one bewildered private, "quickly invisible from the smoke."[75]

The unit cohesion that had served the Second Corps well during the fighting on the Virginia Peninsula mattered less under the weight of the Confederate attack before the West Woods. Brigadier General Oliver Otis Howard, who commanded the Philadelphia Brigade, blamed the disaster on the lack of time to properly train his men. Howard had received charge of the brigade in the late summer, after recovering from a wound suffered on the Virginia Peninsula. Had he only a few more weeks to drill the men, the rout before the West Wood might never have happened. These were troops who already had demonstrated their battlefield discipline and bravery during the fighting before Richmond earlier in the summer, however, so it is hard to see how tramping across the parade ground a few more times would have made any difference. More likely, high officer casualties pushed Sedgwick's men past their breaking point. Sedgwick was badly wounded, and carried from the field. Another 106 officers of all ranks were down, more than the Second Corps had lost during the entire battle at Fair Oaks.[76] In a matter of minutes, only a relatively few officers were left to issue orders.

Taking matters into their own hands, veterans of Ball's Bluff and Fair Oaks broke toward their right, the only side not under fire. Private Andrew Ford of the 15th Massachusetts simply ran. Ford had served with the regiment since the summer of 1861, but nothing in his military career compared to the unequal slaughter at Antietam. He later quipped, "No God Damnded Southerner is going to catch me unless he can run 29 miles an hour." More men seemingly wanted to clear the killing ground rather than to quit the battle. Corporal Edward Walker declared that soldiers of the 1st Minnesota fell back "in pretty good order considering the circumstances." Private Joseph Johnson wrote that survivors of the 82nd New York "marched over a few fields when we again rallied ready on our foe." Walker and Johnson might have been attempting to put a positive spin on an otherwise grim reality. But several of Sedgwick's regiments regrouped to check the Confederate pursuit. Only a new assault swept away these stubborn defenders. Ultimately, the surprise is not that Sedgwick's battle-hardened division collapsed, but that the men had endured the one-sided contest for even the few minutes that they did. The tenacity came at shocking cost. Sedgwick's division had suffered 2,210 casualties, nearly one out of every two men who had first stepped forward.[77]

More than the men, Sumner had the fight taken out of him by the rout suffered in and around the West Woods. When asked for a battle-field update a short while later by one of McClellan's staff members, a distraught Sumner replied, "Go back, young man, and tell General McClellan I have no command." The next day Sumner described Sedgwick's division as still in no shape to renew the offensive, with the men a "good deal scattered and demoralized."[78] The loss of fighting spirit was very much out of character for Sumner. He coped by shifting the blame to McClellan. Sumner curtly cut off any inquires about the possibility of leading another attack on the Confederate left by replying that he was under standing orders from McClellan not to do so. That was true, but missing in the response was the presumably significant role that Sumner's own downbeat assessment had played in convincing McClellan to stand pat. Later in the fall, testifying before the Joint Committee on the Conduct of the War, Sumner attempted to completely remove himself from any blame. He criticized McClellan for deploying the Army of the Potomac at Antietam "in driblets." Had McClellan authorized him to move on the Confederate left in force, he would have driven all before him. When asked if this would have likely led to the destruction of the Confederate army, Sumner confidently asserted, "I think so."[79]

French's soldiers came into their own fight after veering away from the Federal advance toward the West Woods. The men crashed into the center of the Confederate lines at the Sunken Road. This was a rutted wagon road that dipped several feet below ground level and formed a natural defensive position. The attack quickly stalled, because the Confederate defensive fire was, to use the description of Union soldiers on the receiving end, "galling" and an "iron hail." Bullets whizzed by "thicker than bees," and shells exploded with a "deafening roar."[80]

The attack never regained its momentum because, unlike at Fair Oaks that summer, many green soldiers failed to endure the strain of battle. The difference in the two engagements was their duration. At Fair Oaks, the fighting, although sharp, stretched only handfuls of minutes at a time. By contrast, the action before the Sunken Road staggered on for several hours. The men sought shelter along the brow of a low-rising hill that overlooked the Sunken Road, but they still were under almost continuous Confederate defensive fire.[81] Confusion set in. Enlisted men later grumbled that, with only a few days of training prior to receiving assignment to the front, "they didn't know what to do." Some of French's soldiers mistakenly fired into their comrades to the front. As bad, increasing numbers of men excused themselves from the firing line. Major Frederick Hitchcock of the 132nd Pennsylvania later fumed that one man, soon followed by several others, "took counsel of their cowardly legs." The faint of heart bulled through file closers and officers in their rush for the rear. They never came back, suffering from a permanent case of what remaining soldiers termed the "cannon quickstep."[82]

Still, the fighting before the Sunken Road validated Sumner's decision to concentrate new soldiers in French's division. Most important, most of them stayed on the field and fought. None of the green regiments broke, unlike the previously untested 16th Connecticut in the Union Ninth Corps. These rookie soldiers completely collapsed when hit by a Confederate flank attack in the late afternoon. Survivors made no pretense of heading toward the rear, and only regrouped later in the evening.[83] The fire from French's men also took a toll on the Confederate defenders. Here and there a rebel broke toward the rear. The dead and wounded increasingly crowded the unhurt. By the late morning, the high casualties suffered created increasing disorganization among the remaining Confederate defenders.[84]

Soldiers of Richardson's division came up in support of French's now stymied command. The men were anxious, having to listen to the roar of battle as they crossed Antietam Creek and approached the

Sunken Road.[85] They became even more jittery when Confederate artillery opened. Sergeant Charles Hale of the 5th New Hampshire admitted
that when the "big iron bullets went swishing through the air with a
sound as though there were bushels of them, it made me wish that I was
at home." Confederate musketry next came into play, creating a deadly
wall of fire. A lieutenant declared that as Union attackers approached
Confederate defenders, "up went their flags and whiz, whiz came their
bullets."[86]

With casualties mounting, soldiers in two New York regiments
pressed into a wavering group of Confederate infantrymen and entered
the Sunken Road. Richardson's men now had a chance to return the
punishment. Soldiers of the division opened a devastating fire down the
length of the Sunken Road. A sergeant declared that with advantage of
flanking position "we were shooting them like sheep in a pen." After several minutes of the one-sided contest, Lieutenant Colonel Nelson Miles
of the 61st New York attempted to stop the carnage. Miles nervously
went forward yelling for the defenders of the Sunken Road to surrender
or risk death. "They rose up, I scarcely knew if they were going to fight
or surrender," Miles breathlessly described, "they however threw down
their arms and came in." A jubilant Miles later reported sending "almost
300 rebels" to the Union rear as prisoners.[87]

Through superb fighting, Richardson's men had stormed the Sunk-
en Road and torn open the center of the Confederate defensive lines.
Richardson recognized the opportunity to perhaps deal a mortal blow
to the Confederate army, and plunged his men forward. The thrust was
relatively weak, as the division already had suffered nearly one-third of
its men killed, wounded, and missing. The Irish Brigade alone reported
eight color bearers fallen.[88] Many of the remaining soldiers nervously
fiddled with muskets too clogged with gunpowder to properly load and
fire. Had McClellan deployed reinforcements from the army's ample
reserve, the Federal attack might have swept onward. Yet McClellan did
not, fearing a counterattack from hordes of Confederate reserves that
existed only in his imagination.[89] The Confederate artillery posted at
the Piper house, to the front of Richardson's men, was very real, however.
As Confederate gunners began to sweep the field with fire, Richardson's
men halted and dropped to the ground, their attack over. A private noted

Confederate dead in the Sunken Road. The capture of the worn farm lane after bloody fighting by French's and Richardson's divisions tore open the center of the Confederate defensive lines, an opportunity for a decisive Union battlefield victory that ultimately went unexploited. Library of Congress.

that with momentum spent but threat of death and injury still present, soldiers "readily dug their noses into the dirt." The Confederate fire eventually died out, but not before Richardson was mortally wounded while attempting to direct counterfire by Union artillery batteries. The loss of Richardson hit the men hard for, as one private explained, "we had indeed come to love him as a father."[90]

The retreat of the Confederate army back across the Potomac River on the night of September 18–19 freed men to venture across the battlefield. Many likely wished that they had stayed put. Dead and mangled bodies lay thickly across the ground, making, according to one corporal, a "most horrible sight." Sometimes, in an especially jarring experience, soldiers stumbled across dead and mortally wounded friends and family members. Soldiers in the 34th New York discovered a wounded man from their regiment who had shot himself in the head to end his sufferings. The men agreed that the episode was so painful that they would not mention it in their letters home. Other survivors of the fighting around the West Woods helped to carry badly torn Union dead from the field. They realized with horror that the bodies were men from their own regiment after recognizing rings, Bibles, and other personal possessions. In an especially tragic episode, Sergeant John Adams found his brother paralyzed and bleeding from a wound to the neck by the West Woods. "I saw at once that he could not live and had him placed in an ambulance and carried to our field hospital," a distraught Adams wrote. "It was the saddest duty of my life." Even soldiers who chose not to retrace the progress of the battle failed to escape the carnage. The stench from piles of burning horses and unburied bodies permeated food and clothing. "It is awful about here now," surgeon William Child shuddered one week after the fighting had ended. "The odor from the battlefield and hospitals is almost insupportable."[91]

Soldiers counted their own losses in the days that followed the Confederate retreat, making the horrors of the battlefield all the more oppressive. The Second Corps had suffered 5,354 men killed, wounded, and missing. Roughly one out of every three men who had gone into the battle had fallen. Staggering in their own right, casualties in the Second Corps nearly equaled the losses suffered by the other five corps of the Army of the Potomac combined. McClellan drew attention to damage inflicted upon the Second Corps in his official report on the battle. "This splendid veteran corps, in this one battle" was "sadly cut up, scattered, and somewhat demoralized."[92] Sumner's men were all too aware of the extent of the bloodshed. Private George Beidelman noticed the holes in the ranks of the Philadelphia Brigade. He worried that "All the regiments now look but little more than companies, some brigades numbering not over a thousand men." Private Joseph Johnson took a broader view by placing the losses suffered at Antietam into context of past battles. He declared that the battles on the Virginia Peninsula earlier in the summer "are but small in comparison" to the fighting around Antietam Creek. "Such sights never was seen and such terrible slaughter for one day's fight."[93]

Sumner's men might dispute McClellan's claim that they were "somewhat demoralized," because many of them believed the battle at Antietam a Union victory. Some men expressed disappointment that McClellan had allowed Lee to retreat safely back into Virginia. Lieutenant Ephraim Brown fumed that many Union soldiers had remained in reserve during the fighting, even though the Confederate lines had several times appeared near collapse. More men, however, expressed satisfaction in the outcome of the battle. Private Albert Manley argued that Union possession of the field demonstrated beyond doubt that "the rebels got the worst of it." Colonel Edward Cross boldly declared that with thousands of Confederates killed and wounded at Antietam, the battle "has been for the Rebels a Waterloo defeat." Also studying casualty returns, a private in the 72nd Pennsylvania argued that numbers alone now ran solidly in favor of the Union.[94]

Morale also remained high because Sumner's men believed that they had fought well, reinforcing their pride in their units and the Second Corps. There was some criticism over the way that Sedgwick's division had advanced into battle. A bewildered private was uncertain whom to blame, "but there was something wrong about our movement."[95] More men boasted over the battlefield performance of their units. Lieutenant Colonel Nelson Miles, who had helped to end the fighting in the Sunken Road in a Federal triumph, heaped praise upon his regiment. "There was as gallant fighting and as determined spirit displayed by our little band as ever was on any field," Miles declared. "Every man was a hero." A private who had survived the fighting before the West Woods found comfort in the idea that "our men fought with great coolness and courage."[96] General Sumner smartly reinforced this pride. He passed along compliments to several units for their hard fighting, most notably to the four regiments of Kimball's brigade. Sumner praised the men for maintaining before the Sunken Road an "unwavering line during the carnage of a four hours' battle." For the hard fighting, Sumner bestowed upon the unit the title "Gibraltar Brigade."[97]

The praise continued to build a growing awareness regarding the battlefield toughness and resiliency of the Second Corps. As on the Virginia Peninsula, soldiers increasingly recognized that their association with the Second Corps carried its own prestige. A New York private wished that the Second Corps had fought at Harpers Ferry, as well as at Antietam. The Union garrison at Harpers Ferry, under the command of Colonel Dixon Miles, had surrendered on September 15. The Confederate besiegers had rushed in the nick of time to stave off a last Federal attack at Antietam. "I think that old Genl Sumner who is now in command would not surrender upon such considerations," the New Yorker argued. "I would to God he had been there with the Corps instead of Miles and Co. The opinion general in the army is that had Harpers Ferry been held but 10 or 12 hours the War in Virginia would be at an end."[98]

Morale throughout the rest of the Union army is more difficult to discern, obscured by post-battle debate over whether McClellan should have launched a new round of attacks on September 18. What is clear is that, other than the Second Corps, the First Corps and Twelfth Corps on the Union right and the Ninth Corps on the Union left had borne the brunt of the fighting. These men had fought well, but a widespread sense of unit pride seemingly never developed. The high command was in shambles in the First Corps and Twelfth Corps, with Major General Joseph Hooker wounded and Major General Joseph Mansfield mortally wounded. Soldiers also had to contend with their very newness, having served in the Army of the Potomac for only two weeks. In the Ninth Corps, battlefield controversy was the stumbling block to a strong unit cohesion. Hard feelings simmered between McClellan and Major General Ambrose Burnside over why the Ninth Corps had moved with excruciating slowness in attacking the Confederate right around Antietam Creek and Sharpsburg. Combined with the Confederate counterstroke that had sent Burnside's men reeling in the late afternoon, the Ninth Corps ended the campaign with more questions than answers.[99]

Sumner's men commented little on President Lincoln's Emancipation Proclamation, but when they did it generally was positive. Issued in late September, the Emancipation Proclamation declared free all slaves in rebellious sections of the nation as of January 1, 1863. The document set the course for a dramatic broadening of the Union war effort, to include the destruction of slavery. Soldiers made little mention of the evolving Union war aims, perhaps because they hoped that the Union would win the war by the end of 1862.[100] Soldiers who did discuss the Emancipation Proclamation gave surprisingly favorable reviews, given their strong sympathies with the Democratic Party.[101] A private believed that England, France, and other European nations now would never recognize the Confederacy and its fight to uphold slavery. Colonel William Smith of the 1st Delaware took a more earthy view, declaring that with slavery on road toward extinction, "the Southerns will not have the nigger question to harp on." Lieutenant Colonel Elijah Cavins of the 14th Indiana came the closest to seeing slaves as people possessing God-given rights. He rejected out of hand any notion of black social or political equality. Still, "there are certain inalienable rights God had given to them, and they are the right of life, liberty, and the pursuit of happiness."[102]

Soldiers perhaps talked little of the Emancipation Proclamation because they were too busy enjoying camp life around Bolivar Heights and Harpers Ferry. The Second Corps and the rest of the Army of the Potomac had moved to the region in late September, to recuperate from the strains of the Maryland Campaign. Soldiers gushed over the scenery, with the Blue Ridge Mountains and the Shenandoah River running to either side of their encampment. Within short walk was the Potomac River, where men delighted in performing their daily cleanings. Private Albert Manley perhaps enjoyed taking baths and washing clothes more than most soldiers. He claimed that a late September laundry day was the first time that he had put on a clean shirt since leaving the Virginia Peninsula one month earlier.[103] All was not idyllic, however, and soldiers complained that "mouldy and wormy hard tack" was standard fare. Some men attempted to kill the worms through frying, while others attempted to cover the taste of mold by adding salt pork on top. The arrival of the paymaster in mid-October spared men from choosing between worms or mold. Camp settlers offered food for sale, albeit at high prices. Ham ran for twenty-five cents a pound, cheese for thirty cents a pound, cans of fruit for one dollar each, and potatoes for two dollars a bushel.[104]

Rebuilding from the bloodshed suffered in the fall campaigns also took place at Bolivar Heights, starting at the top. Major General Darius Couch assumed command of the Second Corps from Sumner, who had taken temporary leave of absence after the strain of the Peninsula and Maryland Campaigns. Couch came to the Second Corps with a distinguished military background. A graduate of West Point (1846) and veteran of the Mexican War, Couch had led a division of the Fourth Corps during the Peninsula and Maryland Campaigns. Couch also had connections to the very top of the Army of the Potomac, having graduated from West Point in the same class as McClellan.[105] Despite accomplishments and connections, Couch failed to win the hearts of soldiers in the Second Corps. He was extremely blunt in dealing with subordinates; worse, he was simply not Sumner. Veterans of the Peninsula and Maryland Campaigns hoped that they would not lose "our noble commander, the old war-horse Sumner." They especially wanted Sumner back "should it again be our destiny to meet and engage the enemy."[106]

In the First Division, Brigadier General Winfield Scott Hancock assumed command from the mortally wounded Israel Richardson.[107] Hancock on paper looked like many other high-ranking Federal officers. He had graduated from West Point (1844) and had fought in the Mexican War. With the outbreak of the Civil War, Hancock had led a brigade in the Sixth Corps since the fall of 1861. What distinguished Hancock from his contemporaries was his aggressive and fiery leadership. In battle, Hancock was both courageous and unflappable. At the Battle of Williamsburg in early May 1862, Hancock had led his brigade on a daring flank march that helped to smash the Confederate offensive. The quick thinking won Hancock renown across the Union as "Hancock

Darius Couch. Well-qualified for high command by the autumn of 1862, Couch never won the affection of soldiers of the Second Corps. Library of Congress.

the Superb." Equally important, in camp, Hancock was an officer after his men's hearts. He cursed a blue streak, to the chagrin of some men, but to the delight of more. Hancock especially received chuckles when he publicly called his own brother, a member of his staff, the "conventional name a man uses, when he wants to say a mean thing of the other fellow based on the alleged status of his mother." Adding to the aura, Hancock took care to appear immaculately dressed in front of his men. Crisp white shirt cast against the grime of military life cut an inspiring figure.[108]

In stark contrast to Hancock stood Brigadier General Oliver Otis Howard. Howard assumed command of the Second Division after Sedgwick took a leave of absence to recuperate from wounds received in the fighting around the West Woods.[109] Howard was something of an enigma as a military leader. He had ample combat experience. By the early fall of 1862, Howard had fought at Fair Oaks, where his right arm was wounded and amputated, and at Antietam. Howard also had a quick sense of humor. The day that Howard was wounded on the Virginia Peninsula, he informed a fellow officer who had lost his left arm during the Mexican War that they now could wear one pair of gloves together. Battle experience and good-natured jests only went so far, however, and Howard failed to inspire his men. Soldiers viewed their new commander as a prig because, deeply religious, he displayed a crusading spirit to curb drinking, swearing, gambling, and other camp vices. As early as the winter of 1862, Private Herbert Willand described Howard as "an old maid" who should use "less prayers and preaching and more common sense" when dealing with enlisted men. Another private judged Howard "a one wing devil," a word choice that likely would have horrified the pious Second Division commander, because he constantly "preaches to the brigade."[110]

The rebuilding of the Second Corps continued with the arrival of four regiments as reinforcements between late September and late November. Soldiers of the 10th New York and 28th Massachusetts had volunteered in New York City and from Irish-American neighborhoods in Boston, respectively, in the spring and summer of 1861. The two regiments were battle-hardened, having fought at Second Bull Run. By contrast soldiers of the 19th Maine and 116th Pennsylvania had come into the army from southern Maine and Irish-American neighborhoods in

Philadelphia only that summer. As new regiments arrived, the Second Corps, for the first time, had transferred two regiments. The 29th Massachusetts moved to the Ninth Corps, and the 5th Maryland received detachment to the Eighth Corps, permanently stationed in and around Baltimore. The comings and goings of regiments was not exclusive to the Second Corps. Five other regiments received transfer throughout the rest of the army, while at least eleven regiments arrived that same autumn.[111] In the end, the reshuffling of regiments strengthened the Second Corps. On October 10, Couch's command listed 16,345 men. McClellan apparently preferred reinforcing first the commands original to the Army of the Potomac when given the opportunity. By the mid-fall, the three corps that had fought on the Virginia Peninsula (the Second Corps, Fifth Corps, and Sixth Corps) were larger in manpower than the three corps that had only more recently joined the army (the First Corps, Ninth Corps, and Twelfth Corps).[112]

Couch's options of where to send the new regiments were limited. The 28th Massachusetts and 116th Pennsylvania went to the Irish Brigade, replacing the departed 29th Massachusetts. The 10th New York went to Weber's brigade (French's division), rejoining regiments that all had served together on garrison duty at Fort Monroe during the winter of 1861–62. Couch sent the remaining regiment, the 19th Maine, to the Second Division, the hardest hit of the three divisions of the Second Corps during the fighting at Antietam. The newcomers all expressed satisfaction with their assignments. Soldiers in the 10th New York were glad to find familiar faces in their new brigade. Greenhorns in the 19th Maine eagerly listened to advice freely handed out by veterans in Howard's division.[113] Most happy, however, were the largely Irish soldiers of the 28th Massachusetts and 116th Pennsylvania assigned to the Irish Brigade. Newcomers recognized that they joined one of the most celebrated brigades in the Union army. They also enjoyed the reception received from General Thomas Meagher and his veteran Irish soldiers. Private Peter Welsh of the 28th Massachusetts marveled that, even though it was the early morning, Meagher came out and "welcomed us to the brigade." As the New Englanders marched past the drawn-up soldiers of the Irish Brigade, Meagher sang out for three cheers that "were given with a will and were returned by the 28th."[114]

The last step in the rebuilding of the Second Corps occurred with the arrival of handfuls of replacement soldiers to regiments raised in the first year of the war. Veteran officers recruited replacement soldiers in their hometowns while either on detached duty or recuperating from wounds. The newcomers generally received a mixed reception from their battle-tested comrades. A Massachusetts captain complained that replacement soldiers were not worth the effort to enlist because they had to be trained from scratch in every aspect of military life. He griped that "1 man of this Divis. could do the work of 3 recruits." By contrast, a sergeant claimed that new volunteers would make good soldiers with proper training because they wanted to be at the front. He claimed that many of them had waited to enlist, "hoping that the war would be over, and their services would not be required, but seeing the disasters that had come to the army, resolved to come and help us."[115] Replacement soldiers never arrived in large numbers, because men still at home preferred to go to war in their own regiments. Yet the newcomers helped regiments worn down by battle and disease to recuperate at least some of their original vigor. Captain James Sponable of the 34th New York was wounded at the Battle of Fair Oaks on the Virginia Peninsula in late May. While recovering at home, Sponable recruited six volunteers to accompany him back to the front in late September. The numbers in themselves were small, but the volunteers recruited by Sponable doubled the manpower strength of his company to twelve soldiers present for duty. Similarly, in October, the 19th Massachusetts received thirty-one replacement soldiers. These men more than compensated for the ten veterans of the regiment who either received discharge for medical disability or died from wounds suffered at Antietam during the same month.[116]

Commitment to the Union cause remained strong as the rebuilding continued and the autumn progressed. Captain David Beem of the 14th Indiana admitted that he longed to return home. But "however anxious I may be to see the struggle ended, I would not yield an inch to the enemies of our country, and I have yet to see the first hour in which I regretted coming into the service." Homesickness also sometimes struck Private John Lehman of the 7th Michigan. At these moments, Lehman reminded himself "I did not enlist for the fun of it but because my country needs me." John Weiser survived the fighting before the Sunken Road. Even after seeing the carnage of war at its worst, the Pennsylvania private declared, "I am in a good cause and intend to do all for the old Flag that I can."[117]

That soldiers were talking about fighting and dying for the "good cause" in the wake of the bloodiest single-day battle fought in the Civil War indicates that they remained in the ranks for more than just their comrades. The comments also indicate that soldiers were not growing disillusioned with their early war ideals, as sometimes argued in the scholarship.[118] Sumner's men, as much as any Union soldiers, recognized that the courageous often suffered physical harm in battle. Bullets and shells made no distinction in whom they struck. The knowledge that the brave were struck down as often as, perhaps more often than, the shirkers brought acceptance, rather than despair. Sergeant Walter Eames explained that "good soldiers" must accept the death and wounding of their comrades as part of their commitment to preserving the Union. Other men found solace in looking to God. If killed, they might be in a better place. More battles were looming, so soldiers always should "be prepared to meet their Maker in heaven, where there is no more pain, nor sickness, nor death, but all in love." Corporal Amory Allen looked to neither duty nor God, and simply continued on. "I don't know what to write to you," Allen admitted to his wife in late September, "only that I am glad that I am alive."[119]

The Second Corps had undergone a remarkable rebuilding process in the weeks that followed the battle at Antietam. The high command was solid, with Couch, Hancock, and Howard. The ranks were nearly replenished to their early September numbers. The vast majority of the officers and enlisted men now present for duty had fought through the thick of many of the great battles of 1862. Soldiers of the Second Corps had fought well in these engagements, developing a growing sense of unit identity and pride. The initial enthusiasm to go into battle expressed that past winter was gone. But soldiers resolutely looked ahead, determined to continue fighting just as hard toward ultimate Union victory.

3

THE FREDERICKSBURG
CAMPAIGN

Few soldiers in the Second Corps were without opinion when President Lincoln removed General McClellan from command of the Army of the Potomac in early November 1862. To lead the Federal forces, now encamped around Warrenton, Virginia, Lincoln appointed General Ambrose Burnside, the commander of the Ninth Corps. Lincoln made the command change because he believed McClellan too slow and cautious to ever bring Lee to bay.[1] Corporal William Myers of the 106th Pennsylvania worried that partisan politics rather than military strategy now drove the Union war effort. Myers fumed, "It was nothing but the nigar lovers of the North who took [McClellan] from us." Yet more soldiers accepted Lincoln's decision, if not applauding it. Private Joseph Law wished McClellan still in command of the army, but promised to fight just as hard for Burnside. Lieutenant Ephraim Brown of the 64th New York acknowledged that McClellan was a "great commander." But Brown had helped to storm the Sunken Road at Antietam, where his regiment had suffered heavily. Brown was unforgiving that McClellan had seemingly done nothing to exploit the Union breakthrough. All the loss of life, and the Confederate army still was intact and in the field.[2]

AGAINST THE STONE WALL

Couch's men did not have long to sit and stew at Warrenton because Burnside quickly put his stamp upon the Army of the Potomac. Burnside started by reshuffling the army's organization. The new army commander allowed the Twelfth Corps to remain put near Harpers Ferry to help guard Washington. He made good these losses by recalling the Third Corps from the defense of the nation's capital in mid-November, raising the strength of the army to 110,000 men.[3] Next, to better streamline command over the army, Burnside formed his six army corps into three grand divisions. Burnside gave command of each grand division to the senior-ranking officer. He grouped the First Corps and Sixth Corps into the Left Grand Division, under Major General William Franklin; the Third Corps and Fifth Corps into the Center Grand Division, under Major General Joseph Hooker; and the Second Corps and Ninth Corps into the Right Grand Division, under Sumner, recently returned from leave.[4]

In creating the Right Grand Division, Burnside may have wanted his former soldiers of the Ninth Corps to fight alongside the proven veterans of the Second Corps. Burnside never said so, and a combination of several other factors likely influenced his thinking. One reason why Burnside grouped the Ninth Corps with the Second Corps was that he had more reason to trust Sumner than the other two grand division commanders. Sumner was free of the politics and intrigue that often swirled about the high command of the Army of the Potomac. By comparison, Hooker was none too subtly angling to one day assume command of the army, while Franklin was suspect because of his close relationship with McClellan.[5] The other reason why Burnside grouped together the Ninth Corps and the Second Corps was their geographic proximity in camp. Both commands were stationed near Waterloo, Virginia, just to the north of Warrenton. That Burnside paired the various army corps where he found them also is suggested by the unequal manpower of the three grand divisions. The Left Grand Division fielded 43,800 men, the Center Grand Division fielded 36,295 men, and the Right Grand Division fielded 29,908 men.[6]

The leadership of the Second Corps was little affected by Burnside's reshuffling, giving it a greater continuity than most of the rest of the army. This was rather remarkable in itself, since Couch had assumed command only in the aftermath of the Maryland Campaign. Still, four out of the other five corps commanders at Warrenton were new. In the Ninth Corps, Brigadier General Orlando Wilcox filled the command opening after the advancement of Burnside. The same happened in the Sixth Corps, with Major General William "Baldy" Smith replacing Franklin. In the Fifth Corps, Brigadier General Daniel Butterfield assumed command. Butterfield replaced Porter, who soon was to undergo a controversial court-martial for disobeying orders during the fighting at Second Bull Run. Brigadier General George Stoneman assumed command of the Third Corps. The spot needed filling because Heintzelman, the original commander, had received appointment to command the Union defense of Washington during the Confederate invasion of Maryland. Brigadier General John Reynolds of the First Corps was the only Union commander other than Couch to have held his position since the end of the Maryland Campaign. Not since the start of the war had the Union army readied to take the field with as many new corps commanders.[7]

Burnside put the reorganized Army of the Potomac on the march toward Falmouth, Virginia, on November 15. Burnside hoped that soldiers would cover the forty miles between Warrenton in the west and Falmouth in the east before Lee's Confederate forces, encamped near the Blue Ridge Mountains, could react. From Falmouth, Burnside planned to cross the army into Fredericksburg, only a short push from Richmond to the south.[8] Couch's men, in the advance of the army, found the march grueling. Some soldiers complained of weather that turned cold and stormy. Other soldiers complained about the dreary landscape. A private groused that the countryside "is mostly scrub woods, very little good land, and few houses, of any kind. We saw some that looked as if they had been built in the year 1." Another private marching through gloomy woods declared that the only things to see beside trees were wood ticks "that bite one most to death." Seeking relief from stinging bites, unfortunate victims pulled out the tick. Often remaining behind was the head of the tick that festered and made "an itching sore much worse than a boil."[9]

Sumner led the Second Corps into Falmouth two days later, and immediately faced the decision of whether to ford the Rappahannock River. The pontoon bridges that Burnside had requested to be sent from Washington had failed to arrive. Yet the few Confederate gunners who defended Fredericksburg abandoned their battery after coming under Union artillery fire. The temptation to capture the guns and seize

Fredericksburg was "so strong" that Sumner issued orders for the Irish Brigade to cross a nearby ford. The Irish soldiers moved toward the river at a run when Sumner changed his mind. Burnside previously had ordered Sumner not to push ahead the Federal offensive until the entire army had reached Falmouth. Suddenly now remembering this, Sumner halted the Federal advance because he "was rather too old a soldier to disobey a direct order."[10]

Sumner was not one to go off on his own, but he also recognized the strategic opportunity before the Union army. Sumner pressed Burnside later that evening to allow the Second Corps to ford the Rappahannock. He pleaded that the river crossing was shallow, with a cow reportedly wading across easily. Burnside refused. Should heavy rains cause the Rappahannock to rise, the Second Corps might find itself vulnerable to an attack from the entire Army of Northern Virginia. Memory did not need to stretch back far to remember that the Army of the Potomac had nearly suffered a crushing battlefield defeat at Fair Oaks in the summer of 1862 while astride the Chickahominy River. The comparison was not entirely apt, because Union artillery posted outside Falmouth might have provided a near-overwhelming defensive fire against any Confederate attack toward Fredericksburg. In standing pat, Burnside, arguably, had missed an otherwise rare opportunity to strike a daring blow against Lee.[11]

Importantly for the Second Corps and the rest of the Union army, the aggressive counsel offered by Sumner on the evening of November 17 indicated that he had shaken off the disaster before the West Woods at Antietam. Sumner was simply not going to disobey a direct order from Burnside or any other higher-ranking Union officer. But arguing for the seizure of Fredericksburg after Burnside had arrived to take command was very much in keeping with Sumner's emphasis upon quick battlefield action during the Peninsula and Maryland Campaigns. Several weeks later, the mid-November discussion also demonstrated that Sumner was a loyal soldier. Following the disastrous Union battlefield defeat at Fredericksburg on December 13, Sumner publicly declared that Burnside had been right in not fording the Rappahannock. The capture of the town of Fredericksburg was not the end point to Burnside's campaign. Rather, the possession of this geographic point would have allowed Burnside to continue to drive toward Richmond and maintain pressure on Lee. A battle was going to have been fought regardless, whether outside Fredericksburg or Richmond. Other high-ranking officers were far less circumspect, and publicly criticized Burnside for his lack of aggressive action after the Union army first reached Falmouth.[12]

Soldiers were unsympathetic to Burnside's and Sumner's plight as the army marked time at Falmouth. A private in the 10th New York could not determine whether the Federal high command had so far displayed great genius or stupidity. "We hurried from Warrenton to this place as if Old Nick himself were after us," he explained, "over stony and muddy roads and sometimes no roads at all, and—we have laid here five days, doing nothing." Another soldier scoffed that the "'Rapid moving, daring Burnside'" might not be worthy of the praise.[13] Soldiers' mood only darkened in late November, as they watched the arrival of the Army of Northern Virginia and its 75,000 men in Fredericksburg. Private Miles Peabody had fought with the 5th New Hampshire in the thick of the action at Fair Oaks and Antietam. Peabody gloomily readied to add another name to the list. If the Union army now was to take Fredericksburg, "it will be after a hard fight." Private Edward Bassett was one of the few men to keep his sense of humor about him. He wrote tongue-in-cheek that things had not gone nearly as well as expected, "but I suppose there has been enough done to make a few Major Gens., besides any number of Brigadiers and Colonels."[14]

While soldiers talked, Burnside came under intense pressure from the Lincoln administration to launch an offensive. Burnside recognized that the Confederate defensive works behind Fredericksburg were strong, but he decided to assault them anyway in hopes of catching Lee by surprise. In a loosely worded plan of attack that remained fuzzy in detail, Burnside ordered pontoon bridges built across the Rappahannock both above and below Fredericksburg. All the army but Hooker's Center Grand Division was to cross to the far bank on December 12. The next morning, Franklin's Left Grand Division, spearheaded by the First Corps, was to assault and turn Lee's right flank, anchored around Prospect Hill. Simultaneously, Sumner's Right Grand Division, led by the Second Corps, was to push through Fredericksburg and storm Marye's Heights, crushing Lee's left. Hooker's troops, still in reserve, were to

cross the Rappahannock and support whatever attack seemed to be
making the most headway. If all went well, one or more Federal grand
divisions would break through, forcing the Confederate army to retreat
or risk destruction.[15]

Couch's men expressed disbelief as preparations for the Federal
attack became apparent, throwing into some doubt how enthusiastically
they would go forward. Sumner called a meeting of the high-ranking
officers of the Right Grand Division on December 9 to discuss the attack.
Sumner supported Burnside's proposed attack, but Couch declared that
"there were not two opinions among the subordinate officers as to the
rashness of the undertaking." Burnside understandably was concerned
when he heard word of the meeting. He called together the same officers
the next night and tongue-lashed all of them but, presumably, Sumner,
for their perceived opposition to his plans.[16] Soldiers in the ranks made
their shock over the looming attack equally well known. Most vividly, a
distraught private in the Irish Brigade rushed to Father William Corby,
wailing, "'Father, they are going to lead us over in front of those guns
which we have seen them placing, unhindered, for the past three weeks.'
'Do not trouble yourself'"; Corby reassured the man, "'your generals
know better than that.'"[17]

The Second Corps received a wave of reinforcements on the eve of
the planned attack, giving Couch the same organizational headaches as
Sumner had suffered prior to the fighting at Antietam. On December 9,
the Second Corps received the 27th Connecticut, 24th New Jersey, 28th
New Jersey, 127th Pennsylvania, and 145th Pennsylvania. Only five other
regiments arrived throughout the rest of the army in early December,
and four of these units went to the Ninth Corps. The pattern of reinforcements suggests that Burnside expected the Right Grand Division
to carry a full share of the fighting in the upcoming Union assault.[18]

Couch could not place the newly arrived regiments in their own brigades, as Sumner had done prior to Antietam, because each of his divisions already fielded three. Instead, Couch assigned the new regiments
to four brigades that had received no reinforcements in the aftermath
of the Maryland Campaign. General Wilcox followed a similar pattern in the Ninth Corps, distributing reinforcements to three different
brigades. In the Second Corps, the green regiments added nearly full

ranks to their brigades. The 27th Connecticut fielded 829 officers and men present for duty, while the 24th New Jersey mustered 985 officers and men present for duty. The new soldiers also brought an eagerness to see battle. In a typical comment expressed by other newcomers, a private in the 127th Pennsylvania enthused that he had "come down" to Virginia "to kill rebels."[19]

Despite numbers and enthusiasm, the new soldiers were dubious additions. Except for an occasional veteran of a three-months militia unit raised at the start of the war sprinkled here and there, soldiers of the new regiments all had yet to go into battle. Soldiers of the 27th Connecticut were not even equipped to fight well, having received antiquated smoothbore muskets that often failed to fire properly. In words hardly designed to impart confidence, a staff officer inspecting the muskets pronounced, "Boys, if you can't discharge them, you can use the bayonet." Additionally, soldiers in all the new regiments but the 145th Pennsylvania had volunteered for nine-month terms of service in the late summer. Their already short term of enlistment was even shorter by the time that they reached Falmouth, creating a looming organizational problem for the Second Corps. Couch made the best of the decision, and assigned the 24th New Jersey and 28th New Jersey to Kimball's Third Division brigade. The organizational move continued to concentrate the majority of the short-term regiments in French's division.[20]

Soldiers knew that they had reached the point of no return for the Federal attack at Fredericksburg in the pre-dawn darkness on December 11, when Burnside put his offensive into motion. Engineers laying down pontoon bridges across the Rappahannock River met withering fire from Confederate sharpshooters posted in Fredericksburg. To provide covering fire, Burnside ordered Union artillery massed along Stafford Heights to shell the town. Cannon blasts failed to drive the Confederates from cellars and other well-protected defensive positions, and the sharp shooting continued nearly unabated. More immediate measures were needed, prompting Burnside and other high-ranking officers to call for volunteers to row across the Rappahannock River in pontoon boats and clear out the Confederate defenders.[21]

Soldiers from the 7th Michigan pushed off first, followed by the 19th Massachusetts and the 20th Massachusetts. Seemingly unerring

Confederate fire hit the soldiers of Howard's division almost as soon as they were on the water. One horrified observer wrote that killed and wounded men quickly began to tumble among their comrades or, worse, splash into the water. Heavy fire continued to pour into soldiers after they had landed and moved into the streets of Fredericksburg. Lieutenant J. E. Hodgkins described his company moving up a street leading from the river and coming under "a shower of bullets from the enemy, who were posted in the houses, behind the fences and wherever a shelter offered." The men quickly sought cover in an empty lot behind a fence. Even here there was no safety, and another Confederate volley felled two more soldiers.[22]

With Union and Confederate troops swirling through Fredericksburg, the fighting, already intense, turned savage. Howard's men received orders "to bayonet every armed man found firing from a house." Soldiers apparently were reluctant to do so because, as one explained, the order was "contrary to the rules of war." But soldiers of the three attacking regiments were not above meting out their own form of military justice. Members of one regiment received assurance from a young woman that no one was in her house but her "'poor, old blind father.'" After moving on, the group of soldiers came under musket fire from the same house. The men rushed back and stormed into the residence, where they captured a young man with a gun barrel that, literally, was smoking. The outraged men put the unfortunate prisoner at the head of an advancing company of the 20th Massachusetts. When the Massachusetts soldiers rounded a street corner they received a "terrible volley" and the prisoner dropped dead in his tracks. So did many Union soldiers. By the time Howard's men cleared Fredericksburg of sharpshooters by dusk, they had suffered 200 men killed, wounded, and missing.[23]

In addition to gaining Union control of Fredericksburg, the street fighting on December 11 demonstrated that Howard's men, like Sumner, had regained their spirit following the battlefield disaster suffered before the West Woods. Regimental and company officers heaped praise upon their men for "unflinching bravery and splendid discipline." Howard added to the good feeling, extolling soldiers in the three regiments for their "gallantry in crossing the river." Burnside offered perhaps the greatest compliment. Recognizing that a relative handful of Confederate sharpshooters had come close to derailing the entire Union offensive, Burnside was especially pleased to have ended the standoff. He later reportedly described the Union capture of Fredericksburg as "one of the greatest military feats of the war."[24]

Survivors recognized that they had participated in a significant accomplishment, and in later years this led to controversy. Veterans of the 7th Michigan and the 20th Massachusetts argued heatedly over who had first reached the Confederate side of the Rappahannock. The quarrel opened the door for soldiers in other regiments to attempt to claim at least some of the perceived honor. Sergeant E. M. Cafferty declared that soldiers of the 89th New York crossed the river at the same time as any of the three regiments of the Second Corps. "There being a bend in the river, we could not see each other." Another sergeant, but this one in the 50th New York Engineers, settled the matter, if not perhaps to everyone's liking. He helped to row across the first boat, and his passengers were from the 7th Michigan.[25]

The other soldiers of the Second Corps crossed into Fredericksburg the next day, and the scenes that greeted them ranged from the horrific to the ludicrous. Dead Confederates from the recent street fighting lay where they had fallen. Couch's men readily imagined that a similar fate awaited them. If they missed the point, they were reminded when met by an embalmer passing out business cards at the foot of the pontoon bridge in Fredericksburg.[26] Many soldiers chose not to notice dead Confederates or living morticians, and instead busied themselves ransacking abandoned homes and buildings. Many of Couch's men dragged chairs and beds into the street to lounge. Others brought books, tea sets, and clothes into the open to admire or, if especially boisterous, to smash and tear. Inevitably, everything consumable was sampled, and either finished or tossed away. Walking amid the tumult, E. A. Walker admitted that he had read about the plundering of cities in books. However, "Fredericksburg is the first thing in the sacking line that we have seen and it was well done too."[27]

Soldiers of the Second Corps participated in the plundering of Fredericksburg for a variety of reasons, but many seemed freed from restraint by the fighting that had damaged much of the city on the previous day. At least one modern-day scholar argues that the sack of Fredericksburg

represented a policy of "directed severity" on the part of Union soldiers—targeting southern property, rather than southern civilians, to
drive home the costs of war. The violence appears less premeditated in
the Second Corps. Some soldiers did roam the streets engaging in mali-
cious destruction, even carrying off Bibles and other sacred objects from
a local church. More often, soldiers easily rationalized grabbing food,
clothing, or some other bit of private property that might as easily have
been destroyed earlier by bullet or shell. The army's provost guard had
yet to move into Fredericksburg in force, and Couch's men had little
fear of suffering arrest. Yet still some soldiers found relief from anxiety
of impending battle by cavorting through the streets. They often did so
in impromptu bits of street theater, where soldiers dressed up in civilian,
often women's, clothing.[28] Not all soldiers participated. Some soldiers
of the 1st Minnesota even stood guard outside a home where portraits
painted by their commanding officer's father, a well-known artist, hung.
The marauding by the Second Corps embarrassed Couch. He initially
denied that much looting had occurred beyond the taking of "tobacco,
flour, and other eatables," despite the ample evidence to the contrary.[29]

Whatever the reasons behind the plunder of Fredericksburg, the
fact that many of Couch's men freely joined in demonstrates both a
near-complete breakdown in military discipline and a hardening attitude toward the war. Soldiers likely did not move into Fredericksburg
with the intent to rampage. That many of them later did indicates that
more than a few officers also joined in the bedlam. General Howard, the
Second Division commander and one of the more upright leaders in the
Union army, reportedly waved off concerns over the extent of the plundering by remarking that officers and enlisted men "are not expected to
be angels." The quotation must be viewed with some caution, however,
because it comes from a soldier in the Ninth Corps writing well after the
end of the war and perhaps attempting to shift blame. Plenty of contemporary accounts exist about officers helping themselves. Soldiers of the
116th Pennsylvania rolled casks of flour from a bakery into the street.
A "distinguished officer" helped to distribute the foodstuff, quipping,
"Boys, we are surely the flour . . . of the Army of the Potomac now." In
other regiments, captains, lieutenants, and even a chaplain boasted of
stealing books, silver dishware, and other household valuables.[30]

Perhaps even more surprising than the level of involvement in the looting, few soldiers expressed remorse. War meant killing and destruction, and too often Couch's men had been on the receiving end. Tearing apart houses and stores paled by comparison to the horrors witnessed at Fair Oaks and Antietam. Private Roland Bowen of the 15th Massachusetts exemplified the attitude when he passed by several pigs eating the remains of a dead Confederate. Bowen did not stop to shoo away the animals because he was "too busy stealing." The comment was not meant even somewhat in an offhand manner, because "I knew the hogs wanted something to eat (Such is War)." Even new soldiers gave little concern to the level of destruction. Soldiers of the 19th Maine had only arrived at the front in October, and had yet to go into battle. It's unclear if they followed the lead of veterans or exercised their own initiative, but the men literally grabbed any household items not fastened down. If left on their own, the New Englanders would "steal the whole Southern Confederacy in three months."[31]

The chill of a winter dawn on December 13 found the Second Corps weakened in manpower before even much fighting had taken place. The daily vagaries of military life drew some men away from the battle line. Soldiers in two companies of the 10th New York trudged out for predetermined guard duty. And not even all of the men present for duty throughout the rest of the regiment were ready to fight. The regimental historian later declared that "a number of men" remained in camp "for want of shoes and clothing." In the 27th Connecticut, 375 men prepared to advance against the Confederate defensive lines, while 250 men performed picket duty along the Rappahannock River. A recently arrived recruit for the 7th Michigan won a spot in camp because of his inexperience in war. "My captain handed me a gun twice," he explained, "and then withdrew it again because he said it seemed to him like butchering men by taking them into the field without drilling." Other draining of manpower strength occurred on orders. That same morning, Burnside ordered that one division of the Second Corps remain in reserve, to support the attacks made by the other two divisions. In turn, Sumner informed Couch that "as Howard's led into town, it is proper that one of the others take the advance." Although a seemingly fair order, Sumner's decision deprived Couch of one of his largest divisions. This was a serious blow, because the other two divisions of the Second Corps were to attack in successive brigade lines of battle. This was a standard Civil War assault formation that depended upon mass and weight of numbers to overwhelm the opposing lines.[32]

Leading the Federal attack upon Marye's Heights fell to French's division, the larger of the two divisions immediately at hand. The men found themselves in an unusually difficult spot, because the terrain funneled each brigade toward the strength of the Confederate defenses on Marye's Heights.[33] French's men had to cross a fifteen-foot drainage ditch on one of two bridges two hundred yards outside Fredericksburg. Crowded on the bridges, soldiers made easy targets for Confederate artillery posted to the front. An Ohio soldier later commented that no sight depressed the men in his regiment more than the two bridges looming ahead because they recognized the "waste of lives" that would occur in the slow crossing. Respite waited in the shelter of a swale, located about 150 yards beyond the canal. Troops realigned their ranks in relative protection and waited for their hard-breathing comrades to catch up. New obstacles awaited in the open terrain that stretched several hundred yards from the swale to the base of Marye's Heights. Wood and board fences crisscrossed the fields and disrupted attack lines before they tumbled from pushing and cutting. Bogs were many and took those of unwary step "in half leg deep." Worse came when soldiers neared a four-foot stone wall that ran parallel to much of the base of Marye's Heights. Soldiers of the Second Corps were in the open before the stone wall, while their Confederate opponents were sheltered behind what amounted to breastworks. Commenting on the terrain several years after the battle, Confederate General James Longstreet noted that his position formed "an almost unapproachable defense."[34]

Nearly every step of the way from Fredericksburg occurred under blistering Confederate fire. According to one advancing soldier, only moments after his regiment left the town "there is a puff of smoke on the Heights and two men fall; immediately several more cannon belch forth fire and smoke and sixteen more fall." Another Union attacker later remembered how Confederate artillery shells were bursting so rapidly that he pulled up his overcoat collar as if in a driving rain.[35] Confederate fire only increased when French's men came within musket range of the

The stone wall at the foot of Marye's Heights. Soldiers of the Second Corps fought well in their unsuccessful attempts to carry the Confederate defensive position, although they fell like "grass before the scythe." Massachusetts Commandery Military Order of the Loyal Legion and the U.S. Army Military History Institute.

stone wall. "Avalanche of fire," "storm of projectiles," and "leaden storm" were some of the phrases that soldiers used to describe the Confederate shot, shell, and ball received. A New Jersey soldier most remembered the noise, when the "roar of musketry became almost deafening."[36]

With casualties mounting, soldiers simply hit the ground. There was no general collapse as occurred in Sedgwick's division at Antietam, because the Confederates were not actively pressing their battlefield advantage. Longstreet's men did not need to, as their defensive fire was enough to badly disorganize and halt the attacking Union lines. As a private in the 14th Connecticut described it, the "lines dissolved, stragglers or clusters firing here and there, but chiefly dropping upon the ground to be exposed as little as possible." A captain in the 14th Indiana thought the process a bit more orderly, declaring "the line stopped when it came to the rebel infantry." Steeling himself to briefly lift his nose from the mud before the stone wall, Private John Weiser saw enough to decide the Federal assault was "a perfect failure."[37]

Soldiers in Hancock's division suffered nerve-wracking minutes while awaiting their turn to advance after the departure of French's brigades from Fredericksburg. Sergeant Charles Fuller described Confederate artillery fire coming "thick and dangerously near" as his regiment formed in the streets of the town. Looking around the ranks, Fuller noticed a German recruit "who was literally unnerved by fear. His countenance was distorted by terror, and he was shaking in every limb." Private William McCarter declared that clouds of "burning powder" came rolling back through the town and "almost suffocated us in our position." Likely more unnerving to McCarter, one of his squad mates asked a nearby lieutenant about the progress of the battle. The company officer, pulling no punches, responded, "'Well, boys, French is licked to beat hell.'"[38] Words were one thing, but wounded soldiers of French's division streaming back through town were an entirely different matter. Hancock's men gaped as they watched a sergeant from the earlier attack move past with his arm dangling by strands of torn muscle. Close behind came another survivor of French's attack, being pushed in a wheelbarrow. The wounded man was calmly smoking his pipe, seemingly oblivious to the fact that his foot was gone and his stump was pulsing blood. The sights were too much for Private William

Dehaven, who sank to the ground in a faint. Another unsettled soldier declared that the sight of the wounded and maimed "was not calculated to enthuse the men."[39]

Hancock's men faced the wreckage of French's attack strewn across their path of advance, a new and unnerving obstacle on the battlefield. First came the dead and wounded. Soldiers had to move over their less fortunate comrades as best they could, sometimes roughly. There were some patches where the fallen were so thick that oncoming attackers could not help but tread upon them. There were other spots where the dead and dying were less numerous but no less horrifying. Soldiers watched helplessly as a private dragging his mangled leg attempted to pull himself from their line of advance. With his leg now being trampled, the wounded man pleaded for someone to kill him to end the misery. The agony lasted for a while longer because, as one onrushing soldier grimly explained, "no one had time then to attend to one poor wounded fellow."[40] Once over the dead and wounded, advancing Union soldiers ran into survivors from the earlier assault. The lines of the living proved more formidable than the lines of the dead. Hancock's men often went to the ground upon reaching their comrades rather than continuing toward the stone wall. Soldiers from different brigades and regiments became intermingled, and the Union attack lost any remaining momentum. Soldiers of the 5th New Hampshire likely made the farthest advance of any Union attackers, with some men reaching within paces of the stone wall before going to the ground. "Beyond this point we saw no officers," one survivor recalled, "neither did we receive any orders."[41]

Watching the battle unfold from the courthouse steeple, Couch tried to make the best of a fast deteriorating situation. Exclaiming, "Oh, great God! See how our men, our fellows are falling," Couch attempted to shift the weight of the Second Corps assault. He ordered Howard's division to the right of French's and Hancock's divisions, an attempt to put pressure on the flank of the Confederate defenders behind the stone wall.[42] These men accomplished little but to add to the fast-growing list of Union casualties. Soon after, Couch ordered Battery A of the 1st Rhode Island Light Artillery forward from Fredericksburg. The gunners were to provide artillery support for the Union infantry. The battery also made a conspicuous battlefield target, and served to draw

Confederate artillery fire from the hard-hit Union lines. When told that most of the battery likely would be destroyed by Confederate artillery fire, Couch responded, "I would rather lose my guns than my men." The Rhode Islanders advanced forward and took their assigned position, all the while darkly mumbling about being "sacrificed" for the infantry. The gunners withstood a "shower" of Confederate fire, and several fell wounded. The artillerists considered themselves on the receiving end of little less than a miracle that, by the end of the day, none of them had been killed.[43]

The battlefield decisions made by Couch were not, by themselves, going to bring success to the Union assaults. At least Couch, however, was trying to do something to ameliorate the rapidly deteriorating situation before the stone wall. Few other Union commanders displayed the same initiative. Hooker, to his credit, displayed considerable bravery in overseeing the continued Union attacks following the unsuccessful attempts made by the Second Corps. Sensing the futility of any more Federal assaults against the stone wall, Hooker unsuccessfully pleaded with Burnside to stop ordering them. The matter was entirely different on the Union left. After a brief flurry of fighting in the early morning, Franklin, the grand division commander, behaved abysmally. Franklin gave very few orders to the Union forces under his command, even though Reynolds's men appeared to be making some headway. The result was that the First Corps ended the day badly bloodied, while the Sixth Corps and the Third Corps hardly saw any action. Worse, from the perspective of soldiers on the Union right, Lee had to shift no forces from Marye's Heights to bolster other sections of his defensive lines.[44]

Soldiers of the Second Corps fought well at Fredericksburg, despite their failure to storm Marye's Heights. In a point of pride after the battle, many of Couch's men claimed to have made a closer advance against the stone wall than any of the waves of Federal soldiers from the Fifth Corps and Ninth Corps who went into battle later in the day. "No ground was held in advance of our line," Hancock boasted on Christmas Day, "nor did any soldiers fall nearer the enemy than those of the regiments of my division and those of Kimball's brigade, of French's division."[45] Burnside and Sumner also acknowledged that the Second Corps had fought well. The night after the battle, Couch attempted to assure Burnside that, despite the lack of visible battlefield success, "'everything that could be done by troops was done by the Second Corps.'" "'Couch, I know that;'" Burnside replied, "'I am perfectly satisfied that you did your best.'" Several weeks later, Sumner explained that the failure of the Second Corps to capture the stone wall was not from want of bravery on the part of the men. More simply, "No troops could stand such a fire as that."[46]

Brigadier General Andrew Humphreys might disagree. The commander of the Pennsylvania Reserves, an as of yet unbloodied division in the Fifth Corps, Humphreys received orders in the early evening to advance from Fredericksburg against the stone wall. Humphreys led his men over virtually the same ground as crossed earlier in the day by the Second Corps. He later seethed that Couch's men, prone before the stone wall and desperately attempting to wait out the last light of day, broke the momentum of his attack. This disorganized "mass of men" disrupted the Pennsylvanians' advance. There is some truth to the comment. Soldiers from the Second Corps grasped at the pant legs of their Fifth Corps comrades and, in some cases, nearly tackled them down. Had they not done so, Humphreys argued, his division "would have" carried the stone wall. Lost in the complaint is how this might have happened, since no other Federal division had accomplished the task. Humphreys men were no braver than those from Hancock's and French's divisions. And they too faced "furious" Confederate fire that turned the stone wall into a "sheet of flame."[47] No single Union division, at least on that day, before Marye's Heights, was going to break through the Confederate defensive lines.

Soldiers of the Second Corps had fought valiantly but, in the process, had suffered the longest casualty lists in the army. The three brigades of the First Division were the hardest hit. Each of Hancock's brigades had suffered more than 500 casualties, more than any of the other six brigades under Couch's command. Taken all together, the Second Corps had suffered 4,110 men killed, wounded, and missing. This was about one out of every four soldiers who had gone into the fighting. By comparison, casualties throughout the other five corps in the Army of the Potomac ranged in number. The First Corps, which had led the attacks against the Confederate right, suffered the highest, at 3,279 men. The Sixth Corps, which had remained largely in reserve, suffered the fewest, at 444 men. Remove the Second Corps from the casualty totals suffered by the Army of the Potomac, and about one out of every ten Federal solders present at Fredericksburg was killed, wounded, and missing.[48]

Especially hard-hit were commissioned officers and veteran soldiers. No division commanders were killed or wounded, unlike at Antietam. But 321 other officers were hit, the highest number to date. Among regimental commanders, the losses were appalling, at 23 of the 47 officers who first went into battle. The First Division again fared the worst. Among Hancock's seventeen regiments, 25 commanding officers were casualties, meaning that some units lost one or more of their senior-ranking officers. The most bloodied were the 5th New Hampshire, which lost its top four officers, and the 69th New York, which lost its top three officers. "These were veteran regiments, led by able and tried commanders," Hancock lamented after the battle, "and I regret to say that their places cannot soon be filled."[49] Equally hard-hit as officers were soldiers in veteran regiments. The 81st Pennsylvania, whose members had fought through all the battles of the Peninsula and Maryland Campaigns, numbered just 85 men present for duty. The 88th New York, also serving since the start of the war, was in even worse shape, with only 73 men present for duty. Corporal T. Groves of the veteran 5th New Hampshire lamented on December 17, "Have a big company, one sergeant, three corporals, six privates!" Groves's commanding officer, Colonel Edward Cross, was all too well aware. He said that before the stone wall, "the veterans of Fair Oaks, Malvern Hill and Antietam" fell "like grass before the scythe."[50]

The heavy losses suffered at Fredericksburg, coming only three months after the bloodletting at Antietam, left the Second Corps, in the words of Couch, "pretty badly used up." The Second Corps received the 12th New Jersey, 140th Pennsylvania, and 148th Pennsylvania between December 18 and 20, part of a late-arriving reinforcement of the army. The new regiments had full ranks, like the other regiments raised in the summer and fall of 1862 and assigned to the Second Corps. The newcomers constantly fended off the question "What brigade is that?" from veterans unused to regiments with nearly full numbers. Still, the three new regiments boosted the manpower in Couch's command in late December to only 16,201 men. On the same date, only slightly fewer men were absent from Couch's command, either on leave or, more often, recovering from wounds received. The wear and tear of the marching and fighting of the past year is illustrated by looking at past numbers of men present for duty and absent in the Second Corps. In late May, the Second Corps fielded only a few men more present for duty at Fair Oaks than at Fredericksburg. And yet only 3,195 men were listed absent, far fewer than the numbers the intervening seven months would produce.[51]

Casualty figures are abstract, and, as day slowly turned to night on December 13, soldiers of the Second Corps found themselves surrounded by the all too real dead and dying. Captain James Mitchell found himself shivering, whether from the cold or the presence of death he was uncertain. Private Rodney Ramsey found a practical use for the many Union dead nearby. Wounded in the thigh and under Confederate fire, Ramsey and another soldier rolled three bodies in front of them to serve as breastworks. The intense winter cold made the scene even more macabre. General Couch rode along what he described as the "very front line" with several staff officers "just before dark." Veteran of sixteen years in the army, Couch found himself shocked at the sights. "The dead stiffened like sticks of wood," Couch wrote in horror, "and many of my wounded were frozen to death." Soldiers in the 1st Minnesota watched one of their corporals suffer a gunshot wound while on picket duty. Private Isaac Taylor grimly wrote that throughout the remainder of the night "we hear his groans but cannot go to his assistance as he is close to the Rebel lines."[52] Soldiers in Fredericksburg found no relief from the horrors of battle. Nearly every building of size found use as hospital. Surgeons operated through the night by light of candle and lantern. Their handiwork was well apparent, with one soldier gasping that "legs and arms lying in heaps" were visible on sidewalk after sidewalk. All in all, one private decided that for soldiers in the Second Corps, "it was a weary dismal night."[53]

IN THE SHADOW OF MARYE'S HEIGHTS

The agony before Marye's Heights finally came to an end on the night of December 15, when Burnside ordered a retreat back across the Rappahannock River. The atmosphere was tense, because any noise might trigger a fusillade of Confederate fire. Survivors of the Federal attack talked in whispers and wrapped metal items in cloth to avoid clanging. Officers prowled about and grimly cautioned their men to keep as quiet as "the dead who slept near us." Couch's men found luck finally running their way when a thunderstorm broke around midnight. Crashes of thunder nearly rivaled sounds of the battle itself, and the noise covered any sounds of the retreat.[54] Safely back across the Rappahannock and gathered around Falmouth by dawn the next morning, soldiers thought of little more than finding rest. Captain William Plumer recounted to his mother that members of his regiment had found little time to unwind since crossing the Rappahannock River into Fredericksburg on December 11. "You have little idea," Plumer concluded, "how hard a life we have had." Private James Wright quickly found a bed in a nearby house and relished crawling under the covers. The last thing that Wright remembered before drifting off to sleep was someone nearby "singing softly, 'Home, Sweet Home.'"[55]

Fatigue quickly yielded to anger and despair as soldiers of the Second Corps found time to reflect upon the Federal disaster at Fredericksburg. President Lincoln attempted to take some of the sting out of the defeat in his "Congratulations to the Army of the Potomac" issued in late December. With unusually clouded reasoning, Lincoln extolled soldiers, "Although you were not successful, the attempt was not an error, nor the failure other than an accident."[56]

Couch's men, like soldiers throughout the rest of the army, had none of it. "We returned to our old camp and consoled ourselves that we had made another brilliant retreat," one veteran mocked, "and wondering how many more such moves it would take to crush the rebellion." Captain Charles Eager facetiously wondered if in northern newspapers "this fight will be called Burnside's first victory. I consider it the worst defeat and least gained of any fight of the war." Private Joseph Elliott failed to rouse energy even for sarcasm. He glumly described his mood upon arriving back in Falmouth as "defeated, disgusted, disheartened." Private Rodney Ramsey was one who would describe himself as at least "disgusted." Ramsey fumed on Christmas Eve that he would not actually mention the name Fredericksburg, because the "title of the Battle is Burnside's Slaughter House! . . . Our army was badly whipped."[57]

Soldiers heaped particular venom upon Burnside for sacrificing lives in a foolhardy attack. They were less furious that an attack had been made than that they had attacked the heart of the Confederate defenses. Private Augustus Wallen described having to wait out the battle before the stone wall with only mud and gore to offer protection from the unrelenting Confederate fire. He later despaired that "it just looked to me as if we were taken there to be butchered up . . . we aint got no generals worth a dam." A soldier in French's division vowed that he was willing to fight as hard as ever for the Union cause. "But to go into another such battle as Fredericksburg, where they mow men down as they did [there] and then not gain anything, there is not much encouragement in it." Private Edward Cotter felt his anger turn white hot as he watched Union attack wave follow Union attack wave in the hopeless attempt to reach the stone wall. Still choking on rage one month later, he admitted that "I could have went and helped the rebels to think of our men marching right in to the jaws of death without any site to defend themselves." Other survivors stewed that the Federal attack "amounted to Nothing except to slaughter the solgers" and was one of the great "wastes of human life" of the war.[58]

Disgust over the battle only deepened when detachments of soldiers from the Second Corps helped to bury the Union dead before Marye's Heights under a flag of truce several days later. Hancock, in charge of organizing the burial detail, cautioned that grave diggers "will take picks and spaces sufficient to keep them constantly at work."[59] He need not have worried. Soldiers stayed busy digging trenches to bury the roughly 1,100 bodies found, most of them from the Second Corps. The job was gruesome. Many corpses were naked, plundered by thinly clad Confederate soldiers.[60] Other bodies were "shot and blown to pieces in every imaginable way." The horror of burial duty was an experience suffered even by soldiers of the Second Corps who had remained behind. Assistant surgeon A. Stokes Jones could clearly see the Union dead before

Marye's Heights from his hospital outside Falmouth. Stokes lamented, "Oh! What scenes seen when repaid with success, are several fold more horrible should they be in vain." Other soldiers heard that many of the dead lacked identifiable personal possessions and went into the ground marked as "unknown." Upon hearing of the anonymous fate of their comrades, one discouraged soldier declared that "an irrepressible gloom" settled over camp.[61]

No wonder that soldiers of the Second Corps received Burnside coolly during a review held in mid-January. When told of the parade, a captain in the 14th Connecticut asked his men to give three cheers for the army commander. A few diehards responded with weak cheers; most remained silent. The situation deteriorated even more when Burnside, accompanied by Sumner and Couch, rode along the lines of the Second Corps. Burnside met stony faces. A private in the 57th New York wrote that when Burnside passed by "there was not an old regiment in our Division that cheered him." Soldiers of the Irish Brigade broke into wild cheers when the reviewing party rode along, but for Sumner, not Burnside. Normally unflappable, Sumner sent a message instructing regimental commanders to have their men cheer Burnside. Despite the urging, veterans of the Fredericksburg Campaign remained quiet. "French, Sumner, Hooker and several colonels try to get the regt. to cheer Burnside," a corporal in the 1st Minnesota reported. "But they would not." Burnside received cheers from soldiers in recently arrived regiments, but even here the men had to explain themselves. A member of the 140th Pennsylvania pleaded, "We were raw enough—'green enough,' as some one in the Irish Brigade expressed it—to cheer for the brave old commander."[62]

Despondency among Couch's men only deepened when President Lincoln's Emancipation Proclamation went into effect at the start of 1863.[63] Many Union soldiers thoroughly disapproved of the measure. The opposition voiced by members of the Second Corps was surprising, however, given their at least tepid support of the policy when first announced early in the fall.[64] Private John McClure of the 14th Indiana and Sergeant Peter Welsh of the Irish Brigade simply gave voice to a deeply held racism. McClure threatened that if he had his way "I would shoot every nigger I come across. I am thinking if old Abe makes his words come true you folks will have an awful bad smell amonxt you by the time we get home." Similarly, Welsh warned that black troops sent into battle might face fire from Confederate soldiers to their front and Union soldiers to their rear. "The feeling against nigars is intensely strong in this army . . . [and] especially strong in the Irish regiments."[65]

Private William Smith of the Irish-dominated 116th Pennsylvania only confirmed Welsh's point. Smith argued that fighting to free the slaves was a betrayal of why he had gone to war. He protested that he did not come out to fight to free the slaves but to preserve the Union. Working into even greater fury, Smith violently warned "to hell with the Niggers . . . I would shoot one as quick as a wink if he gave me any sase." Venom existed beyond just the Irish Brigade. A New Hampshire private suspected that emancipation was only a ploy by the federal government to grant equal rights to blacks. He insisted that the last reason that he was fighting was to elevate blacks and, for that matter, he cared little whether they remained enslaved or not.[66]

Compounding the ill will all the more, the final Emancipation Proclamation came at an especially bad time for soldiers of the Second Corps. Many men linked the bloodshed suffered at Fredericksburg to the expansion of the Union war effort in a direction that they disliked anyway. Private William Jackson lost his self-described "only friend" before the stone wall, and he failed to see the reason behind the sacrifice. He wondered if the war "will ever amount to a pinch of Sh-t and its nothing anyway but the accursed Nigger. Its all fudge and I am mad." A New Jersey private also found his attitude colored by the recent battlefield carnage. He bemoaned the "heavy freight of destruction, murder, and misery . . . caused by this nigger, abolitionist war."[67]

Other soldiers were mad that they seemed to be doing all of the manual labor around Falmouth, while newly freed blacks stood by and watched. Falmouth had turned into a major Federal supply center, and Couch's men found themselves unloading supplies from barges. Sergeant E. B. Tyler seethed that the white troops, "some slight of frame and weakened in muscle by soldier fare," had to sweat while black onlookers did not. Private Lauren Hotchkiss minded less the heavy labor than watching blacks move freely about Falmouth because, unlike soldiers, they needed no military passes. Hotchkiss complained, "This fighting for the niggars that is thought more of than a white man don't go down very well." Private Joseph Law voiced similar resentment. While white soldiers had to perform military duties day and night, rain and shine, blacks did as they pleased. "We are the slaves now," Law bemoaned, "instead of the negroes."[68]

Other factors compounded the despair, although never to the same depths as discontent over the expansion of Union war aims. Soldiers turned cranky that they worked day after day unloading supplies, and yet often found themselves without. Couch's men complained of short rations and, when food was present, monotonous taste.[69] Stomachs empty of food were one thing, but pockets empty of pay, another. Many men had not received their monthly pay since the early fall, if not longer. Discontent ran high, as soldiers often had to put off purchasing extra foodstuffs, even spare uniform pieces and footwear, for lack of money. Family men fared the worst from missing paymasters. A private declared that many husbands and fathers vowed to "never fire another gun" until they received their pay.[70] On top of everything else, the weather turned bitterly cold and snowy. Pickets stationed along the Rappahannock River suffered the most, especially at night, but even soldiers in log huts sometimes found no relief. A sergeant awoke one morning to find himself covered in snow forced through the cracks in the walls of his shanty by high winds. The now cold, wet, and thoroughly miserable Pennsylvanian wrote that he had "witnessed to satisfaction the romance of soldier life."[71]

Sumner dismissed all of the grumbling as just that. He testified before the Joint Committee in late December that in the Second Corps and throughout the rest of the army, "there is a great deal too much croaking; there is not sufficient confidence." Members of the Joint Committee were skeptical of Burnside's leadership qualities after the debacle at Fredericksburg, and they sensed opportunity in Sumner's comments. Sumner refused to play along. He radiated confidence when pressed about the "general condition and efficiency" of the army. With "sufficient exertion," the army within a few days, by the end of the year at the latest, "will be in excellent order again."[72]

Sumner was right about a lack of confidence throughout much of the army, where infighting among the top commanders badly hurt morale.

The recent defeat at Fredericksburg had splintered the Federal high command, with Generals Hooker and Franklin, as well as others, none too subtly criticizing Burnside. An already bad situation deteriorated more when Burnside again attempted to catch Lee unaware. On January 20, Burnside ordered the Army of the Potomac across the Rappahannock River at Bank's Ford and behind the Confederate left flank. Rain and snow forced Burnside to cancel the offensive, derisively labeled by soldiers as the "Mud March," two days later. Believing his generals had not given him their full support during the recent fiasco, Burnside attempted to clean house. He ordered Hooker, Franklin, and a host of division commanders removed for criticizing their superior officers. None of the names on Burnside's list were from the Second Corps, indicating that Couch and his top lieutenants followed Sumner's lead in exercising discretion. The open squabbling throughout the rest of the army's high command could not help but blacken soldiers' moods. High-ranking officers described their men as "exceedingly dispirited" and "lacking the same spirit" as they earlier had enjoyed.[73]

Unfortunately for the Second Corps, the problems ran far deeper than the low morale suffered by the rest of the army. Most immediately, fallout from the campaigns of the past year had reached near-crippling level. With the start of winter quarters, the pool of regimental officers of the Second Corps, already badly battered during the Federal attacks against Marye's Heights, shrank even further. Couch's command permanently lost seven regimental officers due to wounds and illness and two to promotions and transfers to outside commands in the six weeks following the retreat of the army across the Rappahannock River.[74] Only twenty-six of the forty-seven regiments present in the Second Corps at the end of January 1863 were under the leadership of their colonel or lieutenant colonel. Among the remaining regiments, eleven were under the command of a major, the third-ranking officer. The other ten regiments were led by the senior-ranking captain, a company officer and fourth in line for command. By comparison, one year earlier, during the winter of 1861–62, colonels led all twenty-three regiments present in the Second Corps.[75]

Nearly as damaging, regimental and company officers who remained at their posts often were not up to the task. Some commanders found

themselves stretched too thin. Captain Richard Thompson took turns
commanding the 12th New Jersey with four other captains. Thompson
also had to serve every several days as officer of the guard and commander of the picket line, and complained of exhaustion. More frequently, regimental and company officers created their own problems.
A Pennsylvania captain complained in mid-January that only a handful
of the other officers in his regiment "are not half drunk all the time."
Two months later, Major Jeremiah Rohrer attended a gathering held by
officers of French's division. The celebration ended with the passing of a
bowl of whiskey-laced milk punch, and more than a few of the partakers
stumbling back to their own tents.

Across the camp ground, a Captain Davis took command of the 14th
Connecticut in the early winter of 1863. The honor was tenuous because
Davis, according to one onlooker, could not go "a week without getting
into some scrape that usually led to his being put under arrest." Davis
continually talked his way out of trouble because he had served as a
lawyer before the war. And if legal niceties failed to work, Davis simply
plied members of the court-martial with drink. Either in frustration or
admiration—it's hard to tell for sure—the prosecuting officer claimed
that "it was easier to catch a weasel asleep than to convict Capt. Davis."
Another captain led the regiment while Davis worked his legal charms,
a command arrangement as topsy-turvy as any in the army.[76]

The departure of some regimental officers and the distraction of
others bore evil fruit as discipline in the Second Corps collapsed into
the laxest in the army. The army now numbered seven corps, with the
arrival of the Eleventh Corps and Twelfth Corps in late December and
the departure of the Ninth Corps for Fort Monroe one month later.
The Second Corps found itself at the bottom of the list in an army-wide
inspection held in early February. The emphasis of the pass-through was
on spit-and-polish, designed to promote within each regiment a "proper
state of discipline and efficiency." Six of the twenty-five regiments that
failed to pass the inspection were in the Second Corps (the 34th New
York, 42nd New York, 59th New York, 88th New York, 69th Pennsylvania, and 132nd Pennsylvania), the highest number in the army.[77] The
reviews were scathing. "This regiment has been grossly neglected," the
reviewing officer reported of the 34th New York. "No daily inspections

are made; the arms are in a bad condition; many being deficient." In the 42nd New York, the inspector complained, "Discipline is not good. Officers inefficient. Nothing but a firm hand can ever make their regiment creditable to itself in all respects." Even among regiments that passed the inspection, discipline occasionally wavered. In the Third Division, according to General French, "in many cases the troops while on drill are disorderly and allowed to talk."[78] Taken all together, these comments do not necessarily mean that the Second Corps was unfit for combat. But taken individually, the comments were sharp rebukes to regiments that otherwise had fought well during the past year.

Declining fighting spirit accompanied declining discipline. The Second Corps had suffered more casualties over the past year than any other comparable formation in the Union army, and some men claimed to have had enough. Private Miles Peabody hoped to see battle when he enlisted in the 5th New Hampshire in the fall of 1861. After seeing comrades fall killed and wounded at Fair Oaks, Antietam, and Fredericksburg, his lust for battle was "fully satisfied." Another volunteer of 1861 defiantly concluded that "it is better to be a living Son b-h than a *dead* patriot. Patriotism in the army is played out."[79] More problematic, many men put action behind their words. Couch's men deserted at an alarming rate, as did other soldiers throughout the army. Couch probably suffered no little embarrassment when soldiers in one of his divisions deserted after receiving civilian clothing in the mail, first drawing attention of the army's high command to the all too common practice.[80]

Worse came on the much-derided Mud March. Burnside ordered the Second Corps to remain in reserve because the men were in sight of Confederate soldiers on Marye's Heights. Only when the rest of the army had crossed to the far side of the Rappahannock River and sprung the trap was the Second Corps to march. The point might have been moot, because at least some soldiers declared their intention not to go forward. "The utmost dissatisfaction, almost insubordination, was shown . . . here at the prospect of an attack," a Massachusetts lieutenant ominously described. "Regiments openly said that they would not cross a bridge." Other soldiers jeered when read Burnside's order. Some especially war-weary veterans reportedly "cheered for Jefferson Davis and groaned for President Lincoln."[81]

The Second Corps might not have put up much of a fight even if
the Union offensive had gone forward, because its rates of illness were
among the highest in the army. By late March, 85 out of every 1,000
members of the Second Corps were sick. By comparison, throughout
the rest of the army, only 68 out of every 1,000 men were ill.[82] Most of
the men on the sick rolls of the Second Corps were legitimate cases, victims of various illnesses that spread through the army. Other men broke
under the mental strain of living within eyesight of Marye's Heights. The
ever-looming battlefield was a constant reminder of past bloodshed and,
worse, of more yet to come. A member of the 19th Maine described the
phenomenon. "At the time when sickness prevailed," he wrote, "a few,
though disgustingly healthy, were attacked with low spirits, and a weakness of the knees, to an alarming extent, and were compelled to resort
to the accidental shooting or chopping off of a finger, or some other
accidental injury, in order to get out of the ranks and off to the hospital."
By mid-February, Couch's command numbered only 15,816 men. These
figures were only one-half the aggregate strength of the Second Corps,
the lowest percentage figure in the army.[83]

The first full year of the Civil War had ended especially badly for the
Second Corps. In addition to suffering the worst of the Federal defeat
at the Battle of Fredericksburg, the Second Corps had lost the greatest
number of casualties. The start of the New Year held out little hope for
improvement. Camp discipline all but disappeared, while discontent
over the direction of the Union war effort soared. Few soldiers likely
would have disagreed with a private in the Philadelphia Brigade, who
closed 1862 by wishing "I was at home."[84]

4

THE WINTER ENCAMPMENT
OF 1863 THROUGH THE
GETTYSBURG CAMPAIGN

Morale soared in the Second Corps in late January 1863, when Major General Joseph Hooker replaced Burnside as commander of the Army of the Potomac.[1] Couch's men expressed mixed opinions about yet another command change, their third in nearly as many months, but they almost universally praised Hooker's administrative reforms. Soldiers delighted that better food and full pay followed Hooker's ascension to command. They also praised their new commander for making furloughs easier to obtain. "This was fair-dealing," one soldier declared of the policies implemented by Hooker, "and appreciated by the men."[2]

GOINGS AND COMINGS

Soldiers of the Second Corps and the rest of the Union army experienced a surge in fighting spirit in the early spring for reasons beyond the reforms implemented by Hooker. In part, Couch's men found time to turn their thoughts to activities other than war. The most colorful diversion occurred when soldiers of the Irish Brigade celebrated St. Patrick's Day on March 17. According to one estimate, 20,000 soldiers, including Hooker, attended the festivities. The celebration was replete with horse racing and singing and dancing, as well as ample food and drink. In the words of one ecstatic Irishman, the ethnic revelry "'took' with all the soldiers."[3] Equally important to raising morale, soldiers in the Second Corps and the rest of the Union army closed ranks against the loud harangues of the Peace Democrats back at home. Couch's men

had only recently questioned the purpose of continuing the war, but
they wanted nothing to do with Copperheads. The calls for a negotiated
settlement with the Confederacy would make the Union blood spilled
and treasure spent in vain. "Secesh sympathizers" at home seemed to
forget that "our first great duty is to God, our second to our country."[4]

Soldiers received a tangible reminder of their service in the Second
Corps when Hooker decided to distribute a distinct badge to each corps
serving in the Army of the Potomac. Hooker intended corps badges to
make laggards easily identifiable on both the march and the battlefield.
The Second Corps received a trefoil, color-coded, like the other corps
badges, red, white, or blue, by division.[5] Rumor started in later years
that Hooker issued the trefoil to the Second Corps on the prompting of
General Meagher, the commander of the Irish Brigade. The trefoil made
an ideal way to honor the soldiers of the Second Corps who had "born
aloft in every battle, with the colors of the Nation, the green flag of Erin's
Isle."[6] If this was the case, no official records exist to offer support.

Whatever the rationale behind Hooker's decision, the trefoil badge
was wildly popular in the Second Corps. Soldiers recognized that the
trefoil brought credit to their accomplishments. A private in Howard's
division explained that although the badges did not look like much on
the surface, "they gave an impulse to a good soldier's pride in his own
that helped to create a spirit of emulation in the right direction." Many
of Couch's men took to proudly referring to their new corps emblem as
"the Ace of Clubs." Charles Mills, a staff officer, attempted to make his
badge all the more visible. Rather than cut from flannel, as were most,
Mills sported a velvet trefoil, outlined in gold thread.[7]

Games, politics, and badges were significant, but more important in
boosting morale were two factors distinct to the Second Corps. Praise
from the normally taciturn Sumner was the first factor. Soon after
Hooker's advancement, Sumner had requested and received assignment
from the Army of the Potomac. Sumner was senior in rank to Hooker, so
his removal was only a matter of time.[8] Rather than raise a fuss, Sumner
turned the attention to the hard fighting of the Second Corps. Sumner
reminded his men that they had fought "with credit and honor always."
In doing so, "you have captured so many colors, without losing a single
gun or standard." Sumner urged soldiers to continue to prove worthy of

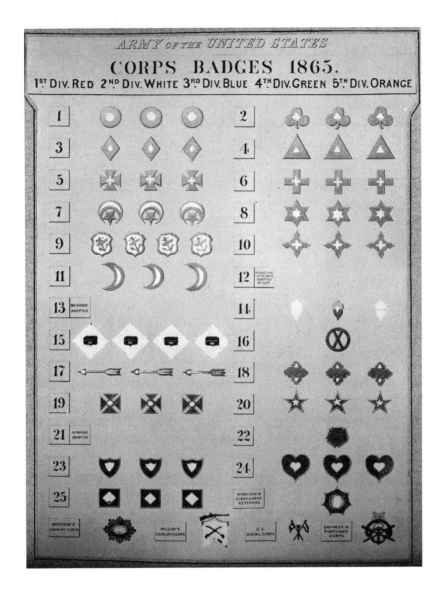

"Clubs are Trump!" The trefoil-shaped badge of the Second Corps boosted morale. Massachusetts Commandery Military Order of the Loyal Legion and the U.S. Army Military History Institute.

their already distinguished record. "It is only in so doing that you can retain for yourselves a reputation well won."[9]

This was the first time that Sumner had talked collectively about the Second Corps, and most of his soldiers responded warmly. The men had served under Sumner since the start of the war, and they recognized that their military fortunes had gone together. Private Charles Hamlin believed this for the bad, judging in the aftermath of Fredericksburg that "Old Sumner . . . seems anxious to get us all shot." Lieutenant Josiah Favill believed the opposite, declaring Sumner "a good man, an excellent soldier and good corps commander, and we shall miss him." In less than a year, Sumner had turned the men from volunteers "to well trained, veteran soldiers." Another soldier shared Favill's assessment of Sumner, writing that the "Second Corps admired him as a general and loved him as a man." President Lincoln still thought highly of Sumner and, in late March, appointed him to command the Department of Missouri. Military service, however, had sapped Sumner's remaining vitality. He died on March 23, while en route to his new post. "I am sorry," a private wrote upon reading about Sumner's death in the newspaper; "he was a good man."[10]

By contrast, Generals William Franklin and Baldy Smith did little to build morale upon receiving assignment from the Army of the Potomac. Franklin and Smith left the Sixth Corps in late January with barely a public word. Unlike Sumner, neither man had requested a transfer. But also unlike Sumner, Franklin and Smith had openly schemed against Burnside. Franklin had the added misfortune of having received his appointment to command from McClellan. In a rapid freefall, McClellan by the spring of 1863 was very much out of favor with Hooker and many other high-ranking Union officers. Franklin received a command in the trans-Mississippi theater that summer. Smith finagled command of the Ninth Corps, recently ordered to Fort Monroe. He eventually would return to the Army of the Potomac. At the moment, however, neither Franklin nor Smith was much missed by officers and men.[11]

The return of at least twenty-seven regimental officers from wounds, illness, and leave was the other factor that boosted the morale of the Second Corps. Colonels and lieutenant colonels led forty regiments of the Second Corps by early April, in stark contrast to the prevalence

Regimental and company officers of the 61st New York, Falmouth, Virginia, April 1863. The return of colonels, lieutenant colonels, and majors from the past year of campaigning helped to restore morale and discipline in their units. Library of Congress.

of company officers commanding regiments in January. The returning regimental officers brought considerable battlefield experience with them. Colonels Edward Cross of the 5th New Hampshire, D. Clinton Baxter of the 72nd Pennsylvania, and Turner Morehead of the 106th Pennsylvania had led their regiments since the start of the war. Colonel Nelson Miles of the 61st New York had won commendation for battlefield gallantry during the Peninsula Campaign, while Colonel Patrick Kelly of the 88th New York had won the affection of his men for his hard fighting from Fair Oaks through Fredericksburg. Beyond these five colonels, twenty-five regimental commanders had led their men in one or more previous campaigns. This was a remarkably high level of battlefield experience given the heavy casualties suffered by the regiments of the Second Corps in past battles.[12]

The return of regimental commanders meant more instruction and better discipline. Five of the six regiments that had failed the army-wide inspection passed at a reinspection in mid-March. The exception was the 132nd Pennsylvania, under the command of Lieutenant Colonel Charles Albright. The failure of Albright and his men was a result more of the difficulty in resupplying muskets and knapsacks lost during the fighting at Fredericksburg than from unsoldierly bearing.[13] Also indicating increased discipline within Couch's command, the numbers of soldiers in arrest and confinement rose sharply throughout the first three months of 1863. Some transgressions were severe, and several soldiers convicted of cowardice were drummed out of the army in a humiliating ceremony. After watching three men publicly dismissed, Sergeant James Walker declared that he would "have infinitely preferred a dose of cold lead" rather than go through such a ceremony himself.[14] Other transgressions were mild, and one unfortunate soldier found himself under arrest for having three loaves of bread speared on his bayonet. The numbers of men under arrest had dropped significantly by late April, suggesting that regimental officers had their commands well in hand.[15]

Soldiers were especially proud of their martial bearing at a review held to honor President Lincoln while on a visit to Falmouth in late April. Captain Isaac Plumb of the 61st New York boasted, "Our corps is in splendid condition, well fed and well disciplined." Colonel William Smith of the 1st Delaware agreed, claiming that the Second Corps had never looked and marched better. The enthusiasm continued after soldiers returned to their camps. A major in the 14th Indiana believed the Second Corps and the rest of the Army of the Potomac ready to again take the offensive. He would not have thought so only a few months ago, in the dark days that had followed the defeat at Fredericksburg. Now, however, "We *must succeed. We will succeed.*" A Pennsylvania private saw only victory ahead. He jauntily predicted that the Federals would soon smash through the Confederates across the Rapidan and "then we will give them a hot chase to Richmond."[16]

Out from the shadow of Marye's Heights, at least figuratively, by the spring of 1863, the Second Corps prepared to go on the offensive with several changes in its high command. Brigadier General John Gibbon assumed command of the Second Division in mid-April, when Hooker advanced Howard to command the Eleventh Corps.[17] Gibbon was a West Point graduate (1847) and a veteran of the Mexican War, like most other Federal division commanders. Gibbon, however, had gained considerable fame in the prewar army. In 1860, he authored the *Artillerist Manual,* a basic text of instruction. Gibbon continued to distinguish himself with the outbreak of the Civil War. He won praise from McClellan and Hooker, who otherwise agreed upon little, for his battlefield leadership. Most notably, Gibbon had forged four western regiments into the famous "Iron Brigade." The unit had earned its nickname well from hard fighting during the Second Manassas and Antietam Campaigns.[18] Adding to these laurels, Gibbon looked and acted the part of a combat officer, overshadowed in the Second Corps only by Hancock. Soldiers variously described the new Second Division commander as a "good looking officer" who "is as cool as a steel knife, . . . unmoved by anything and everything." Yet he also exhibited a warm humanity on occasion. Gibbon kept photographs of his children in his tent, and proudly showed them to all who entered.[19]

At the brigade level the Second Corps underwent three command changes. Colonel Samuel Carroll and Brigadier General William Hays took command of two brigades in French's division. Both men were experienced combat officers. Carroll had served as a brigade commander in the Shenandoah Valley and Second Bull Run Campaigns, while Hays had commanded the reserve artillery of the Army of the Potomac at the Battles of Antietam and Fredericksburg. Carroll was a better fit into the Second Corps than was Hays because Carroll had begun the war as a regimental officer in the 8th Ohio. Colonel Joseph Snyder of the hard-fighting 7th West Virginia fondly remembered the new commander as a "No. 1 military man—he comes nigh knowing it all."[20]

The last new brigade commander was Colonel John Brooke, who advanced from the 53rd Pennsylvania to take command of the newly created Fourth Brigade in the First Division. Hancock created the brigade of five regiments (the 27th Connecticut, 2nd Delaware, 64th New York, 53rd Pennsylvania, and 145th Pennsylvania) solely to give Brooke command. Brooke had fought throughout the war, and he had won Hancock's praise for leading one of the more determined Federal charges against the stone wall at Fredericksburg.[21] That Hooker and

Couch allowed Hancock to reshuffle his division was a testament to their confidence in his ability to spot leadership talent. The permission of Hooker and Couch also demonstrates their faith in Hancock as a combat commander, because only one other division in the army fielded four brigades.[22]

Despite several new faces, the high-ranking officers of the Second Corps were hands-down the most experienced combat leaders in the army. All but one of Couch's thirteen division and brigade officers previously had led an equivalent command.[23] Giving the Second Corps depth of leadership experience, nine of these same commanders had led a division or brigade since the summer of 1862 (five officers within the Second Corps).[24] By contrast, leadership experience was far more difficult to come by throughout the rest of the army. Thirty-nine division and brigade commanders in the other six army corps were serving in the capacity for the first time, nearly one-half the high-ranking officers under Hooker's command. Experience was only marginally greater among the remaining division and brigade officers, where just twelve men had been in command since the previous summer, little more than in the Second Corps alone. The relative lack of leadership experience so worried Hooker that, in early February, he disbanded Burnside's three Grand Divisions. Hooker did so in part because he believed the arrangement cumbersome. But he also did away with the Grand Divisions because he had received promotion, and Franklin and Sumner had received transfer. Hooker would have had to find new commanders for the formations if he had kept them, further diluting the already thin pool of leadership experience among his high-ranking officers.[25]

A potential weakness in the leadership of the Second Corps was that Couch did not number among Hooker's circle of confidants, leaving his command outside the favored of the army.[26] The distance between the two Union generals resulted because Couch had opposed the appointment of Hooker to command the army. Couch, like many other high-ranking Federal officers, believed Hooker guilty of shamelessly scheming to obtain the position.[27] Moreover, Couch was the only remaining corps commander to have received his appointment from McClellan. The seniority hurt more than helped, given the anti-McClellan sentiment held by many Union officers by the spring of 1863. Hooker sometimes acted upon the tension by neglecting the Second Corps. In early February, Hooker attached a newly created Light Division of six regiments to the Sixth Corps. The Light Division was designed for rapid marching and maneuvering and was an experiment in increasing the mobility of the Army of the Potomac. Hooker never explained why he selected the Sixth Corps to receive the Light Division. Explanation might be found in a comment that he reportedly had made earlier, that the Sixth Corps had "*all* the *good* generals." Likely the army commander meant the comment as much a slap at some of his other corps as a compliment to the Sixth Corps, which was among the least bloodied to date.[28] Another instance of Hooker all but ignoring the Second Corps occurred when the army commander stacked many of his favorite officers in the Third Corps, where he had served during the Peninsula Campaign. This included appointing Major General Daniel Sickles, a political crony from New York City, to command the formation.[29]

Geography played a far greater role than politics in determining the role of the Second Corps in the Union's spring offensive. Hooker hoped to outflank and crush Lee west of Fredericksburg. He moved the bulk of the army across the Rappahannock River at Bank's Ford on April 27 and 28.[30] Soldiers of the Second Corps meanwhile continued to go about their daily duties, to avoid tipping Confederate soldiers posted along Marye's Heights that the Union advance had started. Soldiers of Howard's division stayed put for a third day, while members of Hancock's and French's divisions slipped away to join the main army now gathered around Chancellorsville. A brick house and crossroads located nine miles to the west of Lee's army, Chancellorsville was surrounded by thick growths of trees and underbrush. Soldiers complained that in attempting to push through tangled branches and vines, faces and hands were cut, and uniforms and knapsacks were torn. When Lee realized what was afoot, he attacked Hooker on May 1 and 2. Soldiers of the Second Corps formed the Union left, closest to the Rappahannock River, and came under only infrequent Confederate fire. A private in the 5th New Hampshire marveled during the ensuing fighting that "we for a wonder have escaped once."[31]

Hancock's division won one of the few bright spots earned by Union arms the next day, when a defeated Hooker ordered the army to pull back toward the Rappahannock River. Hooker ordered Hancock to hold his men around the critical crossroads at Chancellorsville, to gain time for the Union retreat. Soldiers of the First Division withstood Confederate artillery fire that set woods and the nearby Chancellor mansion to flames. Colonel Orlando Morris of the 66th New York claimed that soldiers found relief from the pounding through action. When Confederate skirmishers advanced, Morris reported that each waiting Union soldier took "careful and steady aim at his object, as if firing at a target for a prize." Lieutenant Josiah Favill found bravery in the person of General Hancock, who always seemed to be in the thick of the action. The Union general rode along the lines shouting encouragement and remaining all but oblivious to the storm of fire around him. To Favill, it seemed that "General Hancock is in his element and at his best in the midst of a fight."[32] The Federal holding action did not go flawlessly, and several hundred soldiers of the 27th Connecticut and 145th Pennsylvania were captured amid the confusion of the battle.[33] Yet Hancock's men had gained valuable time for the rest of the army to fall back in relatively good order before they also joined the retreat. Summing up the action around the Chancellorsville crossroads, Hancock proudly declared, "My division did well."[34]

Hancock's soldiers fought well enough that they fell to squabbling over some of the perceived glory. The arguing sometimes turned heated, indicating, in addition to participation in hard fighting, a strong sense of unit pride. The dispute centered over whether soldiers from the 116th Pennsylvania or the 140th Pennsylvania initiated the rescue of several abandoned artillery pieces of the 5th Maine, attached to the Third Corps. The stakes were high because had the Confederates seized the guns, they might have opened a devastating fire on the Union rear guard. Still, rushing forward to rescue the pieces was not an easy decision to make. Confederate shot and shell whizzed by, making the very air appear, in the words of one nervous private, "alive with deadly missels."[35] Handfuls of soldiers from both regiments eventually ventured forward and hauled the battery off the field by hand. Less easy to establish was who got the first gun rolling toward the safety of the Union lines. The Irish soldiers of the 116th Pennsylvania claimed ultimate victory. Major L. J. Sacriste received a Medal of Honor in the late 1880s for bearing "off in triumph the first gun recovered from the field." Moreover, soldiers of the 116th Pennsylvania and the other three regiments of the Irish Brigade were credited with rescuing "every gun and every caisson."[36]

Spirits in the Second Corps were high for a combination of reasons by the time Hooker withdrew the army back across the Rappahannock River and to Falmouth on May 5. Scapegoats were easy to find. Hooker was a frequent target because his timid leadership after reaching Chancellorsville allowed Lee to go on the offensive.[37] Soldiers not faulting Hooker pinned blame on the poor battlefield showing of the Union Eleventh Corps. On the early evening of May 2, the largely German American soldiers had been surprised and routed by Confederate attackers. Their actions threatened the safety of the entire Federal army by exposing each individual corps to Confederate attack from the right flank and rear. Only darkness finally brought an end to the Confederate threat. Soldiers were unforgiving. A New York private caustically declared that the "frightened Dutchmen" ran so quickly that "we had to prick some of them with the bayonet even to stop them." A Massachusetts captain fumed that "every man" of the Eleventh Corps "ought to be hauled off the face of the Earth."[38]

Spirits also remained buoyant in the aftermath of the Federal defeat at Chancellorsville, because the Second Corps had been only lightly engaged. Hancock's men were the exception, after their hard fighting on May 3. Overall, the Second Corps had suffered 1,940 men killed, wounded, and missing. These were not inconsiderable losses, but they were the lowest suffered by the Second Corps since the Battle of Fair Oaks the previous spring. Couch's men refused to concede defeat, sputtering, "I can't imagine why or how they mastered us." A New Yorker pointedly remarked that despite winning possession of the battlefield, the Confederates were in no position to boast because they also had suffered heavily. Additionally, "Gen. Stonewall Jackson was killed, one of their best generals."[39] Throughout the rest of the Union army, four other corps lost more men than Couch's. Especially hard-hit were Hooker's favorites, with the Sixth Corps losing 4,610 casualties and the Third Corps losing 4,120 casualties.[40]

Escaping the Chancellorsville Campaign in better shape than the rest of the army, the Second Corps also fared better when the two-year

regiments and the nine-month regiments mustered out. That spring
and summer the Second Corps lost nine short-term regiments, among
the lowest numbers in the army.[41] The fighting spirit of soldiers in these
regiments was near-bottom. Soldiers of the 34th New York had threatened to lay down their arms even before the start of the Chancellorsville
Campaign, on the grounds that their term of service had expired. The
New Yorkers argued that their two-year enlistment should date from
when the first company had mustered, not the last company, as claimed
by the War Department. Theirs was a common complaint among many
short-timers, but soldiers of the 34th New York were the only ones to
carry the grievance to such an extreme. Likely, on the eve of a new Federal offensive, they were only too well aware that the Second Corps had
fought in the thick of nearly all the battles of the Army of the Potomac.
The men eventually backed down under threat of arrest. Judging from
their subsequent casualty figures during the Chancellorsville Campaign
they fought with little enthusiasm, losing only two men wounded and
one man missing.[42] Also indicating low morale, none of the short-term
soldiers reenlisted together as a regiment, despite a bounty of between
fifty and one hundred dollars for doing so. Private Benjamin Appleby
was one of the soldiers who chose home over bounty. "If I ever get with
you a gain," Appleby promised his wife, "no money will tempt me to go
and leave you a gain."[43]

In addition to losing fewer soldiers, the departure of both two-year
and nine-month regiments hurt the Second Corps less from an organizational perspective than it did the rest of the army. Six of the nine
regiments that left the Second Corps were from French's division. As
a result, Couch had to reshuffle the composition of only two of his ten
brigades. He disbanded one (MacGregor's) and transferred its remaining regiment, the 1st Delaware, to another (Powers's). Meanwhile, much
of the rest of the army underwent a dramatic reorganization. The shake-
up occurred because the short-term regiments were less concentrated
in the other army corps, an unintended consequence of their earlier
integration into existing divisions and brigades. The commanders of
the Third Corps, Fifth Corps, and Sixth Corps each had disbanded one
division by the late spring, reducing the army from twenty-one divisions to eighteen divisions.[44] The reshuffling went beyond paper and

organizational charts. Soldiers in each of the three downsized corps entered the summer mixed into unfamiliar divisions and brigades, a threat to their hard-won cohesion.[45]

This is not to say that the Second Corps was without problems. Most worrisome, the fighting power of Couch's command was among the most brittle of the army. The problem lay in the failure of Union authorities to recruit veteran regiments back to strength. By May 31 the manpower of the Second Corps had fallen to 12,550 present for duty, a decrease of 25 percent since late April. The rest of the army underwent a similar decline and numbered 74,135 men in the mid-spring. These figures blur the true picture, because Couch's command fielded forty-two regiments at the end of May, among the most in the army. The average strength of each regiment in the Second Corps was 300 men, well below that found in regiments throughout the rest of the army.[46] The most depleted units of the Second Corps were the five regiments of the Irish Brigade. By mid-May, the 69th New York fielded 174 officers and men, and the 63rd New York fielded 183 officers and men. All told, the five Irish regiments fielded 700 men combined, less than the manpower of one regiment at full strength. Rather than fill the ranks with recruits, the War Department consolidated the 63rd New York, 69th New York, and 88th New York into two companies each, and the 116th Pennsylvania into four companies. Furious at the reshuffling, which reduced the command to a brigade in name only, Meagher resigned in protest. "Suffice it to say that, the Irish Brigade no longer existing," the general explained in a farewell letter to his remaining soldiers, "I felt that it would be perpetuating a great deception were I to retain the authority and rank of a brigadier-general nominally commanding the same."[47]

Couch too soon departed, replaced by Hancock. The change benefited the Second Corps because Hooker and Couch had fallen into a bitter feud over the performance of each general during the Chancellorsville Campaign.[48] Hancock avoided the problem, because he was widely respected by his fellow officers for his battlefield exploits. Most recently, Couch had praised Hancock for "his gallantry, energy and his example of marked personal bravery" during the fighting at Chancellorsville. Hancock also had many backers among his civilian superiors. The most influential was Secretary of War Edwin Stanton, who later wrote to

Hancock that no Federal officer "has more sincerely my . . . confidence and respect than yourself."[49] Why Stanton thought so highly of Hancock is uncertain. Most likely, Stanton, an ardent Democrat before the war, respected the fact that Hancock, also a Democrat, put aside politics and focused wholeheartedly on winning the war. This was especially welcome in an army that had known the political intrigues of McClellan and, to a lesser extent, Hooker.[50]

Hancock inherited a command that was becoming ever more modern, in terms of its combined arms capacity. Hooker, unhappy with the performance of the Union artillery during the Chancellorsville campaign, created corps artillery brigades. The organizational move concentrated the artillery batteries and their firepower away from the divisional level. The artillery brigade in the Second Corps fielded four batteries. This actually reduced the artillery strength of the Second Corps by one-half from the Chancellorsville Campaign. Hooker used the extra batteries from the individual corps to create an army artillery reserve with five brigades. The senior battery officer commanded the corps artillery brigades; in the Second Corps, this was Captain John Hazzard. The lack of rank was a potentially serious battlefield problem. The War Department had argued since the start of the war that, because artillery batteries mustered only a relatively small number of men, their commanding officers should not receive a colonelcy. Brigadier General Henry Hunt, the Army of the Potomac's artillery chief, hoped that the creation of artillery brigades might win their commanding officers a higher rank. This did not happen, at least immediately, and higher-ranking infantry officers might still redirect the artillery brigade to support their own units.[51]

Lack of rank was not a problem on Hancock's staff. The Second Corps had a staff of ten officers in the spring of 1863, including a chief of staff, a chief quartermaster, a medical director, and three aide-de-camps. All of the staff members had recently received promotions. Perhaps none was more deserving than Lieutenant Colonel Charles Morgan. A West Point graduate (1857), Morgan served as the assistant inspector general and chief of staff of the Second Corps. The position was, arguably, too big for any one man to fill. But Morgan made a perfect complement to Hancock. In one of his few military weaknesses, Hancock had little

Winfield Scott Hancock. The longest-serving commander of the Second Corps, Hancock led soldiers through some of the most terrible—and, later, most hallowed—spots of the war. Library of Congress.

ability to read the terrain. According to Francis Walker, the then assistant adjutant general of the Second Corps, it was not in Hancock to "know instinctively" the lay of the land beyond the next bend. Morgan possessed that faculty, and in spades. Morgan often directed the Second Corps where to bivouac and where to fight. His ability to quickly size up surrounding streams, roads, and ridges almost as if reading a map proved invaluable to the Second Corps—so much so, that Walker, speaking of Morgan, declared that the fame won by the Second Corps "must always be, in a high degree, his claim to renown."[52]

DEFEATING PICKETT'S CHARGE

Dominating soldiers' attention was not the advancement of Hancock but the march northward of Lee and the pursuing Army of the Potomac.[53] Soldiers of the Second Corps could hardly guess where they might end up as Hooker jockeyed to keep them between Lee's 75,000-man-strong army and Baltimore and Washington. At least one private glumly had Union forces marching across much of the map. The campaign would carry into Pennsylvania, and "possibly to New York." While soldiers speculated over their ultimate destination, they all agreed that the pace of the march northward was grueling. Between June 14 and 29, the Union army marched from Falmouth, Virginia, to Uniontown, Maryland, a distance of nearly 150 miles.[54] A lieutenant in the 145th Pennsylvania claimed that he was so tired after marching twenty-five miles in one day that when he bedded down for the night, "I would not have moved if the whole Reb Army had been there to invite me." Scorching heat and choking dust only made the distances covered seem longer. One New Yorker decided that enduring the noontime sun while marching was nearly as trying an experience as facing Confederate bullets in battle. A Connecticut private, at no loss for words, declared that after choking through "clouds of dirt" day after day any passersby "will think I was a Nig."[55]

On June 25, the Second Corps received reinforcement by Brigadier General Alexander Hays's four regiments (the 39th New York, 111th New York, 125th New York, and 126th New York) near Thoroughfare Gap. Hays's nearly 2,000 newcomers boosted the manpower of Hancock's command to 13,055 present for duty. The totals would have been higher but for the hard marching since leaving Falmouth. Still, the arrival of Hays's brigade made good the earlier departure of the various short-term regiments. Hancock assigned the newcomers to French's division, making each of his three divisions roughly equal in numbers of regiments and men.[56] The rest of the army also received reinforcements while on the march northward, including several brigades of infantry and a cavalry division. The reinforcements helped to boost Hooker's command to 84,710 men.[57]

Hays's soldiers brought several potential troubles with them to the Second Corps. The New Yorkers had compiled a poor war record. This was a new twist for the Second Corps, because all other reinforcements (with the exception of Kimball's brigade) had arrived with little or no prior military experience. In their only combat, soldiers of the New York brigade had surrendered after attempting briefly to defend Harpers Ferry from Confederate attackers during the Maryland Campaign the previous autumn. The men had not taken the field since receiving their parole in late 1862. How well their fighting spirit had recovered, if at all, remained to be seen.[58]

Beyond a poor battlefield record, Hays's newcomers threatened the unit cohesion of French's veterans. The only other option was to break up the brigade, likely creating as many problems as it solved. Signs of strain appeared immediately. The spick-and-span uniforms worn by the Harpers Ferry men were the object of much ridicule. Veterans smirked that the recently arrived soldiers were nothing more than "band box soldiers" with their "dress coats and white gloves." In another instance, soldiers in French's division greeted their new comrades by "hooting at them and calling them white gloved gentry."[59] With catcalls ringing in their ears, Hays's men likely wondered whether they had many friends in the Second Corps beyond their own ranks.

The addition of reinforcements with questionable pasts was a concern also shared throughout much of the rest of the army. The five regiments of Colonel Lewis Grant's Vermont Brigade received assignment to the Sixth Corps. The New Englanders had seen only limited battlefield action by mid-1863, having spent much of their career on garrison duty. In the Fifth Corps, Brigadier General Samuel Crawford's division

of Pennsylvania Reserves expressed little fighting spirit. The Pennsylvanians had fought courageously over the past year, especially through
the Cornfield at Antietam. After spending much of the winter of 1862–63
on guard duty around Washington, Crawford's men expressed little
interest in returning to the front. Whether soldiers of the Vermont Brigade and the Pennsylvania Reserves would fight hard remained open to
speculation as the Union army marched northward.[60]

Two command changes occurred within the Second Corps while
near Thoroughfare Gap, also on June 25. Hays assumed command of
Third Division the same day that he arrived with his brigade, a dizzying jump in command. Hays replaced French, who had requested and
received transfer to command the Federal garrison at Harpers Ferry.
Hays might have had a difficult time winning over soldiers who had
known only French as their division commander. Hays avoided the
potential pitfall because of his record of battlefield experience and bravery. Hays was a well-seasoned combat officer by midsummer of 1863,
having led a regiment during the Peninsula Campaign and a brigade
during the Second Bull Run Campaign, where he was severely wounded.[61] While Hays took his new post, Brigadier General Alexander Webb
assumed command of the Philadelphia Brigade in the Second Division. Webb replaced Joshua Owen, whom Gibbon had placed under
arrest in unclear circumstances. The change from Owen to Webb, if not
benefiting the Philadelphia Brigade, at least did not hurt. Webb was a
combat veteran and a strict disciplinarian, both valuable characteristics
with the army in the field. Most recently, Webb had served as chief of
artillery of the Army of the Potomac during the Peninsula Campaign
and as inspector general of the Fifth Corps during the Chancellorsville
Campaign.[62]

Soldiers learned of yet another command change as they approached
Uniontown in north-central Maryland three days later. Believing Hooker either unwilling or unable to bring Lee to bay, Lincoln replaced him
in command of the Army of the Potomac with Major General George
Meade, the former commander of the Fifth Corps.[63] A few of Hancock's
men criticized the command change. Lieutenant George Finch, a true
diehard, wished that McClellan, the army's first commander, would
regain the position. Lieutenant Thomas Galwey questioned the wisdom

of changing commanders with a battle looming. More soldiers, however, accepted the command change with little, if any, comment. They had seen three commanders come and go since the late fall of 1862, and Meade was only one more in a long line of generals. A soldier in Gibbon's division found himself more concerned with putting one foot in front of the other. He likely expressed the sentiment shared by many of his comrades when he admitted that with the steady marching since leaving Falmouth "we have scarcely time for reflection."[64]

Soldiers' thoughts on Meade were interrupted on July 1, when the advanced portions of the army came under heavy Confederate attack outside Gettysburg, Pennsylvania. Meade had not planned to fight a battle here, and after Major General John Reynolds, the commander of the First Corps, was killed, he had no high-ranking officer on the ground whose judgment he trusted. Meade quickly dispatched Hancock to survey the battlefield and recommend whether the Union army should stay and fight. Hancock believed the ground strong and, working with General Howard, the commander of the Eleventh Corps and the senior Union officer present, he helped to sort the Federal lines.[65] There later emerged significant controversy over whether Hancock or Howard actually selected the high ground running south of Gettysburg at Cemetery Hill and Cemetery Ridge for the Union army to make a stand. The evidence, at the time and after, largely supports Hancock. But, at the moment, the presence of Hancock helped to put the fight back into soldiers of the Union First Corps and Eleventh Corps falling back through Gettysburg. Hancock cut an inspiring battlefield figure, as always. Equally important, according to Brigadier General Henry Hunt, Meade's artillery chief, Hancock's presence also inspired confidence because it "implied . . . the near approach of his army corps."[66] Hunt's few words speak to the reputation of Hancock's men throughout the Army of the Potomac as hard fighters.

The Second Corps took up position on Cemetery Ridge, the center of the Union defensive lines, by the late morning of July 2. The men ate their lunch and quietly talked, but the hours were anything but restful. An ominous silence hung over the field, and soldiers correctly judged that the Confederates were readying to launch an attack. Lieutenant Josiah Favill found the tension nearly unbearable because, unlike at most other battles fought by the Second Corps, "this time it was our turn to await the advance."[67] The strain only increased as soldiers watched Major General Daniel Sickles lead his Third Corps forward from their left. Sickles believed that the wheat field and peach orchard to his front made a more easily defendable position, because the ground was slightly higher. In reality, Sickles had isolated his men and exposed them to attack from the front and both flanks.[68] Hancock, at least, realized the danger. He reportedly silenced debate over the wisdom behind Sickles's advance by declaring, "Wait a moment. You'll see them tumbling back." The expected Confederate attack came soon after, smashing into the exposed Union lines. The fighting quickly earned the Peach Orchard and the Wheatfield a place in American history with capital letters. Watching the carnage unfold, a staff officer to Gibbon gulped, "What a hell is there down that valley!"[69]

Tasked by Meade to help restore the Union left, Hancock ordered Brigadier General John Caldwell to march toward the sound of battle. Caldwell had assumed command of the First Division when Hancock had received his advancement to corps command.[70] Marching toward the front, Caldwell's men brushed past swarms of dispirited Union soldiers streaming back from the killing ground. One jittery private hoped that the division might remain in reserve. He received disappointment from a grizzled veteran of the Irish Brigade who scoffed, "Yis, . . . resarved it is, for the hard fightin'."[71] Soldiers received at least some relief from their anxieties when Father William Corby of the Irish Brigade climbed upon a nearby boulder and offered absolution. One of the faithful declared that the scene of Catholics and Protestants alike bowing their heads in shared reverence "was more than impressive, it was awe-inspiring." To the still wavering, Corby reminded that the Catholic Church "refuses Christian burial to the soldier who turns his back upon the foe or deserts his flag."[72]

Caldwell's men smashed into the Wheatfield in one of the more impressive Union assaults of the war. Within minutes, three of the four brigade commanders of the division became casualties. Soldiers ran low on ammunition and tripped over the Union and Confederate dead that littered the ground from earlier fighting. All the while Confederate fire was "terrific," and the noise of battle was "deafening." Soldiers continued to press forward despite the chaos, sensing that only wounds and death awaited them in the open. Firing as they went, Caldwell's men drove "the rebels before us."[73] Mounting casualties failed to stop the Federal advance. Private George Whipple remembered alternately firing his musket and pushing ahead when a comrade dropped against him, dead from a bullet to the head. Momentarily stunned, Whipple resumed his advance when "Capt. Fuller said 'never mind George, Forward.'" Forward they went, and Caldwell's men crossed the Wheatfield and cleared the bordering Rose Woods and Stony Hill, a low, rocky rise beyond. Soldiers greeted their triumph with "ringing cheers," according to one hoarse Pennsylvanian.[74]

Hard fighting played a role in the success of Caldwell's division in the Wheatfield, but so again did unit cohesion. Sumner, Couch, and, presently, Hancock had attempted to maintain unit identity as much as possible since the start of the war. The result was that twelve of Caldwell's sixteen regiments had served together since the Seven Days Battles on the Virginia Peninsula. Officers and enlisted men were as familiar with one another as they were going to be. Soldiers overcame a "deplorable state of confusion" from the noise and violence of battle because they knew what they, and the men in other units around them, were doing.[75] Few other Union divisions might claim as much, given the many high-ranking officers' practice of almost continuously adding new regiments and brigades. The difficulty in maintaining unit cohesion throughout much of the army became even more pronounced following the organizational shakedown in the aftermath of the Chancellorsville Campaign, and the disbandment of three divisions.[76]

Unit cohesion could do little when new waves of Confederate attackers broke through Union defenders in the Peach Orchard, just to the north of the Wheatfield. Advancing Confederates poured a withering fire into the right flank and rear of Caldwell's men.[77] Survivors of the fusillade streamed back across the Wheatfield, a perilous trip that carried them over their own dead and wounded and through Confederate crossfire. One New Yorker admitted that the short retreat "was awful." Another veteran declared, "It was every man for himself and the rebels took the hindermost." Not Private Stephen Osborne, who claimed that the "most of us made fair time."[78]

Caldwell and his men could not outrun controversy. Survivors of the fighting began to regroup only after reaching Taneytown Road, to the east of Cemetery Ridge. There were not many, with the division having left 1,265 men killed, wounded, and missing in the Wheatfield. Lieutenant Colonel Charles Morgan, the newly appointed chief of staff of the Second Corps, had watched Caldwell's men breaking from the Wheatfield. Morgan could not believe the sight, and he later criticized the division for "flying to the rear." Any attempt to stem the tide "within reach of the enemy's bullets was useless."[79] Worse, other high-ranking Union officers also had noticed. Major General George Sykes had received orders from Meade to move his Fifth Corps to reinforce the Union left even before Caldwell and his men had gone into action. The Fifth Corps soon came under Confederate attack, and barely held its own around Little Round Top. Sykes attributed the close-run affair to a lack of time to prepare, due, in part, to Caldwell's sudden collapse. Brigadier General Romeyn Ayres, one of Sykes's division commanders, contemptuously noted that the Second Corps soldiers had "shut up like a jack-knife."[80] Stung by the accusations, Hancock later investigated the action in the Wheatfield. Hancock pointed out other Union soldiers to the left of the Wheatfield had fallen back, exposing Caldwell's men to a brutal flank attack. Under the circumstances, "no troops on the field had done better." Still, an air of disapproval hung over Caldwell throughout the rest of the army. He received reassignment from division command in the winter of 1863–64, and did not again lead troops in the field.[81]

The rout of Caldwell's division, as well as much of Sickles's Third Corps, threw open a roughly three-quarter mile stretch in the Union lines along Cemetery Ridge. The fluidity of the battlefield situation was new to the Second Corps. Even at Fair Oaks, the closest tactical comparison, the Second Corps reinforced an already existing, albeit tenuous, defensive line. The task at Gettysburg became even greater when, after Sickles was wounded, Meade placed the remnants of the Third Corps under Hancock. Gibbon, under the arrangement, assumed temporary command of the Second Corps.[82]

Hancock was at his best in holding together the patchwork Union lines. According to a nearby General Gibbon, Hancock uttered "some expressions of discontent" when informed that he also was responsible for the Third Corps.[83] He took to the task with a will, however, and was seemingly everywhere to inspire the men. In the early evening, Confederate attackers, under Brigadier General William Barksdale, knocked through Brigadier General Andrew Humphreys's Third Corps division posted along the Emmitsburg Road. The Confederates captured several pieces of Union artillery before continuing to push toward the southern end of Cemetery Ridge. Hancock led Colonel George Willard's brigade to attempt to stem the tide. Hancock pointed to Barksdale's advancing line, and sent Willard's four regiments forward. The Union soldiers were good ones for the task. Hancock had selected the brigade because it otherwise had formed the Union reserve along Cemetery Ridge. Yet, Willard's men, attached to the Second Corps only a few days earlier, were ready. They charged into the attacking Confederates, shouting, "Remember Harper's Ferry!" After a several-minute struggle, Barksdale's men retreated in disorder. Willard was killed in the fighting, but his men beamed in the aftermath.[84] Private Myron Failing claimed that the brigade finally "did prove itself worthy of a place in the old Second Corps." Hays, the division commander, agreed. The brigade's heroism at Gettysburg "is written in blood," blotting out the stain of Harpers Ferry.[85]

Trusting to the outcome of Willard's charge, Hancock rode back north along Cemetery Ridge. He moved to rally some soldiers falling back toward him, presumably from the Third Corps, when he came under fire from the same direction. Recognizing that the troops were Confederate and not Union, and advancing rather than retreating, Hancock rushed to find help. He stumbled across the 262 men of the 1st Minnesota, under the command of Colonel William Colvill. Temporarily giving in to despair, Hancock wailed, "My God! Are these all the men we have here?" Quickly recovering, Hancock barked, "Advance, Colonel, and take those colors." The Minnesotans went forward and into a "galling fire." Colvill's men were heavily outnumbered, going against a Confederate brigade. Yet they had the advantage of surprise, and their advance briefly created a ripple of panic among some of the now halted Confederates. The regiment also received timely artillery support from Union batteries posted along Cemetery Ridge. When more Union infantry began to arrive after about fifteen minutes of fighting, the Confederates fell back. The cost to the 1st Minnesota was extremely high, with nearly 70 percent of those engaged listed as killed, wounded, and missing. But the immediate Confederate threat had passed. A relieved Hancock later gave praise: "I cannot speak too highly of this regiment and its commander."[86]

Soon after the end of the fighting along Cemetery Ridge, the Confederates launched a rare twilight attack against the Union right flank. Fighting had occurred along Cemetery Hill and Culp's Hill throughout much of the day. The Confederates made one last attempt to break the Union lines, held by Howard's Eleventh Corps. Hearing sounds of battle, Hancock, on his own initiative, rushed Colonel Samuel Carroll's brigade of three regiments to the scene. These were the westerners who had reinforced the Second Corps on the Virginia Peninsula. The men again proved their mettle this night. The Confederate attack already was ebbing, as much from the fall of darkness as from Union resistance. Carroll's men swung into the battle, to cheers from Howard's soldiers of "give 'em hell, boys."[87] In a brief but swirling, often hand-to-hand, melee, Carroll's soldiers helped to drive off Confederate attackers attempting to capture a Union artillery battery. The Second Corps soldiers gave chase all the way down to the base of Cemetery Hill, before complete darkness made impractical any further pursuit.[88]

The Second Corps had fought magnificently on July 2. Hancock's men held together the patchwork Union center against repeated Confederate assault. Other Union corps certainly had fought well, especially the Fifth Corps around Little Round Top and Devil's Den, and the Twelfth Corps around Culp's Hill. Only the Second Corps, however, had fought on the offense and defense, and over the greatest distances. Little wonder that in a meeting later that night between Meade and his corps commanders to discuss, among other things, the condition of Lee's Confederate army, Hancock excitedly exclaimed, "General, we have got them nicked!" Perhaps greater praise comes from Confederate General James Longstreet. The two divisions of his corps had carried the bulk of the Confederate effort against the Union center and left. Longstreet boasted that when his 20,000 soldiers went into battle in the late afternoon, they "commenced what I do not hesitate to pronounce the best three hours' fighting ever done by any troops on any battle-field."[89]

Yet the Confederates failed to gain a lodgment in the original Union defensive lines. This was certainly in part due to the stubborn fighting waged by the Union Third Corps and Fifth Corps. The failure of Long-street's attack also was a result of the hard fighting of the Second Corps, both in the Wheatfield and along the slope of Cemetery Ridge.

A relative quiet descended across the battlefield until the early after-noon of the next day. Confederate General Lee used the time to plan for an assault against the Union center on Cemetery Ridge. Lee believed that Meade had weakened his center the previous day to reinforce the flanks. He ordered the Union lines along Cemetery Ridge pounded by 163 artillery pieces and stormed by 13,000 infantry soldiers, an assault forever after known as Pickett's Charge. The aiming point for the assault was a clump of trees and a nearby angled stone wall, soon known more famously as the Copse of Trees and the Angle, where some fighting had occurred on the evening of July 2. Gibbon, still in temporary command of the Second Corps, had at least some warning that Lee's attack was coming. As the meeting among the army's top-ranking commanders was ending on the night of July 2, Meade pulled Gibbon aside to warn him, "If Lee attacks tomorrow, it will be *in your front*." Meade came to the conclusion by using the same logic as Lee in planning the assault. Gibbon was all enthusiasm, according to his postwar account. He con-fidently replied that he hoped that Lee would "try it again," for, "if he did, we would defeat him."[90]

The opening Confederate bombardment came with a fury. This was the most sustained artillery fire that any troops had yet suffered in the eastern theater, if not the war. "It was a terrible fire," an Ohio lieuten-ant declared, "and shot and shell flew around us like hail." A New York private noted the explosion of artillery shells tossing dirt, stones, and body parts into the air. The relentless "storm of iron" made it seem as if the very "heavens were on fire." Another white-knuckled soldier gulped that, amid the pounding, "it did not seem as though a man could get out alive."[91]

Despite the terrors that came with the shriek and explosion of can-non balls, soldiers held their lines. Some men recognized that the Con-federate artillery gunners were overshooting and that the front lines offered more safety than the rear lines. Other men found inspiration in their high-ranking officers, especially Hancock. The Second Corps commander showed no signs of fatigue from the strains of July 2. He rode along the length of his lines, to the cheers of the men. When told by a trailing staff officer that exploding shells knew no rank, Hancock intoned, "There are times a corps commander's life does not count."[92]

Hancock's men felt a range of emotions when Confederate artillery fire relented and Pickett's men started forward from Seminary Ridge. A shell-weary lieutenant jumped to his feet and clapped his hands when he saw the Confederate infantry step off, "shouting 'Hurrah my boys, they are coming, now steady boys!'" An equally battered private exclaimed, "Thank God! There comes the infantry!" Private William Burns expressed admiration as he watched Pickett's men move forward as if on parade. The Confederate advance "was a grand sight and worth a man's while to see it." Lieutenant Chauncey Harris decided that he had never seen soldiers march with more exactitude. Unbroken line followed unbroken line, all punctuated by the fiery red of the Confederate battle flag.[93] As the Confederates continued to approach, however, Sergeant Alexander McNeal worried that the Union defenders were badly outnumbered. Private Calvin Haynes felt just as nervous, admitting that the continued advance of Pickett's men "was a terrible sight for us, fine as it was, for we did not suppose that we could repulse them."[94]

Fortunately for the Union army, calmer heads prevailed as the Confederates came within killing range. Having found themselves all too often in the open and on the wrong side of strong defensive positions, Hancock's men saw a Confederate Fredericksburg in the making. Major Henry Abbott of the 20th Massachusetts boasted that the "moment I saw them I know we should give them Fredericksburg." Another veteran of the fighting before Marye's Heights shouted, "Give them Hell Now We've got you. Sock it to the Blasted Rebels, Fredericksburg on the other leg."[95]

Soldiers did their best to make the Fredericksburg analogy ring true, pouring a withering fire into the oncoming Confederate ranks. Hancock's men gaped at the destruction. A private admitted that "I never saw such slaughter." A captain described Pickett's men falling "like wheat before the garner." Soldiers in the Philadelphia Brigade proved especially formidable. They scavenged any spare and abandoned

The fighting around the Copse of Trees from the Union perspective on July 3, 1863, painted by Edwin Forbes from sketches made at the time. The defeat of Pickett's Charge evoked a particular pride in the Second Corps. Library of Congress.

muskets that they found along Cemetery Ridge, and their extra fire-power made for "dreadful execution" in the Rebel ranks. Despite the blistering fire, some Philadelphians fell back in disorder when handfuls of Confederate attackers cleared the Angle and to their front and pushed into Lieutenant Alonzo Cushing's artillery battery.[96] The breakthrough was short-lived as nearby soldiers from the rest of Gibbon's division, as well as Hays's division, pushed in with fresher, and more numerous, legs. The fighting was savage and confused. Private Frederick Oesterle later recalled that the Union counterattack was the only time during the war that he had fought hand-to-hand. More and more soldiers from the Second Corps all the while surged forward into the gap. "We went up more like a mob than a disciplined force," one participant later recalled; "however we got there in time to help stop Pickett."[97]

The quick defeat of Pickett's Charge caught soldiers of the Second Corps by surprise. Cheers of victory echoing from the Angle alerted one nearby staff officer that the "last and bloodiest fight of the great battle of Gettysburg is ended and won." Soldiers of the 14th Connecticut continued to blaze away at the by now stalled Confederates to their front. Only bits of "white cloth and handkerchiefs" frantically waving alerted the New Englanders that their Confederate opponents had quit fighting. A Massachusetts sergeant was unable to contain his excitement when he realized that Pickett's men were falling back in confusion. He ran before his regiment hollering, "'They've broke, boys! They're running! There they go! See 'em run!'" The sergeant cheered too early; to the horror of onlookers, a bullet struck his head and killed him.[98]

The aftermath of the fighting revealed horrors nearly as trying as the battle itself. The fighting had raged most savagely along the lines of the Second Corps, and dead and dying covered the ground. Amid the bodies, the wounded begged for help. The fortunate at least could move, either crawling upon hands and knees or using their muskets as make-shift crutches. Other wounded men lay where they had fallen, alter-nately gritting their teeth in pain and crying for water and loved ones at home. The sights and sounds around the Angle prompted Corporal Jacob Betchel of the 59th New York to make the previously unthink-able judgment that "Antietam was nothing compared to it." Captain Charles Nash was even more emphatic, claiming that sun had never shone upon a more grisly field.[99] Adding to the misery, Hancock's men found themselves unable to aid the wounded outside their lines for fear of drawing fire from Confederate sharpshooters. Soldiers of the Second Corps clung to their side of Cemetery Ridge and listened in horror. A Pennsylvanian admitted that the cries of Pickett's wounded strewn in the open fields were "piteous" but that "we could not comfort, it was [their] grave yard."[100]

Not all soldiers believed that the fighting had ended, even when firing ceased. Hancock, for one, urged Meade to launch an immedi-ate counterattack. Many Union soldiers had been engaged only light-ly, if at all, in the day's fighting. If these troops immediately pushed forward, "the enemy will be destroyed." Soldiers of the 1st Minnesota shared Hancock's aggressive instinct. They reloaded their muskets and reformed their ranks, expecting at any moment to receive orders to advance.[101]

The Second Corps would have contributed little to any Union coun-terattack. Hancock recognized this, and he meant for other commands to attack the battered Confederate army. His men also quickly realized that the numbers of dead and wounded were staggeringly high. Soldiers of the Philadelphia Brigade began to ask who among their ranks had fallen as soon as "the excitement of the battle was over" on July 3. The next day, an Ohio private glumly estimated that one-half of the soldiers in his regiment had been killed and wounded.[102] He was not far off when the casualty lists were compiled a few days later. Engaged on only two of the three days of the battle, the Second Corps still suffered 4,369 men killed, wounded, and missing. Losses throughout the rest of the army also were heavy, although, as in past battles, they varied greatly by army corps. The First Corps, heavily engaged on July 1 and 2, suffered 6,059 men killed, wounded, and missing. The Sixth Corps, in reserve for most of the fighting, suffered only 242 casualties. Taken all together, the Army of the Potomac lost 23,000 men killed, wounded, and missing, making the fighting at Gettysburg the bloodiest yet experienced.[103]

Further weakening the immediate fighting power of the Second Corps, casualties extended through the ranks. Hancock was severely wounded while helping to repulse Pickett's Charge, as was Gibbon. The two generals took several months to recover and returned to the army only that winter.[104] Six of the ten brigade commanders at the start of the battle were killed or wounded. Among the forty-four officers who led their regiments into the fighting, eight either were killed or died of wounds suffered, and another eleven were wounded. The losses continued after the fighting stopped as the ill went to the hospital and the medically discharged went home.[105] A corporal reported that in one company of the 1st Minnesota, "there wasn't but 9 left" for dinner on July 5. A lieutenant counted "about thirty three muskets left" in the 61st New York. The 8th Ohio was large by comparison, with "106 men left" in mid-July.[106]

Soldiers bore the horrific losses because they believed that Gettysburg made the war's end all that much closer. Moving cautiously, Meade started the Army of the Potomac in pursuit of the defeated and retreating Confederate Army of Northern Virginia. Private Albert Davis admitted that marching mile after mile soon after fighting major battle was hard, but added, "We are in good spirits, and think we shall whip the Rebs in good shape." Reports that recent rains had sent the Potomac River over its banks only fueled speculation among soldiers that a final, decisive battle loomed. A Connecticut private could not imagine how the Confederates might escape across swollen river fords, unless they had somehow discovered an ability to fly. An Irish Brigade private was less imaginative but no less confident. He asserted that "we will be able to keep them from crossing over and give them another good thrashing like at Gettysburg."[107]

The Union pursuit brought only disappointment to soldiers in the Second Corps. They found little gratitude in the Pennsylvania countryside, where they fell victim to exorbitant prices charged by local residents. Meats, breads, and even well water exchanged hands at high prices. Losing much of his monthly pay to mercenary civilians, Captain James Mitchell, a Keystone state native himself, fumed, "I never was so ashamed of anything in my life as I was of Pennsylvania."[108] Worse, Meade was wary of assaulting hastily constructed Confederate defensive works at Falling Waters, Maryland. Meade was a naturally cautious military commander anyway, but his top-ranking subordinates reinforced the tendency. Brigadier General William Hays, who assumed temporary command of the Second Corps after the wounding of Hancock and Gibbon, was among these. Hays, along with four of the army's other six corps commanders, advised Meade against assaulting the Confederate defensive works. While Meade and his generals talked, Lee slipped his army across the Potomac River on the night of July 13.[109] Private Lemuel Jeffries was one of many Union soldiers stunned to find that with coming of sunrise "the rebels entirely disappeared from our front." Lieutenant Samuel Fiske was in for an even ruder shock. He and other soldiers of the Second Division advanced upon the Confederate works at daybreak, expecting any moment to receive a torrent of fire. "Works are ours," Fiske described in disbelief. "Enemy, sitting on the other side of the river, performing various gyrations with his fingers, thumb on his nose."[110]

Outrage and disappointment ran high by mid-July, but both emotions failed to dim the immense pride that soldiers of the Second Corps drew from the Union victory at Gettysburg. The fighting in Pennsylvania demonstrated that the Army of the Potomac could defeat Lee and his Army of Northern Virginia. Captain Augustus Van Dyke declared with almost palpable relief that the "men know now that Lee's army is not invincible and that the Army of the Potomac can win a victory." Private Charles Davis agreed, asserting that "Gettysburg was a magnificent battle, well fought and well contested." A Connecticut sergeant believed that, to date, the greatest Union triumph more than made

up for the greatest Union defeat. "We paid the rebels back, with interest," Alexander McNeil explained, "for our defeat at Fredericksburg."
A private eagerly read more good news for Union arms with newspaper
reports describing the capture of Vicksburg, Mississippi. He gloated
that after the twin Union battlefield victories, the Confederates "are in
a rather tight place."[111]

That the Second Corps had fought well at Gettysburg made the
Union triumph all that much sweeter, but soldiers expected that their
outfits receive proper credit. A Massachusetts soldier griped that readers of Philadelphia-based newspapers, "about the only ones we get,"
received the impression that only "Pennsylvania troops fought the battle—where it is known that they always run if anybody does." Soldiers
of Carroll's brigade seethed that General Howard failed to give them
public recognition for helping to rescue the Union position on Cemetery
Hill on the evening and night of July 2. The men were so incensed that
they began a letter-writing campaign to the *Army and Navy Journal*, an
occasional publication circulated throughout the Union military. One
writer, identified only as "Adjutant," was especially mad. "Our brigade,"
he wrote in February 1864, ". . . *alone* drove the enemy from Cemetery
Hill out of our batteries, and held that portion of the line from which
part of the Eleventh Corps had been driven." Howard relented the next
month, penning an open "Letter of Thanks to Carroll." He admitted
that the Confederates were "just breaking" his "single thin line" when
Carroll and his men arrived. The "prompt support" given by the western
soldiers helped to throw back the attackers and avert a possible disaster.
For this, "I tender you my hearty thanks."[112]

Other soldiers also took to championing their own cause. Captain
William Plumer declared that soldiers in the 15th Massachusetts never
fought better. A lieutenant in the 108th New York asserted that his fellow
soldiers were well aware that they carried a solid reputation won at high
cost on other battlefields. He believed that the knowledge prompted
every man "to do his duty and preserve that name or die then and there,
and indeed many did fall there, but in the front rank facing the enemy."
Survivors of the fighting around the Angle were especially pleased
with themselves. Colonel Robert Penn Smith of the 71st Pennsylvania
recounted that his men poured devastating fire into the Confederates

advancing "in three parallel lines (about 9000)." Smith concluded that
"without flattery it is my regiment that saved the day." Colonel Norman
Hall of the 7th Michigan was more expansive in his praise. He acknowledged that fighting had occurred along much of Cemetery Ridge on
July 3, rather than just at the Angle. Still, the "decision of the rebel commander was upon that point; the concentration of artillery fire was upon
that point; . . . the greatest effort and greatest courage was at that point;
and the victory was at that point."[113]

Satisfaction in a job well done became a particular pride in the
Second Corps. Soldiers believed that they had fought as hard as always
at Gettysburg. The difference was that the effort resulted not just in victory, but in victory widely heralded across the Union. Soldiers linked
the battlefield efforts of their regiments and brigades into the even larger
accomplishments of the Second Corps, as they had done during earlier
campaigns. While fighting around the Copse of Trees with the Philadelphia Brigade, Private George Beidelman had suffered a wound that
eventually would claim his life. Despite the physical pain, Beidelman
was all enthusiasm. "We have just fought, in old Pennsylvania, the greatest battle of the war," Beidelman gushed. "The 2 Corps has covered itself
with glory." Sergeant John Hirst also had reason to be proud, having
fought with the 14th Connecticut to the right of the Angle. The men had
"held our ground bravely." Hirst saw greater fame, however, in the battlefield deeds of the Second Corps. Hancock's men had saved the Union
army. Had Pickett's men pierced the Union defensive lines, "our whole
army would have been cut in two and we should have been flanked upon
all sides." Fighting in the decisive point of the action was not unusual,
because the "Second Corps always held the front in time of peril."[114]

Rejoicing in the hard fighting of the Second Corps extended into
the Union rear lines. Colonel Nelson Miles missed the fighting in Pennsylvania while recuperating from a wound suffered during the Chancellorsville Campaign. Miles beamed that although the Second Corps had
lost heavily at Gettysburg, it "has the credit of saving the day." Surgeon
J. Franklin Dyer pointed out that the ferociousness of the fighting on
July 3 was not new to the Second Corps or, for that matter, the eastern theater. In a matter of hours, Hancock's men had suffered more
casualties than "Grant's army lost in the siege of Vicksburg."[115]

Few other Union soldiers might express as much pride in their army corps. Individual regiments, brigades, and divisions had fought extremely well. But the First Corps ultimately had suffered a rout on July 1, even if largely the fault of the Eleventh Corps collapsing on its right flank. The Third Corps was nearly destroyed in the fighting the next day. The Twelfth Corps had fought well around Culp's Hill but, because of its earlier association with the Union Army of Virginia, always had trouble winning acceptance in the Army of the Potomac. Only two divisions of the Fifth Corps had been heavily engaged, while none of the three divisions of the Sixth Corps had been. Soldiers certainly expressed pride in the clear-cut victory won by the Army of the Potomac. But expressions of corps pride were more muted.

Further distinguishing the Second Corps from the rest of the army, soldiers knew that they had triumphed over the best that Lee's veterans had to offer. Private Albert Emmell of the 12th New Jersey argued that Hancock's men were in no way intimidated when squaring off against their Rebel counterparts. During Pickett's Charge, the Confederate attackers "came trying to strike terror into Yankee hearts by unnatural shrieks and yells. But it was a no go. The old Second is not to be frightened by a little noise coming from rebel throats." Moreover, the Confederates might now themselves be unnerved when facing Hancock and his soldiers in battle. Pickett's men reportedly were unpleasantly surprised to see the trefoil markings of the Second Corps awaiting them as they advanced against Cemetery Ridge. "It appears their officers had told them that the Militia was fighting them, and would break and run at their approach," Corporal Edward Walker of the 1st Minnesota gloated, "*but* they found it *somewhat* different. As one of their men gave himself up he says—'Militia be d-d—we've seen these flags before.'"[116] The story may be apocryphal, but many members of the Second Corps believed it true, giving them a surge of pride and confidence as they entered the third fall of the war.

5

REBUILDING

BRISTOE STATION TO STEVENSBURG

Complaints filled the air as soldiers of the Second Corps marched toward the Rapidan River and temporary encampment in late July 1863, following the conclusion of the Gettysburg Campaign. The past month had brought near-continuous fighting and marching, and fatigue ranked near the top in list of gripes. Estimates varied, but soldiers calculated that they had tromped hundreds of miles through the Maryland and Pennsylvania countryside, in addition to fighting a major battle. Growling stomachs competed with tired feet, and soldiers also bemoaned the lack of food. Difficulty in acquiring salt caused the greatest hardship, because otherwise industrious foragers lacked the means to season and preserve fresh meats.[1] Complaints of too much marching and too little food paled, however, when soldiers contemplated their thinned ranks. The Second Corps mustered only 7,680 men in late July, the smallest number to date. Most of the absent men were recovering from illness and wounds. Veterans wondered if their numbers were too few to help carry the war through to Union victory. In the plaintive cry of Captain Charles Nash of the 19th Maine, "We need more men."[2]

NEWCOMERS AND OLD-TIMERS

Light duty and full rations lifted spirits considerably once the Second Corps arrived at Morrisville, Virginia, and the banks of the Rapidan River. Here the war in the East reached a temporary standstill, as both the Army of the Potomac and the Confederate Army of Northern Virginia recuperated from the bloodletting of Chancellorsville and Gettysburg.[3]

The two armies also each sent reinforcements to north Georgia and Tennessee, one of the few times that the war in the West took the spotlight.
With now ample free time to fill, soldiers of the Second Corps enjoyed
the breathtaking landscape. The Rapidan River to the front and the Blue
Ridge Mountains to the side made for dramatic vistas, especially when
framed against a backdrop of dawn and dusk. The mail caught up with
the army after several weeks' absence, and many soldiers spent their
time reading and rereading letters from family and friends.[4] Making the
stay at Morrisville all the more pleasant, meat, vegetables, hardtack, coffee, and other rations were again ample. Between gulps of food soldiers
noted how they lived "first rate" and "very high."[5]

Amid the leisurely passing of hours, soldiers discussed the federal
draft implemented that summer. Many veterans relished the thought
of their ranks again nearing full strength and impatiently awaited the
arrival of the first draftees. Private Allen Landis explained that the new
waves of Federal soldiers would push the rebellion, already "mighty
weak in the knees," to collapse. More of Hancock's men, however, questioned why the federal government waited as long as it did to roust
perceived stay-at-homes and shirkers to the front. The answer seemed a
lack of urgency, if not outright incompetence, on the Union homefront.
Before suffering a mortal wound in the Wheatfield at Gettysburg, Colonel Edward Cross of the 5th New Hampshire could not understand why
the Union failed to place more men under arms. Only hard blows would
win the war for the Union, and that required more soldiers in the field.
Cross was willing to do his part. But "it is hard fighting against stupidity, foolishness, and treason at home." Private Joseph Graham related a
story circulating widely throughout the army that gives insight into the
poor attitudes many soldiers held toward those in charge of running
the war. In the tale, a group of privates asked a passing general what
they should do with a Confederate spy captured while wearing civilian
clothes. "'Hang him, hang him at once' said the General; 'if I send him
to Washington they will send him back promoted.'"[6]

Such biting attitudes represent a momentary frustration, rather
than a larger breach between soldiers at the front and civilians at home.
Hancock's men expressed gratitude for letters received from family and
friends, as they had since the start of the war. They also acknowledged

that, although they often wished themselves at home, commitment to the Union trumped personal considerations. Isaac Plumb had served through the thick of the war by the autumn of 1863 as a company officer in the 61st New York. Plumb likely shared the sentiments of many of his comrades when he admitted that he would happily see the war over and "myself at home among kindred and friends and comforts." Since that was not the case, Plumb declared that he never expected to derive "greater happiness while I live than I enjoy here while serving my country."[7]

Soldiers remained closely linked to their loved ones at home, but they pulled no punches in criticizing resistance to the draft that had flared across many northern communities. Violence was especially bad in many poorer neighborhoods of New York City, where rioters rampaged, looted, and, sometimes, killed. Many of Hancock's men hoped that the federal government would use force in putting down the upheavals, and that they be allowed to participate.[8]

The draft riots had the potential to create an especially high level of tension within the Second Corps, because many in the mobs were Irish. Northerners quite often drew no distinctions, and savaged the Irish-American community as disloyal and prone to violence. Specific attacks on the perceived lack of patriotism among Irish Americans did not occur in the Second Corps. Instead, soldiers broadly described the rioters as "Butter nuts," "secesh," and "Copperheads." The whys of this are uncertain, but might have had to do with some hostile reaction in the Irish Brigade to the upheavals. Sergeant Peter Welsh of the 28th Massachusetts argued that civil authorities should use canister and grape shot to put down the rioting. The Irish who might be hurt in the ensuing bloodshed were not entirely to blame. "They are to easily led into such snares," Welsh bemoaned, "which give their enemys an opportunity to malighn and abuse them."[9] It is difficult to tell if Welsh was in the majority, because few letters from Irish Brigade soldiers survive. If so, hostility toward the draft riots faded into silence in the postwar era. David Power Conyngham, a staff officer in the Irish Brigade, makes no mention of the episode in his history of the unit, published in 1866.

Soldiers in five regiments (the 14th Indiana, 7th Michigan, 1st Minnesota, 4th Ohio, and 8th Ohio) received assignment in mid-August to help quell the rioting in New York City. The assumption was that soldiers from the Northwest would have fewer emotional misgivings in subduing the upheaval than their comrades from the Northeast.[10] Whether the thinking was accurate never received test, because soldiers arrived several days after the riots had ended. In later years, a fiery talk developed among veterans that they had been disappointed in not receiving an opportunity to crush the riots through force of arms. "[I]t would have been for the admonition of traitors to the end of time," one former staff officer intoned. The talk bore little resemblance to the reality. Hancock's men enjoyed themselves thoroughly in New York City. Many men soaked up the beautiful weather, while others caroused in nearby saloons. The only hostility that soldiers encountered came from store merchants, who feared losing business when city officials closed Broadway for a review parade.[11]

While some soldiers enjoyed New York, the rest of the Second Corps underwent rebuilding from top to bottom. Major General Gouverneur Warren assumed command in mid-August, until Hancock could recover from his Gettysburg wounds. Warren was relatively young at thirty-three years of age, but he already had compiled an impressive battlefield record. Warren had led a brigade during the Second Bull Run and Maryland Campaigns, winning promotion from colonel to brigadier general for his services. During the first half of 1863, Warren served as chief topographical engineer of the army. The Union general had experienced his finest day of the war at the Battle of Gettysburg on July 2. Recognizing the critical importance of the position, Warren had ordered soldiers of the Fifth Corps to occupy the otherwise undefended Little Round Top. For his quick thinking, Warren won promotion to major general. Unfortunately for Warren, however, he suffered inevitable comparisons to Hancock. Few Union generals could fare well in such an evaluation, and Warren was not one of them. Josiah Favill, a staff officer in the First Division, Hancock's old command, downplayed the Union successes at Little Round Top by declaring that Warren "is decidedly a light weight." Warren even paled physically beside the robust and striking Hancock. The new Second Corps commander, Favill described, had a "cast in his look" that marred an already "dusky, sallow face."[12]

The switch from Hancock to Warren weakened the leadership of the Second Corps, but the rest of the army experienced an even greater

Gouverneur Warren. Although leading the Second Corps to one of the few lopsided Union battlefield victories in the East at Bristoe Station during the fall of 1863, Warren paled in soldiers' esteem to the popular Hancock. National Archives.

decline. Major General John Sedgwick, a former division commander under Sumner, was an exception. Sedgwick had assumed command of the Sixth Corps in the spring, and since had provided steady leadership. Major Generals John Newton and George Sykes had led the First Corps and the Fifth Corps through the fighting at Gettysburg. Newton and Sykes were competent officers, but neither was marked for greatness. Newton seemed to undergo an almost complete transformation when away from the battlefield, his energy and fire sapped by heavy drinking. Sykes seemingly worried over every detail before committing to action, a time-consuming punctiliousness that earned him the nickname "Tardy George" throughout the army. Newton and Sykes sometimes drove Meade to near-distraction, but Major General William French, also a former division commander under Sumner, was the true problem child of the Union high command. Assuming command of the Third Corps after Sickles was wounded at Gettysburg, French had by that fall given almost completely away to drink. French now clearly preferred draining whiskey bottles to holding army business, an alcoholism noticed by many of his fellow officers. All in all, Meade fretted that his subordinates, Warren included, were not men he could unflinchingly rely upon to take "care of themselves and commands."[13]

The rebuilding of the Second Corps and the rest of the Union army continued with the arrival of large numbers of replacement soldiers, some of whom were draftees and conscripts. The number of newly arriving soldiers varied depending upon the energy of state officials and the need of the individual unit. By late October, the 64th New York had received 111 replacement soldiers, while the 2nd Delaware had received only 22. The 148th Pennsylvania received 115 replacement soldiers on October 30, and 158 more newcomers three weeks later. The arrival of draftees and substitutes, along with the return of soldiers after recuperation from wounds suffered in earlier campaigns, noticeably swelled the strength of the Second Corps. Warren listed 11,600 men in late December, a nearly one-third increase from the late summer. The rest of the army underwent a similar surge in numbers. The First Corps, Third Corps, Fifth Corps, and Sixth Corps (Meade had transferred westward the Eleventh Corps and Twelfth Corps) reported an increase between August and December from just over 48,500 men to 63,750 men.[14]

Many veterans in the Second Corps and throughout the rest of the Union army questioned the motivations of replacement soldiers, a clear threat to unit cohesion. Warren's men believed that the newcomers had entered the army for any reason but love of nation, and their hostility was palpable. Colonel Nelson Miles scoffed that "nearly all" of the recruits received in the 61st New York "are miserable surly rough fellows and are without patriotism or honor. They seem to have no interest in the cause." Other soldiers referred to new soldiers as "convicts," "mud-mashers," and "a wild lot of fellows with plenty of money." This disdainful attitude toward draftees and substitutes only received confirmation when Meade ordered veterans to look among "detachments of conscripts" to see "if any of them are recognized as deserters or as personnel discharged for disabilities." Meade had hardly given ringing endorsement to the motivation of even well-intentioned replacement soldiers.[15]

Replacement soldiers themselves often lived up to such low expectations. Some of the new men made little effort to fit in, while others were simply inept.[16] Even worse, many draftees and substitutes dodged the dangers inherent to wartime military life. Replacement soldiers often deserted, leaving disgruntled veterans to describe them as "a hard set" who "go to the Rebs most every night." Other replacement soldiers feigned illness. Surgeon William Potter of the 57th New York complained that his days were filled to overflowing by newly arrived soldiers who resorted to the hospital for the least little ailment. More than a few batches of draftees and substitutes adopted both dodges. Major Henry Abbott reported that two hundred replacement soldiers departed Boston for the 20th Massachusetts in the late summer. Twenty men deserted en route. Among the remainder, another seventy men either deserted or joined the sick rolls within days of their arrival. Little wonder that Abbott began to have second thoughts about whether the federal draft was worth the seemingly meager results.[17]

Although much maligned, and often deservedly so, replacement soldiers did bring benefits. The boost in manpower was the most noticeable. A tongue-in-cheek Major Augustus Van Dyke numbered the 14th Indiana at 120 officers and enlisted men in late 1863. Had 200 replacement soldiers not arrived over the past many weeks, "there would be 80 less than nothing left of us." Perhaps even more important than mere numbers, replacement soldiers added a sense of vigor to their regiments. Many veterans had slipped into the doldrums as they sat with little to do. The arrivals of large numbers of new soldiers changed matters dramatically by keeping everyone busy. Colonel James Beaver admitted in the late summer that the 148thPennsylvania "is small—so painfully small that I can find little or nothing to do." The dullness quickly disappeared as more than 250 replacement soldiers arrived during the fall. A glowing Beaver now reported that he had "plenty to occupy my time." Beaver was not alone, and many company officers and noncommissioned officers beamed with pride as replacement soldiers learned the rudiments of unit and individual drill.[18]

The rebuilding process came to an abrupt halt on October 9, when the Union army took the field. Meade was responding to a new Confederate offensive, launched from Warrenton, Virginia. Lee hoped that in marching his 50,000 Confederate soldiers northward, he might force the Union army to fight before Washington at a disadvantage. Some of Warren's men actually welcomed the aggressive Rebel move, arguing that almost any activity beat whiling "along the dull hours." The next several days were anything but dull as soldiers marched hard to shield the nation's capital. After a twenty-two-mile march, one bone-weary private could only write, "very tired and very little rest." On October 13, the Second Corps was marching north along the Orange and Alexandria Railroad tracks and formed the left flank of the army. The pace often received interruptions when soldiers deployed into battle formation to guard against possible Confederate attack. Rumors of impending battle swirled, making sleep hard to achieve after Warren's men went into camp near Auburn, Virginia, later that night.[19]

The early morning of October 14 broke with heavy fog and, to the surprise of Warren's men, Confederate cavalry skirmishers all around. The horse soldiers were leading the advance of two Confederate cavalry brigades, under the overall command of General Jeb Stuart. The troopers were not much of a battlefield threat, by themselves. But Warren did not have the luxury of finding out. He worried that Stuart's cavalry might be masking the attack preparations of a much larger force of Confederate infantry. Warren believed that to stand pat before a potentially combined arms assault was "to await annihilation." A Confederate artillery battery began to find the range, with one shell killing seven men. That decided matters for Warren, and he alertly hurried his men through a fast-closing opening.[20] "I thought that I had been in tight places," one private gulped, "but that was what I call running the gauntlet." New Yorker James Rea found the entire episode "a trying thing."[21]

Warren kept his men moving toward Bristoe Station, several miles to the northeast. Meade earlier had ordered Major General George Sykes to keep his Fifth Corps at the former railroad stop until Warren arrived. Cold feet got the better of Sykes. Upon receiving a report that an approaching Union cavalry squadron was the advance of the Second Corps, Sykes pulled his soldiers out. When Warren and his men arrived at Bristoe Station some time later, they saw only the tail end of the Union army strung out in fording the Broad Run. So did nearly 5,000 pursuing Confederate soldiers from Lieutenant General Ambrose Hill's corps. The Confederates eagerly advanced in line of battle against the slow-moving Union supply wagons and stragglers. "What a sight," an onlooking New Jersey private marveled. "Rebels everywhere, line after line, batteries in position; all ready." Martial spectacle aside, the Second Corps had gone from bad to worse upon reaching Bristoe Station. If the Confederates seized the crossing at Broad Run, they might smash the vulnerable Union force already there. Worse, if the Confederates held Broad Run, they would cut off and isolate the Second Corps from the rest of the Army of the Potomac.[22]

Warren responded with a verve reminiscent of Hancock. Understanding that a several-foot-high railroad embankment that ran perpendicular to the line of the Confederate advance was the key to the battlefield, Warren hustled his men forward. As the Union soldiers reached the embankment, a "most spiteful" Confederate artillery fire began to fall. Lieutenant Fred Brown's Battery A of the 1st Rhode Island opened a counterbattery fire. Brown's guns had briefly suffered capture in the fighting along Cemetery Ridge at Gettysburg on July 2. Now, slightly over three months later, the Union artillerists cheered as their fire drove the Confederates from their guns. "We congratulated ourselves on the fact that our battery had saved the infantry on this occasion," one of Brown's men later remembered, "and we were now on even terms with them." The Second Corps's infantry also held its own. The Confederates had smartly changed the direction of their attack when they received fire from Warren's men on their left flank. The battle raged fiercely for many minutes. Throughout, the bullets flew, according to a Third Division soldier, "about our heads like hail." As in Pickett's Charge at Gettysburg, the Second Corps had the advantage of position. The men were well sheltered behind the railroad embankment, and they poured volley after volley into Hill's lines advancing across the open ground. A battle-hardened volunteer of 1861 gloated that "I never had a better chance to pay them off on the old account, and I did the best I could, as did all the boys." Dead and wounded attackers littered the ground by the time the Confederates retreated from the field in confusion in the late afternoon.[23]

General Hill and his subordinates later spent much energy attempting to explain away their defeat at Bristoe Station, an indication of the thrashing they had received at the hands of the Second Corps. Hill admitted that he ordered his men forward "too hastily." Yet, at the same time, had he reconnoitered the ground to his front more adequately, the retreating Union columns would have escaped anyway. "In that event I believe I should equally have blamed myself for not attacking at once." General Henry Heth, whose division bore the brunt of the fighting, believed that "no military man" who examined the battlefield could blame his troops for suffering defeat. The railroad embankment made an ideal place to form a defensive line. And, as it turns out, the leading Confederate brigades would have suffered even a worse fate had they actually stormed the Union lines. Warren would easily have moved up large numbers of reserves to capture any of the surviving attackers. General Lee had none of it. One month later, he admitted the Confederate defeat at Bristoe Station was a "disaster."[24]

Confederate assessments of the fighting at Bristoe Station were yet in the future, and, as night fell on October 14, Warren's men felt growing unease. The Second Corps had won a lopsided battlefield victory, but it risked attack by the massed Army of Northern Virginia come dawn. Warren's men nervously watched the "anxious, uneasy manner of the general officers" discussing what to do next. The ensuing order by Warren to retreat northward and rejoin the main army around Centreville,

Virginia, brought much hardship. The night turned rainy, and soldiers often slipped and stumbled. Near the Broad Run crossing, the Second Corps marched by Confederate soldiers wounded during the day's fighting. Hill's men called out for water and blankets, but, as an Ohio captain grimly declared, "we had not time then for pity." The sick and just plain tired of the Second Corps lined the route. The provost guard put ill soldiers into ambulances, but gave rough treatment to sleepy men. They hurried along skulkers with curses, threats and, when necessary, point of bayonet. Some worn-out men eluded even these determined efforts. One out of every four of the 546 casualties suffered by the Second Corps at Bristoe Station were men missing. This was second only to the proportion of missing endured during the Seven Days Battles. Despite hardships and straggling, the retreat ended in relief. Soldiers breathed more easily and, according to one survivor, "congratulated one another" on the successful outcome of the day's fighting and marching.[25]

The victory of the Second Corps at Bristoe Station ended the Confederate offensive against Washington, and Meade was appreciative. He issued a general orders throughout the entire Army of the Potomac the next day, praising the hard fighting of the Second Corps. This was a rare occurrence, because congratulatory orders usually addressed all of the soldiers in the army. Arguably even rarer were such clear-cut Union battlefield triumphs. Meade recited that the Second Corps had suffered attack while serving as the army's rear guard. The Confederates—"The enemy," as Meade described them—were repulsed "after a spirited contest," losing two colors, five artillery pieces, and 450 prisoners. Meade concluded that the "skill and promptitude of Major-General Warren, and the gallantry and bearing of the officers and soldiers of the Second Corps, are entitled to high commendation."[26]

Meade's praise added to soldiers' already high morale and confidence. Other Union soldiers found the recent shadow boxing with Lee, full of hard marching but no knock-out blows, discouraging. Not among Warren's men. As during past campaigns, soldiers recognized that the Second Corps had fought well enough to outshine the deeds of any one regiment. Lieutenant Colonel Richard Thompson enthused that the "2nd Army Corps to which I am proud to belong has, during the last week, now more bright laurels." After detailing the recent maneuvers and fighting, Thompson proudly concluded, "Our badge is a Club and 'clubs are trump.'" An Indiana private believed that the Union would win the war quickly "if all the corps fought as well as the 2nd." Private Edward Bassett credited the Confederates with good eyesight at Bristoe Station. Bassett declared that Lee's men "recognized in the white trefoil badge of our men their old antagonist at Gettysburg, and exclaimed, 'Here's those d_____d white clubs again.'" As at Gettysburg, the story of Confederate respect for the trefoil badge of the Second Corps made the rounds in various versions, to the delight of listeners and tellers alike.[27]

The glow of victory strengthened the unit cohesion of the Second Corps, with veterans expressing surprised delight in the generally solid performance of replacement soldiers. Handfuls of the newcomers had broken ranks and fled in panic, especially when the "fire was the hottest." Fortunately for the Union army, these were exceptions. One old hand praised the recruits in the 19th Maine who "stood their ground like veterans." They did more than that, suffering seventeen of the twenty casualties in the regiment. Major Henry Abbott, who had so excoriated new soldiers of the 20th Massachusetts for deserting and taking to the hospital only weeks earlier, changed his opinion at Bristoe Station. He admitted that replacement soldiers who went into the battle fought "as well as could be wished from old troops." Private William Wyman, a replacement soldier in the 64th New York, noticed the change in attitude. He declared that the "boys youst to make fun of us but they did not after we was in a fight—they found that we was the same stuff that they were."[28]

The gulf between veterans and replacements still remained wide throughout the rest of the army. Several regiments from the Union Sixth Corps went into battle at Rappahannock Station in early November. In a sharp engagement, the Union attackers netted 1,600 prisoners and four artillery pieces. The impressive Union triumph was the exception, however, to the marching and countermarching that characterized the fall of 1863. Many veterans of the war's first two years continued to grumble that their new comrades looked and acted as if they might better belong in prison garb rather than military uniform.[29]

The congratulations from the Union victory at Bristoe Station did not extend to everyone, and Warren fumed that Sykes had all but

abandoned him. Proving that battlefield victory often is nearly as acrimonious as battlefield defeat, Warren insisted that Sykes was supposed
to await the arrival of the Second Corps before marching to rejoin
the rest of the army at Centreville. The hasty departure of the Fifth
Corps was somewhat understandable, given that Sykes believed that
the advanced columns of the Second Corps were marching into view.
What Warren found unforgivable was that Sykes had refused to come to
his aid after the battle had concluded. The hour was late. But if Lee had
managed to assemble the Confederate army on the field before nightfall—and for all Warren knew, he had—the assault would have come in
"overwhelming force." Sykes defended himself by pointing out that, by
the late night of October 14, he had marched his men back to Milford,
a short distance north of Bristoe Station. He failed to help his cause
by sending a dispatch to Warren that he was going no farther. If Lee's
army really was in the vicinity, "two corps are little better than one."[30]
Warren had his revenge later while testifying before the Joint Committee, where he criticized Sykes and his seemingly cavalier attitude. The
relations between the two Union generals likely would have continued
to remain frosty, except that Sykes received transfer from the Army of
the Potomac in early 1864.[31]

Meade turned the tables on Lee in late November, when he maneuvered the Army of the Potomac below the Rapidan River and struck
toward Richmond. The advance began well for Warren's men. They
happily discussed newspaper reports detailing the rout of the Peace
Democrats in the recently concluded off-year elections. Captain William Trisler crowed that "Union elections" in his home region of the
Midwest "will prove so great a victory to this Rebellion as heavy fought
battle." Talk turned to cheers when soldiers received word from General
Meade that Union forces in Tennessee had recently won a great victory
at the Battle of Lookout Mountain. "Huzzas" rang forth from the Union
ranks, although some men wondered about the timing of the news.
Private Richard Wright expressed the doubts of many others when he
speculated whether reports from the western theater reached the Army
of the Potomac with unusual speed to "'brace us up'" for heavy fighting
to come.[32]

The goodwill generated by Union political and military victories helped to sustain soldiers as they pushed south and west toward Mine Run, a tributary of the Rapidan River. Carrying several days' rations and ammunition, a load upward of eighty pounds, soldiers soon complained of sore backs and tired feed. Worse, to keep their advanced positions concealed, they had to avoid lighting fires. Cold food was bad enough, but, as Private Charles Davis sourly noted, soldiers also "had to dispense with their Cup of Coffee."[33] Despite the discomforts, soldiers were confident of victory when, in the still small hours of November 30, Meade ordered them to ready to spearhead a Federal assault on the Confederate right. Lee's lines ran along a low rise behind Mine Run, and Warren and his men faced only hastily constructed Confederate rifle pits. Hope for quick victory raised even the spirits of the coffee-deprived Private Davis. The Confederate works several hundred yards ahead were visible by light of full moon, and Davis declared that "we all felt confident that we could take them at a dash."[34]

Expectation turned to dread at dawn, when soldiers got another look at the Confederate defensive lines. Lee's men had used the night hours wisely, strengthening and reinforcing their defenses into as formidable as any yet seen. Warren could not hide his amazement after visually examining the Confederate works. Hastily dug rifle pits "had been re-enforced with all the troops and artillery that could be put in position; the breastworks and . . . abates perfected." Soldiers of the Second Corps well understood that grim work likely lay ahead. Some men could not take their eyes from the open terrain to the front and the Confederate works beyond, morbidly calculating their chances for survival. Other soldiers more busily wrote letters to loved ones at home and pinned slips of paper listing their names on their uniforms.[35] A few men attempted to make the best of a bad situation. Full of determination, Colonel William Fogler ordered his men to take off their knapsacks and blankets so that they might not slow progress "up the fearful hillside." As morning brightened, even Confederate soldiers recognized the likely futility of any Union assault. Gray-clad troops clambered to the top of their works, where they hurled curses, invitations to advance, and defiant glares at Warren's men.[36]

Soldiers of the Second Corps readied to go forward despite the death and destruction that likely awaited them, as great a testament to their fighting spirit as any. Sergeant John Hirst of the 14th Connecticut described the planned Union assault as a "desperate undertaking." The lieutenant colonel of the regiment walked over and put his hands on Hirst's shoulders, asking, "'Jack, do you see those works?' 'Yes,' I replied. 'Well, I want to see you plant those colors right upon those works.' 'I shall go just as far as those Johnnies will let me go alive.'" Nearby, an officer on Warren's staff walked the Union lines and asked a soldier in the 1st Minnesota "what he thought of the prospect" of the Federal attack. The soldier, unaware that he was addressing an officer, declared it "a damned sight worse than Fredericksburg," and added, "I am going as far as we can travel, but we can't get more than two-thirds of the way up that hill." Brigadier General Alexander Hays left little to sheer courage and determination, making sure that soldiers in his division knew that they had to keep moving forward in solid lines if the Federal attack stood any chance of success. Hays ordered soldiers to shoot any unwounded comrade who broke for the rear. Even those men who went forward risked arrest and punishment if they stopped to fire their muskets before ordered to do so by their officers.[37]

At Mine Run, before the Confederate defensive works, waiting for dawn, the fighting power of the Second Corps arguably reached its crest. Soldiers enjoyed their highest morale of the war, fresh from their indisputable battlefield triumphs over the past summer and fall. Veteran soldiers and draftees and conscripts had found common ground in the lopsided victory of the Second Corps at Bristoe Station. The assault tactics that soldiers readied to employ—surging forward without stopping to return fire—promised the best prospects for battlefield success. The next summer, Union Colonel Emory Upton would apply a very similar assault discipline to great success against strong Confederate defensive works near Spotsylvania Court House. Gettysburg represents the pinnacle of the Second Corps's career, because of the severity of the fighting and the magnitude of the victory. Never again, however, would the Second Corps bring the same level of élan and experience to the battlefield that it did at Mine Run.

Soldiers of the Second Corps never had to put their resolve to the test, because Warren, recognizing disaster looming, convinced Meade to call off the planned assault. A few of the army's high-ranking officers criticized Warren for seeing only the battlefield risks, rather than the possibilities. Soldiers on the front lines saw matters differently, and were ecstatic. Private James Stratten cheered, "What glorious news it was to all, the counter manding orders for the charge!" Corporal Edward Walker felt gloom give way to ecstasy. The cancellation of the Federal attack was like gaining a new lease on life because "we never expected to come out alive." Chaplain Thomas Murphey visited with soldiers of the 1st Delaware later in the day. Murphey described officers and men saying to him that if the attack had gone forward, "Our regiment would have been annihilated. We may thank General Warren for our lives."[38]

Warren's men still had plenty of troubles, as they had to retreat back across the Rapidan River the next night. The movement started after sundown to gain the cover of darkness. The tactic worked, but temperatures that plunged to well below freezing proved a greater threat than Confederate pursuit. Soldiers found their canteen water frozen and their hands and feet stinging from the knifelike wind. Making the cold even colder, supply wagons brought dinner late, if at all. "We had no rations," one ravenous private described, "no not one Crumb." Despite more frostbite than biscuits, soldiers likely smiled when they reached the Rapidan River and were greeted by a band playing, "Oh! Ain't you glad you got out of the Wilderness."[39]

The rebuilding process began again soon after the Army of the Potomac went into winter quarters around Stevensburg, Virginia, but the push was especially intense in the Second Corps. Secretary of War Stanton authorized Hancock, still recuperating from his wounds suffered at Gettysburg, to "recruit and fill up" the Second Corps "to the number of 50,000 men." None of the Army of the Potomac's other corps commanders received the same permission, albeit they would have had to receive military leave to do so. Hancock took to the task with a will. The Union general appealed for volunteers in Boston, New York City, Philadelphia, and other cities in the Northeast throughout late 1863 and early 1864.[40] Hancock also requested that Warren, still in temporary

command of the Second Corps, send "details from regiments of Infantry" to recruit volunteers within their hometowns. Apparently not satisfied with the men sent, Hancock later specified that he wanted one
commissioned officer and two enlisted men from each regiment "who
can make public speeches."[41] Rumor swirled throughout the army that
Hancock was enjoying considerable success. When the dust settled by
early April, however, Hancock reported that his recruiters had enlisted
2,040 volunteers. These were respectable numbers, but well short of the
mark anticipated by Stanton.[42]

Not all regiments fared equally well in recruiting their ranks.
Recruiters in the Irish Brigade experienced the most success. Colonel
St. Clair Mulholland of the 116th Pennsylvania had received permission to depart for Philadelphia in the late summer of 1863 to beef up
the regiment. With several months' head start, Mulholland helped to
raise six companies of volunteers."Well we have got the regt pretty well
fill[ed]," Private William Smith gloated; "now it is bigger than it ever
was." Recruiters in the three New York City regiments of the Irish Brigade were no slouches either. On the morning of April 20 alone, the 69th
New York and the 88th New York received forty volunteers between
them. Recruiters from the New York City regiments likely benefited
from the strong military reputation of the Irish Brigade across the Union
as well as fear among many young Irish American men that they might
be the first snapped up in the federal draft slated to begin again in the
spring. Recruiters from the 19th Massachusetts had much less success.
Lieutenant John Adams declared that he and the other soldiers recruiting for the regiment "worked hard" to find volunteers but "made little or
no progress." Adams lost out on many prospective volunteers to recruiters raising regiments and companies to serve in military forts along the
Massachusetts coast. By comparison to garrison duty, Adams found that
his frontline regiment had "no attractions."[43]

More important to the rebuilding of the Union army at Stevensburg
were attempts made by Stanton to reenlist the volunteers of 1861. These
soldiers were hands-down the most experienced fighters in the army,
and Stanton made a concerted effort to convince them to see the war
through. Soldiers who reenlisted received a thirty-days furlough and a
federal bounty of four hundred dollars. In addition to leave and money,

these men received a special chevron to wear on their uniform sleeve, as well as the right to call themselves "veteran volunteers." As a last incentive, if three-quarters of the veterans of a particular regiment reenlisted, they maintained their unit identity. Otherwise soldiers would be transferred to other units when their regiment was mustered out.[44] The result of Stanton's carrot-and-stick approach did not work as well in the Second Corps as throughout the rest of the Union army. By early April, 2,575 volunteers of the Second Corps had reenlisted, about one-third of eligible soldiers. Throughout the rest of the army 23,700 soldiers had reenlisted, about one-half the eligible total.[45]

More veterans of the Second Corps decided to go home than to reenlist, so this side of the question is analyzed first. That a lower percentage of veterans in the Second Corps reenlisted than throughout the rest of the Union army might be seen as a sign of weakening unit cohesion. With many of their comrades long since killed or wounded, the volunteers of 1861 simply wanted to go home. In reality, veterans wanted to go home because they believed that they had done more than their share of the fighting, a claim backed by their casualty totals. The Second Corps was more bloodied than any other Federal corps by the third winter of the war. Since the Battle of Fair Oaks in the early summer of 1862, the Second Corps had lost a staggering 20,000 men killed, wounded, and missing. These numbers represented one-quarter of the casualties suffered in the Army of the Potomac. One Midwestern private worried that more "desperate fighting" lay ahead because the "old 2nd Corps is peculiarly unfortunate in having to bear the brunt of the battle." This being the case, it was someone else's turn to carry the war through to Union victory. Private Richard Wright had served in the 1st Minnesota since the Battle of First Bull Run. By the spring of 1864, Wright believed that the time had come for "the second relief [to] go to the front." Captain David Beem declared that he and other soldiers of the 14th Indiana were going home because they had served faithfully since the start of the war. Should need ever arise, Beem pledged that he and his veteran comrades "will go in for three years or longer with as much patriotism as we first did."[46]

Soldiers needed no more reminder that the Second Corps often went into battle first and suffered the most when they received orders on

February 6 to cross the Rapidan River at Morton's Ford. The aggressive Federal move was designed to divert Confederate attention from a strike toward Richmond by Major General Benjamin Butler and the Army of the James. The task of distracting Lee and his men fell to soldiers of Hays's Third Division, otherwise comfortably ensconced in their winter quarters. In light drizzle soldiers forded the waist-deep water of the Rapidan River, and, in the words of one private, "you had better reckon it was cold." After reaching the far bank, Hays's men entered a shallow ravine from where they could see the Confederate works on high ground beyond. Here they stayed for the rest of the day, dodging Confederate artillery and musket fire. The men withdrew back across the Rapidan River that night, after receiving word that Butler's proposed offensive against Richmond had failed to come off. In the undertaking Hays's division had suffered 261 men killed, wounded, and missing, a not insignificant number for the work involved.[47]

The fighting at Morton's Ford seemed small by Civil War standards, but the clash sounded the death knell for reenlistment efforts that already were faltering in the Second Corps. Only a handful of men had reenlisted in late January, and the fighting at Morton's Ford further dampened any enthusiasm. A mere 175 men enlisted during the remainder of the winter encampment.[48] Soldiers throughout the Second Corps had anxiously listened to the sound of cannon and musketry fire across the Rapidan River, and talked with stragglers who reported heavy Union losses. The possibility that death in battle could strike even in the middle of winter likely prompted at least some men to decide against reenlisting. Equally important, soldiers received an earful from wives and sweethearts visiting the army. Civilians had watched the fighting unfold from the vantage point of nearby Stony Mountain. Many of the spectators later helped to nurse Union wounded carried from the field. The firsthand experience with the aftermath of battle presumably convinced some women to counsel their husbands and friends to come home sooner rather than later.[49]

A significant minority of soldiers did reenlist, motivated by a continuing sense of duty to the Union and their comrades. This argument is in contrast to that put forward by Gerald Linderman now two decades ago, in his influential *Embattled Courage: The Experience of Combat in the*

American Civil War. Linderman asserts that a sense of fatalism, rather than any deeply held ideology beliefs, motivated veteran volunteers. After the horrific bloodshed suffered since the start of the war in 1861, soldiers recognized that they likely would be killed or maimed before their term of service expired. Better to reenlist and at least have the bounty and furlough. If this were the case, however, presumably more veterans in the Second Corps would have agreed to a new term of service after the fighting at Morton's Ford. But the weeks following the February 1864 battle is exactly when the reenlistment efforts in the Second Corps reached their low ebb.

Soldiers who reenlisted often did so because they remained committed to seeing the struggle through to completion. The men were under no illusions, recognizing that hard fighting awaited them in the spring. Josiah Favill acknowledged "more battles to fight, marches to make, and the sacrifice of lives" before the war was won. Despite the risk and hardship, Favill vowed that the "resolve still remains, and until the work is done this army will never lay down its arms." Elijah Cavins agreed. The Indiana lieutenant colonel argued that every man who was a "patriot" had a continuing duty to "add his strength toward maintaining the stability of our country." The payoff was incalculable. According to Captain James Mitchell, the Union triumphant would demonstrate to the rest of the world that the American republic "can live through the most fiery ordeal that ever [a] nation had to contend with." Seeing the struggle through meant that future generations would enjoy peace and prosperity.[50]

Regimental pride stirred the emotions of veterans of the 1st Delaware. Colonel William Smith appealed to soldiers to reenlist because their sacrifices had already moved "the rebellion [to] the brink of destruction." Equally important, keeping up the fight would "avenge the death of our fallen comrades." Veterans who did not reenlist, Smith warned, likely would receive transfer. The move not only would take the recusant from their "old comrades in arms" but also from the "old colors . . . under whose folds you have earned your reputation as soldiers." Smith's various arguments worked. Reenlistments totaled 230 men by late December, enough for the regiment to survive.[51]

Beyond duty and pride, the material benefits of reenlistment proved irresistible to some men. Sergeant James Walker believed that the

federal bounty motivated men "who had scarcely ever seen a ten dollar bill before entering the army." Corporal Amory Allen thought that
his chances for promotion would increase if he reenlisted. With higher
rank came more pay, and Allen hoped to provide his family with a more
comfortable standard of living. Bounty and possible promotion were
attractive, but Private Samuel Maguire most wanted the reenlistment
furlough. As early as the fall of 1862, Maguire had written tongue-in-
cheek to his wife that if kept from her much longer he would be "suf-
ficiently virtuous . . . to become a Catholic Priest, as I can forswear all
connections with Lady's society by that time." Private James Rea had
a different problem. After returning from reenlistment furlough Rea
asked his wife if she blamed him because "I could like a log occupy the
same bed with you and lay still?" The consolation that Rea offered his
now pregnant wife was that she would not have to worry about bearing
another child "for at least 3 years to come."[52]

REORGANIZING FOR THE SPRING

The Second Corps and the rest of the Army of the Potomac underwent major reorganization in midwinter of 1864 to compensate for
manpower losses suffered since the start of the war. General Meade
explained that because "nearly all" of the regiments of the army fielded
less than their authorized strength, he was ordering the "temporary
reduction" of the number of army corps from five to three. Meade had
no precedent to draw upon for the reorganization, because his was the
first time that corps had been disbanded. He plunged ahead all the
same, and ordered the Second Corps, Fifth Corps, and Sixth Corps
consolidated to two divisions. Harder fate awaited the First Corps and
Third Corps, and Meade ordered them disbanded and their soldiers
distributed throughout the rest of the army. Meade attempted to ease
hurt pride by explaining that the reason for breaking apart the First
Corps and Third Corps had nothing to do with "any supposed inferi-
ority of those corps to the other corps of the army. All the corps have
equal claims to the confidence of the Government and of the country." Meade underscored the point by allowing soldiers to continue
to wear the badges of their now disbanded corps. With the reshuffling

the Second Corps swelled to largest in the army, at four divisions and 28,675 soldiers.[53]

Meade believed that by concentrating the striking power of his forces he would avoid the piecemeal assaults that had plagued the Army of the Potomac in past battles. The model for Meade's thinking was, paradoxically, General Lee and his Army of Northern Virginia. Lee had only recently expanded his forces from two army corps to three army corps. The leanness of command had enabled the Confederates on several occasions to launch battlefield attacks with nearly unstoppable numbers of soldiers. Meade also hoped to concentrate his most skilled officers through the reorganization of the army. The corps commanders left standing were Hancock, now back in command of the Second Corps; General Gouverneur Warren, transferred laterally to command the Fifth Corps; and General John Sedgwick, with the Sixth Corps. The three generals all had connections to the Second Corps. Together, they gave Meade the most talented collection of Union corps commanders yet assembled.[54]

In reorganizing the army, Meade sent Hancock two of the three divisions of the former Third Corps. The Second Corps and Third Corps had widely separated winter encampments, so Meade likely did not take proximity into consideration. Perhaps Meade recognized that soldiers of the Second Corps and Third Corps had worked well together during the Mine Run Campaign. Meade had placed the Third Corps under Warren in preparation of the planned Union assault. Warren later praised soldiers of the two commands for working well together. But the Mine Run Campaign was of relatively short duration, and the Third Corps was soon back under its own commander.[55]

More likely, Meade selected soldiers from the Third Corps to go to the Second Corps because he was playing favorites with Hancock. Meade and Hancock got along warmly, and the relationship had been cemented at Gettysburg. One staff officer declared that Meade and Hancock were "great friends" and that when together "they talk, and talk and talk."[56] As such, Meade sent Hancock two divisions with long-standing reputations for hard fighting. Soldiers of one of the former Third Corps divisions (Major General David Birney's) had been under the command of Major General Philip Kearny during the Peninsula Campaign. They had inflicted one of the few defeats suffered by Confederate General Thomas "Stonewall" Jackson at Chantilly, Virginia, on September 1, 1862. Soldiers of the other former Third Corps division (Major General Gershom Mott's) had fought fiercely at the Battle of Williamsburg on May 5, 1862. Here they had won their commander, General Joseph Hooker, the sobriquet "Fighting Joe." Kearny had been killed in action at Chantilly, and Hooker, after an unsuccessful stint as head of the Army of the Potomac, now was serving as a corps commander in the western theater. Memories of past glories remained strong, however. Going into the winter of 1864, soldiers of the Third Corps still referred to themselves as belonging to "Kearny's and Hooker's Divisions."[57]

This is not to say that the other four divisions transferred throughout the rest of the army were poor in quality. Two divisions of the former First Corps were merged into one, and now under the command of Brigadier General James Wadsworth in the Fifth Corps. Serving in the division were the remnants of the Iron Brigade, one of the most stalwart units in the Union army. The other two divisions came with checkered battlefield careers. Brigadier General John Robinson's men, also in the Fifth Corps, had acquired a steady, if not spectacular, battlefield record. The same could not be said for Brigadier General James Ricketts's Sixth Corps division. Soldiers in six regiments had suffered several battlefield defeats, dating all the way back to the Shenandoah Valley in 1862. Known widely throughout the army as "Milroy's weary boys," after their original brigade commander, the soldiers in these regiments needed near-constant vigilance.[58]

The reorganization of the Second Corps presented Hancock with an unprecedented challenge. None of the earlier three commanders of the Second Corps had to confront the disbanding of a division while adding two others from the outside. Meade permitted wide latitude in the process, allowing his subordinates to rearrange their commands "in such manner as they may think best for the service." Hancock worked through the reorganization by attempting to maintain unit cohesion as much as possible, a strategy also followed by Sedgwick and Warren. Hancock started with his own men and disbanded the Third Division, the newest to the Second Corps. He might have assigned the thirteen regiments here and there throughout the remaining two divisions, but did not. Instead, Hancock kept the units together in two newly created brigades (Frank's and Carroll's). Soldiers in each brigade served in a separate division, but at least they fought immediately alongside men already familiar to them. The breakup of the Third Division benefited soldiers from the former Third Corps. The newcomers served in their own divisions, now known as the Third Division and Fourth Division.[59]

Hancock deviated from this policy when he assigned to the Philadelphia Brigade the 152nd New York, one of three regiments (along with the 26th New York and 183rd Pennsylvania) that had arrived as reinforcements over the winter. Hancock had been reluctant to tinker with unit cohesion, drawing back from a proposal in the spring of 1863 to break up the Irish Brigade.[60] Now, with the Philadelphia Brigade, Hancock believed that he had little choice. His decision aroused considerable grumbling among the Philadelphians over the loss of their distinct geographic identity. Yet, more important to Hancock, the New Yorkers added manpower. The Philadelphia Brigade remained the smallest in the Second Division and, for that matter, the Second Corps. With the New York regiment the gap had narrowed, and the Philadelphia Brigade fielded more men than it had for a long time previously.[61]

The artillery brigade and the corps staff also received beefing up, giving Hancock, at least on paper, an unprecedented level of battlefield firepower and flexibility. The reorganized artillery brigade fielded eleven batteries and fifty-four guns. This was a similar number of artillery pieces to those fielded by the Fifth Corps and the Sixth Corps. Should the batteries of the Second Corps ever line up wheel to wheel, they might exert a near-overwhelming concentration of fire on the Confederate lines. Hancock also now had more staff members to help maneuver the regiments and batteries of the Second Corps. The corps staff numbered twenty officers, the highest total yet. Captain I. Thickstun and Lieutenant William Neel served as Hancock's signal officers. The appearance of these slots for the first time as staff positions reflects an increasing commitment on the part of the Union army to speed of maneuver through visual and, especially, telegraphic communications.[62]

On paper, the Second Corps emerged from the reorganization of the army in its strongest shape of the war. Hancock was preparing to take into battle nearly twice as many men as Sumner had upon the organization of the Second Corps two years earlier. The key difference was battlefield experience. Many soldiers, whether they had fought with the Second Corps or the Third Corps at Gettysburg, had seen action in nearly every battle since the start of the war. The knowledge sent morale soaring. A soldier in the 19th Maine marveled that the four divisions of the Second Corps were "composed largely of old soldiers." With these men leading the charge, the "rebels will need a goodly share of Heaven's mercy this coming summer."[63]

The arrival of Lieutenant General Ulysses S. Grant topped the reorganization of the Army of the Potomac and was of the greatest interest to Hancock's men. Grant had won a string of spectacular battlefield triumphs in the West, earning him command of all Union armies in the early winter of 1864. Grant made his headquarters with the Army of the Potomac, even though Meade technically remained in command. Soldiers were uncertain what to make of Grant's appearance. Small in stature and unassuming in dress, Grant flashed little of the polish of McClellan or the dash of Hooker.[64] One veteran claimed that he never would pick Grant out from a crowd as a general, let alone the commander of the most powerful Union army in the East. "But then," he quickly added, "our 'magnificent' men are not always the best soldiers." Soldiers knew, however, of Grant's reputation as a hard fighter. An Irish Brigade private predicted that Grant would fight the army in a manner best suited to winning the war, rather than to meet the arbitrary demands of politicians and newspaper editors. Another enlisted man liked the new commander's reputation as a tenacious fighter, infusing the army with his motto of "Whip them or die." For all the resourcefulness shown by Grant, however, soldiers well recognized that an equally skilled General Lee awaited them to the south. A showdown between the two generals loomed, leaving one New Yorker to nervously anticipate "some hard fighting" with the coming of spring.[65]

Faith in Grant failed to suppress the usual grumbling about the winter weather and continuous drill. Bitterly cold winds swept through the Union encampment at Stevensburg, forcing soldiers to seek shelter in their quarters. Finding warmth seemed in vain to Private Timothy Bateman. Head pulled under his blanket, he shivered away winter nights dreaming "of home and a feather bed." Another soldier grumpily noted that he spent New Year's Day 1864 not lost in thought or feast but in trying to keep warm. He failed, and referred to the passing of 1863 into 1864 as "the cold New Year's." With the arrival of milder weather by the late winter, soldiers found themselves drilling far too much for their taste. Private Timothy Groves moaned that he never seemed to get off the parade ground because "they are drilling and reviewing us to death." Private Isaac Hadden was at least more philosophical about four hours spent at drill every day but Sunday. "I don't like to drill," Hadden decided, "but have to do a great many things which I don't like."[66]

Despite such complaints, one heard little of the divisive backbiting that had occurred the previous winter at Falmouth. The bitter feelings voiced over the implementation of the Emancipation Proclamation in early 1863 had faded. Lieutenant Colonel Elijah Cavins now believed it a positive that the war had lasted long enough for Lincoln's measure to go into effect. "If the rebellion had been crushed during the first year of the war," Cavins argued, "slavery would have been saved, while now it is plain as the 'hand writing on the wall,' that slavery can no longer exist in this country." And, for all the usual grumbling, the logistical situation had improved. The relatively pleasant conditions of the camp at Stevensburg closely resembled those outside Washington in the first winter of the war. The Union supply system worked well, and coffee, bread, vegetables, and other foodstuffs were all widely available. Soldiers not eating worked at two nearby sawmills to build increasingly snug winter quarters. Former woodworkers plied their trade, and several cabins furnished ornate door and window trimmings.[67]

Soldiers also enjoyed a greater range of leisure activities at Stevensburg than at any other encampment. They perhaps most relished seeing female visitors arriving by rail from Washington. "The army flooded with Crinoline," a New Jersey private approvingly wrote. "'Angels in the Wilderness.'" Soldiers escorted their wives, daughters, and sweethearts to parties, dances, and other social occasions, where they received a grand reception. No lady lacked a helping hand, as veterans of Fredericksburg, Gettysburg, and other great battles tripped over themselves offering their services. The highlight of the social season occurred when officers of the Second Corps hosted a ball in a newly constructed "Music Hall" to honor George Washington's birthday on February 22.

The interior of the building was decorated as a "camp scene," replete with artillery pieces, stacks of muskets, shelter tents, and regimental flags. Dancers twirled across the floor, adding movement and color to the laughter and conversation that already filled the room.[68]

Soldiers made their own fun when not attending dances and parties. Some listened to music played by regimental bands. Musicians of the 14th Connecticut performed at dinner parties hosted by their brigade commander. Not to be outdone, the fife and drum corps of the 148th Pennsylvania held occasional evening concerts. One Pennsylvanian proudly declared that strains of "Gentle Annie" and "Faded Flowers" drew men from other regiments encamped several miles distant. When ready to stretch their legs, soldiers held snowball fights. Private Amos Stewart described that after one heavy snowfall in late March, the "boys had quite a jolly time snow balling." A Pennsylvanian in the First Division recalled soldiers in his regiment splitting into two teams and flinging snowballs at one another in "a regular battle." Unlike the real thing, however, combatants exchanged handshakes and pleasantries after.[69]

Soldiers took a more serious tone as the weather warmed and campaign season approached. Members of the Christian Commission, a civilian organization, helped soldiers to construct chapels. Man after man entered to join the "Army of the Great Teacher." Private Joseph Graham found himself one of the many soldiers swept up in the religious emotion. Graham walked one mile to hear "preaching" at a tent pitched by the Christian Commission on three consecutive nights. The tent held one hundred people, and, Graham approvingly noted, "it is well filled." A New York private added that on Sundays he attended church services at division headquarters in the morning and at brigade headquarters in the evening. Such religious devotion prompted another soldier to hope that "we may be drawn from the ways of sin and death."[70]

The culmination of the winter encampment at Stevensburg occurred with a review of the Second Corps and the rest of the Army of the Potomac on April 22. Hancock's men, recognizing that they were parading before the newly arrived General Grant for the first time, nervously stepped onto the parade ground. They need not have worried. These men looked impressive, with bayonets glinting and flags fluttering. Colonel William Smith of the 1st Delaware later boasted that "we

made a fine appearance." Watching from the reviewing stand, Lieutenant Colonel Charles Morgan, the inspector general of the Second Corps,
deemed the parade "the finest corps review that I have ever seen in the
army." Grant apparently agreed, and the next day Hancock praised his
men for their "soldierly bearing."[71]

Soldiers returned to their camps in a buoyant mood, and with reason. The Second Corps at Bristoe Station had scored one of the few
Federal battlefield successes in the East since the conclusion of the Gettysburg Campaign. With the reorganization of the Army of the Potomac
that winter, the Second Corps fielded its greatest numbers of infantry
soldiers, artillery guns, and staff members. Lee's Confederate army still
was a formidable military force. But Hancock's men might be excused
a sense of optimism as they readied to participate in another spring
offensive and another attempt to win the war.

6   CARNAGE

THE OVERLAND CAMPAIGN

The prospect for Union victory looked bright to soldiers of the Second Corps by the spring of 1864. These veterans of many of the war's great battles understood that General Grant intended to make the destruction of the Army of Northern Virginia his primary objective through a campaign of maneuver and assault. The fighting in northern Virginia, when combined with other Union offensives in the eastern and western theaters, would break the Confederacy apart. Captain Isaac Plumb brutally summarized Grant's strategy: "We must crush them."[1] What was less clear was when the campaign would commence. Soldiers tore down winter quarters and pitched shelter tents, all in preparation for a quick move. They watched and conjectured as staff officers galloped back and forth from headquarters with ever-increasing urgency. On the evening of May 3 the suspense ended, when Hancock's men received orders to march for Ely's Ford on the Rapidan River. Soldiers sounded optimistic as they set forth, promising to give the Confederates "hell" and "a good licking."[2]

HOLLOW LEGIONS

Soldiers' confidence belied potential battlefield problems that riddled nearly all levels of the Second Corps, starting with its leadership. Hancock had returned after partially recovering from his Gettysburg wounds in late March, but his physical stamina appeared doubtful. When riding on horseback, Hancock admitted, "I suffer agony." The pain was so great that Hancock received permission from Meade to ride in a wagon when the army undertook a spring offensive. The wagon might have been needed regardless, because Hancock had gained weight from a lack of exercise while recuperating at home. The Union general presented a frumpy appearance to some observers, a far cry from the dashing figure that he had cut earlier. Private John Haley was one less-than-awed observer. "If, as has been asserted, 'all flesh is grass,'" Haley quipped, "General Hancock may be said to be a load of hay." Hancock still held an almost legendary reputation throughout the army for coolness and bravery while under fire. But, for the first time, his health and endurance while in the field were open to question.[3]

Hancock needed a good deal of energy because he had to keep track of three new division commanders, the most in the army.[4] Brigadier General Francis Barlow assumed command of the First Division after Caldwell received assignment to court-martial duty. A New York native who had practiced law after graduating from Harvard in 1855, Barlow did not look much like a combat officer. He was only twenty-nine in the spring of 1864, making him one of the younger Union division commanders. Beyond a youthful step, Barlow was clean-shaven in an army dominated by officers and enlisted men who sported beards, mustaches, and sideburns. Barlow further accentuated himself by wearing checkered flannel shirts and threadbare trousers. According to one observer, Barlow looked more a "highly independent newsboy" than a Union general. Belying appearance, however, Barlow had a reputation as a superb battlefield leader. In the fighting before the Sunken Road at Antietam, Barlow had led the 61st New York in the charge that stormed the seemingly impenetrable Confederate defensive lines. Badly wounded, Barlow returned to the army as a brigadier general in the Eleventh Corps in the winter of 1863. He went on to lead soldiers of his brigade bravely at the Battle of Gettysburg, where he again received a severe wound. Barlow found that his battlefield fame preceded him upon his return to the Second Corps. Soldiers rejoiced that their new division commander, although a strict disciplinarian, is "a triumph" and an officer whom they "believed in."[5]

Major General David Birney and Brigadier General Gershom Mott each brought considerable controversy with him upon assuming command of his division. Birney, an Alabama native and brother to a noted abolitionist crusader, had worked as a lawyer in Philadelphia prior to

Major General Winfield Scott Hancock (seated) and three of the division commanders of the Second Corps, 1864. From left to right: Brigadier General Francis Barlow, Major General David Birney, and Major General John Gibbon. A Second Corps banner is located just behind Birney. Library of Congress.

the war. He had achieved his greatest wartime success when he led a counterattack against Confederate forces that had crumbled the flank of the Union Third Corps on the last day of the fighting at Chancellorsville. The assault allowed the embattled Federal right to reform and won Birney promotion to major general. Birney soon dimmed his otherwise fast-rising star by throwing in his fortunes with Major General Daniel Sickles, his corps commander. The relationship was based upon shared professional ambition, because the openly anti-slavery Birney otherwise meshed poorly with the staunch Democrat Sickles. The unlikely friendship was tested when Sickles publicly squabbled with Meade over the deployment of the Third Corps at the Battle of Gettysburg. The exchanges were bitter, and Birney, perhaps believing Meade ready to fall from command of the Army of the Potomac, remained loyal to Sickles. Birney misread the political and military winds, and with the reorganization of the army, he sought reconciliation with Meade. In a meeting in mid-April that Hancock had helped to set up, Birney mumbled a vague apology and Meade responded coldly. The ongoing feud placed Hancock in an uncomfortable middle between Meade, his friend, and Birney, his subordinate.[6]

The squabbling between Meade and Birney was rivaled only by the command tangle inherited by Mott in coming to the Fourth Division. Mott had acquired a solid record as a combat officer by the spring of 1864. Twice wounded, Mott had led a brigade in the Third Corps through the Chancellorsville and Gettysburg Campaigns. Yet despite demonstrated battlefield bravery, Mott was not the officer Meade wanted in command of the division. Instead, Meade had slated Brigadier General Joseph Carr for the post when he reorganized the army. Carr had led a brigade in the Third Corps through some of the fiercest of the fighting in and around the Peach Orchard at Gettysburg on July 2. Meade assumed that Carr would receive promotion to major general that winter, giving him seniority in rank to Mott. Carr had a long line of other brigadier generals before him, however, and as the days slipped away, the promotion failed to come. By late April, a frustrated Meade simply wanted the matter resolved. He informed Secretary of War Stanton that the uncertainty over who commanded the division "is producing disquiet and bad feeling." The War Department needed to settle the issue "one way or the other before the army moves." Only days later, Carr received transfer to another department. Mott likely found little reason to savor the triumph, clearly winning the position because of his military seniority rather than Meade's backing.[7]

Previous leadership experience improved dramatically at the brigade level, where Hancock's infantry officers ranked among the longest serving and most talented in the army. All eleven had led comparable commands since the Bristoe Station Campaign in the mid-fall of 1863. The continuity in command was remarkable, given the high rate of officer turnover in the Union army. Brigadier General Joshua Owen had regained command of the Philadelphia Brigade following his arrest prior to the Battle of Gettysburg. Colonels Samuel Carroll and John Brooke had also served for nearly a year by the spring of 1864, seeing action at Chancellorsville and Gettysburg. In the case of Colonel Nelson Miles, experience coincided with ability. Born in Massachusetts in 1839, Miles had started the Civil War as a captain. He had quickly won promotion for battlefield gallantry, especially distinguishing himself while fighting the picket line of the First Division at the Battle of Chancellorsville on May 3, 1863. Miles kept probing Confederate infantry at bay, enabling the remainder of the division to retreat and rejoin the main body of the army. Miles suffered a severe wound in the engagement, but his bravery ultimately won him both promotion to brigadier general and a Medal of Honor. Miles was a welcome addition to the army the following spring. A superior officer claimed that Miles possessed a "remarkable talent for fighting battles." Miles was brave under fire, as were many other Union officers. But he "has that perfect coolness and self-possession in danger which is much more uncommon. The sound of cannon clears his head and strengthens his nerves."[8]

Hancock's brigadiers were experienced and talented, but they, too, had some concerns. One was rank. Six brigade commanders in the Second Corps were colonels, among the highest number in any of the three corps of the Army of the Potomac. The danger was that these men would be subject to the battlefield orders of ranking colonels and brigadier generals, combat veterans or not. The prospect of serving under green officers angered veterans. One survivor of the fighting at Fredericksburg and Gettysburg fumed that "I do not care to risk my life in such hands."[9]

The other concern confronted by brigade officers in the Second Corps was the large number of regiments under their command. Each brigade numbered between five and nine regiments, the highest totals to date. The numbers of men in each brigade were no larger than at other points in the war, given the reduced strengths of individual regiments. Brigade commanders now had more layers of command to contend with, a liability when promptness of action often determined the difference between success and failure on the battlefield.[10]

Some officers found distraction from their increased responsibilities in the bottle. Officers attempted to keep their men from drinking, but they seemed to have plenty of alcohol at hand. Libations purchased from a camp sutler or sent from home flowed freely when officers met to while away the hours. An Indiana captain expressed dismay that the "flowing bowl" often begat other problems, including gambling and cursing.[11] Imbibing in camp was one thing, but some soldiers who fought at Morton's Ford in early February swore that their officers reeked of alcohol. Captain William Hawley of the 14th Connecticut charged that General Warren had been "so drunk" that he could not leave his tent for most of the day. Warren allegedly had drinking companions in General Alexander Hays, the division commander, and Colonel Charles Powers, the brigade commander. Hawley charged that Hays had enough drink to "make him reckless." Powers was even deeper in his cups and "unfit to command" for much of the battle. Private Levander Sawtelle was more circumspect in his accusations. He named no one, but criticized that some officers "think they must have whiskey to give them courage." The problem was that "some gets so much courage they cant tell the front from the rear." A Connecticut private fumed that the hypocrisy involved when it came to drink "is enough to disgust the whole army."[12]

Potential battlefield problems also stemmed from the recent reorganization of the army, with many soldiers of the Third Corps livid over losing their distinct identity. To be sure, veterans of the First Corps also were upset over their disbandment. Major General John Newton, the outgoing commander, reminded his men that they had fought bravely in holding off Lee's army during the first day at Gettysburg. The heavy losses suffered attest to the First Corps's "supreme devotion to the country." Although the command "has lost its distinctive name by the present changes, history will not be silent upon the magnitude of its service." And, just as much, some veterans like Robert Robertson of the 93rd New York appreciated the opportunity to serve in the "grand old" Second Corps. Robertson gloated upon receiving assignment to Hancock's command, "Our badge was the far-famed red trefoil, the boys called it 'the ace of clubs,' and in all our campaigns clubs were trumps."[13]

More soldiers seethed, recognizing that the Third Corps had as long a history with the Army of the Potomac as any of the three surviving corps. From Yorktown through Gettysburg, the Third Corps, "this famous fighting corps," as described by Major William Green of the 17th Maine, had made its mark. The knowledge that the diamond-shaped badge of the Third Corps no longer represented an independent command caused among its wearers "many heart burnings." Disgruntled soldiers in the now Fourth Division held a mock funeral to protest the "killing" of the Third Corps. They thought little of Meade's argument that the heavy losses suffered by the Army of the Potomac necessitated the reorganization. Instead, an unspecified combination of "Personal Malice, Spite and Jealousy" spelled the end. Other soldiers made their displeasure most publicly known when they wore their new trefoil badge on the seat of their pants during the review before Grant in late April. These diehards stubbornly insisted until the end of the war that they fought in the Third Corps.[14]

Discipline in the former Third Corps dropped to almost nonexistent, as discovered by Major Henry Abbott of the 20th Massachusetts. Abbott served as the corps officer of the day on March 24 and 25. He inspected the picket lines of the two divisions newly assigned to the Second Corps, and was horrified by what he found. The pickets lounged before roaring fires, failed to salute, and seemed completely oblivious as to what they were about. Abbott chose to let matters continue in slipshod fashion, because he did not know even where to begin to make the needed corrections. He confessed that "my efforts against an evil so universal would have seemed so puny as to have been merely laughed at." Nor did Abbott appeal to any of the officers from the Third Corps for help. Most of the regimental and company commanders he encountered were "careless, indifferent, and ignorant." Abbott's blistering report shocked Hancock, who immediately forwarded it along to Meade. This

Soldiers of the 71st New York, 1861. Many soldiers of the Excelsior Brigade and other units of the Third Corps were furious at the reorganization of the Army of the Potomac three years later, weakening the otherwise hard-won cohesion of the Second Corps. Library of Congress.

was an unusual move, because the problems now became external. A worried Hancock was more concerned with informing Meade of the condition of affairs among the troops newly assigned to his command.[15]

Other potential battlefield problems extended into the ranks, and one of the most daunting was the arrival of droves of replacement soldiers on the eve of Grant's spring offensive. Draftees and substitutes again were prevalent in number, and they brought the same training and disciplinary issues as they had in the fall. Many of the newcomers seemed incapable of learning the art of soldiering, or anything else. One veteran quipped that in his regiment the replacement soldiers generally were good men—except for one who was blind and one who died from old age. Lieutenant Colonel John Hammell gave up on many of the recruits received in the 66th New York and grouped them into a self-described "awkward squad." When asked by the regimental surgeon for nurses, Hammell replied that he could look over the misfits and "take what you want." The poor quality of replacement soldiers reached the point where medical inspectors in the Second Corps and the rest of the army received orders from headquarters to administer rigorous exams. They were warned to watch for "the many" who suffered from "defects" in health and "intellectual capacity." The number of recruits weeded out in subsequent inspections is uncertain, but they must have been hard cases in an army hungry for manpower.[16]

Worse than their seeming ineptness, replacement soldiers weakened the unit cohesion that the Second Corps had gained from its victory at Bristoe Station. Veterans and newcomers had only a few weeks, if that, to become acquainted. Back was the gulf in military experience that had separated greenhorns from old-timers in the later summer of 1863. Private Jacob Cole recovered from wounds suffered at Gettysburg to return in April to the 57th New York. Plenty of soldiers were present, but few of them had volunteered with Cole when the regiment first had organized in 1861. "I met with new faces unknown to them and they unknown to me, excepting that I was a member of Company A." The weakening of unit cohesion was unavoidable with the 116 recruits who arrived in mid-April at the camp of the 20th Massachusetts. Nearly all of the newcomers spoke only German, leaving their officers to conduct rudimentary drill through example.[17]

The volunteers of 1861 also sometimes proved of shaky resolve, with many of them reluctant to risk their lives only days before going home. An Indiana captain admitted that his men talked often about whether they would go into battle before their muster-out date in mid-June. The fervent hope was to avoid battle because "the boys . . . don't like the idea of getting killed or getting a limb shot off just as their three years is about to expire." Private Charles Hamlin, due to leave the army with the rest of the 57th New York in mid-July, heard rumors that the Second Corps would be assigned garrison duty to recuperate from its exceptionally high battlefield losses in 1862 and 1863. Hamlin decided that the remoter the post the better. Another private was approached repeatedly by his company officers to reenlist and receive a furlough home. He flatly refused, explaining that he could wait until his muster out on the "seventh day of June and then I will take a big furlough."[18]

Soldiers of the 8th Ohio were driven to mutiny from fear of going into battle before their term of service expired in mid-July. The Buckeyes ranked among the most stalwart in the army, having fought well at every engagement since joining the Second Corps on the Virginia Peninsula in the late summer of 1862. Yet some men refused to do any more military duty in late April, claiming that their federal service should date from the muster of individual companies rather than the entire regiment. The gap between the muster of the first company and the last company sometimes stretched into weeks. Showing their desperation, the Ohioans were advancing the same argument that two-year soldiers had put forth unsuccessfully in the early spring of 1863. In this case, General Gibbon, the Second Division commander, reacted decisively. Gibbon quelled the disturbance by arresting and placing in irons the twelve perceived ringleaders of the protest. The thwarted mutiny had enough worrisome ramifications among other veterans that Meade felt obliged to weigh in. He grimly warned that any soldier "who refuses to do duty on a similar plea will instantly be shot without any form of trial whatever."[19] The iron-fisted tactics worked, because no further protests occurred in the Second Corps. But many short-time soldiers likely went into battle that spring with both eyes fixed firmly on the calendar.

The potential departure of so many veterans threatened to devastate the fighting strength of the Second Corps. Twenty-two regiments were slated to leave for home during the summer and fall, from the 1st Massachusetts on May 25 through the 5th New Jersey on November 6 (see table 3). Most of the short-service regiments would leave during the six-week period between June 13 and July 30, the height of the summer campaign season. Adding to the headache, the muster-out of regiments would occur unequally. The hardest hit would be the Fourth Division,

Table 3. Reenlistment Status and Muster-out Date of the Fifty-seven Regiments of the Second Corps Organized during 1861, by Division

Unit	Reenlisted (Yes/No) and Muster-out Date	Unit	Reenlisted (Yes/No) and Muster-out Date
First Division		*Third Division*	
28th Massachusetts	Yes, 6/29/65	20th Indiana	Yes, 6/12/65
39th New York	Yes, 7/1/65	5th Michigan	Yes, 7/5/65
52nd New York	Yes, 7/25/65	40th New York	Yes, 6/27/65
61st New York	Yes, 7/14/65	86th New York	Yes, 6/27/65
63rd New York	Yes, 6/30/65	93rd New York	Yes, 6/29/65
64th New York	Yes, 7/14/65	57th Pennsylvania	Yes, 6/29/65
66th New York	Yes, 8/30/65	99th Pennsylvania	Yes, 7/1/65
69th New York	Yes, 6/30/65	105th Pennsylvania	Yes, 7/11/65
88th New York	Yes, 6/30/65	110th Pennsylvania	Yes, 6/28/65
53rd Pennsylvania			
81st Pennsylvania	Yes, 6/29/65	3rd Maine	No, 6/28/64
		4th Maine	No, 7/19/64
2nd Delaware	No, 7/1/64	3rd Michigan	No, 6/13/64
57th New York	No, 7/14/64	63rd Pennsylvania	No, 9/9/64

Table 3, continued

Unit	Reenlisted (Yes/No) and Muster-out Date	Unit	Reenlisted (Yes/No) and Muster-out Date
Second Division		*Fourth Division*	
1st Delaware	Yes, 7/12/65	11th Massachusetts	Yes, 6/14/65
19th Massachusetts	Yes, 6/30/65	7th New Jersey	Yes, 7/17/65
20th Massachusetts	Yes, 7/16/65	8th New Jersey	Yes, 7/17/65
7th Michigan	Yes, 7/5/65	73rd New York	Yes, 6/29/65
59th New York	Yes, 6/30/65	84th Pennsylvania	Yes, 6/29/65
4th Ohio	Yes, 7/12/65	115th Pennsylvania	Yes, 6/28/65
69th Pennsylvania	Yes, 7/1/65		
106th Pennsylvania	Yes, 6/30/65	1st Massachusetts	No, 5/25/64
7th West Virginia	Yes, 7/1/65	16th Massachusetts	No, 7/27/64
		5th New Jersey	No, 11/6/64
14th Indiana	No, 6/16/64	6th New Jersey	No, 9/7/64
15th Massachusetts	No, 7/28/64	70th New York	No, 7/7/64
42nd New York	No, 7/13/64	71st New York	No, 7/30/64
82nd New York	No, 6/25/64	72nd New York	No, 6/20/64
8th Ohio	No, 7/13/64	74th New York	No, 6/19/64
71st Pennsylvania	No, 7/2/64	26th Pennsylvania	No, 6/18/64
72nd Pennsylvania	No, 8/24/64		

Source: The muster-out date of each regiment is listed in the corresponding entry of Dyer, *A Compendium of the War of the Rebellion,* vol. 1.

where one-half of the regiments had not reenlisted. The departure of veteran regiments was less of a concern throughout the rest of the army because reenlistment rates had reached higher levels. Soldiers of thirty regiments were preparing to leave the Fifth Corps and Sixth Corps over the remainder of the year, little more than in the Second Corps alone.[20]

ATTACKING LEE'S ARMY

A sense of gloom quickly overtook soldiers as they started toward Ely's Ford and the start of Grant's spring offensive on the evening of May 3. Forming the left wing of the army, Hancock's men pushed south of the Rapidan River and into the dense tangle of the Wilderness. The terrain was unnerving. A thick tree canopy blocked out much of the natural light, and vines and underbrush tripped the feet and tore the uniforms of the unwary. Tired and sweating soldiers made the route into the Wilderness even more treacherous by discarding any item they believed unnecessary. Overcoats, blankets, and knapsacks littered the ground for miles along the route of march.[21] Soldiers found little relief when they finally halted on the late morning of May 4 near the old Chancellor family manor. Bits of uniform, broken muskets, and abandoned gun carriages were everywhere scattered, vivid reminders of the fighting that had raged across the same ground nearly one year before to the day. Most gruesome were remains of former comrades identified by some distinctive feature. Various markings on boots, shoulder straps, and headgear all identified the remains of men killed in the fighting. Many of the living found their sleep haunted by memories of now gone friends. Other men dug graves and buried bones for much of the remainder of the day. "What memories do these scenes awaken," one Pennsylvanian concluded.[22]

Hancock's men had nearly cleared the Wilderness by the midmorning of May 5, and the open ground beyond decidedly favored Union numbers. Soldiers halted for a brief rest from the fast-warming morning sun at Todd's Tavern, a small clearing along the north-south-running Brock Road. Here the Union advance halted, when the Second Corps received orders to march back the way that it had come. The reason for the change of direction soon became apparent when soldiers heard sounds of artillery and musket fire coming from the Orange

Plank Road. That west-east-running thoroughfare intersected the Brock Road at roughly the center of the Union lines. Sedgwick's Sixth Corps had crashed into Confederate forces just west of the vital intersection, unleashing a savage fight.[23]

Francis Walker, the historian of the Second Corps, later claimed that Grant made a strategic blunder in halting the advance of Hancock and his men at Todd's Tavern. Had the Union soldiers continued to go forward, they would have pushed past the right flank of the Confederates fighting in the Wilderness. Such a maneuver might have helped to deal Lee's army a crushing blow at the outset of the campaign. Modern-day scholars give significantly less weight to the claim. Had the Union lost control of the Brock Road intersection, the Army of the Potomac might have been cut in half. All of this was in the future, and, at the time, Hancock's men felt a lifting of spirits as they marched toward the sound of battle. Every step carried them back deeper into the Wilderness, but soldiers correctly recognized that the long-anticipated showdown between Grant and Lee finally had come. As usual, action brought relief. "Well boys," a hard-bitten sergeant reassured his men as they jostled along, "the sooner it comes, the sooner it will be over."[24]

Soldiers of the former Third Corps plunged first into the fighting, and they showed far less spirit in fighting Lee's men than they had in fighting the army's reorganization that winter. The wooded terrain disrupted formations, and heavy Confederate fire dropped Union soldiers "on all sides." As disruptive, however, many short-termers hardly wished to risk life and limb only a few days before going home. Soldiers of the 1st Massachusetts, only twenty days away from becoming civilians, broke first after receiving a "terrific volley" of Confederate musketry. The Bay Staters melted back toward the perceived safety of the Union rear, halting only upon reaching breastworks that fronted the Brock Road. Other survivors of Birney's and Mott's divisions soon followed. Colonel Robert McAllister found the shaky performance of the otherwise reliable troops in his brigade of Mott's division "impossible" to explain, "unless it was from the fact that a large number of troops were about to leave the service."[25] Only hard fighting by Barlow's and Gibbon's men later that evening succeeded in pushing the Confederate defenders back and away from the Brock Road.[26]

In later years, soldiers of the former Third Corps blamed the failure of the Union attack on everything but their own poor showing. Mott's men, who had broken first, blamed the difficult terrain and the deadly Confederate shooting. Soldiers in Birney's division argued that they would have held firm, had anyone else in the Union assault done so. John Bloodgood, a sergeant in the 141st Pennsylvania, barely acknowledged that the setback to the west of the Brock Road had occurred at all. Bloodgood claimed that he and his comrades fell back only to allow Union reinforcements to continue the attack. Otherwise, the Pennsylvanians would have continued pressing forward. Still, to be fair, short-timers in the Second Corps were not the only veterans to fight poorly in the Union attacks on May 5. Soldiers in the Iron Brigade, widely regarded as one of the hardest-fighting units in the Union army, had broken earlier under Confederate fire. These men too had fled backward, before finally rallying and constructing entrenchments.[27]

Whether they had fought well or poorly, soldiers of the Second Corps showed considerable inner steel in enduring the night of May 5–6. Hancock's men had spent many a night on previous battlefields, most recently at Gettysburg. The Wilderness added new horrors to the experience. Nervous pickets fired often at bushes and trees that seemed to take human shape in the darkness, keeping their comrades to the rear awake and jittery. Wounded men who were only yards away, maybe tens of yards away—in the pitch black of the Wilderness it was impossible to tell—groaned and called for help and water. One distraught captain called out repeatedly into the darkness, "do, do hear those men, do hear those men." Groans and calls turned to shrieks of terror as fires set by the day's fighting swept the ground. Men unable to move from their wounds and injuries burned to death. Private Joseph Wicklein described listening to the "lamentations of hundreds" of badly wounded men as night fell. Approaching flames brought new pleas and, as grim silence settled, Wicklein declared that the "pains and embarrassments" that the wounded had suffered "are indescribable."[28]

Dawn broke to birds screeching in fright and soldiers of the Second Corps again advancing into the attack. Grant ordered Hancock to throw three divisions from the Second Corps and one division of the Sixth Corps down both sides of the Orange Plank Road and against the

Confederate lines. Upward of 30,000 Union soldiers swept all before them and threatened to smash Lee's right flank.[29] Opportunity proved fleeting as the day wore on. Hancock claimed to have ordered Barlow's First Division, stationed on the Union left flank along the Brock Road, to reinforce the morning's success. General John Gibbon, in charge of the Union forces on this section of the front, never received the order. The two officers argued bitterly in the postwar era about whether the order actually was sent and received. The stakes were high because Hancock believed that had Barlow's men arrived in a timely manner, the "overthrow of the enemy would have been assured."[30] The Federal advance lost its momentum as terrain jumbled battle lines and Confederate reinforcements under the command of Lieutenant General James Longstreet rushed onto the field. In the ensuing fighting around the Tapp farm clearing, the Confederates exploited the opening in the Union lines where Barlow's men should have been. Suffering a devastating flank attack, soldiers of the Second Corps went reeling. Hancock later admitted that Longstreet's assault "rolled up" his lines "like a wet blanket."[31]

The battlefield situation before the Brock Road now turned decidedly dangerous for the Second Corps. The men streamed back to the Union lines in "broken little squads" and "fragments." Brigadier General Alexander Webb believed this not the time to stand on military protocol. Webb variously shouted for his men to "get out of there as damned quick as you can!" and to "break like partridges" for the Brock Road.[32] From the other side of the lines, the Confederates sensed a rare opportunity to score a major, perhaps decisive, battlefield triumph. Watching the Union lines crumble into confusion, Brigadier General Micah Jenkins jubilantly shouted, "We shall smash them now." Fate intervened on the side of the Union. While making arrangements to continue the Confederate counterattack, Longstreet and his aides were mistaken for Union soldiers and fired upon. Longstreet fell badly wounded, and, as a consequence, Lee delayed the planned Confederate assault. After the battle, one Confederate staff officer termed the wounding of Longstreet a "catastrophe." Colonel Porter Alexander, Longstreet's chief of artillery, agreed. The "time was ripe" for the Confederate attack, because the Union Second Corps was panicked and "'on the jump.'"[33]

Not for long. Showing a battlefield resiliency that had marked the Second Corps throughout much of the war, soldiers quickly regrouped after reaching the Union defensive lines along Brock Road. Hancock was instrumental in the rally, shouting for his troops to form a line of battle wherever they stood and "hold these works." The men were tired, but they were ready to receive a Confederate assault that came in the late afternoon.[34] The Rebels advanced in numbers, according to one private, "thicker than hairs on a dog." The Confederate attackers relentlessly pressed through a withering musketry fire. When a section of the Union parapet caught fire, handfuls of gray-clad attackers stormed through. The outcome of the battle now hung in the balance. At least twelve pieces of artillery earlier massed by Hancock opened fire with canister, a benefit of the corps artillery system.[35] Nearby Federal defenders rallied amid the fire and smoke and quickly breached the gap. After a few more minutes of fighting, Hancock's men reported that those Confederates not left on the works "writhing in the agonies of death" fled back into the thickets "howling."[36]

The repulse of the Confederate attack on the Brock Road very much buoyed soldiers' spirits after an otherwise long and disheartening day. The success had been limited, but it marked one of the few clear-cut Union triumphs in the two days of battle in the Wilderness. "Our Corps has done some hard fighting," a Pennsylvania sergeant wrote. "Prisoners say General Lee took his best troops and tried to break our center, but failed." Another Pennsylvanian declared that at Brock Road the Confederates were "badly whipped." Even the Confederates acknowledged their rough handling. Colonel Porter Alexander, who earlier had believed Hancock's men on "the jump," bemoaned the sudden turn of events. The early evening attack "ought *never, never* have been made." The Union defense was simply too stout, and the resulting loss in veteran troops killed and wounded was one the Confederates "could not spare."[37]

Soldiers of the Union Sixth Corps found no similar consolation, after suffering a flank attack north of the Orange Plank Road later that same evening. Three Confederate brigades, under the command of General John B. Gordon, crumpled the poorly anchored Union right flank. Darkness as much as mounting Union resistance finally brought the Confederate attack to a close. Gordon later claimed that had he the benefit of even one extra hour of daylight, his assault would have scored "the crushing defeat of General Grant's army." That overstates the case, given the relative paucity of Confederate numbers. But many of the Union defenders had not fought especially well, streaming away from the front almost as soon as coming under attack. Where Hancock's men could rightly claim a triumph to take some of the sting from their earlier defeat, Sedgwick's men could not. Regimental officers attempting to hold along the Union right criticized their commands for falling back in "wild disorder" and "panic and confusion." Lieutenant Colonel Theodore Lyman, a staff officer to General Meade, offered a similarly grim assessment. Lyman judged the rout along the Orange Plank Road the "most disgraceful thing that happened to the celebrated 6th corps during my experience of it."[38]

Hancock's men were tired by the morning of May 7, having served in the thick of the action since crossing the Rapidan River three days earlier. They were even more tired by day's end, building entrenchments and skirmishing with Confederate pickets as Grant and Lee planned their next moves. "Foot sore, weary and hungry," one captain groused, "we work day after day and night after night." Yet spirits soared that evening, when Grant put the army in motion toward Spotsylvania Court House. The line of march meant that Grant was trying to clear the Wilderness and maneuver around Lee's right flank rather than abandoning the campaign. Lieutenant Nathanial Stanton was delighted at the aggressiveness displayed by the Army of the Potomac. He had served under all the past commanders but believed that Grant, finally, "is the man for the rebs to fear."[39]

Soldiers of the Second Corps turned in a mixed battlefield performance on May 10, when Grant launched a series of assaults outside Spotsylvania Court House. Hancock's men went forward at Po River, Laurel Hill, and Spotsylvania, all to the left of the Mule Shoe and the center of newly constructed Confederate defensive lines. The Mule Shoe was a salient that jutted forward as an inverted U, offering Confederate defenders clear fields of fire over approaching terrain.[40] Barlow's division probed Lee's defenses across the Po River. Hit by a Confederate counterattack, the Union soldiers held their own before receiving orders to retreat.[41] That same afternoon, members of Gibbon's division made two unsuccessful attacks against strong Confederate entrenchments on Laurel Hill, aided in the second attempt by soldiers from Birney's division. The attackers fought poorly the second time around. They seemed to think that if one attempt to carry the Confederate works had failed with heavy losses, a second assault would fare no better. Soldiers in Mott's division fought with even less enthusiasm when ordered to support an attack by elements of the Union Sixth Corps against the western face of the Mule Shoe. The Second Corps soldiers advanced alone, due to a miscommunication. They moved forward only a short distance before falling back "in confusion to the rear" when hit by Confederate fire.[42]

The Union attacks on May 10 had failed, and un-reenlisted veterans bear the blame. These men fought poorly, and there were lots of them. In the three divisions of the Second Corps but for Barlow's, nearly one-half of the regiments raised at the start of the war were due to soon go home. Men in these units showed an understandable reluctance to risk life and limb, especially in assaulting formidable-looking Confederate defensive works. The situation was especially pronounced in Mott's division, where most of the volunteers of 1861 were short-term. Colonel Robert McAllister, a brigade commander, thought the sooner these soldiers gone, the better. "The troops whose term of service is just coming to a close do not fight well," McAllister admitted after the failed Federal assault. "I am sorry to say that in our Division we have too many of this kind."[43] Others throughout the rest of the Union army were less charitable in their assessment. Meade proposed later that evening to keep Mott's division on the flank of the Sixth Corps. Brigadier General Horatio Wright, who had assumed command after Sedgwick was killed by a Confederate sharpshooter on May 9, exploded into a rage. "General, I don't want Mott's men on my left"; Wright fumed, "they are not a support; I would rather have no troops there." Meade agreed, and Mott's division soon rejoined the Second Corps.[44]

Hancock's men found little relief from their labors the next morning. Some soldiers built entrenchments and skirmished with Confederate pickets, as they had done following the Battle of the Wilderness. Other men nervously fingered their muskets in preparation for a possible

Confederate assault. All attempted to keep warm, most unsuccessfully, as heavy rains came down by the early evening. One veteran recalled that by sunset, "we were just about as disconsolate and miserable a set of men as ever were seen." Later that night, soldiers received orders to march to about a half-mile above the Mule Shoe and spearhead a Federal assault to go forward at 4 o'clock in the morning. The distance seemed greater than the miles. The night was "exceedingly dark," and the roads were "very rough."[45] Men accidentally bumped into comrades who had stopped suddenly, only to find themselves jostled by unsuspecting marchers coming behind. The rain continued and the footing proved treacherous, with soldiers slipping, falling, and rising again, but this time covered in mud. Grunts and curses filled the air, even though orders called for silence. Finally, with an hour or two to spare, Hancock's men filed into position. Sleep proved frustratingly elusive amid the chill night air. "Our teeth chattered," one exhausted private recalled, "and our frames shook like leaves."[46]

Thick fog and darkness prevented soldiers from seeing the Mule Shoe, but they had no illusions about the nature of the work before them. Hancock's men had assaulted breastworks enough over the past week and a half to give them a sense of foreboding. A Pennsylvanian declared that a "funeral like silence" hung over the gathering Union troops. A New Yorker feared that "we all must perish" in the upcoming attack. The lucky few soldiers who did manage to doze off found little escape. A captain griped that his one hour of sleep, which "seemed but about 5 minutes," was cut short by orders to fall in for the attack.[47] Any man who still hoped for an easy assault had his hopes dashed by officers who walked among the ranks, massed by divisions with Birney and Barlow to the front and Mott and Gibbon to the rear. Soldiers received instructions to advance with bayonet fixed and "to do their duty." A colonel of the Irish Brigade promised Sergeant John Dillon a promotion if he planted the colors of the 63rd New York upon the Confederate entrenchments. "Promotion or no promotion," Dillon replied, "there is not a man in this brigade shall get a head of me if the Lord will spare me or I will die in the attempt."[48]

Officers quietly ordered their men "forward" in the predawn darkness, and the 19,000 soldiers of the Second Corps stepped off. The men

advanced steadily at first, as if on parade. As they neared the Confederate entrenchments, they "opened the yell that always accompanies a
charge."[49] Soldiers dashed forward at a dead run and tore away at felled
trees, sharpened branches, and other man-made obstacles. A Union
attacker later recalled that officers and enlisted men all around him recognized that the "success of the movement was involved in passing over
this ground in the shortest time possible." Private Isaac Hadden was
more succinct, declaring that he ran as fast as his legs could carry him
because he "felt rather tickelish" in the killing ground before the Confederate works. Nearly simultaneously, scattered Confederate shots rang
out, and a new round of Union cheers lifted. Before either had quieted,
the Federal attack lines had rolled up and into the Mule Shoe. In some
spots along the works the fighting was hand-to-hand.[50] More often,
Hancock's men caught the Confederate defenders unaware. Union soldiers rounded up thousands of sleepy-eyed Confederate prisoners and
drove others pell-mell to the rear. A New Jersey private gloated that the
Union attackers had "pounced upon the Johnnies before many of them
were out of bed and took [several] thousands prisoners and 20 pieces of
Artillery." Other nearby soldiers shook hands and judged the Federal
attack a "complete success."[51]

With the Confederate center split open, Hancock began to over-
manage the battlefield. He sent assault wave after assault wave spilling
into the captured works to attempt to secure the triumphs already won.
Barlow attempted to at least temporarily stem the rush forward, pleading with Hancock, "For God's sake, do not send any more troops in
here!" Hancock paid little heed, desperate to avoid a lack of support that
he believed had repeatedly helped battlefield victory elude the Union
army. In the meantime the Union Sixth Corps advanced and took up
position along the western face of the captured works.[52] Inside the Mule
Shoe soldiers milled about and moved off in every direction. Officers
vainly tried to re-form their men. Colonel James Beaver admitted that in
the confusion of victory the "whole mass of troops became thoroughly
mixed up." Captain Benjamin Peck declared that "all organization was
lost." Into the confusion came a counterattack by Confederate soldiers,
now regrouped and reinforced. The tables turned, Hancock's men found
themselves giving ground to what one New Yorker described as "this

Gen Hancock

Captured guns.

Prisoners from the front by A. Stewart's Div. C.S.A.

Gen'l Edward Johnson

of Hancock's Corps. In front of Spottsylvania C.H.
Rainy day—   7 A.M.   May 12" 1864   E.F.
Union troops about to make the charge from this
or from this

"Charge of Hancock's Corps in front of Spottsylvania Court House," a sketch made by Edwin Forbes on May 12, 1864. Confederate soldiers and artillery captured by the Second Corps are in the foreground, while Hancock, mounted on horseback, is to the left and center. The capture of the Mule Shoe was a spectacular battlefield success, buoying sprits amid the otherwise heavy casualties and hard marching of the Overland Campaign. Library of Congress.

living tide streaming in upon us." They fell back, but not far. Union soldiers planted their colors on top of the outward face of the Mule Shoe and from there "bid defiance to the whole rebel army."[53]

The ensuing fighting around the outer tip of the Mule Shoe was brutal, with rifle butts, bayonets, and fists all freely used. Only a few feet separated the Union and Confederate lines, and battle flags and colors sometimes flapped against one another in the breeze. Rain again had started falling, causing dead and wounded soldiers to slide into a morass of mud, blood, and vomit. The noise was appalling. The "furious cannonade and musketry" reminded a Union surgeon of "Gettysburg over again." Individual acts of heroism were plenty amid the carnage. A lieutenant in the 116th Pennsylvania killed a Confederate color bearer with his sword and captured the flag. Later in the day, Corporal Charles Russell of the 93rd New York clambered to the top of the entrenchments to grapple with a Confederate colonel defiantly waving a battle flag. The scuffle lasted for several minutes before Russell threw the officer "headlong, flag and all over into our line." Russell was as fortunate as brave, clambering back down "without a scratch."[54] Only well after nightfall did the Confederates pull back to newly constructed defensive lines. Hancock's men expressed shock at the severity of the fighting as quiet finally settled over the Mule Shoe, forever after known as the Bloody Angle. Lieutenant Thomas Galwey declared that of all the battles he had fought in since the start of the war, the struggle at the Bloody Angle "exceeded all the rest in stubbornness, ferocity, and in carnage." Private A. B. Ramsey wondered if the battle had not been fought at Spotsylvania but "right in the core of Hades."[55]

The next morning brought the first sunny skies in several days, but the pleasant change meant little amid scenes of almost unbelievable horror and suffering. Soldiers of the Second Corps still clung to the captured Confederate works at the Bloody Angle, and they struggled to describe what they saw. A few men, perhaps overwhelmed by the death and dying around them, focused upon the landscape of the battlefield. Trees not "cut to pieces" by bullets were stripped of foliage "as though an army of locusts had passed during the night." Bushes and underbrush were mowed down "as with a scythe."[56] More men lingered over the human destruction. Bodies were spread as thick as "pumpkins in a cornfield in autumn" and the "leaves of autumn" before and to the rear of the Bloody Angle.[57] Immediately inside the works, the dead were piled "thick" and "three deep." Many of the bodies were "shot to pieces as to be totally unrecognizable." A few wounded men feebly moved arms and legs, while others gazed at their Bibles and family pictures as strength ebbed away. All together, the scenes around the Bloody Angle were "ghastly" and "sickening." One Union observer claimed that nearly everyone who observed the aftermath of the fighting pleaded, "God forbid that I should ever gaze upon such a sight again."[58]

The misery only deepened as Grant and Lee skirmished around Spotsylvania over much of the next week. Soldiers seemed almost constantly in motion as they dug entrenchments and marched to and from picket lines. Grant's offensive now stretched into the end of a second full week, and physical strain became nearly overwhelming. "I cannot describe and you cannot imagine," one Pennsylvanian admitted on May 16, "the labors and suffering we have undergone." Another soldier pleaded with his family that he could not write more often because, after marching for two consecutive nights, "I am too sleepy."[59] Even in rare quiet moments, soldiers found no reprieve. Rations were inexplicably scarce. When the men did stop to eat, the smell of the hastily buried dead from the recent fighting at the Bloody Angle often took away their appetite. The heavens again opened after a few hours of sunshine on May 13, and soldiers worked and slept in damp and clammy uniforms and shoes. Even for those with iron constitutions, the ever-present threat of Confederate attack provided no break from what one private described as a state of "mental excitement."[60]

Confederate artillery and musket fire compounded the daily suffering. Picket firing was as intense as any time since the two armies had dug in outside Richmond following the Battle of Fair Oaks in the late spring of 1862. Only tens of yards sometimes separated Union and Confederate picket lines. Hancock's men sometimes hoisted hats on sticks just high enough above the breastworks to tempt their southern counterparts to fire. "If we can get one to come out from a tree," Private Benjamin Draper grimly described, "we shoot him."[61] Sustained combat occurred less often, but with more deadly results. Soldiers of the Second Corps probed Confederate defenses on May 13 and again five days later. Neither time did Hancock's men fight especially well, failing to press forward with much enthusiasm. Union soldiers found their fighting spirit drained quickly as they received "most determined" Confederate fire while attempting to claw their way through wood abatises. Equally demoralizing, soldiers of the Second Corps moved across ground strewn with bodies still unburied from the fighting on May 12. The "overpowering and sickening" stench of decaying corpses all too vividly reminded soldiers of their potential fate if too careless in exposing themselves before the Confederate works.[62]

Despite abundant trial and sacrifice, morale in the Second Corps remained among the highest in the army. Soldiers recognized that their losses had been substantial since the army crossed the Rapidan River and started the Overland Campaign on May 4. Hancock's command had lost 11,734 men killed, wounded, and missing through the fighting at Spotsylvania. These figures totaled a staggering one-third of the losses suffered by the army to date. Losses were unusually high in the Fourth Division, when combined with a stream of veterans mustering out and returning home. Rather than have the manpower of the division continue to drain away, Hancock transferred Mott's two brigades to Birney's division. The reorganization, while bumping the Third Division to four brigades, reduced the Second Corps itself to three divisions.[63]

The human costs from the killing fields of the Wilderness and Spotsylvania had been staggering, but many soldiers argued that the triumphs won were greater.[64] The successes were, ultimately, localized. But Hancock's men believed they had inflicted worse than they had received. Unlike the bloodletting before the stone wall at Fredericksburg, soldiers in Grant's 1864 offensive pointed to tangible battlefield accomplishments. Colonel William Smith admitted that losses in the 1st Delaware had been heavy in the recent battles and maneuvers. Yet the payoff was that "we have whipped the rebels every day." An Indiana captain declared the fighting through Spotsylvania the "greatest man slaughter" that he had seen. "However," he quickly added, "we have been victorious in every attempt." A private in the 42nd New York believed the fighting ferocious so far because the Confederates "are as good fighting men as we." That just made the triumphs all the greater because "we get the best of them on every turn in this Corps." A Pennsylvanian looking at the gruesome aftermath of the fighting around the Bloody Angle estimated that Confederate losses have been "large, if not larger, than our own." Using grim arithmetic, he calculated that "if we could deal them two or three more such blows, I should hope for an early end of the campaign."[65]

Others, both inside and outside the Union army, also recognized the hard fighting of the Second Corps. Only hours after the fighting around the Bloody Angle had ceased, Grant recommended Hancock for a promotion in the Regular Army.[66] Several days later, an artillery soldier in the Fifth Corps reported a rumor that Hancock's men had again stormed the Confederate defensive lines during the fighting on May 13.

The scuttlebutt ultimately proved wrong. The mistake might easily be forgiven, however, because "we are all the time hearing about successful movements by the Second Corps." Confederate survivors of the carnage around the Bloody Angle also chimed in. One Virginian admitted that the struggle in the mud and gore was the "hardest fight we had fought since the war." Lieutenant General Richard Ewell, whose Confederate corps bore the brunt of much of the back-and-forth fighting, described the battle with Hancock's men as "most desperate."[67]

Spirits varied throughout Grant's other three army corps. Soldiers in the Sixth Corps had fought ferociously since leaving the Wilderness, especially in helping to hold the Union battlefield gains at Spotsylvania. Impressed by the accomplishments, Grant also recommended Wright for promotion. In the Fifth Corps and the Ninth Cops, soldiers had compiled a relatively lackluster record. The fault rested more with Warren and Burnside than with the men. The two Union corps commanders became increasingly disillusioned with the bloodshed and the lack of any major battlefield successes in the campaign so far. Warren became especially ill-humored, and took to questioning the leadership skills of both Grant and Meade. The lack of resolve seemingly trickled into the ranks. Warren's and Burnside's soldiers turned in uninspired battlefield performances at Spotsylvania, although losing heavily in casualties.[68]

Grant reinforced the Second Corps heavily in late May, after combing the Union for reinforcements. Much of the new manpower came from converting regiments of heavy artillery into infantry in the late spring. These units previously had served on garrison duty in the ring of Federal forts protecting Washington, D.C. Among the group the Second Corps received was the 1st Massachusetts Heavy Artillery, 1st Maine Heavy Artillery, 2nd New York Heavy Artillery, 7th New York Heavy Artillery, and 8th New York Heavy Artillery. Each of the newly arrived regiments numbered close to their authorized strength of 1,800 men. In addition to the heavy artillery regiments, the Second Corps received the 5th New Hampshire, back from recruiting duty, and the 36th Wisconsin. More notable because of the manpower involved, the Second Corps also received the four regiments (the 155th New York, 164th New York, 170th New York, and 182nd New York) of the Corcoran Legion. The late Brigadier General Michael Corcoran had raised his self-named legion from Irish-American neighborhoods in New York City in 1862. These men had helped defend Union-occupied Suffolk, Virginia, from Confederate siege in the spring of 1863. With these additions the Second Corps numbered 28,350 men, thus recouping the losses suffered through the fighting at Spotsylvania. In contrast, the other three Federal army corps also received reinforcements, but not enough to make good their previous manpower losses. The Fifth Corps was the worst off, having declined by a third in strength since the start of the campaign.[69]

Newly arriving soldiers benefited the Second Corps more than the rest of the Union army because they brought with them at least some prior combat experience. Brigadier General Robert Tyler's heavy artillerists were the exception, but not for long. The newcomers marched to head off a Confederate flanking attempt on May 19, only one day after they had arrived at the front. The collision occurred at Harris Farm, on the extreme Union left. The heavy artillery soldiers fought confusedly in their first battle. Green troops sometimes fired into their own men and formed battle lines raggedly. Yet, by the end of the day, they had turned back the Confederate movement. They also had left nine hundred of their comrades on the field. Many of the new men expressed horror at their sudden immersion "into the mysteries of war." More survivors voiced pride, however, that the "baptism of fire" at Harris Farm "was all that was needed to make us soldiers."[70] By contrast, at least some green soldiers throughout the rest of the army brought with them little more than numbers. Grant earlier had pleaded with Major General Henry Halleck, the chief of staff of the Union army, to send him all the reinforcements that he could "rake and scrap" from rear-line duties. Halleck did as asked, but he warned Grant that "considerable dissatisfaction" existed among many of the garrison troops now pressed into front-line service.[71]

Grant again attempted to outflank Lee in the late hours of May 20, with Hancock's men in the van. Soldiers welcomed the change of scenery as they approached the North Anna River, about twenty miles to the north of Richmond. Encounters with die-hard Confederates failed to detract from the beauty of green fields and bountiful farms in the region. After encountering strong Confederate defensive lines running back in an inverted V shape from the North Anna River on May 24 and 25, Grant once more marched south.[72] And once more he found the Confederate

army already entrenched, this time behind Totopotomoy Creek. Undeterred, Grant ordered the Army of the Potomac to begin to concentrate
around Cold Harbor, a crossroads town about nine miles to the south.[73]

Marching away from Totopotomoy Creek, Hancock's men rarely
added to a small, but growing, criticism of Grant and his generalship
throughout the rest of the Union army. The Union army had fought and
marched nearly every day since crossing into the Wilderness, and no end
seemed in sight. Soldiers of the Vermont Brigade grew frustrated at the
lack of Union progress toward winning the war. These were men who
had served well on the Virginia Peninsula and at Gettysburg. Now, with
the fall of Richmond seemingly as far away as ever, the New Englanders
took to dismissing Grant as "Old Useless." A chaplain in the 15th New
Jersey later remembered that the bloodshed and physical strain since
crossing the Rapidan River had "produced a feeling of listlessness and
discouragement" throughout the Union army. "The men felt they were
doomed to slaughter."[74]

Soldiers of the Second Corps more often voiced strong confidence in
Grant. They especially approved of Grant's continuing attempt to slide
around Lee's left flank, to force a decisive showdown in the open. Some
of Hancock's men certainly were frustrated that the Union offensive
appeared stymied in everything but high casualty totals. More soldiers
appreciated maneuvering rather than fighting, given their long casualty
lists since the start of the campaign. "As a general thing," Private James
Rea explained, "charging costs a good many lives while flanking does
not." If Lee refused to come into the open, siege of Richmond and death
of his army would commence. A Maine sergeant predicted the operation
would prove "long and tedious." If happening, however, "we expect to
celebrate the 4th of July" in the Confederate capital.[75]

Such determination was needed because the grind of daily existence
on the front lines continued unabated. Soldiers went on picket duty,
dug entrenchments, and readied for battle. At night, they marched and
grabbed whatever sleep they could. The physical strain was awful. Private Herbert Willand complained that the "plan so far on this campaign
is to fight days and march by night a method of wearing us out on short
notice." After an especially grueling night march, Private Timothy Bateman grimaced, "Never had such sore feet in my life." Another enlisted

man believed that the nonstop toil and anxiety "is killing me." Nature made matters worse. Thunderstorms soaked soldiers one day, while summer sun scorched them the next. In between cooler nighttime temperatures made, Sergeant John Hirst admitted, "for a rough time of it."[76] When not soaking, sweating, or shivering, soldiers were hungry. Supply wagons failed to keep pace with the fast-moving Federal offensive. Generals Meade and Hancock rode through the camp of the 141st Pennsylvania on the evening of May 30. Rather than cheer the two Union officers, soldiers shouted, "'Hard Tack! Hard Tack!'" Meade promised bread, but instead the empty-bellied Pennsylvanians received "orders to move immediately." Hungry soldiers in the Irish Brigade took matters into their own hands. They ate through much of a nearby apple orchard, only to later suffer from diarrhea from the still unripened fruit.[77]

Soldiers were not impervious to the daily strains, and discipline began to falter. Some men used cries of "going for water" as an excuse to straggle. Others, when battlefield action loomed, "have shot their own fingers off as an excuse to go to the rear."[78] The three division commanders of the Second Corps had a known dislike of men failing in their duty, and they took stern countermeasures to limit the occurrence. Gibbon had a battlefield deserter shot by firing squad, the only execution yet held by the Army of the Potomac while actively campaigning. Barlow would have staged the second, had not President Lincoln commuted the sentence of a private found guilty of "cowardly conduct" from execution to "some other form of punishment." Birney adopted a less ceremonial approach when dealing with soldiers who recently had mutilated themselves to avoid combat. Birney ordered that men with suspiciously wounded fingers, toes, and other body parts be placed in the "foremost rank" in any future battle. Should any again falter, the unfortunate transgressor was to be "shot on the spot."[79] The savage punishments made a point. Soldiers reported that fewer of their comrades straggled as the army pressed toward Richmond. At the same time, many officers throughout the rest of the army voiced increasing frustration that some of their men almost routinely absented themselves from lines of battle and routes of march.[80]

Fatigue proved the greater problem on the night of June 1–2, when the Second Corps marched to join the main body of the army at Cold

Harbor. The men had spent the day glaring at their Confederate counterparts entrenched along Totopotomoy Creek. They trudged toward
Cold Harbor after dark, where humid and still air further drained their
strength. Dust stirred up by thousands of marching feet filled the air in
"choking and sickening" quantity, covering everything and everyone. A
Massachusetts soldier quipped that "a more veritable set of Graybacks,
to the eye, than we were, would not be found outside the Rebel lines."[81]
To top everything off, many soldiers followed the guide sent by Grant
down a wrong road. By the time the Second Corps had backtracked and
filed onto the Union left at about sunup, the men were worn out. Grant
took notice, and commented on "the exhausted state of the 2nd Corps."
The fatigue factored into Grant's decision to delay a planned full-scale
Union assault on Confederate entrenchments already going up before
Cold Harbor from that afternoon until early morning. Later analysts of
the battle bemoaned the delay, as Lee's men continued to extend and
strengthen their defensive works. But a badly winded Second Corps
was not alone, and Grant believed that the rest of the army also needed
more time to prepare for the assault. Any second-guessing came later
from Hancock's men, who, according to one Ohioan, "were more in a
mood to sleep than to do any hard fighting."[82]

Soldiers spent the remainder of the day in varied fashion, and here
the strains of the past month's campaigning again became apparent.
After hastily throwing up entrenchments, many soldiers slept. Other
men stared gloomily across the way, and with reason. The Confederate
works at Cold Harbor were strong, with rifle pits and entrenchments
running six miles along a low ridge and hills.[83] Often before, soldiers
had whiled away pre-battle hours by sleeping and fretting. Now at Cold
Harbor, men could not help dwelling on the past. The losses suffered
since the start of the campaign haunted survivors. Private William
Haines bemoaned that the tired and dirty soldiers of the 12th New Jersey
"only took up the space of a company." Ominously for the Union cause,
Haines declared that the "few who were left were not very hungry for
more fighting." Also that day, General David Birney calculated that the
Third Division had suffered nearly 6,000 casualties since crossing the
Rapidan River. "Is that not a large enough butcher's bill?" Birney wailed.
"My God how many faces I miss." Disappointed expectations made

other men gloomy. Veterans of the Peninsula Campaign sourly noted that they had believed victory close when they had encamped close by Cold Harbor in early June 1862. Here they were again two years later, but the fighting and killing still continuing. The knowledge did little, according to one volunteer of 1861, "to brighten the minds" of men.[84]

The Second Corps helped lead off the Union assault at 4:30 the next morning. Also attacking, but to the right of Hancock's men, were: Wright's Sixth Corps; the Eighteenth Corps, recently arrived to the front and under the command of Major General William "Baldy" Smith; Warren's Fifth Corps; and Burnside's Ninth Corps. Grant recognized that the Confederate defensive works at Cold Harbor were strong. He also believed that a straight-ahead attack was the best strategic option available. A further move to the left would carry the Union army into the swamps and bottomlands of the Chickahominy River. Additionally, Lee's army had fought almost continuously on the defensive, perhaps lowering morale. With a hard push, the Confederate army might be driven into the Chickahominy and destroyed piecemeal.[85]

So Hancock's men moved forward, and their subsequent performance depended upon whether they had fought at the Wilderness and Spotsylvania. Men who had arrived at the front after the earlier two battles charged bravely against the Confederate works. Barlow and Gibbon, whose divisions led the Federal attack on the Confederate right (with Birney's division posted in reserve), often placed their less bloodied regiments to the front. In part they did so because these units fielded the fullest ranks. Barlow and Gibbon also placed more recently arrived regiments well forward because they believed that the soldiers in them pressed their attacks with the most "enthusiasm." In the van of the Union assault, soldiers spared the slaughter of the Brock Road and the Bloody Angle breasted pulverizing Confederate fire. "Storm of lead and iron" tore into the ranks of the 7th New York Heavy Artillery, while air "full of messengers of death" mowed down the lines of the 8th New York Heavy Artillery "as wheat falls before the reaper." Almost unbelievably, some Union attackers stormed the Confederate lines. Soldiers in both New York Heavy Artillery regiments as well as in the 5th New Hampshire and the 164th New York cleared the Confederate parapets and drove back the defenders. Their success proved fleeting. No reserves exploited

"7th N.Y. Heavy Arty. in Barlows charge nr. Cold Harbor," sketched by Edwin Forbes on June 3, 1864. The battlefield success enjoyed by the New York regiment was brief, but was one of the few bright spots won by the Union army during the fighting. Library of Congress.

the Union breakthrough as a savage Confederate counterattack threw back the Federals. After some hand-to-hand fighting, Hancock's men fell back in confusion and under blistering Confederate fire. "Green soldiers though we were," one Heavy Artillery private later recounted, "our short experience had taught us to know just when to run, and run we did, I assure you."[86]

Soldiers who had survived the Wilderness and Spotsylvania advanced more begrudgingly. They, too, faced Confederate fire variously described as "awful," "death-dealing," and "destructive." Calculating the chances for Union success as not very good, experienced soldiers quickly hit the ground. Confederate sharpshooters targeted anyone who moved, while occasional blasts by artillery and musketry continued to take a toll.[87] Survivors hurriedly constructed breastworks that varied in stoutness. Soldiers in the 14th Connecticut had overrun the Confederate picket line before halting under "intolerable" fire from the main works. Survivors used tin plates to pile dirt over dead picket soldiers and sought shelter as best they could. A "few rods" back, soldiers of the 4th Ohio stopped their advance along a tree line. They industriously used "timber and whatever came first to hand" to build works that they proudly noted "were virtually bullet-proof."[88] Here they stayed put and, like other veteran soldiers both close to and far from the Confederate lines, prayed for the sun to go down.

Hancock, after the failure of the initial assault launched by the Second Corps, did his best to limit the carnage for the remainder of the day. By as early as 6:00 AM, Hancock informed Meade that his men were stopped cold before the Confederate lines. He might order another general advance, but not with much hope for success. "If the first dash in an assault fails," Hancock reminded Meade, "others are not apt to succeed better." Meade decided to press forward, although, to be fair, he received little overall guidance from Grant. A weakness had to exist somewhere in the Confederate lines, and Meade believed that another full-out Union assault might exploit it. From the front lines, however, Hancock again advised caution. Barlow and Gibbon reported that their divisions would make little headway against Confederate defensive fire directed at their front and flanks, unless the other four Union corps involved in the assault carried the works to their immediate fronts. That was unlikely, given that they also faced grim odds. Any more attacks by the Second Corps therefore seemed doomed to failure, prompting Hancock to conclude, "I do not advise persistence here."[89] The bad news at least was honest, unlike some of the hedging and self-serving reports sent by Wright, Burnside, and Smith. The stalled Federal battlefield offensive finally brought Grant to the front, where he visited individually with Hancock and many of the other high-ranking Union officers. Hancock had not changed his mind from the morning, and openly stated that "in his front the enemy was too strong to make any further assault promise success." Shortly after noon, Grant issued orders suspending any more Union attacks.[90]

Well after the battle, stories circulated that Meade had ordered more Union assaults and that soldiers, in the Second Corps especially, had refused to advance forward. The claim finds backing from, among other sources, two postwar accounts, penned by Private Frank Wilkenson of the 11th New York Light Artillery and Captain George Bowen of the 12th

New Jersey.[91] Wilkenson claims to have observed soldiers from unidentified units in the Second Corps refuse orders to charge. Bowen provides more specifics, claiming that members of his regiment "positively
refused to attempt another assault, notwithstanding all we could do in
the way of driving or exhortation."[92] No other sources from the Second
Corps support the accusations. Francis Walker dismisses the charges
as "unprincipled" and "erroneous." Bowen's fellow soldiers in the 12th
New Jersey, whether writing at the time or after, make no mention of any
breakdown in discipline. Certainly some men did not advance with the
élan that they had shown at Antietam and Fredericksburg. But, remembering days later the heaps of dead and wounded from the Second Corps
both in and before the Confederate works, one survivor judged that "it
can not be said that these assaults were feebley delivered."[93]

Hancock's men gained a chance to settle some of the score in the late
evening, when they repulsed a half-hearted counterattack by Brigadier
General James Martin's brigade of three North Carolina regiments.
Why the Confederates launched the attack is unclear, and Martin's
men quickly abandoned the field. "We checked them," Private Daniel
Chisholm gloated as the firing sputtered to a stop, "and gave hundreds
of them their last check."[94]

The triumph on the evening of June 3 soon grew far out of proportion, as soldiers grasped for any bright spots to come from the fighting
at Cold Harbor. Colonel Robert McAllister breathlessly described the
attack the next day. "The Rebel horde moved up towards our works,"
McAllister wrote. "Then our lines—infantry and artillery—poured into
them and repulsed with great slaughter." Confederate numbers and
losses only increased in the postwar era. Regimental historians variously described Martin's soldiers advancing in "some three lines deep,"
and making "vigorous assaults upon our lines." However, "the enemy
was hurled back again and again, with severe losses."[95]

The fighting at Cold Harbor badly bloodied the Second Corps,
although casualties were concentrated most heavily in the newer regiments. The 7th New York Heavy Artillery, 8th New York Heavy Artillery,
155th New York, 164th New York, and 5th New Hampshire lost more than
one-half of the 2,500 casualties suffered by the entire Second Corps. Four
of the eight colonels killed and wounded fell at the head of regiments

that joined the Second Corps after the fighting at Spotsylvania in mid-May. Handfuls of survivors in the most bloodied regiments could not quite bring themselves to believe that their sacrifices had been in vain. Private Herbert Willand stubbornly insisted that had supports reached the Confederate works stormed by the 5th New Hampshire, "they could have carried all successfully before them and the attack would have been a success."[96] Far more new men, however, complained that they had done the bulk of the fighting and dying in an assault doomed from the very start. A private in the Corcoran Legion bitterly judged the Union attacks "murder, not war." Other survivors claimed that the battle "was simply a butcher" and that "my heart pains me to think of the opporation." Lieutenant Henry Swan believed it a miracle that he and any other soldiers of the 8th New York Heavy Artillery had survived unhurt. The "hail storm of bullets and shell," he shuddered, "was horrible."[97]

Worse than heavy casualty lists, Hancock and many of his other high-ranking officers later argued that the fighting spirit of the Second Corps seemed to die at Cold Harbor. Coming on the heels of the bloodletting at the Wilderness and Spotsylvania, the fighting at Cold Harbor was a "blow to the corps from which it did not soon recover." Lieutenant Colonel Charles Morgan, Hancock's chief of staff, seconded the assessment. The Second Corps at Cold Harbor "received a mortal blow, and never again was the same body of men."[98] Yet Hancock and Morgan were writing after the fact, in an attempt to trace the root of various battlefield disasters suffered in the late summer and fall. In reality, the Second Corps had fought well since crossing the Rapidan little over one month earlier. There were some blemishes, especially the performance of short-term soldiers in the former Third Corps at the Wilderness and Laurel Hill. But these incidents stood out precisely because they were the rare defeat experienced by the Second Corps. Otherwise, Hancock's men won almost all of the Union successes achieved in the campaign. That the rest of the army had failed to achieve more—if that even was possible, given the formidable Confederate defensive works now confronted at nearly every turn—was not a fault of their making.

Some modern-day writers have taken up Hancock's claim, arguing that the battlefield spirit of the entire Union army received a shattering blow during the fighting on June 3. Memory of the seemingly useless slaughter at Cold Harbor remained fresh throughout the remainder of the war, with soldiers demonstrating a reluctance to assault Confederate defensive works. A Union officer who had survived the one-sided contest perhaps most forcibly expressed the sentiment. Stumbling back into the Union lines, he declared that he "would not take his regiment into another such charge, if Jesus Christ himself should order it."[99]

The "Cold Harbor syndrome" never took deep root in the Second Corps. Soldiers were discouraged in the aftermath of the fighting, and some men openly questioned the generalship of Grant, as many of their comrades throughout the rest of the army had done even before the Union disaster at Cold Harbor. The blue mood, however, although deep, was temporary. Hancock's men would go on to fight well during the initial Union assaults upon the Confederate-occupied city of Petersburg, Virginia, in mid-June. The men would make a determined charge against Confederate defensive works described by one modern-day historian as "more formidable than those at Cold Harbor."[100] Long casualty lists at Petersburg testify that the fighting spirit of the Second Corps had not died at Cold Harbor.

In the short run, the aftermath of the battle at Cold Harbor hurt morale nearly as much as the fighting itself. Union wounded lay trapped on the ground, enduring heat, thirst, and other near-unimaginable sufferings. The agony was brought about in part by Confederate sharpshooters, who fired even at Union soldiers attempting to bring relief to the wounded. The suffering lasted even longer because General Grant believed that asking General Lee for truce to bury the dead was open acknowledgment of defeat. The prayers, and screams, and whimpers became so bad that Hancock pointedly asked Grant on June 5 if "any arrangements" could be made to remove the wounded before his lines. Truce negotiations dragged on until finally successful by the evening of June 7.[101] The ensuing sights sickened Hancock's men. Bodies were turned "black as coal" from exposure and emitted a smell of decay that "was terrible." The few men found alive proved more a source of anguish than cheer. One rescued soldier survived the ordeal of his four-day abandonment by pulling up and eating grass. As the story made the rounds, soldier after soldier vowed to avoid running any battlefield risk that might place them "in the same position."[102]

Daily life that was hard before the fighting at Cold Harbor took an even harder turn after. Federal soldiers dug entrenchments largely where they had gone to the ground during the battle, sometimes only tens of yards from the Confederate lines. Soldiers in the 148th Pennsylvania were only a "biscuits toss" from the opposing works; those of the Philadelphia Brigade were so close that they listened to their Confederate counterparts carry on conversation. At such close range sharpshooting was especially deadly. Anyone careless or foolish enough to expose part of his body found that the "bullets come in zip zip all around." Caps placed on ramrods and held barely aloft quickly drew Confederate fire.[103] While soldiers hid from sharpshooters they were often soaked by the rain. Wet uniforms made for a clammy feeling on days when the temperature soared and an uncomfortable chill on nights when the temperature dropped. The torment pushed some sleepless men to the breaking point. A private in the Irish Brigade admitted that he had trouble even writing letters home because "for want of proper sleep I am very nervous." A Massachusetts lieutenant doubted he could "stand it in the trenches much longer, deprived of sleep and rest."[104]

Soldiers withstood by attempting to take control of their circumstances as much as possible. Hancock's men more than occasionally shouted to the Confederates across the lines to cease firing. "'If you'uns won't fire, we'uns won't,'" started many cease fires, as did this one between the 14th Connecticut and 42nd North Carolina. The truces never were comprehensive. Some soldiers resumed firing when ordered to do so by their commanders; other soldiers continued to target mounted officers. Yet soldiers took full advantage of any respite from the fighting. Often bags of Union coffee and packages of Confederate tobacco passed one another in the air as they sailed toward the opposite trench line. More intrepid spirits conversed and swapped camp gossip. On one section of the front, Pennsylvanians and South Carolinians met to talk and trade "as if they had never been enemies." When a Union officer approached, the men all airily sang out, "Good-morning, captain," before they dispersed and headed back to their respective lines. The men apparently were undeterred from future meetings, because the same captain later recorded that "quite peaceable times" prevailed along the regiment's front.[105]

Truces notwithstanding, soldiers of the Second Corps furtively abandoned their trenches and slipped to the Union rear on the night of June 12. The men were soon tramping toward the James River as part of a new Federal flanking movement. The night march meant sore feet and sleepy eyes by the next morning. No one, however, seemed to complain. Lieutenant George Salmon caught the prevailing mood as Cold Harbor faded from sight. "For the grace of God," Salmon praised, "I am marching out of this damnable place."[106]

7   VICTORY

THE PETERSBURG AND
APPOMATTOX CAMPAIGNS

The march toward the James River on the night of June 12 quickly turned more grueling than soldiers of the Second Corps had anticipated. This was no march of a few miles to clear the Confederate right flank, as the Union army had attempted at Cold Harbor. Rather, Grant hoped to cross the James River and capture Petersburg, Virginia, before Lee had time to counter. Petersburg was a major Confederate transportation center, connecting Richmond, twenty miles to the north, to the southern heartland. Grant correctly believed that capture of this key point would force Lee either to abandon Richmond or to submit to a debilitating siege. Both Confederate choices favored Union numbers and logistics, and would hasten the war's end. For the moment, however, the grand strategy was lost on soldiers of the Second Corps. Trudging behind General Baldy Smith's Eighteenth Corps in the lead of the army, Hancock's men marched through heat and dust before reaching the James River on the evening of June 13. The next day and the following morning were spent aboard transports to Windmill Point on the river's south bank. The marching and sailing was nearly too much for one Pennsylvania sergeant. Not only did the fast pace from Cold Harbor make his feet "very sore," but the choppy voyage across the James River gave him "a headache also."[1]

SEASONS OF DISAPPOINTMENT

Grant had stolen a march, and by the predawn hours of June 15, Smith's Eighteenth Corps pressed toward Petersburg and its ragtag defenders. Assistant Secretary of War Charles Dana was at army headquarters to report to Stanton on the progress of the Union offensive. "All goes on like a miracle," Dana breathlessly described at 8:00 AM; ". . . Hancock moves out instantly for Petersburg to support Smith's attack on that place, which was to have been made at daylight." Few reports have held forth so much promise. Few, also, have ultimately brought so much heartbreak. Grant, inexplicably, had failed to inform anyone but Smith that he hoped to capture Petersburg that day. Smith was not a man to show much initiative, and he let the hours go by as he reconnoitered the ground.[2] Hancock's men, meanwhile, unaware of the looming Federal assault on Petersburg, sat at Windmill Point and waited for three days' rations. The foodstuffs, through a series of clerical mishaps, never arrived. Less-than-urgent-sounding orders from Meade did, with the Second Corps to take up positions around Petersburg, about fifteen miles distant. Men sweated and cursed as they plodded along through the already intense heat, their feet churning up clouds of dust. The tramping took soldiers nowhere in particular because the maps provided were, a disgusted Hancock noted, "utterly worthless." After spending considerable time and energy searching for misplaced and nonexistent landmarks, Hancock turned to local blacks to head him in the right direction.[3]

Hancock showed little fire when he belatedly received orders from Grant to support Smith's assault on Petersburg, a slump that largely doomed the Union effort. Smith hoped that the Second Corps would reach his lines, a few miles east of Petersburg, "in time to make an assault tonight after dark."[4] Hancock had all of his men up between 9:00 and 10:00 PM but for Barlow's troops, who took a wrong turn in a wood and became hopelessly lost. Hancock was in charge of the field because of his seniority in rank, a situation that suited his tendency to issue orders anyway. The battlefield situation was promising, with soldiers from the Eighteenth Corps earlier having captured over one mile of lightly held Confederate entrenchments. Yet here, with Petersburg all but for the taking, Hancock allowed Smith to maintain command. The reasons were many, ranging from the lateness of the hour to Smith's familiarity with the ground. Hancock also missed Charles Morgan, his chief of staff, who was busy hurrying troops to the front. Morgan had the better capacity to grasp the depth of a battlefield, an intuition that might now have served the Union cause well. With Hancock taking a pass, Smith, despite his earlier bravado, ordered Birney's and Gibbon's men to replace his own on the front lines. Once completed, the Union offensive halted for the remainder of the night.[5]

Hancock received much criticism in the following days for his timid behavior before Petersburg, and the attacks bothered him greatly. Theodore Lyman, a colonel on Meade's staff, granted that Smith's and Hancock's men had marched far and eaten little on June 15. "But, oh! that they had attacked at once," Lyman bemoaned. "Petersburg would have gone like a rotten branch." Worse attacks came from Smith. One of the great gossipers in the army, Smith was not going to take the fall for the Union failure to capture Petersburg. In articles that ran in late June in the *New York Times* and the *New York Tribune,* Smith showered praises on the Eighteenth Corps. These soldiers had fought hard all day. Had Hancock pushed his troops harder, they might have reached the Confederate-held city in time to launch a decisive assault. Smith was clever enough that all of the particulars he fed to the newspaper correspondents attached to his headquarters were vaguely worded. The inference was clear enough, however. Hancock and the Second Corps had turned in a lackluster performance, and thereby were to blame for the missed opportunities before Petersburg.[6]

Hancock, furious at Smith's loose words, reacted defensively. After reading the *Times* and *Tribune* articles, Hancock called for an investigation into his actions on June 15. Grant declined to do so, generously noting that the "reputation of the Second Corps and its commander is so high, both with the public and in the army, that an investigation could not add to it. It cannot be tarnished by newspaper articles or scribblers."[7]

Hancock could not let the matter rest, a loss of focus that ultimately splintered the high command of the Second Corps. He sent a poorly worded circular to each of his division commanders, asking them to explain their actions during the initial approach of the Second Corps

to Petersburg. Hancock seemingly meant the request as a way to gather
more ammunition in his fight against Smith. The division commanders
saw it differently, and believed their battlefield performance was under
critique. Barlow was especially combative, since his division had gotten
lost on the march to Petersburg. The men had gone down the wrong
road, Barlow admitted, but only because Morgan had directed them
to do so. Morgan defended himself, and a nasty exchange between the
two Union officers followed. With tensions escalating, Hancock had to
step in. This involved deciding who was to blame, and Hancock pinned
Barlow for an "error of judgment" in getting lost. Hancock closed by
attempting to strike a conciliatory tone. Barlow "is certainly responsible" for the division traveling in the wrong direction, but only "so far
as responsibility may attach to it." Hancock was mistaken if he thought
that the argument now would go away. Barlow fired back, lodging that
he "very respectfully, but very firmly" disagreed. If the matter went any
farther, Barlow baldly warned that he would take his case directly to
Meade.[8]

There still seemed time for a quick strike against Petersburg as the
first light of dawn broke on June 16, a possibility that had soldiers of the
Second Corps in high spirits. Many men found their breakfast when
African American soldiers of the Eighteenth Corps shared their rations.
While enjoying biscuits and coffee, Hancock's men voiced a sense of
excitement when they peered out from their lines. The Confederate
defensive works before Petersburg clearly were strong. Finished in the
fall of 1863, the Confederate lines featured redoubts for artillery and
six-foot-high walls with firing steps for infantry. Running along all
was a fifteen-foot-wide and six-foot-deep ditch that any attacking force
would have to cross.[9] Normally the sight of such strong works would
have quelled even the strongest of fighting spirits. But Hancock's men,
through talking with soldiers of the Eighteenth Corps and looking with
their own eyes, correctly judged that the Confederate Army of Northern Virginia had yet to arrive. Manning the works before them were
not battle-hardened veterans but a thin assortment of militia troops.
The colonel of the 145th Pennsylvania excitedly reported that among
the Confederates he saw only handfuls of "cannoniers, no infantry."
He decided that the opposing works only looked formidable and that a

line of Union skirmishers could carry them "with but little loss." Private
Herbert Willand agreed, declaring that "our forces are confident of
capturing the city."[10]

Optimistic about scoring a battlefield triumph, soldiers of the
Second Corps spearheaded a major Federal assault delayed until the
late afternoon. Hancock's men charged forward "in quick time" while
"keeping the alignment beautifully," a verve not seen since the fighting
around Spotsylvania in mid-May. Unfortunately, there were now many
more Rebels behind the works than there had been earlier. Confederate General Pierre Beauregard, in charge of holding off the Union army
until Lee arrived, had rounded up troops here and there as quickly
as he could find them. By late afternoon, roughly 14,000 Confederate
troops held the line. These men still were not veterans from the Army of
Northern Virginia. But, fighting behind the formidable defensive works
of Petersburg, they did not have to be model soldiers.[11] Hancock's men
described Confederate fire as "terrific" and "a perfect shower of shot
and shell." Many quickly fell, creating "fearful" gaps in the ranks. Some
attacking lines ground to a halt, and others pressed forward. Soldiers
in Barlow's division made the most progress. The men captured several
advanced Confederate rifle trenches before falling back under a counterattack. One stunned survivor considered the Confederate defenses
the most formidable works "we ever charged, the stone wall on Marye's
Heights at Fredericksburg not excepted."[12]

Coming hard on the heels of the Overland Campaign, the failed
Union assaults on Petersburg shattered the Second Corps as a combat
organization for weeks to come. Overall casualty totals for the fighting
on June 16 are unrecorded. For the ten-day period June 10–19, however,
the Second Corps lost 4,322 officers and men killed, wounded, and
missing. These losses totaled about 20 percent of the men who had
gone into action. Such losses were heavy but, by this point in the war,
not unusually so for the Second Corps. What was more damaging
was who was hit. Many of the best remaining officers in Hancock's
command suffered death or serious wounds. Colonel Patrick Kelly of
the Irish Brigade was killed leading a charge on an artillery redoubt,
while Colonel James Beaver, another brigade commander, fell badly
wounded. Nineteen other officers of all grades were killed and mortally

Colonel Patrick Kelly, killed in action while leading the Irish Brigade at Petersburg during June 1864. Heavy casualties suffered during that spring and summer left the Second Corps without "enough good officers" to continue the Union assaults against the Confederate-held city. Massachusetts Commandery Military Order of the Loyal Legion and the U.S. Army Military History Institute.

wounded.[13] The officer casualties caught the notice of the high command. Barlow reported that after the fighting on June 16, "there are scarcely any officers in the brigades." Two days later, Hancock, suffering still from his Gettysburg wound, temporarily relinquished command of the Second Corps. Birney took charge, and was aghast at what he found. He cautioned Meade that the offensive force of the Second

Corps was weakened, with not "enough good officers" to lead the men into any more assaults.[14]

This is not to say that soldiers no longer expressed faith in the Union war effort, because they did. Private James Martell of the 19th Maine took a bullet in the stomach in one Union assault. Sensing that the wound was mortal, Martell penned some final lines to his family. "The battle rages terribly," he explained, "but, my dears, I die for my country, and I pray God take me to that home in heaven where I hope to meet you all." Lieutenant Cornelius Moore had served through the war in the 57th New York, one of the hardest-fighting regiments in the Union army. Despite seeing much of the horrors of war, Moore still prayed outside Petersburg, "May God bless our efforts to maintain the right!" The men also remained strong in their belief in ultimate Union triumph. A private declared that even though the Army of the Potomac was temporarily stymied, he and other soldiers of the 86th New York believed that "Richmond must fall this time." To the rear, surgeon William Potter treated scores of wounded men as the Federal assaults on Petersburg continued. Union losses were heavy, but so must be Confederate. Potter concluded that the "enemy has certainly reached very nearly, if not quite, his last ditch."[15]

What all but disappeared in the heat, and the mud, and the blood outside Petersburg was the aggressive battlefield instinct so often displayed before by soldiers of the Second Corps. Men who had stormed the Sunken Road at Antietam and the Mule Shoe at Spotsylvania now hesitated to approach Confederate works. General Hancock acknowledged that "the men do not attack with persistence," but blamed the problem on fatigue. Soldiers certainly were tired, some of them dropping off to sleep almost as soon they retreated back to Union lines following the fighting on June 16. Worse than heavy eyelids, the problems before Petersburg had become more psychological. Colonel George Hopper of the 10th New York believed that his soldiers still would willingly attack, but only if they could hit the Confederates before they had much chance to construct their earthworks. Colonel Guy Watkins of the 141st Pennsylvania thought even that a stretch. He described his men encamped in a pine woods off the front lines the next day and leading an "idle life." No one was "at all anxious to be more busily occupied, if to do so we have to charge the enemy's breastworks or rifle pits."[16] In other words, a "Petersburg syndrome" now afflicted the Second Corps.

The depth to which morale had plummeted became all too apparent on June 18, during a new series of Federal assaults launched against Petersburg. Union numbers finally had overlapped the Confederate flanks, forcing Beauregard to pull his forces back to new lines closer to Petersburg in the small hours of the morning. Meade assigned the Second Corps the task of capturing a low ridge across from the Hare house, located in the heart of the Confederate defenses. The lines curved inward to form a half-moon shape, providing awaiting infantry and artillery from Lee's now fast-arriving army a near-perfect killing zone.[17] When soldiers of the Second Corps went forward as part of a general Union assault in the late morning and early afternoon, they met pulverizing Confederate fire. Colonel Robert McAllister described encountering a storm of "lead and iron" that "cut our men down like hail cut the grain and the grass." A private watched in horror as entire lines disappeared in a "perfectly murderous fire of musketry, canister and spherical case." Soldiers quickly hit the ground and dug in as best they could, as they had done at Cold Harbor.[18]

When Meade ordered a new assault beyond Hare house hill in the late evening, many, perhaps most, of the men balked. Soldiers in one brigade of Mott's division briefly advanced before taking shelter behind a nearby barn. They caught their breath for the remainder of the battle, and, noted one disgusted onlooker, "not half of them fired a shot." A captain in Gibbon's division declared that when ordered to charge, "our men positively refused to attempt it and no urging could get them to make even a show of going." A fellow company officer shrugged off the inaction by explaining that veterans in the division "'had seen the wolf and bore his scars.'" In the second brigade of Mott's division, soldiers shouted, "Played out!" and refused to advance.[19] When the relatively green soldiers of the 1st Maine Heavy Artillery did move forward, veterans attempted to disrupt the attack by hissing loudly, "Lie down, you damn fools, you can't take them forts!" The New Englanders tumbled back in confusion after only a few minutes, leaving behind 600 of their comrades killed and wounded.[20]

The rest of the army also fought poorly outside Petersburg, although with far less bloodshed than the Second Corps. Major General Quincy Gillmore's Tenth Corps from the Union Army of the James had only recently arrived at the front, giving Grant five other army corps. From this total, Burnside's Ninth Corps had suffered the highest casualties, at 3,000 men (between June 15 and 30). These were fewer than one-half the total suffered by the Second Corps. Wright's Sixth Corps and Gillmore's Tenth Corps suffered, combined, only 1,500 casualties. Soldiers through-out the rest of the army described the Union assaults on Petersburg as a "horrid massacre," with men sent forward to "get shot." The casualty fig-ures more testify that many soldiers fought with little enthusiasm, when confronted by the strong Confederate defensive works to their front.[21]

Soldiers of the Second Corps enjoyed a respite following the debacle around Hare house hill until June 21, when they received new orders. Conceding that siege of Petersburg now had begun, General Grant attempted to push his lines south and west of the city. Extending the zone of operations outward stretched the 110,000 Union attackers less thinly than the 64,000 Confederate defenders. Equally important, expanding the siege lines threatened both the Petersburg and Weldon Railroad and the Southside Railroad. Cutting the two rail lines would deal a near-mortal blow to the Army of Northern Virginia by sever-ing the Richmond-Petersburg front from the lower South. Grant sent the Second Corps, still under the temporary command of Birney, and Wright's Sixth Corps against the Weldon Railroad. The day was hot and water was scarce. Soldiers dug holes where they hoped an underground spring might be located. Sometimes they were rewarded by a refreshing gurgle; more often they had to wait patiently as "warm milky-colored" water oozed forth "drop by drop." Exacerbating heat and thirst, soldiers were fatigued from near-nonstop campaigning over the past six weeks. Nelson Miles, now a brigadier general and as hard a fighter as any in the Union army, believed that no man had enjoyed a full night's rest "for a long time. You can not imagine how worn and tired the army is."[22] Fight-ing sleep and dripping sweat, soldiers pushed through woods and across the Jerusalem Plank Road on the afternoon of June 22.

A wide gap opened between the left flank of the Second Corps and the right flank of the Sixth Corps in the press to reach the Weldon

Railroad, about two miles distant. The Second Corps bore little of the blame for the potentially dangerous lack of cooperation. Wright's men had advanced forward sluggishly, as much from a general lack of energy as from Confederate skirmishing. Meade, frustrated by the slow pace of the Union offensive, ordered the Second Corps to keep pressing toward the Weldon Railroad without waiting "on any movement of the Sixth Corps." Charles Morgan, this time at the point of the advance, questioned the decision. The dangling Union left flank might "imperil very much" the entire Second Corps. When Meade became aware of the disjointed Federal advance, he reportedly brushed it off by replying that "each corps must look out for itself."[23]

The "whiz! bang!" of bullets and "Ki-yi" of Confederate yells suggested that two of Lee's divisions had exploited the opening. Taken completely by surprise, soldiers of the Second Corps collapsed. Men ran rearward as fast as they could. One soldier claimed to have bolted "like a blue streak," while another man said that his legs carried him so fast that he outran flying musket balls. A brigade commander reportedly urged on the less than fleet of foot by shouting *"Run boys, run! Run like the devil!"*[24] Rearward-streaming men did not represent the Second Corps at its finest, but at least they attempted to get away. Private Allen Landis recalled seeing many men decide against braving the "shower of bullets" by sitting down and awaiting capture. Casualty figures bear Landis out. The rout stopped when soldiers of the Second Corps reached the line of breastworks that they had built the previous evening and turned to deliver fire into their Confederate pursuers. In the few minutes required to reach the breastworks, however, the Second Corps lost 1,700 men captured. The total is higher than their number captured at the Battles of Antietam, Fredericksburg, and Chancellorsville combined. General Grant perhaps best summarized the fighting around Jerusalem Plank Road several days later. Sputtering in frustration, the Union commander described the disaster suffered by the Second Corps as "a stampede."[25]

Embarrassing defeat was a new experience in the Second Corps, and finger pointing began soon after Grant halted the Union offensive two days later. General Birney blamed un-reenlisted veterans, complaining that "they will not fight." Barlow, whose division broke first, blamed

Gibbon. Gibbon, whose division broke last, blamed Barlow.[26] Soldiers in the ranks went to the top and faulted Birney. A New York private fumed that the temporary corps commander "never went to the front during all the fight." The criticism is unfair, since the battle started and ended quickly. Yet the benchmark in the Second Corps was high. Had Hancock been in command, one private argued, "this disagreeable affair would never have taken place."[27]

Still, soldiers often grumbled about their commanders, and their griping might be excused. More ominous for the hard-won cohesion of the Second Corps was the internal bickering. The fault line pitted veterans of the old Second Corps questioning the fighting prowess of veterans of the old Third Corps. Soldiers in Barlow's and Gibbon's divisions did so in part to cover their own poor performance at the Jerusalem Plank Road. Each of their commands had more men captured than Mott's division. More damaging to unit cohesion, Barlow's and Gibbon's soldiers believed that they were in a bad fix because their comrades in Mott's division, holding the very center of the line, collapsed along with everyone else. Lieutenant Colonel Richard Thompson of the 12th New Jersey admitted that the Second Corps suffered from "bad luck" in the recent fighting. However, "Our boys say that the loss is the 3rd Corps' doings and there is a very bad feeling on account of it."[28]

Hancock acknowledged that the fighting at Jerusalem Plank Road had "seriously tarnished the fame" of the Second Corps when he reassumed command later in June. That was the least of it. The Second Corps had fought very badly at Jerusalem Plank Road, demonstrating that the poor battlefield showing before Petersburg on June 18 was anything but an aberration. Even more disquieting, Barlow and Gibbon admitted that they placed little confidence in their men to do anything that required initiative and daring on the battlefield. These were the troops original to the Second Corps, who had fought ferociously in attacking at Antietam, Fredericksburg, and Gettysburg. The news that the greatest days of the Second Corps had passed likely was little surprise to Hancock. While listening to the sounds of the fighting around Jerusalem Plank Road from his sickbed, Hancock attempted several times to ride to the front. The doctors refused consent, only to have Hancock vainly plead, "I am afraid something will happen to the Corps."[29]

Hancock soon found his thoughts more occupied by daily returns. The Second Corps numbered 17,201 men on June 30, a decrease of 40 percent since the start of the campaign. Some of the manpower drain came as volunteers of 1861 left for home. Hancock reported that since May 1, eighteen regiments and 2,095 officers and enlisted men had mustered out. Other losses occurred as substitutes and draftees continued to desert. Confederate pickets taunted their Union counterparts that they ought to "send over the flag and the colonel" of this and that regiment "as the greater part of it had come over to them." To no one's surprise, however, the greatest manpower drain came from the toll taken by the fighting since the army crossed the Rapidan River on May 4. More wounded men were absent during the intervening seven weeks than at any other time in the career of the Second Corps.[30] One officer mournfully noted that the soldiers who had begun the campaign were "now principally in heaven and in hospitals." The rest of the army also had suffered. But by late June, both the Fifth Corps and the Sixth Corps fielded more men present for duty than the Second Corps.[31]

Hancock responded by ruthlessly consolidating units. All eleven brigades in the Second Corps in mid-June underwent reshuffling, some almost entirely. Hancock never officially explained his actions, but an order that he issued upon reassuming command of the Second Corps is revealing. The war had become "one of endurance." Given that Union numbers "are greater" than Confederate numbers, "it is only required that each one should do his duty . . . to insure success." Numbers, in other words, at long last had trumped élan. The most controversial moves came with the consolidation of the Irish Brigade and the Philadelphia Brigade into other commands. The fate of the Philadelphia Brigade likely was sealed when veterans of the 71st Pennsylvania and 72nd Pennsylvania had decided against reenlisting the previous winter. The disappearance of the Irish Brigade was more surprising. The Irish soldiers had not only compiled an exceptionally distinguished fighting record, but also had reenlisted for another term of service. The men were furious. They cussed something "awful" and "swore they would never charge again."[32]

The rest of the Army of the Potomac underwent only minor organizational changes during late June, because losses had been less severe.

Warren, Wright, and Burnside all shifted a handful of units throughout
their commands, as regiments raised at the start of the war continued
to depart the army. The drain in veteran manpower would prove the
undoing of the Iron Brigade that autumn, when with the muster-out of
several of the western regiments, Warren would consolidate the remnants of the once-powerful brigade into another unit. That was weeks
off, however. At least as organized on paper, the three other corps of the
Army of the Potomac were essentially unchanged from Cold Harbor
through Petersburg.[33]

Nearly as much as recent battlefield defeat and reorganization, life
in the trenches before Petersburg sapped the morale of Hancock's men.
The heat was the worst aspect, with temperatures soaring and no rain
falling day after day. When soldiers looked up they saw "brassy" sky and
"hot" sun; when they looked to any side they saw "clouds of dust." A
New Jersey private gave up attempting to describe the unrelenting heat
beyond reporting "hot and dusty" one day and "very hot and dusty" the
next. Even soldiers who managed to find shade failed to escape torment.
One regimental officer claimed that his arms were tired by day's end
from constantly shooing away flies. All the time the men continued to
work on the trenches. By mid-July, the Union lines extended mile after
mile as they curved gradually westward around Petersburg. Soldiers
grimly quipped that in the maze of dugouts and trenches they soon
would not be able to find the way to the front or, once there, to find the
way back again.[34] There were, to be sure, some enjoyable moments, if not
days, around Petersburg. Freely flowing supplies and contributions from
the United States Sanitary Commission improved the diet consumed.
Soldiers enjoyed canned meats, lemons, cabbages, onions, bread, and
other foodstuffs in adequate quantity. The Fourth of July and a National
Fast Day in early August brought music and church services. But, in
general, daily life just had to be endured. Some soldiers simply wished
they were with their families, and speculated that "if I can live a year
from this time you may expect to see me at home."[35]

Soldiers were more than a little tired and discouraged when Grant
sent them north of the James River in late July. Designed to draw Confederate forces away from Petersburg and to threaten Richmond, the
Deep Bottom operation (named after the Federal crossing point over

the James River) represented the first time that Hancock exercised independent command. Normally as aggressive as any Union officer, Hancock acted tentatively. He lethargically put his troops into the field against outnumbered Confederate defenders on July 27, all the while supported by Union cavalry. No extensive fighting occurred, although the presence of the Second Corps close to Richmond did draw some of Lee's men northward. The Second Corps pulled back across the James River on orders from Grant two days later. Rumors swirled that Hancock had acted cautiously because of an "excessive fear" that his men might again suffer a bruising attack like the recent affair at Jerusalem Plank Road.[36] The tentativeness perhaps came back to haunt Hancock a few days later. Confederate forces had pushed into the Shenandoah Valley and were threatening Washington. Grant put General Philip Sheridan, his cavalry commander, in charge of the Union defenses. The assignment of Sheridan to the Valley meant that Meade, who hoped for the command, would stay with the Army of the Potomac. In turn, Hancock, who hoped for Meade's spot, would stay with the Second Corps. Whether Grant picked Sheridan for the assignment because he feared Hancock assuming command of the Army of the Potomac after the uninspiring showing at Deep Bottom is uncertain. When Meade informed Hancock that they both would be staying put, his friend and confidant seemed "quite put out."[37]

Hancock's men arrived back in their entrenchments in time to witness an assault launched on July 30 by the black and white soldiers of the Union Ninth Corps, arguably the most famous of the Federal attempts to storm Petersburg. Burnside's troops ingeniously had dug a mine and placed four tons of explosives under the Confederate lines. The ensuing explosion shot flame, bodies, and equipment into the air and sounded "like the sudden eruption of a vast volcano." Union artillery added to the noise by pounding everything around the now massive crater splitting open the Confederate lines. Burnside's men rushed forward, only to enter the crater and mill about aimlessly. Inside essentially a deep bowl, the Union soldiers proved easy targets when Confederate attackers seized the surrounding rim. The ensuing slaughter was especially brutal when the black soldiers of the Ninth Corps were on the receiving end.[38] To the rear, Hancock's men watched the unfolding disaster in disbelief. Colonel Robert McAllister believed that had the star-crossed soldiers of the Ninth Corps pushed anywhere beyond the crater, "we could have advanced and went into the city." A New Hampshire private argued that had the Second Corps made the assault instead, "the fort would have been held and the result altogether different." Displaying thick skin, Private William Myers asserted that when Union forces finally succeeded in the taking of Petersburg, "or the blowing of it up, it will be our turn to laugh and rejoice."[39]

Tough talk about seizing Petersburg found little form in mid-August, when the Second Corps received orders to board steamers and transports at nearby City Point, Virginia. Rumors flew regarding their final destination. A few men admitted having "no idea where we were going." More men brightly predicted that the Second Corps was bound for Washington, D.C., and the Union defense of the Shenandoah Valley. Assignment to the nation's capital likely meant more fighting, but anything to get away from the trenches and the filth of Petersburg. The rumored change of base likely meant some uncomfortable moments for soldiers who had roundly criticized their fellow countrymen for failing to defend their own homes. Private Ansell White even hoped that "the rebs will be able to throw a few shells into some of the northern cities— and then they will begin to realize that we have a war before us."[40] Such fantasies never came to fruition because Grant intended the steamers as a ruse to draw Confederate attention away from Deep Bottom, the expedition's real objective. Grant believed that another push north of the James River would force the Confederates to weaken the Petersburg front and risk perhaps a decisive Federal assault. Hancock's men discovered their true destination on the early morning of August 14, when the crossing at Deep Bottom heaved into view. Rather than receiving the hoped-for greeting from cheering northern crowds, soldiers were met instead by shells from long-range Confederate artillery fire "dropping in the water around us."[41]

Marching into oppressive early afternoon heat, soldiers of the Second Corps bumped into thinly held Confederate entrenchments running across the Darbytown Road near Fussell's Mill. General Barlow, leading the advance, ordered the men in his division forward as they arrived. The Union assault was helter-skelter, but Barlow believed speed critical in seizing the Confederate works before reinforcements arrived. Many of his men, veterans of some of the hardest fighting at Spotsylvania, Cold Harbor, and Petersburg, thought otherwise. The colonel of one regiment flatly refused to advance beyond a line of captured Confederate rifle pits because the "enemy were in strong force and getting artillery into position." Soldiers in another brigade deployed for an assault with such little enthusiasm that Barlow gave up the idea of sending them forward. Later in the day, Colonel George Macy's brigade struggled across both blackberry vines and gulches and pierced the Confederate lines. After a hand-to-hand struggle the men retreated, their triumph short-lived. Despite the bravery exhibited by Macy's men, Barlow was livid. He complained that soldiers in his division "behaved disgracefully" and failed to "show their usual vigor and gallantry under fire."[42] After glaring at the Confederate lines for the next several days, soldiers of the Second Corps began to retreat back across the James River on the night of August 20–21. The march occurred after a full day spent in blazing sun and, with the onset of darkness, a drenching rain. "This has been a very hard march," one veteran groused, "even for us." Soldiers collapsed to the ground after reaching the Union lines around Petersburg that same morning in "sheer weariness" and "exhaustion."[43]

A few hours later, Hancock's men, almost unbelievably, received orders to prepare to march. They were to journey beyond the left of the Union army and help in the destruction of the Weldon Railroad. The Union Fifth Corps had seized control of the vital Confederate supply route days earlier and, when not fending off Rebel counterattacks, was busily tearing up track. The order to march to the other flank of the army elicited grumbles from Hancock's men, who were tired and worn down. Soldiers murmured that they might as well be called "Hancock's Cavalry" because they were "seldom long at rest." The quip drew wry smiles, but, in reality, Grant was leaning heavily on the entire army to squeeze the Petersburg defenses. The Second Corps had begun to march by the early afternoon, with Mott's Third Division remaining behind to man the Petersburg trenches. The journey south quickly turned into a surprisingly pleasant experience. Soldiers found green corn, apples, and potatoes in the less heavily fought-over countryside. Perhaps even more welcome, commissary officers distributed whiskey rations to help ward off "chill" on one especially rainy afternoon. The destruction of several miles of the Weldon Railroad also brought some enjoyment. The work was hot and dirty, as soldiers lighted fires to bend rails in the middle. Men passed the time by puzzling over ways to try to twist hot iron into the trefoil shape that marked the Second Corps, an attempt to one-up soldiers of the Fifth Corps, who had fashioned heated rails to resemble a Maltese Cross.[44]

The Confederates again attempted to regain control of the Weldon Railroad on August 25, when they launched a new attack. The 6,000 soldiers of the Second Corps fought behind U-shaped entrenchments constructed earlier in the campaign. The men "handsomely repulsed" two Confederate assaults "with terrible slaughter." A third assault pressed forward through heavy fire "with great impetuosity." A Connecticut soldier admitted that "it was a time of terror" as the Rebels continued to close. Under the fierce assault, "it seemed impossible for our men to hold their line."[45] The strain proved too much for soldiers in a recently consolidated brigade in the First Division.[46] Directly in the path of the attack, the men panicked and gave way. The Confederates swept into the gap and opened fire into the flank and rear of the remaining defenders. Some of Hancock's men continued to resist fiercely. Just as many either threw down their arms and surrendered or ran pell-mell to the rear. Fearing Confederate prison more than Confederate fire, one private admitted that the rearward rush marked "the fastest time I ever made." Hancock rode into the wreckage, pleading, "Come on! we can beat them yet," and "Men, will you leave me?" Few men stopped to heed the appeal. By the time that darkness ended the fighting, the Second Corps had suffered 559 men killed and wounded and 2,046 men captured and missing. The numbers of men headed into Confederate captivity were even greater than those captured around Jerusalem Plank Road two months earlier. Making this defeat at Ream's Station all the more dismal, the Second Corps lost twelve colors and nine cannon, several times over the numbers lost at any previous engagement.[47]

Meade attempted to take away some of the sting, and took the unusual step of writing to Hancock later that night. Meade explained that he had not sent any reinforcements during the day's fighting because he was worried that the Confederates were working their way around Hancock's flanks. Should that have happened and no reserves been at hand for a counterattack, the Second Corps might have been cut off from the rest of the Army of the Potomac. The Confederate attackers had launched frontal attacks instead, and Meade went on to express sympathy with Hancock in the "misfortunes of this evening." Hancock and his men should not worry that anyone thought the less of them. "Though you have met with a reverse, the honor and escutcheons of the old Second are as bright as ever, and will on some future occasion prove it is only when enormous odds are brought against them that they can be moved."[48] Meade likely had the recent poor battlefield showings of the Second Corps before Petersburg in mind when he wrote the last line. But he might have recognized the good fortune for the Union that he was not penning the same thought in the aftermath of Pickett's Charge at Gettysburg.

Soldiers of the Second Corps had none of it, and recriminations over the disaster at Ream's Station began almost immediately. Some men admitted that they had fought poorly, but blamed the trying conditions of the Petersburg Campaign. Weeks spent marching and fighting and digging had sapped their stamina, with disastrous results. Still, the Second Corps had successfully fought before against fatigue and long odds. More men took to blaming one another, as they had following the defeat at Jerusalem Plank Road. Brigadier General Nelson Miles, who commanded the First Division due to illness of Barlow, blamed the disaster on the poor performance of recently drafted soldiers in the heavily German 7th New York. He fumed that "it was the fault of a few Dutch cowards that we did not win a glorious victory." Colonel James Beaver agreed. He argued that Union victory was only minutes away when a "full regiment [of] mostly drafted men, was seized with panic, broke from the line and ran, like a flock of sheep."[49] Hancock, suffering the worst defeat in his otherwise distinguished career and seeing his possible hopes for nomination on the Democratic Party ticket for the 1864 presidential election destroyed, railed against everything. Poorly constructed entrenchments, heavy casualties suffered in the Overland Campaign, and late-arriving reinforcements all received his execration. But the poor showing of his soldiers was the main factor in the rout. Still smarting several days later, Hancock admitted that "we ought to have whipped them."[50]

Hancock overlooked several critical factors in the Union disaster at Ream's Station, beginning with his own questionable decision to stay and fight. Hancock might have pulled back his two divisions on the night of August 24. Meade earlier had sent warning that large numbers of Confederate infantry were gathering in the vicinity. Hancock stayed put, however, possibly hoping to win redemption for the recent poor battlefield showings by the Second Corps. Francis Walker, Hancock's biographer and admirer, dismissed the claim for a nighttime withdrawal out of hand. Walker argued that "it was for headquarters to re-enforce or to withdraw him." This is true, but it is unclear what Hancock was hoping to gain by remaining at Ream's Station. By midmorning, his men had stopped tearing up the track to assume a defensive crouch. Hancock might have stood pat because he had a newspaper correspondent at headquarters. The Second Corps appeared to benefit by the late afternoon, when the reporter departed to wire his line. Three days later, the headlines trumpeted a hard-fought Union victory.[51] As news of the bruising Union defeat became more widely known, Hancock had lost the gamble. The embarrassment suffered from the disappointed public expectations far outweighed the little publicity that simply twisting rails and retreating would have garnered.

Conjecture on what a Civil War general might have done sets too high a bar. The Second Corps might have won a tidy victory at Ream's Station anyway, had veteran soldiers fought with more determination. In placing the blame on draftees, the volunteers of 1861 and 1862 avoided some hard truths. Many of them streamed away from the fighting as quickly as had replacement soldiers. In part, this was the fault of Hancock. The reorganization of the Second Corps without regard to previous unit identity had badly hurt morale. The Consolidated Brigade that broke first listed regiments from three previously independent brigades. Equally to blame, many veterans were simply fought out. Soldiers in Lieutenant Colonel Horace Rugg's Second Division brigade refused to attempt to seal off the Confederate breach when ordered to do so by General Miles. These men came from the 15th Massachusetts, 7th Michigan, 82nd New York, and other regiments with distinguished battlefield records. Francis Walker later claimed that had the Union dead and wounded from the fighting at Cold Harbor still been in the ranks, the

Second Corps would have held its defensive lines for as long as needed. More accurately, had the survivors of the fighting at Cold Harbor displayed anywhere near the same level of determination at Ream's Station, they might have scored a Union triumph.[52]

The one thing that soldiers agreed on was that the defeat at Ream's Station was the most embarrassing battlefield setback yet suffered by the Second Corps. Fredericksburg still topped the list as the bloodiest defeat, but soldiers there had won praise for their valor and bravery. The recent poor showing at Jerusalem Plank Road occurred after the Second Corps had lost the advantage of position. No similar excuse eased the sting of the defeat at Ream's. The Second Corps not only was beaten while fighting behind entrenchments, but was beaten by a head-on attack. A private acknowledged that the Second Corps "got the worst whipping that it has had since the war began." A surgeon regretted that "the 2 Corps for the first time in its history behaved disgracefully, some of the men running like sheep."[53] It was perhaps just as well that Hancock's men were unaware of the Confederate take on the fighting. A North Carolina major argued that the Union soldiers his regiment encountered "did not show the determination which had generally marked the conduct of Hancock's Corps." More searing, other triumphant Confederates joked that with so many soldiers of the Second Corps surrendered, Grant would have to send Hancock back home to recruit.[54]

The infighting within the Second Corps soon turned especially vicious, an indication of the emotional toll that the repeated Union failures before Petersburg was taking. Hancock and Gibbon took to quarreling almost as soon as the battle had ended. Demonstrating little tact, Gibbon suggested to Hancock that the entire Second Corps needed to be revamped. If matters continued as before, the Second Corps "could never again do efficient service." Hancock, believing the suggested reorganization to be a comment on his leadership, unloaded on Gibbon and his men. Had the Second Division fought with any spirit at Ream's Station, the entire defeat might have been avoided. Both jibes hurt but, to their credit, Hancock and Gibbon later met to attempt to patch over the hard feelings. They were only partially successful. The two Union officers shook hands and, according to Gibbon, "parted on tolerably good terms." Despite the surface friendliness, however, a "soreness of feeling" lingered between them and "never entirely disappeared"[55]

With time to cool down, Gibbon saw some merit to Hancock's criticism of his division at Ream's Station. Gibbon took punitive action against the 164th New York, 8th New York Heavy Artillery, and 36th Wisconsin, all of which had left their colors on the field. These regiments were deprived of the right to carry new banners "until they show themselves competent to protect them." This was a decidedly harsh measure, since regimental colors were a tangible symbol of soldiers' unit pride. Gibbon lectured the guilty officers and men that they should never have abandoned their colors without a stout fight. Well-disciplined soldiers should recognize as much, and it was a "disgrace for the majority of the command to return from the field of battle" without their flags.[56]

The Second Corps had come into hard luck, because the disciplinary measures undertaken by Gibbon actually worsened, rather than improved, his relations with Hancock. Soldiers in the three affected regiments were outraged, and argued that Gibbon had exceeded his authority as a division commander.[57] Their protest threw the matter higher. In carefully chosen words, Hancock backed his subordinate. He also argued that the practice of depriving regiments that had lost their colors the right to carry new ones should be applied throughout the entire army. Other Union regiments had certainly lost their colors before Petersburg. Meade agreed, but instituted the new policy to begin with Ream's Station. The timing greatly embarrassed Hancock, because it initially punished only the three regiments of the Second Corps. Worse, Meade handed the list of offending regiments to newspaper reporters. Hancock became increasingly grumpy over the turn of affairs, and he expressed little regret when Meade transferred Gibbon to temporarily command the Eighteenth Corps in early September.[58]

The perceived shame became too much for Hancock to bear by later in the month, and he elegantly defended the Second Corps in appealing for Meade to reconsider his new policy. The public singling out of the three regiments, when many others deserved the same fate, was a "slur cast upon the corps." The Second Corps "never lost a gun or a color previous to this campaign, though oftener and more desperately engaged than any other corps in this army, or perhaps any other in the country." The command had captured thirty-four Confederate flags at Gettysburg alone, and over fifty prior to the spring of 1864. Since crossing the Rapidan River in May, the Second Corps "has captured more guns and colors than all the army combined." Its reverses had been few, and began only when the "corps had dissolved to a remnant of its former strength." Hancock concluded by arguing that given the otherwise illustrious record of the Second Corps, "it is in the highest degree unjust by a retrospective order to publish a part of it as unworthy to bear colors." Meade agreed, and allowed all of the regiments of the Second Corps to again carry their flags.[59]

The internal troubles for the Second Corps were not yet finished, and a new fault line appeared when Hancock clashed with Brigadier General Philippe Regis de Trobriand. A French aristocrat, de Trobriand had immigrated to New York before the outbreak of the Civil War. He enjoyed making the rounds on the social scene before taking command of the 55th New York in the spring of 1861. Leading his men without much flash, de Trobriand still managed to win promotion to brigadier general for his battlefield performance with the Union Third Corps at Gettysburg. As much from seniority as from skill, de Trobriand had advanced to brigade command in the Third Division by the late summer of 1864. While he was chatting one evening with other high-ranking officers of the Second Corps, the subject turned to the Peninsula Campaign. De Trobriand wondered if Hancock might have won some of his fame at the Battle of Williamsburg in the spring of 1862 at the expense of generals in the Third Corps. Showing a complete lack of awareness for a man of his social graces, de Trobriand continued to press the point. Hancock finally had enough. "I understand," he snapped. "You are all alike in the old Third Corps. In your eyes, you have done everything in this war, and all others nothing." With that the gathering broke up, although de Trobriand belatedly recognized that he had won few points from Hancock for himself and for the Third Division.[60]

With the Second Corps in a free fall by the autumn of 1864, soldiers resumed siege operations. Elements of the Second Corps participated in a successful attempt to seize Confederate rifle pits around Jerusalem Plank Road in early September and an unsuccessful attempt to break the Southside Railroad in late October.[61] Otherwise, the men dug to expand and strengthen the Union siege lines and stood guard to prevent a Confederate attack. Hancock protested the seemingly never-ending fatigue and picket duty less because of its severity than because the men had little time for drill and rest. "The effect on the morale of the troops," Hancock warned, "I believe to be unfortunate." The digging and watching continued, with Hancock ultimately proved right about low spirits. The lines of the Second Corps were within several hundred yards of the Confederate trenches, and soldiers faced threat of death and injury from sharpshooter and artillery blast. Corporal Amory Allen wearily complained that a soldier could not walk anywhere beyond deeply dug entrenchments "without a ball whizzing past his head." An enlisted man in the 10th New York suffered perhaps the ultimate indignity when he was wounded in the head and fell into a latrine trench. He floundered in the filth for several hours before rescuers came to his aid.[62] All the while those alive and well battled insects and rats and waited out the days behind their entrenchments. Sometimes soldiers made unofficial truces with their Confederate counterparts. More often the men kept their heads down and hoped for the best. For most men the best was reduced to very little by the autumn of 1864. A New Hampshire private longed for the luxury of stretching his arms and legs without fear of Confederate ball sending him on his "long march." Private James Rea of the 52nd New York asked even less, promising, "If my life is only spared it will be all I ask."[63]

Morale waned further in late November, when Hancock left the Second Corps to take command of the Veteran Volunteer Corps. Still being organized at the time of Hancock's appointment, the Veteran Volunteer Corps was to field a minimum of 20,000 volunteers. These men all were to have at least two years' military experience. Grant believed that the military reputation of Hancock would quickly bring former soldiers back into the ranks. "It will prove a success," he boasted, "and will give us a body of men equal to any army now in service." Hancock accepted the new command because he desired independent assignment.[64] The honor made it no more easy to depart the Second Corps, where he had gained distinction since arriving at the Battle of Antietam more than two years earlier. "Conscious that whatever military honor has fallen to me during my association with the Second Corps has been won by

the gallantry of the officers and soldiers I have commanded," Hancock
declared in his farewell order, "I feel that in parting from them I am sev-
ering the strongest ties of my military life." Soldiers felt just as strongly.
One veteran described Hancock as a "man of most perfect bravery." His
departure was "greatly regretted." Another veteran admitted that the
transfer of Hancock "was a matter of much regret" because the renown
of the Second Corps "was so indissolubly connected with his name."[65]

DEFEATING LEE'S ARMY

Soldiers persevered in the autumn of 1864 because they believed
ultimate Union victory was growing ever closer. On their own front,
they now recognized that Petersburg was not going to fall overnight.
Yet Grant clearly was gaining the upper hand. The Union army had
squeezed the Petersburg defenders down to the Southside Railroad
as their only supply route by the late summer. Cut that link, an Indiana private asserted, and the Confederates would have to "starve or
come out and fight us, where we will have the advantage." Private John
Haley believed that whatever option the resourceful Lee chose, he was
finally facing the end. Grant had no intention of backing off from the
Rebel army until he had "choked the life out of it."[66] While the Army
of the Potomac dug closer to victory at Petersburg, soldiers cheered
more immediate triumphs in other theaters of the war. Union General
Sheridan smashed Confederate forces in a series of battles and secured
control of the Shenandoah Valley by mid-fall. Soldiers in the Army of
the Potomac declared that repeated reports of "great victory" won by
Sheridan put them "in high spirits."[67] More glorious, Union General
William T. Sherman captured Atlanta in early September. Atlanta was
a major Confederate supply and transportation center, and its capture
marked a much-heralded Union triumph. Union soldiers around Petersburg celebrated the success won by their western comrades by firing a
"shotted salute" toward the Confederate lines at midnight. The sight of
hundreds of artillery bombs and shells sailing simultaneously across
the nighttime sky was "truly and grandly sublime." For still sleepy-eyed
Confederates who missed the commotion, Union soldiers followed with
shouts of "Atlanta! Atlanta!"[68]

Soldiers also persevered because they remained committed to maintaining the Union. A New York lieutenant found himself day-dreaming about his regiment and "the scenes it had passed through" since its recruitment in 1861. There had been many hard moments over the intervening three years, but he would not have missed them "for a great deal." The hope to "see the end" of "this Slave-holder's Rebellion" still came above all else. Captain James Mitchell declared that he looked forward to the day that peace would again "bless our beloved country." More important than ending the fighting, Union victory would serve as "proof to all nations of the earth that our republican form of government can live through the most fiery ordeal that ever [a] nation had to contend with."[69]

Seeing the war through came easier to Hancock's men as they gained respect for the fighting qualities of black soldiers serving in the Union army around Petersburg. African American soldiers served in two divisions that eventually comprised the Twenty-Fifth Corps. They fought in several battles, most notably in the Union charge at the Crater, and made a good impression.[70] Soldiers in the Second Corps praised their black comrades-in-arms as "good soldiers" and "soldierly looking." When black troops went into battle they made a "grand charge" and "won laurels surpassed by none." Hancock's men still seemed slow to embrace emancipation as a Union war aim, as few of them mentioned it when discussing why they fought. And, like most white northerners, they were not fighting to achieve black equality. Pickets in the Irish Brigade reportedly were so incensed by Confederate taunts of "'keep still, or we'll send a niggah after you'" that they called for a duel between the lines. Yet an Ohio private admitted that in the many Union attempts to take Petersburg, African American troops "fought desperately." Their bravery won the respect and praise of even "the most prejudiced of Negro haters."[71]

Soldiers demonstrated their commitment to preserving the Union, even if accomplished with the help of black defenders, when they voted for Lincoln in large numbers in the presidential election in 1864. Hancock's men gave Lincoln approximately two-thirds of their votes. The tally put the Second Corps in line with the rest of the Army of the Potomac. The decisive results surprised at least Lieutenant Charles Mills. A staff

officer to Hancock, Mills admitted that he felt "great relief" upon learning the outcome of the vote in the otherwise Democratic-leaning Second
Corps.[72] The tallies for Lincoln might have run even higher had soldiers
let go their prewar political loyalties. The 81st Pennsylvania, raised in
Philadelphia, and the 116th Pennsylvania, recruited in Irish-American
neighborhoods, were two of the regiments that went for McClellan. Else-
where Lincoln ran much stronger. In the 26th Michigan, Lincoln won all
but 28 of the 150 votes cast. The President achieved similar success in the
19th Maine, where he carried 129 out of the 160 ballots counted.[73]

Soldiers believed that the reelection of Lincoln sent a clear message of determination, to their delight. Captain Ansell White argued
that Democrats and Republicans would put aside their differences at
the ballot box to concentrate on the task at hand and "make these rebs
succumb." Private Daniel Chisholm explained that he knew that he was
right in voting for "Old Abe and the Stars and Stripes" because, across
the lines, the "Johnnies would take off their hats by the hundreds and
shout for McClellan." Another Lincoln supporter declared with more
than a little satisfaction, "I guess the copperheads and butternuts know
who is who and what is what now."[74]

At the same time, soldiers pondered the downfall of McClellan.
The Union general once had been the idol of the army. He had fallen far
and quickly, and, by the winter of 1864, one New Yorker asserted that
"he is to us only Mr. McClellan." Soldiers gave many reasons for their
former commander's decline in popularity. McClellan had backpedaled
from the peace plank crafted by the Democratic Party, but George Pendleton, his running mate, had not. That was enough for most soldiers.
They railed that they "don't like" Pendleton because he mingled "with
the enemies of his country." Accepting the claim by McClellan that he
would negotiate peace with the Confederacy only after receiving pledge
of reunion, another soldier despaired of war with no end. The Confederates would hold out through thick and thin, recognizing that the Union
lacked the unity and resolve to win the war. With Lincoln safely back in
the White House the war soon would be over because the Confederates
will "see the foolery of trying to hold out longer."[75]

While soldiers discussed the virtues of Lincoln and the flaws of
McClellan, they received a new commander when Major General

Andrew Humphreys took over the Second Corps.[76] Born in Philadelphia in 1810 and graduated from West Point (1831), Humphreys began the Civil War as an engineering officer. He served as staff officer for McClellan before winning division command during the Maryland Campaign. Humphreys led his men well enough at the Battles of Fredericksburg and Gettysburg to earn him promotion to major general and assignment as Meade's chief of staff in midsummer of 1863. With as distinguished a record as any other high-ranking Union officer, Humphreys still had big shoes to fill. At first glance, he appeared a poor second by comparison with Hancock. Slight of build and bespectacled, the new Second Corps commander appeared more "philosopher" than combat officer. Looks were deceiving, though, and Humphreys came into his own in battle. One onlooker described him as "a fighter"; another as "cool and brave in battle." Away from the crash of guns, Humphreys took exceptional care to make sure that his men received adequate food and timely pay. Humphreys also had a short fuse, to the delight of soldiers not suffering his wrath. The general had "flaming outbreaks" during which he spoke with "all the vigor known or unknown to the English language." Humphreys raised his voice to a level that belied his small frame during these outbursts, earning him distinction as "one of the loudest swearers" in the army.[77]

Humphreys soon found his hands full with a command burgeoning in manpower but weak in staying power. The Second Corps swelled in strength over the winter, numbering 21,157 men in late March 1865. No new regiments had arrived, so the increase in numbers was largely due to the return of wounded veterans and the assignment of replacement soldiers. The other five corps in the Army of the Potomac also increased in manpower, reaching 114,335 men in the late winter. The Union army had made good nearly all the manpower losses suffered since the start of the Overland Campaign the previous spring. Yet concerns persisted about the fighting quality of the very soldiers who helped to revitalize the Second Corps, especially the replacements. Veterans griped that the new men were "professional 'bounty jumpers'" who held "very slight" love of the American flag.[78] Many of the old-timers complaining most loudly had themselves been newly arriving soldiers only one year earlier, so some of the grousing was just that. Sometimes, however, they had

Andrew Humphreys. Humphreys faced a difficult challenge in taking command of the Second Corps after the departure of Hancock during late 1864. Diligence in looking to daily necessities, and a creative use of the English language, soon won the hearts of the men. Library of Congress.

reason. Replacement soldiers continued to desert in large numbers, just as they had during the summer. On one night in early December alone, twelve newcomers deserted. Driven to distraction, Humphreys asked his division commanders "whether measures cannot be devised to prevent these desertions or to ensure the shooting of any man making the attempt." Apparently the answer was no, because less than one week later, eight more replacement soldiers deserted. Some of the soldiers who deserted in December and throughout the rest of the winter crossed the lines and surrendered to Confederate pickets. That they were willing to risk life in now notorious Andersonville prison only shows their desperation to avoid battle at all cost.[79]

Division and brigade commanders, normally sources of strength in the Second Corps, were mediocre by the early winter of 1865. There were exceptions, certainly. Nelson Miles, the commander of the First Division and now a major general, Colonel Robert Nugent, leading a newly reestablished Irish Brigade, and Brigadier Generals Robert McAllister and Thomas Smyth were long-serving and talented. The other officers were undistinguished, especially Brigadier Generals William Hays and Gershom Mott, the commanders of the Second and Third Divisions. Hays had received command in early September, when General John Gibbon received permanent transfer to command the Twenty-Fourth Corps. Hays had briefly led the Second Corps following Hancock's wounding at the Battle of Gettysburg. He earlier had been captured while leading a brigade in the Second Corps at the Battle of Chancellorsville, in still unclear circumstances. What was known was that Hays was the highest-ranking Federal officer captured in the fighting. In the Third Division, Mott replaced General David Birney, who now commanded the Tenth Corps. Mott was the only division commander in the Second Corps who had started the Overland Campaign to hold the position as the Union army wintered outside Petersburg. But in this case, he might attribute his longevity to seniority rather than to battlefield skill.[80]

Leadership only became worse at the regimental level, where the casualties suffered during the previous year's fighting still bore heavily. By late March 1865, colonels and lieutenant colonels commanded fewer than one-half of the fifty-seven regiments. Captains, even though only company officers, commanded most of the remaining regiments.

Leadership experience had not been so short in the Second Corps since the winter following the disastrous defeat at the Battle of Fredericksburg. In some cases the lack of rank was unavoidable because of unit consolidation. Captain Patrick Bird commanded the five companies of the 28th Massachusetts, while Captain Frank Houston commanded the two companies of the 1st Minnesota. In more cases these were the officers left after the past year's campaigning. The Corcoran Legion, which had joined the Second Corps after the fighting at Spotsylvania, was worst off by that March, with captains leading four of the five regiments. Leadership experience was far less thin throughout the rest of the Army of the Potomac. The Fifth Corps, Sixth Corps, and Ninth Corps had suffered significant bloodshed over the past year, but to less punishing depths than the Second Corps. More high-ranking officers survived, and colonels and lieutenant colonels commanded most of the regiments.[81]

A slowdown in military operations and an upswing in morale masked the uneven manpower and leadership that characterized the Second Corps outside Petersburg. Grant's army maintained the Union siege lines already established by late 1864. Soldiers of the Second Corps destroyed more track along the Weldon Railroad in early December and helped to repulse a Confederate thrust that had shattered two divisions of the Union Fifth Corps along Hatcher's Run in early February. Beyond these few days of campaigning, Humphreys's men huddled against the cold and helped to hold the left of the Union siege lines.[82] In the meantime soldiers often experienced moments of discomfort and terror. Confederate artillery shells, especially mortar shells, seemed to land close by too often, while sharpshooters continued to pick off the unwary. None of these encounters, however, required the initiative and stamina of a more active campaign. Describing the pace of the Union siege by midwinter, a Connecticut private declared that "everything appears to be at a stand still." Another soldier agreed, remembering the winter months as "monotonous and without special activity."[83]

The rhythms of daily life picked up farther back from the front lines, boosting soldiers' morale for the first time in months. At regular intervals pay arrived and soldiers departed for home on furlough. In between came the holidays. Soldiers celebrated Christmas with "extra dinners and amusements," and St. Patrick's Day with horse racing, sandwiches, and whiskey punch "to the invited guests." These were fine celebrations, but Thanksgiving ranked as the most popular holiday. Soldiers received turkey, chicken, canned peaches, apples, pastry, and other foodstuffs in amounts that "seemed to be inexhaustible" from both the Sanitary Commission and home-front donations.[84] The food mattered less to soldiers than the thought that those at home had not forgotten them. "Could the generous donors have beheld [soldiers'] enjoyment of the good things," one onlooker declared, "they would have been amply repaid for their kindness." Humphreys's men were not dependent solely upon the goodwill of others for entertainment. They visited friends in nearby regiments and listened to music in bands that they had helped to organize. The more athletically inclined played "ten-pins." Participants tied a branch or other nearby piece of wood to two trees "as high as possible from the ground." A fuseless artillery shell hung from the end of a rope attached to the crosspiece. Players scored points by swinging the shell and knocking down pins on the return arc. The game continued until a predetermined score had been reached. Some games never went that long, when Confederate artillery pieces interrupted by "trying to knock down the players with shell not fastened to a rope."[85]

Soldiers put down their ten-pins when preparations for a new Union offensive began in the early spring. Visiting civilians and sutlers headed to the rear lines following a review of the Second Corps on March 24, a sure sign that a campaign was looming. Soldiers optimistically looked ahead to the coming contest, believing ultimate Union victory fast approaching. Confederate deserters brought tales of hunger and other hardships in Lee's army. Newspapers brought word that Union General Sherman's Army of the Tennessee had pushed deep into South Carolina, the very starting point of the war. Humphreys's men recognized that breaking the Confederate army at Petersburg would require ferocious struggle. In the words of a New Jersey captain, "hurt it may." Yet, "we are anxiously awaiting the order to commence the campaign—which we hope will wind up the affairs of the Confederacy." News that the Union Ninth Corps had soundly repulsed Confederate attack around Fort Stedman on March 25 boosted spirits even more. "The rebs were thoroughly whipped," Lieutenant J. E. Hodgkins gloated.[86]

The Union offensive began on March 29, when Grant sent the Second Corps to help smash the Confederate right flank at Five Forks. Under the overall command of General Philip Sheridan, the Federal thrust aimed to unhinge the Petersburg defenses and cut the Southside Railroad. The Second Corps formed the right wing of the Union offensive, and for several days the men battled rainy weather more than Confederate defenders. Soldiers huddled beneath any shelter and wondered whether the ground beneath them "contained more of earth or water."[87] When the clouds broke on April 1, Humphreys's men tried to make sense of the fighting now raging to their front and left. Initial reports ranged from crushing defeat to overwhelming victory. The truth became known as streams of Confederate prisoners began to trudge by, heading for the Union rear. A soldier in the 1st Delaware found the sight of Lee's defeated veterans "a cheering spectacle" because it gave visible proof that "the Rebellion was nearing its 'last ditch.'" Watching the same sight, a chaplain in the 7th New Jersey proclaimed "everything a bright glorious day for the Army of the Potomac."[88]

The Federal victory at Five Forks cleared a path for the Second Corps to push toward the Southside Railroad and the lifeblood of Lee's Army of Northern Virginia. Miles's First Division led the surge forward. Soldiers advancing at daylight on April 2 heard Union artillery pounding the crumbling Confederate defensive lines around much of the rest of Petersburg. "It was a terrible roar," Private Frederick Oesterle claimed; "the cannonading of Fredericksburg and Gettysburg sank into insignificance in comparison with this." The men reached the inner line of Confederate defensive works around Sutherland Station by the early afternoon with a mounting sense of anticipation. The Confederate works were strong, running across a low hill and covering open ground to the front. Yet the men exuded an almost palpable sense that the decisive moment of the campaign and the war was at hand. Regimental officers reported their men as "exhausted" from "loss of sleep" the night before and "rapid marching" that morning. But the "excitement was such that the desire prevailed to charge." Union attackers hastily moved forward, only to just as quickly fall back in the face of heavy fire. Regrouped and rested by the late afternoon, Miles's men again undertook the attack. An onlooking newspaper correspondent declared that this time the men went "sweeping forward across the open space, regardless of the hailstorm of bullets and shell which met their advance." The Confederate defenders broke and fled in confusion. With the triumph, the Union army had struck a near-mortal blow at Lee's army. Reflecting, after a long and distinguished career, on the capture of the Southside Railroad, Miles still glowed. He never would forget "the exultation that thrilled my very soul" as his men stormed the Confederate lines "on that memorable day."[89]

Good news came in abundance in the days that followed the triumph of the Second Corps at Sutherland Station. Humphreys's men joined in the Union pursuit as the Confederate army abandoned defense of Petersburg and Richmond and retreated toward Danville, Virginia. Soldiers were tired and hungry as they moved westward on the morning of April 3. They drew motivation to keep the pace from the signs of Confederate demoralization found nearly everywhere. The roads were strewn with dead horses, broken muskets, and abandoned wagons and other equipment. More telling, soldiers captured Confederate prisoners by the hundreds. This turned into the thousands when the Second Corps arrived at the tail end of the smashing Union triumph at Sayler's Creek on April 6. The next day soldiers reached High Bridge, Virginia. Here they seized a wooden wagon bridge that allowed them to cross the Appomattox River and continue to harry Lee's flanks. Throughout the Union pursuit, soldiers exuberantly described themselves as enjoying "a magnificent day," "an exciting day," and "splendid times."[90]

As impressive as soldiers believed the chase of Lee's army from Petersburg had been, they nervously filed into fields north of Appomattox Court House on the late morning of April 9. The men cooked coffee and discussed a rumor that Lee was in the process of seeking arrangements from Grant to surrender the Army of Northern Virginia. Some men doubted the talk as "too good to be true"; others preferred to wait and see. When news came that rumor indeed was true and that Lee had surrendered, soldiers showed the "wildest enthusiasm." Men cheered and tossed their hats into the air, and bands struck up the tunes of "Home, Sweet Home" and "Yankee Doodle."[91] Captain Ansell White believed soldiers so delirious upon realizing that the war was over that they lost the true meaning of the moment and "acted like insane men."

Humphreys and his staff leading the Second Corps during the review parade of the Army of the Potomac in Washington, D.C., soon after the end of the Civil War. The photograph is the only known unit image of the Second Corps. Library of Congress.

Private Robert Morehead well realized the enormity of the day to him. He declared, "Happy! Happy! . . . [I] never saw such a happier day in my life." Corporal William Baker was equally aware. "Such a happy day and such joyful scenes I never have witnessed," he asserted, "nor do I expect to witness . . . as long as I live."[92]

Soldiers excitedly discussed their role in helping to destroy Lee's army, renewing their pride in the Second Corps for a last time in the war. Humphreys started things off, as the only Union corps commander to issue a congratulatory order to his troops. "I cannot refrain from expressions of admiration at the noble spirit that has animated you throughout," Humphreys praised, "at the brilliant exhibition of the soldierly qualities for which the Second Corps has been conspicuous." The aggressive fighting and marching during the pursuit of Lee "have, I believe, been unexampled." The Second Corps captured thirty-five cannon, fifteen flags, and five thousand prisoners. Additionally, "you have contributed eminently to the general success, and to captures made by other corps, by hemming in the enemy and preventing his escape." Humphreys concluded by declaring, "It is a source of intense gratification to us all—that the greatest military feat of the country was reserved as a fitting climax to the great deeds of that army of which this corps has always formed a part—the Army of the Potomac." Humphreys's men echoed the theme. Captain James Mitchell declared, "What a glorious campaign we have had. I would not have missed it for anything." Private George Senfert agreed, gloating that "I would not have been absent that last campaign for any money in the world." The sight of Lee's army surrendering "was never before witnessed in any war and will perhaps never again be seen for Generations to come."[93]

Soldiers had little time to dwell upon the scene of their triumph. The Second Corps left Appomattox Court House to march to Washington, D.C., on April 11. The journey culminated with a grand review with the rest of the Army of the Potomac down Pennsylvania Avenue on May 23. Five weeks later, Lieutenant Charles Whittier, the assistant adjutant general, closed his books by noting, "Second corps ceased to exist."[94]

MEMORIES

THE POSTWAR ERA

Soldiers of the Second Corps demonstrated a strong desire to record their stories even before the guns had fallen silent around Appomattox Court House. As early as the winter of 1864, soldiers of the 57th New York eagerly snapped up a history of their regiment published in a local newspaper. Lieutenant Cornelius Moore believed that the men were almost as excited about obtaining a copy of the history "as they would their discharge." That fall, veterans of the 15th Massachusetts formed a regimental association only weeks after they had mustered out. The purpose of the organization was to "keep alive the good feeling which always existed among its members while comrades-in-arms." Attendees made toasts and listened to speeches while dining on oysters, beef, chicken, and partridge. Only late evening brought an end to the ceremonies. Participants agreed to meet the next year and beyond, pledging, "Hereafter it will delight us to remember."[1]

WRITING THE HISTORY OF THE SECOND CORPS

Other veterans were nearly as quick to record their stories, and their wide focus initially threatened to overshadow the memory of the Second Corps. By the late 1860s and early 1870s, former soldiers were reminiscing about their military careers. The eagerness to tell about the war suggests that many of these men did not undergo a period of "hibernation," where otherwise hard memories softened. Yet, in the glow of Union victory, Hancock's former soldiers focused mostly on comradeship and remembrance.[2] Veterans of the 14th Connecticut met "for the purpose of perpetuating reminiscences of the past." Those attending a

reunion of the 108th New York pledged to "perpetuate the friendly feeling and aid that so closely allied them in the field." Amid the convivial
atmosphere, veterans expressed determination that their comrades who
had been killed in battle and died of disease and wounds would not slip
forgotten into the mists of time. They exalted their dead as "heroes"
and "martyrs" whose "figures loom up grandly in our memories." One
speaker declared that the dead were dead only in body. "Forgotten! no!"
he exclaimed, "for at the mere mention of our dead comrades, lo! they
are here with us again." Those resurrected in memory did not form "dim
and ghostly procession," but images "so vivid and life-like that we almost
reach forward to grasp in our own their embrowned and sturdy hands."[3]

Some Second Corps veterans had even broader ambitions in
remembering the war. Thomas Murphey published his history of the
1st Delaware in 1866. A chaplain in the regiment, Murphey attempted
to impart moral lessons as much as to trace the unit's history. Those
soldiers who kept their faith in God often survived the war unscathed.
And when a Godly man fell, it was because "he had done and suffered
all that was appointed for him here." Disbelievers who flaunted the Ten
Commandments, most commonly by "taking the name of God in vain,"
often met a grisly end. "Judgment may be slow," Murphey warned, "but
it is sure to follow the guilty." The next year, David Power Conyngham published *The Irish Brigade and Its Campaigns*. Conyngham had
served in late 1862 and early 1863 as an aide to Thomas Meagher, the
brigade's commander. Now, in the postwar era, he hoped to bring recognition to the sacrifices made by Irish soldiers in preserving the Union.
Conyngham described the Irish soldier as a "patriot" who went to war
to protect the "safety and welfare of his adopted country and its glorious
Constitution." The willingness of ethnic soldiers to fight and die for the
Union merited "stronger claim to the protection and gratitude of the
American nation."[4]

Charles Morgan worried whether the memories were becoming too
diffuse, and in the late 1860s, he began to chronicle the Second Corps
and its doings. Morgan had a good vantage point to write from, having
served as the inspector general and chief of staff of the Second Corps. He
also had precedent to draw upon, with surgeon George Stevens of the
77th New York publishing a history of the Sixth Corps in 1866. Stevens

claimed that throughout his writings he had "endeavored without par-
tiality to give the story of the Corps." The attempt proved difficult,
because Stevens wrote the narrative largely based upon his own wartime notes. Readers were through nearly one-third of the book before
Stevens shifted from detailing the career of his regiment and division
to discussing the creation of the Sixth Corps.[5]

Morgan initially made some headway before finding the obstacles
too many to overcome. Most difficult, as an officer in the postwar army,
Morgan felt it a breach of professionalism to speak his mind "on some
points as I would like to." He especially disapproved of General Meade's
failure to reinforce the Second Corps during the Battle of Ream's Station in the late summer of 1864. But even if comfortable offering opinion
freely, Morgan believed that the history of the Second Corps was "so
interwoven" with the rest of the Army of the Potomac as to make its
story "fragmentary" if told alone. He feared writing "not a complete"
history by including either too much or too little about the operations
of the other Union army corps.[6]

Morgan's retreat left the task of directly remembering the war to
the Society of the Second Corps, founded in 1869. The Society of the
Second Corps met with eight other corps societies, including one for the
"Cavalry Corps," at the annual reunions of the Society of the Army of
the Potomac.[7] The declared purpose of the Society of the Second Corps
was to "freshen and perpetuate the memories and history of a common
service in the face of uncommon dangers."[8] Membership in the organization was open to any veteran who demonstrated "faithful service in
the field" in the Second Corps and "an honorable discharge therefrom."
The two-dollar dues were divided evenly between the Society of the
Army of the Potomac and the Society of the Second Army Corps. Many
former high-ranking officers joined, including Winfield Scott Hancock,
Nelson Miles, John Brooke, and Alexander Webb. Attendance at the
meetings varied, but the 1882 meeting in Detroit, Michigan, attracted
fifty participants. Three years later, the Baltimore reunion boasted "full
and enthusiastic attendance."[9]

Members of the Society of the Second Army Corps touted their
wartime service with a great deal of pride. One speaker asserted that "no
other corps ever went further or oftener to the front" than the "grand

15th Reunion, Second Army Corps Association, Brooklyn, New York, May 1884. Veterans such as these helped to preserve the memory of the sacrifices and accomplishments of the Second Corps. Massachusetts Commandery Military Order of the Loyal Legion and the U.S. Army Military History Institute.

old Second Corps." Another man boasted that the hard fighting of the Second Corps resulted in a Union "grander and more august than even its founders dreamed." Those who missed the speeches picked up the same sense of pride when they looked around the meeting room. Hanging on the walls were American flags and a "new Corps headquarters flag," purchased from the Society's funds. Veterans claimed that their corps flag was the first purchased by any of the corps societies. Outside the meeting rooms, members wore an approved corps badge. Fashioned in the shape of the "old trefoil," the badge was, to the eyes of one proud wearer, "beautiful."[10]

Society members proved adept at backroom dealings, and they exercised more influence at the annual meetings than any of their other comrades. Reunion attendees voted on who should serve as president at the following meeting. The first four presidents elected after the initial 1869 meeting (Meade, Hooker, Burnside, and McDowell) all had at one time commanded the Army of the Potomac. Candidates nominated by the Society of the Second Corps carried three of the next seven elections (Hancock in 1874, Charles Devens in 1881, and Humphreys in 1882). These successes were greater than those enjoyed by any other comparable command. The push to have Humphreys elected aroused the most concerted effort, because at no other time had candidates from the same army corps won consecutive elections. Members of the Society of the Second Army Corps received instructions to "present" Humphreys to their colleagues as the best choice for their vote. The Second Corps had its electoral steamroller halted only in the mid-1880s, when Grant swept into the presidency for consecutive terms.[11]

Veterans had opportunity to harness their pride in the Second Corps to the political benefit of Hancock in 1880, when he won the Democratic presidential nomination. Hancock before had sought to top the ticket, only to fall just short in 1868 and 1876. Now, running as a war hero, Hancock helped revitalize a Democratic Party still tainted by charges of wartime treason. Supporters often referenced the general's military exploits. One fellow Democrat reminded his listeners that Hancock "on the field of battle was styled 'The Superb.'" Having served as a Reconstruction commander in New Orleans in the late 1860s, "the soldier-statesman" had achieved "a record as stainless as his sword." Another politician predicted to Hancock that after he became president, "your civic honor will rank with your military achievements."[12]

Many veterans supported their former commander's campaign, especially St. Clair Mulholland. The former colonel of the 116th Pennsylvania, Mulholland had built a wartime friendship with Hancock that carried into the presidential election. Mulholland formed the "Hancock Veterans Association of Pennsylvania" in 1880 to rally the soldier vote. The same year he also penned a pamphlet on the Gettysburg Campaign, subtitled "Hancock's Heroism under Fire." Published in the *Philadelphia Times* and later on its own, the recounting lauded Hancock for his role in winning the "battle that was really the death-blow to the rebellion." Mulholland included in the essay a discussion of Hancock's respectful attitude when Father Corby blessed the soldiers of the Irish Brigade before the fighting in the Wheatfield. The religious ceremony was "more

than impressive, it was awe-inspiring." Of more immediate concern to
the presidential race, the description might have allayed charges that
Hancock harbored anti-Catholic sentiments. Mulholland was not alone
in his efforts to help Hancock, and other Second Corps veterans gave at
least moral support. They sent telegrams reading, "Heartfelt congratulations from old members of [the] Second Corps," "Second Corps ahead
as usual," and "Gettysburg and victory."[13]

Yet, to some veterans, personal concerns and party politics trumped
corps loyalty. William McCarter continued to worry over Hancock's
profanity. Other Union officers had cursed. But Hancock did so nearly
around the clock, and often chose his blue streaks poorly. "Indeed, he
seemed to have got into such a habit of indulging in profane language,"
McCarter speculated, "that he could never address the troops without
taking God's name in vain." Elijah Cavins worried more over a resur-
gent Democratic Party. He admitted that Hancock and many other
northern Democrats had fought bravely and sincerely for the Union.
Still, the "great mass of the Democratic party was either in open arms
against their country, or were giving the enemies of our country aid and
comfort." Union veterans should not forgive. "So it is with Hancock's
old soldiers. They honor him for his gallantry during the war, but now
that he has been put in a flock with those who are afflicted with the rot
of treason, . . . they say farewell." Losing veterans' votes hurt Hancock
as he narrowly lost the election to James Garfield, a congressman from
Ohio and, equally important, a former Union general.[14]

The lack of a strong postwar identification in the Second Corps,
other than among Society members, was not true throughout the rest
of the Army of the Potomac. The critical difference was that other
veterans believed that they had old scores to settle.[15] Often, ironically,
these were with the Second Corps. Former soldiers of the Third Corps
were the most upset, believing that their fellow veterans, as well as the
American public at large, were virtually ignoring their military career
prior to the reorganization of the army in early 1864. They took their
case to the *National Tribune*, a weekly newspaper for Union veterans.
William Deacon of the 87th New York wondered in 1884, "Why do
historians seem to ignore [the Third Corps]?" The answer was that
postwar writers simply lumped the battlefield accomplishments of the

Third Corps in with the Second Corps. "The Second has a record of which any member may well be proud," Deacon admitted, "but I apprehend that veterans of the old Third Corps consider it a higher honor to be able to say that they were members of Kearny's or Hooker's Divisions than of any other command to which they were subsequently attached." The next year, veterans of the Sixth Corps returned to the stone wall at the base of Marye's Heights. The men had stormed the Confederate-defended position while much of the rest of the army was fighting around Chancellorsville. "Standing on top of the heights you are impressed with it being a position impregnable," one observer noted, "but the old Sixth Corps had the honor to take it." This despite the fact that the "same troops that were in position and so ably and successfully defended it," in December 1862 were the "same ones that took the racket" that spring.[16]

The absence of a spirited rejoinder worried members of the Society of the Second Corps. Union veterans were helping to shape the early understanding of the war, and the Second Corps was in danger of standing on the outside looking in. Attempting to turn the tide, Society members ran a column in the *National Tribune* only weeks after the Sixth Corps veterans had reported on their Virginia trip. They grandly hoped every surviving member of the "Iron Second Corps" would join with them in membership. They had much to discuss, since the Second Corps had "amid the smoke of battle and the deadly shock of columns, by its brilliant fighting won the admiration of friends and the respect of its foes." The appeal clearly never brought all survivors into the ranks. Yet the advertisement tapped an interest in remembering the Second Corps. In March 1885, David Newcomb of the 19th Massachusetts admitted that he "feels his heart warm" toward his former comrades. "He thinks that the boys of the old 'White Club Division' should speak up." Late in the same year, S. H. Aldrich of the 1st Rhode Island Artillery wondered "whether the boys of the old Second Corps were all dead, or whether they are ashamed of their record or have fallen into a condition of indifference." Believing that veterans might be "waiting . . . for someone to call out to them," Aldrich recounted the exploits of his battery at Gettysburg. He concluded by declaring, "Let us hear from more comrades of the old Second Corps."[17]

The spark took and, by the mid-1880s, veterans of the Second Corps were actively joining the quest to shape the public memory of the Civil War. The debates over past battles sometimes seemed trivial, but they reflected the desire to have a place in the recounting of the war. William Driver, a former lieutenant colonel and staff officer to Hancock, argued that the Second Corps had participated in the thickest of the fighting around the Bloody Angle at Spotsylvania. Driver was engaging Lewis Grant, who had commanded a brigade in the Union Sixth Corps during the fighting. Grant earlier had suggested that his men had done much of the fighting after the initial Union battlefield successes.[18] Driver gave short shrift to the claims, detailing at length that Hancock's men were in the fight from start to finish. Moreover, at Spotsylvania, the Second Corps was "an organization whose capacity for striking a decisive blow was, I believe, unequaled by any formed at any other time during the campaign."[19]

Other veterans of the Second Corps lobbied hard for their regiments to be included in any listing of units "which lost the most men." The debated swirled until William Fox published his listing of "300 Fighting Regiments" in 1889. Veterans of the Gibraltar Brigade asserted that "in any claim for 'gore'" they "can well come in for a share." Samuel Blummer claimed for the 1st Minnesota the distinction of losing the most men in the fighting on July 2 at Gettysburg. Even if so, E. W. Smith counted that the 5th New Hampshire had suffered 1,500 casualties between 1861 and 1865. That surely must rank the regiment near, if not at, the top of any most-bloodied list. "Can we, the few survivors," Smith concluded, "help it if we feel proud of its record?"[20]

Even more important in helping to initiate renewed discussion of the war, members of the Society of the Second Corps appointed Francis Walker to complete Morgan's now abandoned history. Walker made an ideal choice to restart the project, having served as assistant adjutant general in the Second Corps for much of the war. He had earned high praise, with General Hancock reportedly declaring him "the best Adjutant-General that I ever knew."[21] Walker continued to excel professionally in the postwar era, publishing widely on scholarly topics and becoming the president of the Massachusetts Institute of Technology. The only concern that members of the Society expressed over Walker's

Francis Walker during the postwar era. Walker stirred veterans' memories by preserving in writing the "history of the grand old 2nd Corps." Reprinted from James Phinney Munroe, *A Life of Francis Amasa Walker.*

appointment was whether too much time already had passed to write a truthful history. They encouraged Walker to begin documenting the career of the Second Corps immediately, "while so many who took part in its operations are living and able and willing to give important information pertaining to such a work." To show the importance attached to the effort, members of the organization unanimously voted Walker the "Historian of the Second Corps." Hancock especially was "very desirous" that a corps history be written, perhaps because he had an eye toward another run at the White House.[22]

Walker searched widely for sources, attempting to write for the "general reader" rather than the "military student." Walker acquired much of his material by corresponding with his former comrades about events, places, and dates. He found the exchange straining as he sometimes had to wade through letter after letter to determine "with approximate accuracy the course of a thunderbolt on some summer's evening of 1862 or 3 or 4."[23] The veterans on the other end, however, found the experience cathartic. Lieutenant Colonel James Brady of the Irish Brigade wrote about the failed assault of his men against Confederate entrenchments at Cold Harbor over the course of two days, far longer than the battle itself. Brady concluded by admitting that although "I am now old," his memories of the war "are as bright as they were when I was Horse racing with the other boy officers of the Army of the Potomac." T. F. Brown had served in an artillery battery attached to the Second Corps before resuming work in the postwar era as a merchant. Small in physical stature and painfully shy, Brown seldom mentioned his military service. So reticent was he that "very many of my big friends here do not know that I even was in the army." Brown finally broke his self-imposed silence to "give a little account" of his experiences in the fall of 1863 during the Bristoe Station Campaign. The experience of remembering was enough to satisfy this momentary urge, and Brown gave Walker permission to "throw aside" his account "if it does not serve."[24]

Walker also collected source material provided by former Confederate officers, following an increasingly popular trend in the national discussion of the war. Walker praised high-ranking members of Lee's Confederate army for their "great assistance" in providing "valuable information." Letters from Henry Heth, a former brigadier general, were especially useful to Walker in constructing an account of the fighting at Bristoe Station and Ream's Station. Heth had led the Confederate forces that had clashed with Walker's Second Corps in each of the two engagements. In addition to Heth, Walker quoted from Confederate battle reports printed in the fast-appearing *Official Records*. Most frequently, Walker added to his description of the Union assaults before Marye's Heights by drawing upon the accountings of General Robert E. Lee and several of his brigade commanders. Drawing upon recollections from one-time adversaries might have been controversial, but national publishing houses already had blazed the way. Most notably, Clarence C. Buel and Robert Underwood Johnson, associate editors at the *Century* magazine, had discovered tremendous popular interest in the mid-1880s in publishing both Union and Confederate reminiscences about the war. The essays proved so popular that Buel and Johnson later published many of them in *Battles and Leaders of the Civil War,* a four-volume set.[25]

Walker demonstrated that he would champion the Second Corps in a speech on Ream's Station even before he had finished writing his history. Presenting in early 1884 to the Military Historical Society of Massachusetts, Walker declared that the defeat at Ream's was "of peculiar though painful interest" to veterans of the Second Corps. This was because the defeat of Hancock's command seemed so unexpected. Through the late summer of 1864, the Second Corps "had borne an unusually conspicuous part in the operations of the Army of the Potomac, and had deservedly won a unique reputation for headlong daring and persistent courage." But the rout at Ream's happened, and Walker gave a listing of the many reasons why. Only one focused on the poor resistance offered by many of the Second Corps's soldiers. Even this required qualification. Hancock's command was the most bloodied in the Union army since the start of the Overland Campaign. Had even a handful of the many fallen officers and men been present, rather than their poorly motivated and trained replacements, the outcome at Ream's would have been much different. The Confederates "might have charged till the sun went down, all to no purpose."[26]

Walker utilized a highly selective memory in describing the fighting at Ream's Station, to the benefit of the Second Corps. A range of factors had contributed to the Union defeat, not the least of all the courage and determination of the Confederate attackers. Even Hancock, however, acknowledged a few days after the battle that his men had fought poorly. In claiming that "we ought to have whipped them," Hancock offered no caveats. Walker might have played loose with the facts innocently enough, having suffered capture on the night of the battle while carrying orders to the Union picket line. He therefore missed the bitter infighting that had racked the Second Corps in the late summer of 1864. Walker also likely placed the blame off from the Second Corps to spare any additional embarrassment to Hancock. Even well after the end of the war, Hancock still smarted over the disaster at Ream's. In 1880, Hancock met with Henry Heth. The two officers talked over much about the war, but for the fighting in the late summer of 1864. This was a deliberate decision at least by Heth, who sensed that "if Hancock's heart could have been examined there would have been written on it 'REAMS', as plainly as the deep scars received at Gettysburg."[27]

Three years later Walker finished his *History of the Second Army Corps,* providing a generally straightforward narrative. Walker penned his lines with "intense enthusiasm," but he studiously avoided criticizing anyone in the Second Corps, especially the high-ranking officers. The only hint of second-guessing comes in describing Sumner and his decision to advance into the West Woods at Antietam. Sumner knew that he had little support, yet he advanced Sedgwick's division anyway. Here Walker reminded his readers that Sumner had spent "all his life in the cavalry, he has the instincts of a cavalry commander. What shall stay him?" Still, the resulting slaughter from Sumner's "ill-regulated ardor" is "terrible." Otherwise, Walker even refused to print accompanying portraits of "some of the most meritorious officers" of the Second Corps if a good wartime likeness could not be found. Some prewar "ambrotypes and photographs" were available, but these often were "scarcely less than caricatures."[28] Walker's discretion came to the benefit of Hancock, who had died the preceding year. The listed picture portrays Hancock "how he appeared during the war." This meant "tall, slender, with brown hair mustache and goatee, more spirited and martial in appearance than during the latter days of his life." Along with Hancock appeared pictures of Sumner, Couch, Humphreys, and twenty-seven other officers.[29]

What troops had made the farthest advance against the stone wall at Fredericksburg was the exception to Walker's otherwise attempt at dispassionate analysis. Veterans of Humphreys's Pennsylvania Reserves, who had fought with the Fifth Corps, claimed after the war that they "went nearer to that stone wall (on that day) than any other troops." The point was an especially sensitive one to raise, because Humphreys had openly criticized the Second Corps after the battle for disrupting the advance of his men. Walker aggressively took each charge in turn. Walker had no friendship to lose here as he did with Hancock, because he had suffered Confederate capture several months before Humphreys took command of the Second Corps in November 1864. The claim that soldiers from the Second Corps had irreparably disrupted the Pennsylvanians' advance Walker dismissed as "the tale" of some regimental or company officer attempting to excuse the "breaking of his own command." That soldiers from the Second Corps did not gain the farthest approach to the stone wall went against "a hundred officers who witnessed" the fighting. If one did not believe testimony from the living, Union burial parties later reported that the bodies closest to the stone wall were from the 5th New Hampshire, 69th New York, and 53rd Pennsylvania, all from Hancock's division. Walker concluded by stating that he disliked introducing "controversial matters into this history." But the importance of the matter mandated "a sacred duty to the dead not to keep silence."[30]

Walker's history received some acclaim when published. John Ropes, a well-respected military historian at Harvard, praised the book as the "most interesting" title to yet appear "on the subject of our great Civil War." Another reviewer gushed that the work is the "most romantic, picturesque and stirring example of literature ever inspired by the campaigns of the Army of the Potomac."[31] Perhaps more important to Walker, praise from his fellow veterans was equally flattering. Francis Barlow, a former division commander in the Second Corps and now the secretary of the Society of the Second Corps, could hardly contain his enthusiasm. He declared that everything about Walker's history, from its organization to its accuracy, was "worthy of the highest commendation." The Second Corps was "fortunate" not only in its officers and men and "its actual achievements," but also in "having one within its organization a soldier and scholar so notably fitted to suitably narrate its glorious deeds." Robert Nugent, who led the Irish Brigade as a colonel in 1863–64, thanked Walker for completing the "history of the grand old 2nd Corps."[32] Even veterans of other commands were impressed. Frederick Locke, who had served as a regimental commander in the Fifth Corps, showed that he had no hard feelings over the stone wall controversy. Locke congratulated Walker for not portraying the Second Corps as fighting and winning the war alone. The willingness to credit other commands "shows that you were animated by a true soldierly spirit." Locke concluded by declaring, "Your history is in brief one of the best histories of the Army of the Potomac yet written—and many of our old army friends with whom I have spoken are loud in their praises of your book."[33]

MEMORIALIZING THE SECOND CORPS

Veterans began to feel a pull to return to the battlefields that had defined their military careers about the same time as the publication of Walker's history. National and state officials in part stimulated the urge, appropriating money to build monuments and otherwise commemorate the anniversaries of various battles. More important than the financial assistance, veterans wanted to return. Soldiers of the 14th Connecticut had discussed meeting again at Antietam almost as soon as they had fired their last shots at the 1862 battle. The mood soon turned, however, and by the end of the war, the men "had grown weary of the sight of battlefields." Only in the early 1890s, with the benefit of perspective, did "hearts begin to burn and talk to flow" about returning to the "scenes of [our] war experiences."[34]

Former soldiers showed considerable determination to revisit the scenes of their youth. Reunion committees aroused enthusiasm for the sometimes several-day trip by mailing circulars to veterans and their families. Veterans of the 108th New York were urged to make "the effort of your life" to meet in reunion the "boys of our old brigade" in Maryland and Virginia. The prodding worked, and 150 New Yorkers and their families made the excursion. Rousing enthusiasm was not always enough, and reunion committees also had to secure inexpensive transportation and lodging for their parties. Traveling southward in 1886, 150 veterans and family members of the 15th Massachusetts boarded a specially booked train and steamer. Five years later, on their return to Antietam, the reunion committee of the 14th Connecticut secured a "special train of six well appointed cars" to carry the 300 participants. When touring concluded for the day, the New Englanders paid one dollar each for board and lodging in private houses and hotels in nearby towns. Quality varied, with bachelors receiving more rough-and-tumble quarters than their married counterparts. For the unmarried who balked at paying lodging costs, tents were provided for camping.[35]

Veterans most often returned to Gettysburg because here, they argued, occurred the decisive battle of the war, if not of world history. Charles Devens, the former colonel of the 15th Massachusetts, declared Gettysburg the "high-water mark of the rebellion." More fighting and sacrifice lay ahead, but the "culminating point" of the war "was here and it was here that the tide was turned." John Reilly of the Philadelphia Brigade believed Gettysburg the "Mecca of American Patriotism." The 1863 battle "is conceded by all historians and military authorities to have been the turning point in favor of the Union cause during the war." Other Second Corps veterans only added to the praise. They described Gettysburg as "one of the great battles" of history, ranking right alongside the pantheon of "Marathon, Austerlitz, and Waterloo." The focus on Gettysburg did not leave veterans of the 130th Pennsylvania silent when they visited Antietam in 1894. The Pennsylvanians argued that England and France would have intervened in the Civil War if Lee's army had triumphed in Maryland. Had that happened, the negotiated peace that followed "would have culminated in an inevitable dissolution of the Union."[36]

Veterans became almost boundless in their pride as they walked the ground where their regiments had fought. The most prized terrain was the Angle on Cemetery Ridge, where Pickett's Charge had reached its apogee. Here the "hardest blows were given" and "victory was finally secured." Other Union soldiers had fought bravely across the rest of the battlefield. Yet "there was but one Pickett's charge, and on this spot . . . was that charge met, and the floodtide of rebellion checked."[37] Soldiers who had fought in the Wheatfield reminded listeners of the chaos that they had endured. "Terrible beyond words to picture" was the "tempestuous rattle of the musketry, as it sweeps over our heads in the heavy timber and plows through the ranks." Darkness finally halted the fighting, and the "sickening story of the wheat-field . . . had passed into history." Survivors of the fighting against the Confederate center at Antietam admitted that other spots of the battlefield involved more troops. But nowhere else was the fighting as savage as it was in and before the Sunken Road. The fields on either side of the lane "presented a harvest of death." Blood from the dead and dying soaked the ground, so thickly in some spots that it "lay in pools."[38]

Sometimes there was not enough glory to go around, and veterans sniped at one another. Who had advanced farthest into the Wheatfield caused argument among some soldiers in Caldwell's division. William Glenny of the 64th New York upped the stakes by claiming that his men had advanced "farthest to the front of any who fought on that day."[39] Survivors of the Philadelphia Brigade waged a campaign against published accounts implying that they had quailed before Pickett's Charge. Charles Banes, the unit historian, dismissed the charges as "grossly misrepresenting the heroic efforts of the brigade." Most ferociously, the Pennsylvanians took aim at Lieutenant Frank Haskell. A member of Gibbon's staff during the battle, Haskell had cast the behavior of the Philadelphia Brigade in a decidedly poor light. Veterans of the brigade replied by wondering caustically whether to Haskell and "Dick," his horse, alone "'belong the honor of meeting and repulsing Pickett's Division.'" If so, Dick "was plugged with enough Confederate lead" that Haskell might have made a fortune if he had begun mining operations. Harry Wilson of the 81st Pennsylvania believed that the Philadelphia Brigade received too much public attention anyway. The former captain claimed that his regiment never received the same newspaper acclaim, even though also recruited in Philadelphia, because its commanding officers lacked the necessary political influence. The year upon year of neglect "was somewhat aggravating."[40]

Many veterans let their memories rewrite history to gain the upper hand in these disputes. William Helmbold had the 2nd Delaware taking on practically the entire Confederate army at Antietam. By the late afternoon, "our whole army appears to have been badly cut up and every available fighting regiment had been put in, and things hung in the balance." With one more Union attack possibly forcing the issue, McClellan ordered in the regiment. "We smashed everything in our front," Helmbold recalled, "and practically cut Lee's line in two." This included erasing "pretty nearly all that was left of A. P. Hill's Corps." Never mind that the 2nd Delaware had launched no recorded attack by itself, and that Hill's Confederate soldiers had fought against the Federal left. Helmbold likely had confused the attack by elements of Richardson's division, including his own regiment, toward the Piper house after the storming of the Sunken Road. The point was that Antietam marked the high point in the career of the 2nd Delaware. Helmbold reminded his listeners that, as matters now stood, "historically our name is not mentioned." Survivors must go to Antietam and "put tablets, even if they are but those that we can scratch ourselves, that will serve to show the important work that we did that day." In doing so, "a proper pride may be satisfied . . . and interesting historical facts may be made known."[41]

Helmbold was not alone, and survivors of the fighting around the Angle at Gettysburg were equally prone to enhancing their battlefield accomplishments. The Second Corps had scored one of its greatest battlefield triumphs in the defeat of Pickett's Charge. As the years rolled by, however, the numbers of Union defenders dropped almost as quickly as those of the Confederate attackers soared. Writers seemed to think that the more desperate the odds, the greater the victory. Richard Thompson, the former colonel of the 12th New Jersey, was one. The Second Corps was "singled out" to receive the heaviest artillery bombardment of the war, "to be followed by the most determined charge the Army of the Potomac had ever encountered." A New Yorker remembered that in his regiment there was "hardly enough left" to even form a skirmish line. The few Union defenders faced a Confederate "line moving forward like a victorious giant." Some of Hancock's veterans placed the number of Confederate attackers at 25,000 men, almost double the actual strength.[42] Perhaps not surprisingly given the hyped-up atmosphere, some veterans whose regiments had played little actual role in the fighting on July 3 now thought differently. L. H. Fassett and the other soldiers of the 64th New York had served well to the left of Pickett's Charge. By 1890, however, Fassett proudly declared, "We stopped the tidal wave at Gettysburg." Clinton MacDougall fought to the right of the Angle while serving as the colonel of the 111th New York. That was the pivotal spot in the Union lines, because the main point of the Confederate attack "seemed to be Ziegler's Grove, just on our right and rear." Another regimental officer who served in the same brigade as MacDougall disagreed, claiming that the Confederate attackers were attempting to "march through my command and seize Cemetery Hill."[43]

All this seemed a bit too much for other Union veterans. The counterattack came especially fierce at Gettysburg, where veterans of the Third Corps determined to make a stand. These men claimed that their fight in the Wheatfield and Peach Orchard on July 2 was "*the* battle-day of Gettysburg." Had General Sickles not advanced the Third Corps forward in the early afternoon, the Confederates likely would have gained possession of Little Round Top and turned the Union left flank. The maneuver would have planted Lee "as master, across the communication of the Army of the Potomac with Washington." Only the advanced position and fierce fighting of the Third Corps prevented Lee from achieving his plans. The story of the "self-sacrificing heroism of the Third Corps" was not better known because jealous West Point officers refused to extend any credit to the politician-turned-soldier Sickles. Refusing to concede anything themselves, partisans of the Third Corps claimed that by the end of their fight on the second day, "the field was decided and the battle was won, and the North and the Nation were saved." Pickett's Charge, therefore, although capturing much public attention, was little more than "a thirty minute incident in a three days' contest."[44]

Soldiers from throughout the rest of the Army of the Potomac also chimed in. Veterans of the First Corps, like their comrades in the Third Corps, believed that the "true history" of their command was not yet known. Their hard fighting on July 1, especially in defense of McPherson's Ridge, north of Gettysburg, was the critical moment of the battle. Had their resistance been less stout, "the position of Cemetery Hill could not have been secured and the great battle of Gettysburg would not have been fought." A. D. Stewart bravely trumpeted the contributions of the Eleventh Corps to the Union victory. General Howard's command had fought "until we were all cut to pieces" in attempting to delay the Confederate advance toward Culp's Hill and the Union right on the afternoon of July 1. Stewart was not trying to detract from the battlefield accomplishments of any other command. Yet each Union corps had contributed in its own way to the Union triumph, and "they are entitled each to their share of the credit." Veterans of the Fifth Corps and, even, Berdan's sharpshooters all later claimed that they had made "the" decisive contributions to the success of the Army of the Potomac at Gettysburg.[45]

Hancock's men closed ranks in the face of these competing claims, drawing upon a shared pride in the hard fighting of the Second Corps. As during the war, former soldiers recognized that association with the Second Corps carried its own prestige. Veterans variously described their former command as the "grand old corps," a "gallant corps," a "fighting corps," and the "old fighting Second Corps."[46] Clinton Mac-Dougall, who earlier had claimed that the 111th New York had held the

pivotal spot in the Union lines during Pickett's Charge, now walked
veterans and their families along the rest of Cemetery Ridge. "The
flower of the Army of the Potomac, if such a distinction may be made,"
MacDougall praised, "were upon this crest and lay along these stone
walls—the gallant Second Corps, a corps that up to this time had never
given a color or a gun to the enemy." New Yorkers Clinton Rogers and
Sherman Richardson set forth in poem their affection for the Second
Corps. Rogers penned:

> I was a soldier of the old Second Corps,
> Her grand record, we'll ever adore;
> In passing over to the other shore
> We'll give the countersign—Old Second Corps.

The equally versatile Richardson wrote, in a verse describing the
defeat of Pickett's Charge:

> The "Clover Leaf" again reveals
> Its undimmed fame. The day is won!
> No grander victory neath the sun!

Bloody Lane provided the meeting spot for former soldiers of the 130th
Pennsylvania. Amid the peaceful chirp of birds, survivors recounted
how they and the rest of the Second Corps had led the Union charge
against the Confederate center. This was because Sumner's corps was
the "'Fighting Corps' of the army and for that reason was selected for
the advance in most of the engagements of the Army of the Potomac."
The cost in blood was high, and the casualties of the Second Corps were
"double that of any other corps engaged."[47]

The Second Corps almost always emerged triumphant in these conflicts of memory, primarily because others also recognized their version
of the past. A correspondent for the *National Tribune* attended a reunion
of Union veterans at Gettysburg in 1882. Touring the battlefield, he
declared that the hard fighting of Caldwell's division in the Wheatfield
on July 2 "saved Little Round Top." This was not to overshadow the
fighting of Gibbon's and Hays's men around the Angle on Cemetery
Ridge, which was "an ever-memorable point in the death-struggle of
the war." Almost all the pivotal spots on the battlefield reflected the
glory of the "well-known trefoil of Hancock's men." Three years later,

another sight-seer toured Cemetery Ridge, where the "thin blue line of the Second Corps" had "stood like a wall of adamant." E. H. Ropes of the 3rd New Jersey agreed. The former major in the Sixth Corps watched Pickett's Charge unfold to his left, a sight "such as a man is privileged to look upon but once in a lifetime." Ropes described the suspense as "maddening" as the fight swirled around the Angle. "The fate of the army—of Washington—of the country—hangs upon a thread." When Hancock's men ultimately triumphed, Ropes vowed "never to cease telling my countrymen how that handful of heroes fought for the dear old flag."[48]

Perhaps more impressively, Lee's veterans recognized the hard fighting done by Hancock's men. The Second Corps was "celebrated" and the one "generally chosen by Grant for perilous enterprises." James Poindexter, a former captain in the 38th Virginia, described the role played by Brigadier General Richard Garnett during Pickett's Charge. Garnett led his five Virginia regiments through a "murderous fire" to the stone wall on Cemetery Ridge. Handfuls of Confederate attackers began to push into the Union lines, and "victory seemed within their grasp." But the Union defenders did not turn and run because, in the Second Corps, Garnett had found foemen "'worthy of his steel.'" In the ensuing melee, Garnett fell mortally wounded. The general's blood, shed against the defensive lines of the Second Corps, marked the "high-water mark of the Confederate cause." George Rogers remembered the Second Corps fighting ferociously throughout much of the battle at Ream's Station the following summer. The former colonel had little reason to exaggerate the stoutness of the Federal resistance, because his 6th Virginia had remained in reserve during the fighting. Watching from the rear lines, Rogers described the fire of Hancock's men as "deadly" and "withering." Only the bravery of soldiers in a North Carolina brigade, who launched a third Confederate assault, eventually carried the day.[49]

The Second Corps further won the battle over memory because it had Winfield Scott Hancock. Despite his failed presidential bid, Hancock remained a military hero to his veterans. The men lavished praise on their former commander as "The hero of Gettysburg" and the "most conspicuous officer who served and bled upon this field." A veteran of the 82nd New York claimed that Hancock turned the tide of the battle when he rode along the Union lines during the Confederate bombardment that preceded Pickett's Charge. Soldiers of the Second Corps were "flat on the ground" nervously attempting to wait out the "bursting shells and storm of missiles." Hancock slowly passed along the lines, trailed by an aide carrying the Second Corps banner. The sight of the general moving "coolly amid that direful storm of death quickened the pulse of every soldier." Loud cheers went up, and the men found new courage, knowing that Hancock "was personally attending to affairs." George Vickers of the 106th Pennsylvania put his praise for Hancock to verse:

> Thee and thine! Was there not one whom men have learned to know
> As "the superb," whose deeds resplendent friend and foe alike to praise!
> Hancock! Thy bright genius here did on thy loyal men bestow—
> The fire of thy brave heart, all-pervading as the sun's fierce rays.

Vickers also extolled some of the other Union corps commanders for their contributions to the battlefield victory. But he advised his listeners that if they went "where smoke and death were thickest . . . there was Hancock's ground."[50]

The death of Hancock from complications of diabetes in 1886 brought renewed national attention to both him and the Second Corps. William Sherman, the hero of the Atlanta Campaign and a tremendously popular figure among Union veterans, remembered Hancock as "one of the greatest soldiers in history." Francis Walker described Hancock as "that gallant soldier, that brilliant tactician, that great leader of men." Other mourners declared Hancock the "greatest of all corps command-ers" and a "great political leader and brave officer." When Hancock "first drew his sword at the head" of the Second Corps in the early summer of 1863, he did so before a command that, although already suffering 15,000 casualties, "had never lost a color or a gun." Hancock only took the repu-tation of the Second Corps higher. At Gettysburg, "the grand charge of Pickett's Division fell full upon Hancock's Corps. It was met gallantly and repulsed." After storming the Mule Shoe at Spotsylvania the next year, Hancock's men "hurled back" repeated Confederate counterattacks "with terrible slaughter." There had been some battlefield defeats, most notably with Ream's Station as "that blackest of days." Dark days were few, and John Newton, a former commander of the Union First Corps, praised Hancock for leading the Second Corps to a "splendid record."[51]

Veterans of the Second Corps also notably helped their own cause the next July, when survivors of the Philadelphia Brigade hosted their Confederate counterparts in Pickett's Division at Gettysburg. This was the first Blue-Gray reunion held on the Pennsylvania battlefield, and marked the twenty-fourth anniversary of the defeat of Pickett's Charge. Despite the lapse in time, some northern observers criticized that it still was too early to forgive those men who had taken up arms against the Union. The Philadelphians thought otherwise, and they proved gracious hosts. The nearly seven hundred Union and Confederate veterans and family members mingled freely over the battlefield. Despite the summer heat, one observer noted that the "hurrah business" was "visible everywhere." The reunion culminated at the Angle on the morning of July 3. Underneath the flap of a "faded standard" of the Second Corps, Hancock's and Pickett's men shook hands in "Fraternity, Charity, and Loyalty." The scene played well nationally, and, for many Americans, provided a defining image of national reconciliation. By 1913 and the fiftieth anniversary of the battle, the Angle had become synonymous with Gettysburg and the Civil War. That kept veterans of the Second Corps in the center of national memories as, in the words of distinguished guest and Speaker of the House Champs Clark, "those unconquerable men in blue."[52]

The Second Corps did not win all of its postwar battles, and in the early twentieth century, the Fifth Corps claimed ultimate victory at Fredericksburg. A. K. McClure, a veteran of Humphreys's division, dedicated a monument in 1908 to Pennsylvania soldiers who fell in the various Union assaults on Marye's Heights. McClure used the ceremony to highlight the battlefield sacrifices of the Pennsylvania Reserves. When ordered to the "hopeless task" of assaulting the Confederate defensive lines posted behind the stone wall, soldiers of the two Pennsylvania brigades started forward with "hearty cheers." The results were near-predictable, and, after Pickett's Charge at Gettysburg, the Union advance at Fredericksburg "was the most bloody and disastrous assault of our Civil War." The point was not to criticize Burnside or, for that matter, Lee. Rather, Pickett's Charge at Gettysburg and Humphreys's assault at Fredericksburg "both stand in history, and will ever so stand as high-water marks of the heroism of American soldiery." Yet McClure at least implicitly acknowledged that the tide was running against the Fifth Corps on other battlefields. McClure recognized that other Pennsylvania regiments beyond those in Humphreys's division had fought before Marye's Heights. But these regiments "have or will have monuments on other fields in which they had been in the flame of battle."[53] Go to Gettysburg and Antietam, as many Americans did, and the markers bore the trefoil of the Second Corps.

The pride in the Second Corps especially mattered when veterans discussed the meaning of the Union victory in the war. Hancock's former soldiers believed that the triumph had preserved republican government in the United States. R. H. Forster wondered whether he could adequately describe the accomplishments of his comrades in the 148th Pennsylvania. These men had not only helped to win the Battle of Gettysburg, their heroism had "rendered this field hollowed ground, dear to every lover of liberty and the cause of free, constitutional government." Not to be outdone, Harry Wilson thanked veterans of the 81st Pennsylvania for their "self-sacrificing devotion" in preserving the nation passed down by the Revolutionary generation "as a precious heritage." That the American flag presently floated across the land was proof that the Pennsylvanians had more than met their obligation in perpetuating "our glorious Union."[54]

The plight of African Americans in the postwar South rarely clouded the celebration over the glories of the Union. Veterans often patted themselves on the back for helping to bring an end to the institution of slavery. Talk flowed freely about slavery as a "foul blot wiped out forever" and America as a land "where all mankind are free." Yet the transition of millions of blacks from slavery to freedom simply was not these veterans' concern. William Glenny and Ely Parker were two of the few speakers who broached the topic. Glenny maintained that the results of the war "are stupendous." The Union triumphant "effected the freedom of 4,000,000 bondmen, and effaced from our fair Columbia the foul blot of slavery forever and forever." Glenny sounded almost apologetic, however, in describing the results of the peace. Gaining the constitutional right to vote, members of "the late enslaved race" elected politicians who "create scenes upon the floor of Congress that would disgrace the lowest of New York dives." Parker took a more controversial tack. He praised his fellow veterans for freeing the slaves and making them "citizens, equal with you." The deed accomplished, Parker passed the responsibility. Soldiers were off the hook in the effort to uphold citizenship for blacks, because they had sacrificed enough already in their efforts to "preserve the country and government." To future generations fell the weight, a task that they should strive to achieve "by every means consistent with justice and the general constitution."[55]

The focus on the Civil War as a white man's war placed soldiers of the Second Corps in line with other Union veterans.[56] While the focus remained on the battlefield, especially at Gettysburg, where no African American regiments had fought, white Americans dominated the landscape. Hancock's veterans had little room to maneuver otherwise. They willingly refought old battles because that is where the Second Corps had won its fame. That many of these men had fought to preserve the Union only made their willingness to recognize the contributions of black Union soldiers all the less.

Memories remembered and friendships renewed, veterans published many of their unit histories upon returning from their battlefield reunions. They undertook the task in part to keep alive the memory of their fallen comrades, a theme that stretched back to the earliest regimental reunions. Authors variously dedicated their books to the "cherished memories of our departed comrades" and the "memory of our comrades who died in the bloom of their young manhood before the morning came." Henry Roback comforted his readers by declaring that the dead of the 152nd New York were not even really gone; they simply awaited their comrades at "the last roll call." Many veterans had other purposes, and they wrote to build their historical legacy. Enough war histories had been published by the late nineteenth century to prompt some veterans to ask if there needed to be yet another added "to the apparently endless list of books upon this subject." The answer was a resounding "yes." Histories were needed to set a timeless example. Veterans believed that if readers across the years "shall be led to 'highly resolve'" to emulate the life and examples "of the fathers as herein written, the object of our book will be accomplished."[57]

Veterans were less sure whether to offer opinion on their content. John Day Smith thought "yes" in writing the history of the 19th Maine.

The former Corporal Smith warned that he had been "free in his comments and criticisms." He was not trying to be mean-spirited or judgmental. Rather, Smith was trying to meet a challenge issued earlier by Ulysses S. Grant, that a "truthful history" of the war be written in his lifetime. Smith went on to show the typical disdain that many enlisted men felt toward their superior officers. He especially lambasted General Burnside, General Hooker, and Major General Henry Halleck ("as a commander of troops in the field he was a grievous failure"). Jasper Searles and Matthew Taylor took the opposite approach in their history of the 1st Minnesota. The two veterans argued that it was easy to judge commanding officers and their decisions well after the fact, when more and more materials about the war came to public light. The true test was to try to place oneself in a general's shoes, with the information that he had at hand at the time. Since this was impossible to do, "we have studiously aimed to avoid criticism of commanding officers—preferring to observe the old maxim, 'Say nothing of the dead, unless it be good.'" Ernest Waitt avoided offering any unnecessary comment because it was as easy to fall into flattery as criticism. He believed it best to avoid either pitfall by offering instead "a 'plain, unvarnished tale.'"[58]

Veterans felt fewer qualms about allowing modern-day concerns to creep into their narratives, especially when attempting to correct perceived wrongs. These generally were over relatively minor issues. A New Jersey veteran wanted it made known that a lieutenant in his regiment accused of drunkenness at the Battle of the Wilderness was instead suffering from sunstroke. The malady explained why the officer appeared "scarcely conscious of what he was doing." Louis Chapin told the tale of George Moss, who had gained admittance at a Soldier's Home in Bath, New York, until his death in 1897. The tale had an odd twist, because the George Moss in the 34th New York had suffered a mortal wound in the summer of 1862 at Malvern Hill. Chapin decided to "do some investigating," including writing letters to Moss's boyhood friends and family. The results left "no doubt that the man who died at Bath was a fraud." Another New Yorker was out to settle a larger score. He was furious that some politicians argued against granting veterans' pensions, claiming that the payout would bankrupt the nation. The veteran failed to see the math, reminding his readers "about the great surplus of money they got lined away at Washington in their vaults." The federal government could foot the pension bills, if it really "wanted to do so."[59]

Many of Hancock's men felt a lingering sense of unease about releasing their work to the public, despite their intentions to right the wrong. George Washburn drew heavily upon the words of his former comrades to write the history of the 108th New York. He reminded the "kind reader" that many soldiers had lacked educational opportunity. "They tell their stories in their own way," Washburn cautioned, "always breathing love of country and comrade, but not always in language that would meet the approval of a professor of English Literature." These were men who had fought for their country, and "I am sure that imperfection of this nature will be overlooked." Worries only increased over time. The more veterans aged, the more they worried about their memory as an accurate source. George Whipple tackled the issue head on, admitting in his opening sentence that "thirty-three years is a good while to remember dates and names correctly and it will not be a wonder if I do not keep entirely straight on that line." Penning his memoir in the early twentieth century, James Wright readily admitted that he could not hope to avoid all factual errors. He hedged his bets, however, and offered to correct any passage that his fellow veterans found at fault. They only needed to write, and "I earnestly desire to hear from them all."[60]

Easing some of the concerns, veterans often turned to Walker's history for help when foggy about dates and maneuvers. Charles Page quoted Walker to help describe the assault of the 14th Connecticut against the Sunken Road at Antietam. Ezra Simons relied upon Walker to describe the 125th New York joining the Second Corps in the early summer of 1863, on the march to Gettysburg. In detailing the career of the 140th Pennsylvania, Robert Laird Stewart claimed that Walker's narrative had helped him to achieve "an accurate, concise and readable history." Ernest Waitt was one of the few regimental historians to pick a quarrel with Walker. Waitt believed that Walker diminished the role of his brigade, and by extension the 19th Massachusetts, in storming the Mule Shoe at Spotsylvania Court House. Waitt huffed that any reader of Walker's book came away with the impression that the First Brigade was held in reserve throughout the fighting. Yet, by Waitt's recounting, the unit had gained "the farthest point reached that day."[61]

The glimpse into the war offered by some soldiers-turned-authors conformed to public expectations. Battles often received perfunctory treatment. One veteran of the Appomattox Campaign remembered making a "flank movement" on a pail of pork and beans cooked by a group of Union soldiers to the left of his unit. He failed to remember what regiment the aggrieved men belonged to. "That is one of the things that has passed from my memory; but the beans—no, never." A volunteer of 1861 remembered that regardless how fierce a battle, "there is always a humorous side to it." In this case, a captain called for volunteers to help fill in for wounded and killed artillerymen during the Confederate bombardment that preceded Pickett's Charge. "'Every man is to go of his own free will and accord,' the officer growled. 'Come out here, John Dougherty, McGiveran and you Corrigan, and work those guns.'" Even in lightly treated battles, men suffered harm. But the wounded "endured their sufferings with scarce a murmur." The dead met their fate as the "best soldiers and truest Christians in the regiment."[62] Reflecting the move toward national reconciliation by the late nineteenth century, the Confederates in these accounts were "as brave as ourselves" and "foemen 'worthy of our steel.'" Throughout the struggle "it was American against American." As the estimation of Confederate soldiers rose, that of African Americans fell even lower. Blacks were variously described as "niggers," "darkeys," and "wooly headed pickaninys."[63]

More veterans at least attempted to describe the grim reality of battle, having seen so much of it while serving in the Second Corps. Some gave up in frustration. One man wailed that whenever he tried to write his memoirs, "I get stuck; in fact a battle is a plaguey poor thing to put on paper—some how it won't *fight*." The many veterans who persevered gave a remarkable "feel" to the experience of battle. They vividly recalled the noise and the sights. Confederate artillery shells made a "shrieking" sound as they tore through the air, and the subsequent crashes and explosions seemed "like a volcanic upheaval of nature." Confederate bullets made a "buzzing sound like bees" and, when they struck flesh and bone, made a "tearing sound." A low buzz soon permeated all, as the wounded and dying writhed "under our feet groaning with pain." Soldiers under fire attempted to make themselves as "thin" as possible but, simultaneously, felt as if "ten or twelve feet high." They persevered to fight on, despite seeing wounded comrades with their eyes thrown "fairly out of their sockets" and corpses "slowly cooking" from fires set by exploding artillery shells.[64]

More than the horror of battle, veterans remembered their pride in serving in the Second Corps. John Hays bemoaned that regiments from other commands were claiming some of the glory for storming the Sunken Road at Antietam. A quick run through the casualty lists proved otherwise. "The heaviest fighting at Antietam was done by the 2nd Corps. It made 'Bloody Lane.'" The thickly strewn Confederate dead hid the ground below. The grisly sight was "unsurpassed in warfare and attested to the deadly character of the fight made by the Corps." Benjamin Child declared that it had been his "good fortune" to be "connected with the grand Old Second Corps." The Second Corps "did more hard fighting and lost more men than any other corps of the Army of the Potomac." Throughout the war the Second Corps had "covered itself with immortal honors by its constancy and courage." Richard Thompson pointed out that sometimes an army corps might suffer great loss and yet still fail to accomplish its battlefield objective. This was not the case with the Second Corps. "What it was given to do it did." William Lochren knew that the reason why was because the Second Corps fielded "sturdy veterans."[65]

By the late nineteenth century, veterans began to shift their focus away from the Second Corps toward the role of the United States in the world. William Haines met with many of his former comrades in writing the history of the 12th New Jersey, published in 1897. William Adams reportedly talked on about his sons, who were ready to follow in his footsteps "in support of our own grand old flag, or that of poor suffering Cuba." Another man was "an earnest advocate" of Cuban independence. John Brooke, speaking before the Society of the Army of the Potomac, warned European nations not to take lightly the fighting qualities of American troops. "The American soldier," he opined, "is the best disciplined, is the most efficient, the most thoroughly capable of all the soldiers of all the world." The attention returned squarely back to the Second Corps for one last time in 1897, with the death of Walker. Members of the Society of the Second Army Corps passed a resolution the following year expressing their "high appreciation" for Walker.

The Second Corps had achieved a "position unequaled" in the Civil War because of its hard fighting. "It was fitting, therefore, that those deeds should have a faithful inscription in the annals of the nation." But Walker did more than merely recount names and dates. His work was "so complete, so thrilling and so accurate, as to make it an enduring monument to himself as well as to his comrades-in-arms." Veterans closed by hoping that the "high standard and lofty virtues" possessed by Walker "animate those who survive him to keep untarnished the name of the volunteer soldier of the Second Army Corps."[66] They already had, in monument and in printed and spoken word.

APPENDICES

♣

Appendix 1. Organization of the Thirty-two Regiments and Batteries of the Second Corps, Fall and Winter 1861

BRIGADIER GENERAL
CHARLES STONE'S DIVISION
(*Organized on October 3, 1861*)

First Brigade:
Brigadier General Willis Gorman
15th Massachusetts (early August)*
34th New York (early July)
1st Minnesota (late June)
82nd New York (mid-June)

Second "Philadelphia" Brigade:
Colonel Edward Baker
69th Pennsylvania (mid-September)
72nd Pennsylvania (mid-September)
71st Pennsylvania (early August)
106th Pennsylvania (early November)

Third Brigade:
Brigadier General Napoleon Dana
19th Massachusetts (early September)
7th Michigan (early September)
20th Massachusetts (early September)
42nd New York (mid-July)**

BRIGADIER GENERAL
EDWIN SUMNER'S DIVISION
(*Organized on November 25, 1861*)

First Brigade:
Brigadier General Oliver Otis Howard
5th New Hampshire (late October)
64th New York (mid-December)#
61st New York (early November)
81st Pennsylvania (mid-October)

Second "Irish" Brigade:
Brigadier General Thomas Francis Meagher
63rd New York (early November)
88th New York (late November)
69th New York (mid-November)

Third Brigade:
Brigadier General William French
52nd New York (mid-November)
66th New York (mid-November)
57th New York (mid-November)
53rd Pennsylvania (early November)

Artillery Brigade:
Captain George W. Hazzard
Batteries B and G, 1st New York
Batteries A and C, 4th United States
Battery A, 2nd Battalion New York

Artillery Brigade:
Colonel C. H. Tompkins
Batteries A, B, and G, 1st Rhode Island
Battery I, 1st United States

Notes:

*Dates in parentheses represent the general time period when regiments arrived in Washington.

**McClellan transferred the 42nd New York from Gorman's to Dana's brigade in the winter of 1861.

#The 64th New York replaced the 4th Rhode Island, detached to an outside military department in the winter of 1861.

Source: The arrival date in Washington of each regiment is taken from sources cited in the text.

Appendix 2.1. Organization and Casualties of the Thirty-one Regiments and Batteries of the Second Corps, Battle of Fair Oaks, May 31–June 1, 1862

SECOND CORPS: Brig. Gen. Edwin Sumner

FIRST DIVISION:
Brig. Gen. Israel Richardson
(*Men Present: 8,050*)

First Brigade
Brig. Gen. O. O. Howard (w)
Col. T. Parker
5th New Hampshire
61st New York
64th New York
81st Pennsylvania
Casualties: 557
K 95 W 398 M 64

Second Brigade
Brig. Gen. T. F. Meagher
63rd New York
69th New York
88th New York
Casualties: 39
K 7 W 31 M 1

SECOND DIVISION:
Brig. Gen. John Sedgwick
(*Men Present: 9,362*)

First Brigade*
Brig. Gen. W. Gorman
15th Massachusetts
1st Minnesota
34th New York
82nd New York
Casualties: 196
K 40 W 153 M 3

Second Brigade
Brig. Gen. W. Burns
69th Pennsylvania
71st Pennsylvania
72nd Pennsylvania
106th Pennsylvania
Casualties: 35
K 5 W 30 M 0

TOTAL CASUALTIES OF THE SECOND CORPS:
K 195 (17%) W 895 (76%) M 90 (8%)
1,185 casualties of 17,412 men present (7%)

TOTAL CASUALTIES IN THE THIRD CORPS,
FOURTH CORPS, FIFTH CORPS, AND SIXTH
CORPS:**
K 595 (13%) W 2,701 (70%) M 557 (15%)
3,853 casualties of 34,131 men present (11%)

Third Brigade
Brig. Gen. W. French
52nd New York
57th New York
66th New York
53rd Pennsylvania
Casualties: 242
K 32 W 188 M 22

Artillery Brigade
Capt. G. Hazzard
Batteries A and C
4th United States
Batteries B and G
1st New York
Light
Casualties: 0

Third Brigade
Brig. Gen. N. Dana
19th Massachusetts
20th Massachusetts
7th Michigan
42nd New York
Casualties: 111
K 16 W 95 M 0

Artillery Brigade
Col. C. Tompkins
Battery I
1st United States
Batteries A, B, and G
1st Rhode Island
Light
Casualties: 5
K 1 W 4 M 0

Notes:
*The 1st Company, Massachusetts Sharpshooters also served in Gorman's brigade, suffering a total of one casualty.
**Besides the Second Corps, only the Federal Third Corps and Fourth Corps were engaged during the fighting.
Sources: Number of Men Composing the Army of the Potomac, May 31, 1862, *O.R.*, vol. 11, pt. 2, 204; Return of the Casualties of the Army of the Potomac, Battle of Fair Oaks, *O.R.*, vol. 11, pt. 1, 757–62.

Appendix 2.2. Organization and Casualties of the Thirty-four Regiments and Batteries of the Second Corps, Seven Days Battles, June 25–July 1, 1862

SECOND CORPS: Brig. Gen. Edwin Sumner

FIRST DIVISION:
Brig. Gen. Israel Richardson
(*Men Present: 8,071*)

First Brigade
Brig. Gen. John Caldwell
5th New Hampshire
7th New York
61st New York
81st Pennsylvania
Casualties: 554
K 61 W 356 M 137

Second Brigade
Brig. Gen. Thomas F. Meagher
63rd New York
69th New York
88th New York
29th Massachusetts
Casualties: 493
K 34 W 227 M 232

SECOND DIVISION:
Brig. Gen. John Sedgwick
(*Men Present: 9,144*)

First Brigade*
Brig. Gen. Willis Gorman
15th Massachusetts
1st Minnesota
34th New York
82nd New York
Casualties: 246
K 12 W 82 M 152

Second Brigade
Brig. Gen. William Burns
69th Pennsylvania
71st Pennsylvania
72nd Pennsylvania
106th Pennsylvania
Casualties: 405
K 40 W 193 M 172

TOTAL CASUALTIES OF THE SECOND CORPS:
K 201 (8%) W 1,195 (49%) M 1,024 (42%)
2,420 casualties of 17,581 men present (14%)

TOTAL CASUALTIES IN THE THIRD CORPS, FOURTH CORPS, FIFTH CORPS, AND SIXTH CORPS:
K 1,533 (11%) W 6,867 (51%) M 5,029 (38%)
13,430 casualties of 97,865 men present (14%)

Third Brigade
Brig. Gen. William French
2nd Delaware
52nd New York
57th New York
64th New York
66th New York
53rd Pennsylvania
Casualties: 208
K 3 W 43 M 162

Artillery Brigade
Capt. George Hazzard
Batteries A and C
4th United States
Battery B
1st New York
Light
Casualties: 29
K 0 W 19 M 10

Artillery Reserve
Battery G, 1st New York Light
Batteries B and G, 1st Rhode Island Light
Casualties: 2
K 0 W 0 M 2

Third Brigade
Brig. Gen. Napoleon Dana
19th Massachusetts
20th Massachusetts
7th Michigan
42nd New York
Casualties: 467
K 51 W 262 M 153

Artillery Brigade
Col. Charles Tompkins
Battery I
1st United States
Battery A
1st Rhode Island
Casualties: 16
K 0 W 12 M 4

Note:
*The 1st Company, Massachusetts Sharpshooters, and Russell's Company, Sharpshooters, also served in Gorman's brigade, suffering a combined total of one casualty.

Sources: Abstract from Return of the Army of the Potomac, June 20, 1862, *O.R.,* vol. 11, pt. 3, 238; Organization of Troops and Return of Casualties, June 25–July 2, 1862, *O.R.,* vol. 11, pt. 2, 24–37.

Appendix 2.3. Organization and Casualties of the Forty-five Regiments and Batteries of the Second Corps, Battle of Antietam, September 17, 1862

SECOND CORPS: Maj. Gen. Edwin Sumner

FIRST DIVISION:
Maj. Gen. Israel Richardson (mw)
Brig. Gen. Winfield Scott Hancock
(Number of Men Engaged: 4,029)

First Brigade
Brig. Gen. John Caldwell
5th New Hampshire
7th New York
61st New York
64th New York
81st Pennsylvania
Casualties: 316
K 44 W 270 M 2

Second Brigade
Brig. Gen. Thomas F. Meagher (w)
Col. John Burke
29th Massachusetts
63rd New York
69th New York
88th New York
Casualties: 540
K 113 W 422 M 5

SECOND DIVISION:
Maj. Gen. John Sedgwick (w)
Brig. Gen. Oliver O. Howard
(Number of Men Engaged: 5,437)

First Brigade*
Brig. Gen. Willis Gorman
15th Massachusetts
1st Minnesota
34th New York
82nd New York
Casualties: 740
K 134 W 539 M 67

Second Brigade
Brig. Gen. Oliver O. Howard
Col. Joshua Owen
69th Pennsylvania
71st Pennsylvania
72nd Pennsylvania
106th Pennsylvania
Casualties: 545
K 93 W 379 M 73

THIRD DIVISION:
Brig. Gen. William French
(Number of Men Engaged: 5,740)

First Brigade
Brig. Gen. Nathan Kimball
14th Indiana
8th Ohio
132nd Pennsylvania
7th West Virginia
Casualties: 639
K 121 W 510 M 8

Second Brigade
Col. Dwight Morris
14th Connecticut
108th New York
130th Pennsylvania
Casualties: 529
K 78 W 356 W 95

TOTAL CASUALTIES OF THE SECOND CORPS:
K 914 (17%) W 4,029 (75%) M 411 (8%)
5,354 casualties out of 15,206 men engaged and 18,813 men present (29%)

TOTAL CASUALTIES OF THE FIRST CORPS, FIFTH CORPS, SIXTH CORPS, NINTH CORPS, TWELFTH CORPS:
K 1,243 (16%) W 5,748 (76%) M 599 (8%)
7,590 casualties out of 38,426 men engaged and 68,351 men present (11%)

Third Brigade
Col. John Brooke
2nd Delaware
52nd New York
57th New York
66th New York
53rd Pennsylvania
Casualties: 305
K 52 W 244 M 9

Artillery Brigade
Battery B, 1st New York Light
Batteries A and C, 4th United States
Casualties: 4
K 1 W 3 M 0

Third Brigade
Brig. Gen. Napoleon Dana (w)
Col. Norman Hall
19th Massachusetts
20th Massachusetts
7th Michigan
42nd New York
59th New York
Casualties: 898
K 142 W 652 M 104

Artillery Brigade
Battery A, 1st Rhode Island Light
Battery I, 1st United States
Casualties: 25
K 4 W 21 M 0

Third Brigade
Brig. Gen. Max Weber (w)
Col. John Andrews
1st Delaware
5th Maryland
4th New York
Casualties: 802
K 131 W 623 M 48

Artillery Reserve
Battery G, 1st New York Light
Batteries B and G, 1st Rhode Island
 Light
Casualties: 10
K 1 W 9 M 0

Note:
*The 1st Company, Massachusetts
Sharpshooters, and 2nd Company,
Minnesota Sharpshooters, also
served in Gorman's brigade, suffering
a combined total of 50 casualties.
Sources: Report of Casualties in the
Army of the Potomac in the Battle of
Antietam, *O.R.,* vol. 19, pt. 1, 189–200;
Priest, *Antietam,* 333–43.

Appendix 3. Organization and Casualties of the Fifty-two Regiments and Batteries of the Second Corps, Battle of Fredericksburg, December 13, 1862

SECOND CORPS: Maj. Gen. Darius Couch

FIRST DIVISION:
Brig. Gen. Winfield Scott Hancock
(Men Present: 5,006)*

First Brigade
Brig. Gen. John Caldwell (w)
Col. George Von Schack
5th New Hampshire
7th New York
61st New York
64th New York
81st Pennsylvania
145th Pennsylvania
Casualties: 952
K 108 W 729 M 115

Second Brigade
Brig. Gen. Thomas F. Meagher
28th Massachusetts
63rd New York
69th New York
88th New York
116th Pennsylvania

SECOND DIVISION:
Brig. Gen. Oliver O. Howard

First Brigade**
Brig. Gen. Alfred Sully
19th Maine
15th Massachusetts
1st Minnesota
34th New York
82nd New York
Casualties: 122
K 14 W 77 M 31

Second Brigade
Brig. Gen. Joshua Owen
69th Pennsylvania
71st Pennsylvania
72nd Pennsylvania
106th Pennsylvania
Casualties: 258
K 27 W 203 M 28

THIRD DIVISION:
Brig. Gen. William French

First Brigade
Brig. General N. Kimball (w)
14th Indiana
24th New Jersey
28th New Jersey
4th Ohio
8th Ohio
7th West Virginia
Casualties: 520
K 36 W 420 M 64

Second Brigade
Col. Oliver Palmer
14th Connecticut
108th New York
130th Pennsylvania
Casualties: 291
K 20 W 207 M 64

TOTAL CASUALTIES OF THE SECOND CORPS:
K 412 (10%) W 3,207 (78%) M 488 (12%)
4,107 casualties out of 15,383 men present (27%)

TOTAL CASUALTIES OF THE FIRST CORPS, THIRD CORPS, FIFTH CORPS, SIXTH CORPS, AND NINTH CORPS:
K 874 (10%) W 6,433 (75%) M 1,277 (15%)
8,584 casualties out of 94,846 men present (9%)

Casualties: 545
K 50 W 421 M 74

Third Brigade
Brig. Gen. Samuel Zook
27th Connecticut
2nd Delaware
52nd New York
57th New York
66th New York
53rd Pennsylvania
Casualties: 527
K 60 W 427 M 40

Artillery Brigade
4th United States, Battery C
Casualties: 5
K 1 W 4 M 0

Third Brigade
Col. Norman Hall
19th Massachusetts
20th Massachusetts
7th Michigan
42nd New York
59th New York
127th Pennsylvania
Casualties: 515
K 63 W 419 M 33

Artillery Brigade
1st Rhode Island Light, Batteries A and B
Casualties: 18
K 0 W 18 M 0

Third Brigade
Col. John Andrews
1st Delaware
4th New York
10th New York
132nd Pennsylvania
Casualties: 342
K 32 W 271 M 39

Artillery Brigade
1st New York Light, Battery G
1st Rhode Island Light, Battery G
Casualties: 7
K 1 W 6 M 0

Corps Artillery Reserve
1st United States, Battery I
4th United States, Battery A
Casualties: 7
K 0 W 7 M 0

Notes:
*The numbers of men present in each division are unavailable, except for Hancock's division.
**The 1st Company, Massachusetts Sharpshooters, and 2nd Company, Minnesota Sharpshooters, also served in Hall's brigade, suffering a combined total of 2 casualties.
Sources: Report of Brigadier General Winfield Scott Hancock, December 25, 1862; Return of Casualties in the Union Forces, Battle of Fredericksburg, O.R., vol. 21, 129–42; 229–31; Stackpole, *The Fredericksburg Campaign,* 277.

Appendix 4.1. Organization and Leadership of the Forty-seven Regiments of the Second Corps, Winter and Spring 1863

REGIMENT	COMMANDING OFFICER, JANUARY 31, 1863	COMMANDING OFFICER, MAY 31, 1863
FIRST DIVISION		
First Brigade		
5th New Hampshire	Capt. J. Larkin	Col. E. Cross
7th New York*	Capt. G. von Bransen	NA*
61st New York	Lt. Col. K. Broady	Col. N. Miles
64th New York	Capt. H. Hunt	Col. D. Bingham
81st Pennsylvania	Lt. Col. R. Lee, Jr.	Col. H. McKeen
145th Pennsylvania	Lt. Col. D. McCreary	Col. H. Brown
148th Pennsylvania	Col. J. Beaver	Same
Second Brigade		
28th Massachusetts	Lt. Col. G. Cartwright	Col. R. Byrnes
63rd New York	Lt. Col. R. Bentley	Same
69th New York	Capt. J. Whitty	Capt. J. McGee
88th New York	Maj. John Smith	Col. P. Kelly
116th Pennsylvania	Capt. J. McNamara	Maj. S. Mullholland
Third Brigade		
27th Connecticut	Lt. Col. H. Merwin	Col. R. Bostwick
2nd Delaware	Lt. Col. D. Stricker	Same
52nd New York	Capt. F. Benzler	Col. P. Frank
57th New York	Capt. J. Britt	Lt. Col. A. Chapman
66th New York	Col. O. Morris	Same
53rd Pennsylvania	Lt. Col. R. McMichael	Same

SECOND DIVISION

First Brigade

19th Maine	Maj. H. Cummings	Col. F. Heath
15th Massachusetts	Maj. T. Baird	Maj. G. Joslin
1st Minnesota	Lt. Col. W. Colvill, Jr.	Same
34th New York	Maj. J. Beverly	Col. B. Laflin
82nd New York	Lt. Col. J. Huston	Col. H. Hudson

Second Brigade

69th Pennsylvania	Lt. Col. D. O'Kane**	Same
71st Pennsylvania	Lt. Col. J. Markoe	Col. R. Smith
72nd Pennsylvania	Maj. S. Roberts	Col. D. Baxter
106th Pennsylvania	Lt. Col. W. Curry	Col. T. Morehead

Third Brigade

19th Massachusetts	Lt. Col. A. Devereux	Same
20th Massachusetts	Maj. G. Macy	Same
7th Michigan	Capt. A. Steele, Jr.	Same
42nd New York	Lt. Col. G. Bomford	Col. J. Mallon
59th New York	Lt. Col. W. Northedge	Lt. Col. M. Thoman
127th Pennsylvania	Col. W. Jennings	Same

THIRD DIVISION

First Brigade

14th Indiana	Maj. E. Cavins	Col. J. Coons
24th New Jersey	Lt. Col. F. Knight	Col. W. Robertson
28th New Jersey	Maj. S. Wilson	Lt. Col. J. Wildrick

Appendix 4.1, continued

4th Ohio	Maj. L. Carpenter	Same
8th Ohio	Lt. Col. F. Sawyer	Same
7th West Virginia	Lt. Col. J. Lockwood	Col. J. Snider
Second Brigade		
14th Connecticut	Capt. I. Bronson	Maj. T. Ellis
12th New Jersey	Col. R. Johnson	Col. J. Willets
108th New York	Maj. F. Pierce	Col. C. Powers
130th Pennsylvania	Capt. W. Porter	Col. L. Maish
Third Brigade		
1st Delaware	Col. J. Andrews	Col. T. Smyth
4th New York	Maj. C. Kruger	Lt. Col. W. Jameson
10th New York	Col. J. Bendix	Maj. G. Hopper
132nd Pennsylvania	Lt. Col. C. Albright	Same

Notes:

*The 7th New York mustered out from a two-year term of service in the early spring of 1863, prior to the start of the Chancellorsville Campaign.

**The following officers received promotions in the winter of 1863: Lieutenant Colonel (to Colonel) D. O'Kane, 69th Pennsylvania; Major (to Lieutenant Colonel) G. Macy, 20th Massachusetts; Major (to Lieutenant Colonel) L. Carpenter, 4th Ohio; and Lieutenant Colonel (to Colonel) C. Albright, 132nd Pennsylvania.

Sources: Organization of the Army of the Potomac, January 31, 1863, *O.R.*, vol. 25, pt. 2, 17–18; Organization of the Army of the Potomac, May 1–6, 1863, *O.R.*, vol. 25, pt. 1, 159–60.

Appendix 4.2. Organization and Casualties of the Fifty-four Regiments and Batteries of the Second Corps, Battle of Chancellorsville, May 1–4, 1863

SECOND CORPS: Maj. Gen. Darius Couch

FIRST DIVISION:
Maj. Gen. Winfield S. Hancock
(*Men Present: 5,900*)*

First Brigade
Brig. Gen. John Caldwell
5th New Hampshire**
61st New York
81st Pennsylvania
148th Pennsylvania
Casualties: 278
K 36 W 205 M 46

Second Brigade
Brig. Gen. Thomas Meagher
28th Massachusetts
63rd New York
69th New York
88th New York
116th Pennsylvania
Casualties: 102
K 8 W 63 M 31

SECOND DIVISION:
Brig. Gen. John Gibbon
(*Men Present: 5,196*)

First Brigade
Brig. Gen. Alfred Sully
19th Maine
15th Massachusetts
1st Minnesota
34th New York
82nd New York
Casualties: 20
K 0 W 16 M 4

Second Brigade
Brig. Gen. Joshua Owen
69th Pennsylvania
71st Pennsylvania
72nd Pennsylvania
106th Pennsylvania
Casualties: 0

THIRD DIVISION:
Maj. Gen. William French
(*Men Present: 5,797*)

First Brigade
Col. Samuel Carroll
14th Indiana
24th New Jersey
28th New Jersey
4th Ohio
8th Ohio
7th West Virginia
Casualties: 268
K 29 W 182 M 57

Second Brigade
Brig. Gen. William Hays (captured)
Col. Charles Powers
14th Connecticut
12th New Jersey
108th New York
130th Pennsylvania
Casualties: 319
K 26 W 242 M 51

TOTAL CASUALTIES IN THE SECOND CORPS:
K 157 (8%) W 1,033 (54%) M 750 (38%)
1,940 casualties out of 16,893 men present (12%)

TOTAL CASUALTIES IN THE FIRST CORPS, THIRD CORPS, FIFTH CORPS, SIXTH CORPS, ELEVENTH CORPS, TWELFTH CORPS, CAVALRY CORPS, AND ARTILLERY RESERVE:
K 1,537 (10%) W 8,369 (55%) M 5,205 (35%)
15,111 casualties out of 116,975 men present (13%)

Appendix 4.2, continued

Third Brigade
Brig. Gen. Samuel Zook
52nd New York
57th New York
66th New York
140th Pennsylvania
Casualties: 188
K 13 W 97 M 78

Fourth Brigade
Col. John Brooke
27th Connecticut
2nd Delaware
64th New York
53rd Pennsylvania
145th Pennsylvania
Casualties: 529
K 19 W 64 M 446

Artillery Brigade
Battery B, 1st New York Light
Battery C, 4th United States
Casualties: 27
K 2 W 25 M 0

Third Brigade
Col. Norman Hall
19th Massachusetts
20th Massachusetts
7th Michigan
42nd New York
59th New York
127th Pennsylvania
Casualties: 67
K 4 W 55 M 8

Artillery Brigade
Batteries A and B,
  1st Rhode Island Light
Casualties: 23
K 5 W 18 M 0

Third Brigade
Col. John MacGregor
1st Delaware
10th New York
132nd Pennsylvania
Casualties: 99
K 8 W 80 M 11

Artillery Brigade
Battery G, 1st New York
Battery G, 1st Rhode Island
Casualties: 2
K 0 W 2 M 0

Corps Artillery Reserve
Battery I, 1st United States
Battery A, 4th United States

Notes:

*The manpower figures of the First and Second Divisions are taken from sources listed below, although no comparable listing is given for the Third Division. To determine the manpower strength of French's command, the manpower of Hancock's and Gibbon's divisions were subtracted from the number of men present in the Second Corps on April 30 (16,893 − 11,096 = 5,797).

**During the battle, Hancock temporarily formed the 5th New Hampshire, 81st Pennsylvania, and 88th New York into a brigade (attached), under the command of Colonel Cross (5th New Hampshire).

Sources: Return of Casualties in the Union Forces, Battle of Chancellorsville, O.R., vol. 25, pt. 1, 174–85, and 188–91; and Bigelow, *Chancellorsville*, 473–74.

Appendix 4.3. Organization and Casualties of the Forty-nine Regiments and Batteries of the Second Corps, Battle of Gettysburg, July 1–3, 1863

SECOND CORPS: Maj. Gen. Winfield S. Hancock

FIRST DIVISION:
Brig. Gen. John Caldwell
(*Men Present: 4,006*)

First Brigade
Col. Edward Cross (K)
Col. H. Boyd McKeen
5th New Hampshire
61st New York
81st Pennsylvania
148th Pennsylvania
Casualties: 330
K 57 W 260 M 13

Second Brigade
Col. Patrick Kelly
Col. John Fraser
28th Massachusetts
63rd New York
69th New York
88th New York
116th Pennsylvania
Casualties: 198
K 27 W 109 M 62

SECOND DIVISION:*
Brig. Gen. John Gibbon (w)
Brig. Gen. W. Harrow
(*Men Present: 4,389*)

First Brigade
Brig. Gen. William Harrow
Col. Francis Heath
19th Maine
15th Massachusetts
1st Minnesota
82nd New York
Casualties: 768
K 147 W 573 M 48

Second Brigade
Brig. Gen. Alexander Webb (w)
69th Pennsylvania
71st Pennsylvania
72nd Pennsylvania
106th Pennsylvania
Casualties: 491
K 114 W 338 M 39

THIRD DIVISION:
Brig. Gen. Alexander Hays
(*Men Present: 4,390*)

First Brigade
Brig. Gen. Samuel Carroll
14th Indiana
4th Ohio
8th Ohio
7th West Virginia
Casualties: 211
K 38 W 166 M 7

Second Brigade
Col. Thomas Smyth (w)
Col. Francis Pierce
Lt. Col. James Bull
14th Connecticut
1st Delaware
12th New Jersey
10th New York
108th New York
Casualties: 366
K 61 W 279 M 26

TOTAL CASUALTIES IN THE SECOND CORPS:
K 797 (18%) W 3,194 (73%) M 378 (9%)
4,369 casualties out of 13,631 men present (32%)

TOTAL CASUALTIES IN THE FIRST CORPS, THIRD CORPS, FIFTH CORPS, SIXTH CORPS, ELEVENTH CORPS, TWELFTH CORPS, CAVALRY CORPS, AND ARTILLERY RESERVE:
K 2,358 (13%) W 11,335 (61%) M 4,987 (26%)
18,680 casualties out of 71,079 men present (26%)

Appendix 4.3, continued

Third Brigade
Brig. Gen. Samuel Zook (w)
52nd New York
57th New York
66th New York
140th Pennsylvania
Casualties: 358
K 49 W 227 M 82

Fourth Brigade
Col. John Brooke (w)
27th Connecticut
2nd Delaware
64th New York
53rd Pennsylvania
145th Pennsylvania
Casualties: 389
K 54 W 284 W 51

Third Brigade
Col. Norman Hall
19th Massachusetts
20th Massachusetts
7th Michigan
42nd New York
59th New York
Casualties: 377
K 81 W 282 M 14

Third Brigade
Col. George Willard (k)
Col. Eliakim Sherrill (k)
39th New York
11th New York
125th New York
126th New York
Casualties: 714
K 139 W 542 M 33

Artillery Brigade
Capt. John Hazzard
Battery B, 1st New York Light
Batteries A and B,
   1st Rhode Island Light
Battery I, 1st United States
Battery A, 4th United States
Casualties: 149
K 27 W 119 M 3

Note: *The 1st Company, Massachusetts Sharpshooters also served in Gibbon's division, suffering a total of 8 casualties.

Sources: The casualties of the Army of the Potomac are listed in Return of Casualties in the Union Forces, Battle of Gettysburg, July 1–3, 1863, *O.R.*, vol. 27, pt. 1, 173–87. The number of men in each of the three divisions of the Second Corps is taken from Busey and Martin, *Regimental Losses at Gettysburg*, 31.

Appendix 5.1. Organization and Casualties of the Forty-seven Regiments and Batteries of the Second Corps, Battle of Bristoe Station, October 14, 1863

SECOND CORPS: Maj. Gen. Gouverneur Warren

FIRST DIVISION:
Brig. Gen. John Caldwell
(*Men Present: 3,428*)*

First Brigade
Col. Nelson Miles
61st New York
81st Pennsylvania
140th Pennsylvania
Casualties: 15
K 0 W 11 M 4

Second Brigade
Col. Patrick Kelly
28th Massachusetts
63rd New York
69th New York
88th New York
116th Pennsylvania
Casualties: 15
K 0 W 1 M 14

SECOND DIVISION:
Brig. Gen. Alexander Webb
(*Men Present: 3,276*)

First Brigade
Col. Francis Heath
19th Maine
15th Massachusetts
1st Minnesota
82nd New York
Casualties: 72
K 11 W 60 M 1

Second Brigade
Col. DeWitt Baxter
Lt. Col. Ansel Wass
69th Pennsylvania
71st Pennsylvania
72nd Pennsylvania
106th Pennsylvania
Casualties: 0

THIRD DIVISION:
Brig. Gen. Alexander Hays
(*Men Present: 3,394*)

First Brigade
Brig. Gen. Samuel Carroll
14th Indiana
4th Ohio
8th Ohio
7th West Virginia
Casualties: 8
K 0 W 2 M 6

Second Brigade
Col. Thomas Smyth
14th Connecticut
1st Delaware
12th New Jersey
10th New York
108th New York
Casualties: 68
K 8 W 51 M 9

TOTAL CASUALTIES IN THE SECOND CORPS:
K 50 (9%) W 335 (62%) M 161 (29%)
546 casualties out of 9,383 men present (6%)

Appendix 5.1, continued

Third Brigade
Col. Paul Frank
52nd New York
57th New York
66th New York
148th Pennsylvania
Casualties: 39
K 3 W 17 M 19

Fourth Brigade
Col. John Brooke
2nd Delaware
64th New York
53rd Pennsylvania
145th Pennsylvania
Casualties: 115
K 8 W 36 M 71

Third Brigade**
Col. James Mallon (k)
19th Massachusetts
20th Massachusetts
7th Michigan
42nd New York
59th New York
Casualties: 59
K 5 W 40 M 14

Third Brigade
Brig. Gen. Joshua Owen
39th New York
11th New York
125th New York
126th New York
Casualties: 125
K 12 W 91 M 22

Artillery Brigade
Capt. John Hazzard
Batteries F and G,
1st Pennsylvania Light
Batteries A and B,
1st Rhode Island Light
Battery I, 1st United States
Casualties: 27
K 2 W 24 M 1

Notes:

*The manpower figures of each division are estimates. They were calculated by multiplying the aggregate strength of each division by the percentage of men present, both listed in Walker, for late September. The resulting manpower totals (10,098 men) are slightly higher than those listed for the battle by Warren (9,383 men) in late September.

**The 1st Company, Massachusetts Sharpshooters also served in Mallon's brigade, losing a total of 2 casualties.

Sources: Walker, *History of the Second Army Corps*, 392–93; Report of Major General Gouverneur Warren, October 25, 1863, *O.R.*, vol. 29, pt. 1, 235, 248–50.

Appendix 5.2. Organization and Manpower of the Eighty-nine Regiments and Batteries of the Second Corps, May 4, 1864

SECOND CORPS: Maj. Gen. Winfield Scott Hancock

FIRST DIVISION: Brig. Gen. Francis Barlow	SECOND DIVISION: Brig. Gen. John Gibbon	THIRD DIVISION: Maj. Gen. David Birney	FOURTH DIVISION: Brig. Gen. Gershom Mott	ARTILLERY BRIGADE: Col. John Tidball
First Brigade: Col. Nelson Miles	First Brigade: Brig. Gen. Alexander Webb	First Brigade:* Brig. Gen. J. Hobart Ward	First Brigade: Col. Robert McAllister	10th Massachusetts Light
26th Michigan	19th Maine	20th Indiana	1st Massachusetts	Battery F, 6th Maine Light
61st New York	15th Massachusetts	3rd Maine	16th Massachusetts	1st New Hampshire Light
81st Pennsylvania	19th Massachusetts	40th New York	5th New Jersey	Battery G, 1st New York Light
140th Pennsylvania	20th Massachusetts	86th New York	6th New Jersey	Battery F, 1st Pennsylvania Light
183rd Pennsylvania	7th Michigan	99th Pennsylvania	7th New Jersey	Batteries A and B, 1st Rhode Island Light
Number of Men Present: 1,995	42nd New York	110th Pennsylvania	8th New Jersey	Battery K, 4th United States
	59th New York	124th New York	11th New Jersey	Batteries C and I, 5th United States
Second "Irish" Brigade: Col. Thomas Smyth	82nd New York	141st Pennsylvania	26th Pennsylvania	3rd Battalion, 4th New York Heavy
28th Massachusetts	*Number of Men Present: 2,429*	*Number of Men Present: 3,499*	115th Pennsylvania	*Number of Men Present: 1,601 and 54 Guns*
63rd New York			*Number of Men Present: 2,511*	
69th New York	Second "Philadelphia" Brigade: Brig. Gen. Joshua Owen	Second Brigade:** Brig. Gen. Alexander Hays		
88th New York	69th Pennsylvania	4th Maine	Second "Excelsior" Brigade: Col. William Brewster	
116th Pennsylvania	71st Pennsylvania	17th Maine	11th Massachusetts	
Number of Men Present: 1,676	72nd Pennsylvania	3rd Michigan	70th New York	
		5th Michigan	71st New York	

Appendix 5.2, continued

Third Brigade:
Col. Paul Frank
7th New York
  (battalion)
39th New York
52nd New York
57th New York
111th New York
125th New York
126th New York
Number of Men
  Present: 2,041

Fourth Brigade:
Col. John Brooke
2nd Delaware
64th New York
66th New York
53rd Pennsylvania
145th Pennsylvania
148th Pennsylvania
Number of Men
  Present: 2,355

106th Pennsylvania
152nd New York
Number of Men
  Present: 1,416

Third Brigade:
Col. Samuel Carroll
14th Connecticut
1st Delaware
14th Indiana
12th New Jersey
10th New York
  (battalion)
108th New York
4th Ohio
8th Ohio
7th West Virginia
Number of Men
  Present: 2,853

57th Pennsylvania
63rd Pennsylvania
68th Pennsylvania
105th Pennsylvania
Number of Men
  Present: 3,687

72nd New York
73rd New York
74th New York
120th New York
84th Pennsylvania
Number of Men
  Present: 2,488

Notes:
*The 2nd United States Sharpshooters also served in Ward's brigade.
**The 1st United States Sharpshooters also served in Hays's brigade.
Sources: Organization of the Army of the Potomac, April 30, 1864, *O.R.*, vol. 33, pt. 1, 1037–44; Priest, *Victory without Triumph*, 232–36.

Appendix 6. Organization and Casualties of the Ninety-seven Regiments and Batteries of the Second Corps, Battles around Cold Harbor, June 2–15, 1864

SECOND CORPS: Maj. Gen. Winfield S. Hancock

FIRST DIVISION:
Brig. Gen. Francis Barlow
(Men Present: 7,786)

First Brigade
Col. Nelson Miles
26th Michigan
5th New Hampshire
61st New York
81st Pennsylvania
140th Pennsylvania
183rd Pennsylvania
2nd New York
Heavy Artillery
Casualties: 675
K 87 W 493 M 95

Second Brigade
Col. Richard Byrnes (w)
Col. Patrick Kelly
28th Massachusetts
63rd New York
69th New York

SECOND DIVISION:
Maj. Gen. John Gibbon
(Men Present: 8,595)

First Brigade*
Col. H. Boyd McKeen (w)
Col. Frank Haskell (k)
Brig. Gen. Byron Pierce**
19th Maine
15th Massachusetts
19th Massachusetts
20th Massachusetts
7th Michigan
42nd New York
59th New York
82nd New York
184th Pennsylvania
36th Wisconsin
Casualties: 396
K 78 W 304 M 14

THIRD DIVISION:
Maj. Gen. David Birney
(Men Present: 8,458)

First Brigade^
Col. Thomas Egan
20th Indiana
17th Maine^^
40th New York
86th New York
124th New York
99th Pennsylvania
110th Pennsylvania
141st Pennsylvania
Casualties: 64
K 9 W 27 M 28

Second Brigade^^^
Col. T. Tannatt
4th Maine
3rd Michigan
5th Michigan
93rd New York

TOTAL CASUALTIES IN THE SECOND CORPS:
K 494 (14%) W 2,442 (70%) M 574 (16%)
3,510 casualties out of 26,986 officers and enlisted men present (13%)

TOTAL CASUALTIES IN THE FIFTH CORPS; SIXTH CORPS; NINTH CORPS; EIGHTEENTH CORPS; CAVALRY CORPS, AND ARTILLERY RESERVE:
K 1,351 (15%) W 6,635 (72%) M 1,242 (13%)
9,228 casualties out of 76,889 officers and enlisted men present (12%)

Appendix 6, continued

88th New York
116th Pennsylvania
Casualties: 194
K 20 W 157 M 17

Third Brigade
Col. Clinton MacDougall
39th New York
7th New York
52nd New York
11th New York
125th New York
126th New York
Casualties: 34
K 3 W 26 M 5

Fourth Brigade
Col. John Brooke (w)
Col. Orlando Morris (k)
Col. Lewis Morris (k)
Col. James Beaver
2nd Delaware
64th New York
66th New York
53rd Pennsylvania
145th Pennsylvania

Second Brigade
Brig. Gen. Joshua Owen
Col. John Fraser#
152nd New York
69th Pennsylvania
71st Pennsylvania
72nd Pennsylvania
106th Pennsylvania
Casualties: 122
K 26 W 90 M 6

Third Brigade
Col. Thomas Smyth
14th Connecticut
1st Delaware
14th Indiana
12th New Jersey
10th New York
108th New York
4th Ohio
8th Ohio
7th West Virginia
Casualties: 227
K 46 W 173 M 8

57th Pennsylvania
63rd Pennsylvania
105th Pennsylvania
1st Massachusetts
Heavy Artillery
Casualties: 71
K 10 W 37 M 24

Third Brigade
Brig. Gen. Gershom Mott
16th Massachusetts
5th New Jersey
6th New Jersey
7th New Jersey
8th New Jersey
11th New Jersey
115th Pennsylvania
1st Maine
Heavy Artillery
Casualties: 50
K 5 W 35 M 10

Fourth Brigade
Col. W. Brewster
11th Massachusetts

148th Pennsylvania
7th New York
Heavy Artillery
Casualties: 658
K 80 W 432 M 146

Fourth Brigade
Brig. Gen. R. Tyler (w)
Col. James McIvor
Col. John Ramsey##
155th New York
164th New York
170th New York
182nd New York
8th New York
Heavy Artillery
Casualties: 922
K 122 W 586 M 214

71st New York
72nd New York
73rd New York
74th New York
120th New York
84th Pennsylvania
Casualties: 36
K 1 W 31 M 4

Artillery Brigade:
Col. John Tidball
Battery F, 6th Maine Light
1st Battery, New Hampshire Light
Battery B, 1st New Jersey Light
4th New York Heavy
11th Battery, New York Light
12th Battery, New York Light
Battery F, Pennsylvania Light
Batteries A and B, 1st Rhode Island
Battery K, 4th United States
Batteries C and I, 5th United States
Casualties: 54
K 7 W 47 M 0

Notes:

* The 1st Company, Massachusetts Sharpshooters also served in McKeen's brigade, suffering a total of 3 casualties.

**Byron assumed command on June 4.

#Fraser assumed command on June 12.

##Ramsey assumed command on June 7.

^The 2nd United States Sharpshooters also served in Egan's brigade, suffering a total of 12 casualties.

^^The 17th Maine received transfer from the Second Brigade on June 5.

^^^The 1st United States Sharpshooters also served in Tannatt's brigade, suffering a total of 15 casualties.

Sources: Return of Casualties, Cold Harbor, Bethesda Church, etc., June 2–15, 1864; Field Return of the Army of the Potomac for June 1, 1864, *O.R.*, vol. 36, pt. 1, 166–80, 209; Walker, *History of the Second Army Corps,* 504.

Appendix 7.1. Organization and Casualties of the Ninety-seven Regiments and Batteries of the Second Corps, Battles of Petersburg, June 15–30, 1864

SECOND CORPS: Maj. Gen. Winfield S. Hancock*

FIRST DIVISION:
Brig. Gen. Francis Barlow
(*Men Present for Duty: 5,570*)**

First Brigade
Brig. Gen. Nelson Miles
26th Michigan
5th New Hampshire
61st New York
81st Pennsylvania
140th Pennsylvania
183rd Pennsylvania
2nd New York
Heavy Artillery
Casualties: 558
K 65 W 403 M 90

Second Brigade
Col. Patrick Kelly (k)
28th Massachusetts
63rd New York#
69th New York
88th New York

SECOND DIVISION:
Maj. Gen. John Gibbon
(*Men Present for Duty: 5,540*)

First Brigade##
Brig. Gen. Byron Pierce
Maj. William Smith
19th Maine
15th Massachusetts
19th Massachusetts
20th Massachusetts
7th Michigan
1st Minnesota
42nd New York
59th New York
82nd New York
184th Pennsylvania
36th Wisconsin
Casualties: 1,115
K 51 W 221 M 843

THIRD DIVISION:
Maj. Gen. David Birney
(*Men Present for Duty: 6,837*)

First Brigade^
Col. Thomas Egan (w)
Col. Henry Madill
20th Indiana
17th Maine
40th New York
86th New York
124th New York
99th Pennsylvania
110th Pennsylvania
141st Pennsylvania
Casualties: 373
K 55 W 276 M 42

Second Brigade^^
Col. Thomas Tannatt (w)
Maj. Levi Duff
5th Michigan
93rd New York

TOTAL CASUALTIES IN THE SECOND CORPS:
K 679 (10%) W 3,510 (53%) M 2,435 (37%)
6,624 casualties out of 21,190 men present for duty (31%)

TOTAL CASUALTIES IN THE FIFTH CORPS, SIXTH CORPS, NINTH CORPS, TENTH CORPS, EIGH-TEENTH CORPS, CAVALRY CORPS, AND ARTILLERY RESERVE:^^^
K 1,334 (13%) W 6,425 (65%) M 2,168 (22%)
9,927 casualties out of 98,999 men present for duty (10%)

116th Pennsylvania
Casualties: 221
K 16 W 106 M 99

Third Brigade
Col. Clinton MacDougall
39th New York
52nd New York
57th New York
111th New York
125th New York
126th New York
Casualties: 353
K 52 W 223 M 78

Fourth Brigade
Col. James Beaver (w)
Col. J. Fraser (captured)
Lt. Col. John Hastings
2nd Delaware
64th New York
66th New York
53rd Pennsylvania
145th Pennsylvania
148th Pennsylvania
7th New York
Heavy Artillery

Second Brigade
Col. J. Fraser (Transferred)
Maj. Timothy O'Brien
152nd New York
69th Pennsylvania
72nd Pennsylvania
106th Pennsylvania
Casualties: 365
K 21 W 116 M 228

Third Brigade
Col. Thomas Smyth
4th Connecticut
1st Delaware
12th New Jersey
10th New York
108th New York
4th Ohio
8th Ohio
7th West Virginia
Casualties: 78
K 7 W 62 M 9

Fourth Brigade
Col. John Ramsey (w)
Col. W. Blaisdell (k)
Col. James McIvor

57th Pennsylvania
63rd Pennsylvania
105th Pennsylvania
1st Massachusetts
Heavy Artillery
Casualties: 737
K 83 W 391 M 263

Third Brigade
Brig. Gen. Gershom Mott
16th Massachusetts
5th New Jersey
6th New Jersey
7th New Jersey
8th New Jersey
11th New Jersey
115th Pennsylvania
1st Maine
Heavy Artillery
Casualties: 922
K 122 W 683 M 117

Fourth Brigade
Col. W. Brewster
11th Massachusetts
71st New York
72nd New York

Notes:
*Hancock received sick leave June 18–26. During these eight days, Birney commanded the Second Corps and Mott commanded the Third Division.
**The number of men present for duty for each of the three divisions of the Second Corps is taken from manpower returns on June 21, 1864.
#The following regiments were consolidated during late spring and early summer 1864: 2nd Delaware, five

Appendix 7.1, continued

Casualties: 971
K 64 W 275 M 632

155th New York
164th New York
170th New York
182nd New York
8th New York
Heavy Artillery
Casualties: 690
K 105 W 563 M 22

73rd New York
74th New York
120th New York
84th Pennsylvania
Casualties: 96
K 16 W 77 M 3

Artillery Brigade
Col. John Tidball
6th Battery, Maine Light
10th Battery, Massachusetts Light
1st Battery, New Hampshire Light
Battery B, 1st New Jersey Light
3rd Battery, New Jersey Light
4th New York Heavy
Battery G, 1st New York Light
11th and 12th Batteries,
   New York Light
Battery F, 1st Pennsylvania Light
Batteries A and B,
   1st Rhode Island Light
Battery K, 4th United States
Batteries C and I, 5th United States
Casualties: 144
K 21 M 114 M 9

cos.; 11th Massachusetts, five cos.;
1st Minnesota, two cos.; 10th New
York, six cos.; 59th New York, four
cos.; 63rd New York, six cos.; 72nd
New York, three cos.; 74th New
York, six cos.; 82nd New York, four
cos.; 88th New York, three cos.; 4th
Ohio, four cos.; 7th West Virginia,
four cos.

##The 1st Company, Massachusetts
Sharpshooters also served in
Pierce's brigade, losing a total of one
casualty.

^The 2nd United States Sharpshooters
also served in Egan's brigade, losing
a total of 72 casualties.

^^The 1st United States Sharpshooters
also served in Tannatt's brigade,
losing a total of 34 casualties.

^^^On paper, the Tenth Corps and
Eighteenth Corps were part of the
Union Army of the James.

Sources: Return of Casualties in
the Union Forces, June 15–30,
1864; Abstract from Tri-Monthly
Returns, June 30, 1864, O.R., vol. 40,
pt. 1, 177, 218–38; David Birney to
Seth Williams, June 21, 1864, O.R.,
vol. 40 pt. 2, 277.

Appendix 7.2. Organization and Casualties of the Seventy-five Regiments and Batteries of the Second Corps, Appomattox Campaign, March 29–April 9, 1865

SECOND CORPS: Maj. Gen. Andrew Humphreys

FIRST DIVISION:
Maj. Gen. Nelson Miles
(Men Present for Duty: 7,192)

First Brigade
Col. George Scott
26th Michigan
5th New Hampshire*
61st New York
81st Pennsylvania
140th Pennsylvania
2nd New York
Heavy Artillery
Casualties: 579
K 45 W 247 M 287

Second Brigade
Col. Robert Nugent
28th Massachusetts
63rd New York
69th New York
88th New York
4th New York

SECOND DIVISION:
Brig. Gen. William Hays
Brig. Gen. Thomas Smith
(Men Present for Duty: 5,999)

First Brigade
Col. William Olmsted
19th Maine
19th Massachusetts
20th Massachusetts
7th Michigan
1st Minnesota
59th New York
152nd New York
184th Pennsylvania
36th Wisconsin
Casualties: 26
K 2 W 24 M 0

Second Brigade
Col. James McIvor
155th New York
164th New York

THIRD DIVISION:
Maj. Gen. Gershom Mott (w)
Brig. Gen. Regis de Trobriand
(Men Present for Duty: 7,776)

First Brigade
Brig. Gen. R. de Trobriand
Col. Russell Shepherd
20th Indiana
40th New York
73rd New York
86th New York
124th New York
99th Pennsylvania
110th Pennsylvania
1st Maine
Heavy Artillery
Casualties: 182
K 26 W 134 M 22

Second Brigade
Brig. Gen. Byron Pierce
17th Maine

TOTAL CASUALTIES IN THE SECOND CORPS:
K 197 (11%) W 1,228 (67%) M 408 (22%)
1,833 casualties out of 21,167 men present for duty (9%)

TOTAL CASUALTIES IN THE FIFTH CORPS, SIXTH CORPS, NINTH CORPS, TWENTY-FOURTH CORPS, TWENTY-FIFTH CORPS, CAVALRY CORPS, AND ARTILLERY RESERVE:**
K 1,119 (13%) W 6,522 (73%) M 1,306 (10%)
8,947 casualties out of 93,168 men present for duty (10%)

Appendix 7.2, continued

Heavy Artillery
Casualties: 147
K 12 W 132 M 3

Third Brigade
Brig. Gen. Henry Madill (w)
Brig. Gen. C. MacDougall
7th New York
39th New York
52nd New York
111th New York
125th New York
126th New York
Casualties: 356
K 48 W 278 M 30

Fourth Brigade
Brig. Gen. John Ramsey
64th New York
66th New York
53rd Pennsylvania
116th Pennsylvania
145th Pennsylvania
148th Pennsylvania
183rd Pennsylvania

170th New York
182nd New York
8th New York
Heavy Artillery
Casualties: 7
K 0 W 7 M 0

Third Brigade
Brig. Gen. T. Smyth (mw)
Col. Daniel Woodall
14th Connecticut
1st Delaware
12th New Jersey
10th New York
108th New York
4th Ohio
69th Pennsylvania
106th Pennsylvania
7th West Virginia
Casualties: 31
K 2 W 28 M 1

5th Michigan
93rd New York
57th Pennsylvania
105th Pennsylvania
141st Pennsylvania
1st Massachusetts
Heavy Artillery
Casualties: 127
K 15 W 111 M 1

Third Brigade
Brig. Gen. Robert McAllister
11th Massachusetts
7th New Jersey
8th New Jersey
11th New Jersey
120th New York
Casualties: 149
K 12 W 88 M 49

Artillery Brigade
Lt. Col. John Hazzard
10th Battery, Massachusetts Light
Battery M, 1st New Hampshire
Battery B, 1st New Jersey Light

Casualties: 214
K 34 W 166 M 14

11th Battery, New York Light
Companies C and L,
   4th New York Heavy
Battery B, 1st Rhode Island
Battery K, 4th United States
Casualties: 12
K 0 W 11 M 1

Notes:

*The following regiments were consolidated during early spring 1864: 28th Massachusetts, five cos.; 1st Minnesota, two cos.; 5th New Hampshire, battalion; 10th New York, battalion; 63rd New York, six cos.; 64th New York, battalion; 88th New York, five cos.; 126th New York, battalion; 4th Ohio, four cos.; 106th Pennsylvania, three cos.; 7th West Virginia, four cos.

**On paper, the Twenty-Fourth Corps and Twenty-Fifth Corps were part of the Union Army of the James.

Sources: Major General Andrew Humphreys to Major General Webb, March 30, 1865, *O.R.*, vol. 46, pt. 2, 291; Abstract from Tri-Monthly Return, March 31, 1865; Return of Casualties in the Union Forces, March 29–April 9, 1865, *O.R.*, vol. 46, pt. 1, 61–62, 581–97.

NOTES

PREFACE

1. Among the best and most recent unit histories include: Coffin, *Nine Months to Gettysburg*; Daniel, *Days of Glory*; Dreese, *The 151st Pennsylvania Volunteers at Gettysburg*; Gaff, *On Many a Bloody Field*; Gibbs, *Three Years in the Bloody Eleventh*; Glatthaar, *The March to the Sea and Beyond*; Hagerty, *Collis' Zouaves*; Herdegen, *The Men Stood Like Iron*; Jones, *Giants in the Cornfield*; Overmyer, *A Stupendous Effort*; Wert, *The Sword of Lincoln*; and Woodworth, *Nothing but Victory*. A standard history of the Iron Brigade remains Nolan, *The Iron Brigade*. For a comparative work, see Wert, *A Brotherhood of Valor*. Unit histories on the Second Corps are cited in the text.

2. Union veterans authored six corps histories: Stevens, *Three Years in the Sixth Corps*; Woodbury, *Major General Ambrose Burnside and the Ninth Army Corps*; Irwin, *History of the Nineteenth Army Corps*; Hyde, *Following the Greek Cross*; and Powell, *The Fifth Army Corps (Army of the Potomac)*; Walker, *History of the Second Army Corps in the Army of the Potomac*. For a recent study of the Union Sixth Corps during the Chancellorsville Campaign, see Parsons, *The Union Sixth Army Corps in the Chancellorsville Campaign*.

3. For a brief history of each Union corps, see Welcher, *The Union Army*.

4. Walker, *History of the Second Army Corps in the Army of the Potomac*, 1–2; Fox, *Regimental Losses*, 67; Rhea, *The Battle of the Wilderness*, 38. Also see Wert, *The Sword of Lincoln*, 412.

5. Walker, *History of the Second Army Corps*, iv; Fox, *Regimental Losses*, 69.

6. The literature on why Civil War soldiers fought is extensive. Two of the more influential, and controversial, early works are: Wiley, *The Life of Billy Yank*; and Linderman, *Embattled Courage*. Wiley argues that soldiers had little idea why they were fighting, other than for their comrades. Linderman argues that a cluster of values, centering around the concept of courage, initially motivated soldiers. By the last full year of the war, however, courage had lost its meaning. Linderman asserts that the war "regularly betrayed the confidence with which Union and Confederate soldiers sought to fight it; much that they encountered was at odds with their expectations. As they wrestled with the unforeseen, they were changed. The experience of combat frustrated their attempts to fight the war as an expression of their values and generated in them a harsh disillusionment." Two books by nationally recognized scholars that refute Wiley and Linderman are: Hess, *The Union Soldier in Battle*, and McPherson, *For Cause and Comrades*. Hess and McPherson both

argue that ideology played the major role in motivating soldiers throughout the war. The exception that McPherson makes is with combat motivation, where unit pride and comrades played as important a role as ideology. Other important works that deal with soldiers' motivations are: Mitchell, *The Vacant Chair* and *Civil War Soldiers*; Robertson, *Soldiers Blue and Gray*. For a historiographical essay on the wartime experiences of the common soldiers of both armies, see Mitchell, "'Not the General but the Soldier,'" 81–95.

7. Cowley, ed., *With My Face to the Enemy*, 61. The standard work on the mobilization of the Union army is the now dated Shannon, *The Organization and Administration of the Union Army, 1861–1865*. An excellent study on the creation of military force at the start of the war in the western theater is Prokopowicz, *All for the Regiment*. Mobilization during the Civil War is placed in an international context in Hattaway, "The Civil War Armies." For an overview of manpower mobilization in other American wars, Kreidberg and Henry, *History of Military Mobilization in the United States Army*.

8. Major General Winfield Scott Hancock, General Orders, No. 44, Headquarters Second Army Corps, November 26, 1864, in *O.R.*, vol. 42, pt. 3, 713–14.

1. BEGINNINGS

1. George McClellan to Edwin Stanton, January 31, 1862, in *The Civil War Papers of George B. McClellan*, 163. McClellan added that when he arrived in Washington, the Union soldiers present were "undisciplined, undrilled & dispirited." The best biography of McClellan is Sears, *George B. McClellan*. Also see Rafuse, *McClellan's War*. For a sympathetic treatment of the Union general, see Hassler, *General George B. McClellan*. The perspective of McClellan is found in his *McClellan's Own Story*.

2. For a description of McClellan in western Virginia, see Sears, *George B. McClellan*, 89–93. Also see Cox, "McClellan in West Virginia."

3. Report of Major General George McClellan, July 27, 1861–November 9, 1862, *O.R.*, vol. 5, 13; George McClellan to Edwin Stanton, January 31, 1862, in *The Civil War Papers of George B. McClellan*, 163. McClellan claimed that when he arrived in Washington in the summer of 1861, the "city was almost in a condition to have been taken by a dash of a single regiment of cavalry." The initial organization of the Army of the Potomac by McClellan is described in Beatie, *The Army of the Potomac*, 425–26.

4. The manpower of the divisions of the Army of the Potomac is taken from Major General George McClellan, Abstract from Consolidated Morning Report of the Army of the Potomac, November 12, 1861, *O.R.*, vol. 5, no. 1, 650.

5. Epstein, "Patterns of Change and Continuity in Nineteenth-Century Warfare." Also see Epstein's *Napoleon's Last Victory and the Emergence of Modern War*.

6. George McClellan to Mary Ellen McClellan, August 8, 1861, in *The Civil War Papers of George B. McClellan*, 81. For a recent biography of Scott, see Peskin, *Winfield Scott and the Profession of Arms*.

7. McClellan, *McClellan's Own Story*, 113. An excellent discussion on the political and military considerations behind the creation of corps within the Army of the Potomac is Taaffe, *Commanding the Army of the Potomac*.

8. Williams, *Lincoln and His Generals*, 42–43, 46; George McClellan to Abraham Lincoln, August 2, 1861, in *The Civil War Papers of George B. McClellan*, 74.

9. John Hay, diary entry, November 1861, in *Lincoln and the Civil War in the Diaries and Letters of John Hay*, 32–33.

10. Report of Major General George McClellan, July 27, 1861 to November

9, 1862, *O.R.*, vol. 5, pt. 1, 50; Rafuse, *McClellan's War*, 191.

11. George McClellan to Simon Cameron, October 31, 1861, and George McClellan to Samuel Barlow, November 8, 1861, in *The Civil War Papers of George B. McClellan*, 116, 128. McClellan estimated the Confederate army in northern Virginia at 150,000 men.

12. Taaffe, *Commanding the Army of the Potomac*, 8–9; Williams, *Lincoln and His Generals*, 68–69.

13. *CCW*, vol. 1, 6–7, 144, 218; Epstein, "The Creation and Evolution of the Army Corps in the American Civil War," 28–32. For a history of the Joint Committee, see Tap, *Over Lincoln's Shoulder*.

14. *CCW*, vol. 1, 86.

15. Abraham Lincoln, President's General War Order, No. 2, March 8, 1862, *O.R.*, vol. 5, pt. 1, 18; Williams, *Lincoln and the Radicals*, 118–19.

16. Wert, *The Sword of Lincoln*, 415.

17. The argument expressed above agrees with Taaffe, *Commanding the Army of the Potomac*, 12. Taaffe asserts that expediency was the primary factor in appointing the corps commanders. Appointing officers other than by seniority "would have caused all sorts of problems that the president undoubtedly hoped to avoid."

18. "An ideal soldier," quoted in Sears, *To the Gates of Richmond*, 71; George McClellan to Mary Ellen McClellan, May 6, 1862, in *The Civil War Papers of George B. McClellan*, 257–58. McClellan had brief contact with Sumner in the prewar army. McClellan received appointment as captain in the 1st Cavalry in 1855, when Sumner assigned him by letter to recruiting duty in the Northeast. Whether the two men met in person is unclear. For a brief description of the interaction, see Myers, *General George Brinton McClellan*, 84–85.

19. The Comte de Paris, a French nobleman serving as a member of McClellan's headquarters staff during 1862,

commented that Sumner "has an air of stupidity that perfectly expresses his mental state." The quotation is taken from Sears, *To the Gates of Richmond*, 71. Even Francis Walker, in describing Sumner in his history of the Second Corps, wrote, "much may be said upon either side of the question whether, with his mental habits and at his advanced age, he should have been designated for the command of twenty thousand new troops in the field." Walker, *History of the Second Army Corps*, 11.

20. A description of Sumner as "Bull" is found in Chalfant, *Cheyennes and Horse Soldiers*, 192 and 321. The birth years of the other three Union corps commanders are: Samuel Heintzelman, 1805; Erasmus Keyes, 1810; and Irving McDowell, 1818. For summaries of the military careers of these men, see Warner, *Generals in Blue*, 227–28, 264–65, 297–98.

21. Welsh, *Medical Histories of Union Generals*, 329.

22. Description of Lincoln's train trip from Springfield to Washington and Sumner's advice regarding the rumored assassination plot in Baltimore is found in Donald, *Lincoln*, 273–79.

23. Edwin Sumner to Samuel Cooper, November 3, 1854, Sumner Family Papers, LC.

24. Abraham Lincoln, President's General War Orders, No. 2, March 8, 1862, *O.R.*, vol. 5, pt. 1, 18.

25. Walker, *History of the Second Army Corps*, 14.

26. Chalfant, *Cheyennes and Horse Soldiers*, 71–103.

27. The transfer of Blenker's division is discussed in Williams, *Lincoln and His Generals*, 76–77.

28. Richardson's prewar career is detailed in Warner, *Generals in Blue*, 402–403; and Walker, *History of the Second Army Corps*, 7.

29. Herbert Willand, diary entry, March 30–31, 1862, Willand Diary, NHSL; Charles Hamlin to Sister, April 5, 1862, Hamlin Papers, NYSLA; Cole, *Under Five Commanders*, 16–17; Fuller, *Personal Recollections of the War of 1861*, 14.

30. Small, *The Road to Richmond*, 30. Descriptions of the prewar careers of Richardson and Sedgwick are found in Warner, *Generals in Blue*, 402–403, 430–31; and Walker, *History of the Second Army Corps*, 5, 7. Sedgwick's role in establishing Fort Wise is discussed in Chalfant, *Cheyennes and Horse Soldiers*, 282–83. The most recent biography of Sedgwick is Winslow, *General John Sedgwick*.

31. John Sedgwick to Sister, February 18, 1862, in *Correspondence of John Sedgwick*, 38; Wert, *The Sword of Lincoln*, 58–59; Sears, *Controversies and Commanders*, 27–50.

32. Hattaway and Jones, *How the North Won*, 29–30.

33. Conyngham, *The Irish Brigade and Its Campaigns*, 36–37; 536.

34. Hattaway and Jones, *How the North Won*, 30. Details regarding the backgrounds of the brigade commanders of the Second Corps are taken from the relevant sections of Warner, *Generals in Blue*.

35. McClellan, *McClellan's Own Story*, 114–15; Naisawald, *Grape and Canister*, 21–28. For an overview of Union and Confederate artillery in the eastern theater, also see Naisawald's *Cannon Blasts*.

36. Epstein, "The Creation and Evolution of the Army Corps," 35.

37. Report of Major General George McClellan, July 27, 1861–November 9, 1862, *O.R.*, vol. 5, pt. 1, 13–17; Starr, *The Union Cavalry in the Civil War*, vol. 1, 235–37.

38. McClellan, *McClellan's Own Story*, 122, 136; Walker, *History of the Second Army Corps*, 13.

39. Walker, *History of the Second Army Corps*, 3–7.

40. An excellent discussion of military companies as an extension of home communities is found in Mitchell, *The Vacant Chair*.

41. The manpower figures of the regiments of the Second Corps are taken from: 15th Massachusetts, 19th Massachusetts, 42nd New York—Fox, *Regimental Losses*, 161, 163, 193; 20th Massachusetts—Bruce, *The Twentieth Regiment of Massachusetts Volunteer Infantry*, 12; 7th Michigan—Tivy, *Souvenir of the Seventh . . .*, 8; 1st Minnesota—Holcombe, *History of the First Regiment Minnesota Volunteer Infantry*, 6–7; 5th New Hampshire—Child, *A History of the Fifth Regiment New Hampshire Volunteers*, 9; 34th New York—Chapin, *A Brief History of the Thirty-Fourth Regiment N.Y.S.V.*, 17; 52nd New York, 57th New York—Fox, *New York at Gettysburg*, vol. 1, 394, 409; 61st New York, 64th New York, 66th New York—Fox, *New York at Gettysburg*, vol. 2, 461, 548, 552; 63rd New York, 69th New York, 88th New York—Conyngham, *The Irish Brigade and Its Campaigns*, 68; 71st Pennsylvania—Bates, *History of Pennsylvania Volunteers*, vol. 5, 789; 72nd Pennsylvania, 81st Pennsylvania—Nicholson and Beitler, eds., *Pennsylvania at Gettysburg*, vol. 1, 387, 411; 106th Pennsylvania—Nicholson and Beitler, eds., *Pennsylvania at Gettysburg*, vol. 2, 540. The manpower figures for the 82nd New York, 53rd Pennsylvania, 69th Pennsylvania are taken from Headquarters, Army of the Potomac, Medical Director's Office, February 6, 1862, in *O.R.*, vol. 5, 714, 720. The manpower figures for the three regiments listed above date from several months after each unit mustered, so they likely represent the minimum manpower present.

42. The population data cited above is taken from Series A 57–72, "Population in Urban and Rural Territory, by Size of Place: 1790–1970," in United States

Bureau of the Census, *Historical Statistics of the United States*, vol. 1, 11–12.

43. Burton, *Melting Pot Soldiers*, 44. Burton defines an ethnic regiment as displaying three characteristics: a large number of its soldiers were either foreign born or first generation; soldiers in the regiment identified themselves as an ethnic organization; and the larger community regarded the regiment as an ethnic organization. The standard study of the immigrant experience in the Union army is Lonn, *Foreigners in the Union Army and Navy*.

44. Robertson, *Soldiers Blue and Gray*, 27–28. When created in late 1862, the Union Eleventh Corps fielded a majority of German regiments.

45. Cavanagh, *Memoirs of Gen. Thomas Francis Meagher*, 438. The best biography of Meagher's life remains Athearn, *Thomas Francis Meagher*.

46. Conyngham, *The Irish Brigade and Its Campaigns*, 53–54. Also see Lonn, *Foreigners in the Union Army*, 42–43.

47. *Fourth Annual Report of the Bureau of Military Statistics*, 164–65; Lonn, *Foreigners in the Union Army*, 97. Sigel had no known connection to the 52nd New York beyond inspiring many of his countrymen to enlist in the Union cause. The only full-length biography of Sigel is Engle, *Yankee Dutchman*.

48. Burton, *Melting Pot Soldier*, 148–49; Conyngham, *The Irish Brigade*, 55–67.

49. *Fourth Annual Report of the Bureau of Military Statistics*, 61–62; Fox, *New York at Gettysburg*, vol. 1, 312.

50. Banes, *History of the Philadelphia Brigade*, 7–13; Nicholson and Beitler, eds., *Pennsylvania at Gettysburg*, vol. 1, 389.

51. For a modern-day study of the Philadelphia Brigade, see Gottfried, *Stopping Pickett*.

52. *Fifth Annual Report of the Chief of the Bureau of Military Statistics*, 124–25; Fox, *New York at Gettysburg*, vol. 2, 518;

Holcombe, *History of the First Regiment Minnesota Volunteer Infantry*, 13–14; Child, *A History of the Fifth Regiment New Hampshire Volunteers*, 211–12.

53. Ford, *The Story of the Fifteenth Regiment, Massachusetts Volunteer Infantry*, 21–23.

54. Robert McAllister to Wife, October 15, 1864, in *The Civil War Letters of General Robert McAllister*, 520; McPherson, *For Cause and Comrades*, 176–77. McPherson writes that "40 to 45 percent of soldiers had been Democrats (or came from Democratic families) in 1860."

55. The Democratic sympathies of voters in Philadelphia and New York in the Civil War era are discussed in Burrows and Wallace, *Gotham*, 864–65; Dusinberre, *Civil War Issues in Philadelphia*, 98–103; Gallman, *Mastering Wartime*, 2; Spann, *Gotham at War*, 2–5; Weigley, "The Border City in the Civil War, 1854–1865," 363–416.

56. Irish Americans' fear of economic competition posed by free blacks and, later, emancipated blacks is discussed in Kenny, *The American Irish*, 123–26; and Ignatiev, *How the Irish Became White*, 164–67. A strong discussion of Irish American political attitudes in general during the prewar period is found in Bruce, *The Harp and the Eagle*.

57. For a recent and strong study of the 20th Massachusetts, see Miller, *Harvard's Civil War*.

58. Charles Benson, diary entry, December 31, 1861, in *The Civil War Diaries of Charles E. Benson*, 33; Henry Law to Brother, December 14, 1861, 106th Pennsylvania regimental file, GNMP; Casper Crowninshield, diary entry, August 1861, Crowninshield-Magnus Papers, MHS; Jonathan Stowe, diary entry, December 31, 1861, Stowe Diary, CWTI, USAMHI.

59. *Red Wing Sentinel*, April 24, 1861, quoted in Wright, *No More Gallant a Deed*, xv; Herbert Willand, diary entry,

October 28, 1861, Willand Diary, NHSL; George Beidelman to Father, May 15, 1861, in *The Civil War Letters of George Washington Beidelman*, 14.

60. Manning, *What This Cruel War Was Over*.

61. Edward Bassett letter, December 1861, in *From Bull Run to Bristow Station*, 13.

62. For the most recent exploration of soldiers' religious outlooks, see Woodworth, *While God Is Marching On*.

63. Chapin, *A Brief History of the Thirty-Fourth Regiment N.Y.S.V.*, 9; Gorham Coffin to Father and Sister, December 7, 1861, in "Civil War Letters of Gorham Coffin," 71; Cornelius Moore to Sister, August 21, 1861, in *Cornie*, 6.

64. Allan Zacharias, letter, June 28, 1862, in *Michigan in the War*, 271; Henry Taylor to Isaac Taylor, May 4, 1861, in Taylor, "Campaigning with the First Minnesota," 14; Martin Sigman, undated diary entry, Sigman Diary, vol. 320, FSNMP; Chapin, *A Brief History of the Thirty-Fourth Regiment N.Y.S.V.*, 10; Samuel Sexton to Hannah Sexton, July 28, 1862, Sexton Papers, OHS.

65. Alfred Wheeler to Mother, August 1861, Wheeler Letters, CWMC, USAMHI; George Whipple, Civil War reminiscences, 64th New York regimental file, GNMP. The relation between the economic downturn of the 1850s and the coming of the Civil War is detailed in Huston, *The Panic of 1857 and the Coming of the Civil War*.

66. Benjamin Chase to Mother, June 15, 1862, 5th New Hampshire regimental file, ANMP; Wistar, *Autobiography of Isaac Jones Wistar*, 356–57.

67. Francis Barlow to Mother, December 12, 1861, Barlow Papers, MHS; Herbert Willand, diary entry, February 7–17, 1862, Willand Diary, NHSL; James Turrill to Wife, January 30, 1862, 7th Michigan regimental file, ANMP.

68. Josiah Favill, diary entry, December 7, 1861, in *Diary of a Young Army Officer*, 56–57; Walker, *History of the Second Army Corps*, 8. The Second Corps had only 88 men under arrest in late March, an extremely small percentage of the total number of men present for duty.

69. Beatie, *McClellan Takes Command*, 354, 478–79. In late 1861, McClellan criticized soldiers in Brigadier General George McCall's division for their poor "state of discipline." Soon after a brigade commander in Brigadier General Frederick Lander's division criticized the men because "they knew nothing of garrison, or other military duty, and were literally a mob."

70. For a description of the fighting that also provides numerous official reports, see Patch, *The Battle of Ball's Bluff*. More recent descriptions of the fighting at Ball's Bluff and its aftermath are: Marvel, *Mr. Lincoln Goes to War*, 216–80; and Ballard, *Battle of Ball's Bluff*.

71. Francis Adams Donaldson, narrative of the Battle of Ball's Bluff, summer 1862, in *Inside the Army of the Potomac*, 34; Adams, *Reminiscences of the Nineteenth Massachusetts Regiment*, 16; Wert, *Sword of Lincoln*, 47.

72. Walter Eames to Wife, October 22, 1861, Eames Letters, USAMHI; George Beidelman to Father, October 24, 1861, in *The Civil War Writings of George Washington Beidelman*, 45; Henry Abbott to Father, February 5, 1862, in *Fallen Leaves*, 100–101.

73. For descriptions of soldiers' meals at Thanksgiving and Christmas, see Gorham Coffin to Father and Sister, November 16, 1861, in "The Civil War Letters of Gorham Coffin," 69; and Herbert Willand, diary entry, December 25, 1861, Willand diary, NHSL. For a leaner description of Christmas dinner, see Charles Benson, diary entry, December 25, 1861, in *The Civil War Diaries of Charles E. Benson*,

32. Benson writes, "Christmas. How different from a Christmas at home. Our dinner was hard crackers. Rather hard for a Christmas dinner."

74. Adams, *Reminiscences of the Nineteenth Massachusetts Regiment*, 17–18; Child, *A History of the Fifth Regiment New Hampshire Volunteers*, 19–20. Festivities marking George Washington's birthday are found in Herbert Willand, diary entry, February 22, 1862, Willand diary, NHSL; Henry Lyon, diary entry, February 22, 1862, in *"Desolating This Fair Country,"* 71.

75. J. N. Searles, "The First Minnesota Volunteer Infantry," 89; Walter Eames to Wife, November 30, 1861, Eames Letters, USAMHI; Henry Lyon to Brother and Friends, August 1, 1861, in *"Desolating This Fair Country,"* 30. Mail services in Stone's and Sumner's divisions were excellent if anything like those enjoyed by soldiers in the 1st Minnesota. Soldiers in the regiment received 1,800 letters weekly.

76. Livermore, *Days and Events*, 46. For description of Federal successes in Tennessee and coastal North Carolina in the winter of 1862, see Cooling, *Forts Henry and Donelson;* and Sauers, "Laurels for Burnside."

77. Charles Johnson to Wife, March 12, 1862, Johnson Papers, USAMHI; Chalkly Garrett to Wife and Children, March 21, 1862, Garrett Letters, vol. 321, FSNMP; Arnold Daines to Wife, March 2, 1862, Daines Letters, CWMC, USAMHI; McPherson, *Battle Cry of Freedom*, 356–57.

2. APPRENTICESHIP

1. McClellan gives description of his strategy for the Peninsula Campaign in George McClellan to Edwin Stanton, March 19, 1862, in Sears, *The Civil War Papers of George B. McClellan*, 215–16. The best scholarly studies of the Peninsula Campaign include Sears, *To the Gates of Richmond;* and Gallagher, ed., *The Richmond Campaign of 1862.* Also see Miller, *The Peninsula Campaign of 1862;* and Webb, *The Peninsula.*

2. Unidentified soldier, 64th New York, Civil War reminiscences, IU; Charles Eager to Wife, March 31, 1862, Eager Letters, Leigh Collection, USAMHI; Henry Ropes to Father, April 1, 1862, Ropes Letters, BPL; Henry Lyons, diary entry, April 1, 1862, in *"Desolating This Fair Country,"* 85.

3. Sears, *To the Gates of Richmond,* 36–43.

4. Jacob Pyewell to Mother, May 4, 1862, Pyewell Letters, CWMC, USAMHI; Charles Benson to Father, May 8, 1862, in *The Civil War Diaries of Charles E. Benson,* 70; Chapin, *A Brief History of the Thirty-Fourth Regiment N.Y.S.V.,* 38; Francis Adams Donaldson to Brother, May 18, 1862, in *Inside the Army of the Potomac,* 78; Herbert Willand, diary entry, May 23, 1862, Willand Diary, NHSL; Waitt, *History of the Nineteenth Regiment, Massachusetts Volunteer Infantry,* 72–73; Arnold Daines to Wife, May 13, 1862, Daines Letters, CWMC, USAMHI; Joseph Dimock to Wife, May 28, 1862, Dimock Family Papers, Emory.

5. Sears, *To the Gates of Richmond,* 106–107; Taaffe, *Commanding the Army of the Potomac,* 17–18; Abstract from the Return of the Army of the Potomac, May 20, 1862, *O.R.,* vol. 11, pt. 3, 184; Major General George McClellan, General Orders, No. 125, May 18, 1862, *O.R.,* vol. 11, no. 3, 181. McClellan earlier had received permission from Lincoln to make temporary reorganization to the Army of the Potomac, if he believed it a military necessary. The two new corps were listed as "provisional" until that summer, when they became permanent.

6. Paul Revere to Lucretia Revere, May 22, 1862, Revere Family Papers, MHS. For a contrasting view to the general optimism among soldiers of the Second Corps in late May, see Edgar Newcomb

to Sister, May 24, 1862, in *A Memorial Sketch of Lieut. Edgar M. Newcomb of the Nineteenth Mass. Vols.,* 62. Newcomb writes, "The men are sick of soldiering. ... Even I, who till within a week never had a thought of homesickness, want to go home and get something to eat. And notice, once at home I'll never go again for a soldier."

7. Sears, *To the Gates of Richmond,* 124–28; Wert, *The Sword of Lincoln,* 84–85. The Confederate plan of attack is detailed in Newton, *Joseph E. Johnston and the Defense of Richmond,* 174–75.

8. Report of Brigadier General Edwin Sumner, June 9, 1862, *O.R.,* vol. 11, pt. 1, 763; Howard, *Autobiography,* 237; Report of Colonel Charles Tompkins, June 4, 1862, *O.R.,* vol. 11, pt. 1, 793–94; Ames, *Battery A, First Rhode Island Light Artillery,* 82; Walker, *History of the Second Army Corps,* 27–28.

9. Howard, *Autobiography,* 237; Walker, *History of the Second Army Corps,* 27–28; Van Ness, "Gen. Sumner"; Report of Brigadier General Darius Couch, June 7, 1862, *O.R.,* vol. 11, pt. 1, 880.

10. For description of the two-day battle, see Newton, *The Battle of Seven Pines.*

11. Neill, "Incidents of the Battles of Fair Oaks and Malvern Hill," 460; Benjamin Chase to Mother, June 15, 1862, 5th New Hampshire Regimental File, ANMP; W. H. Lucas to Mother, June 3, 1862, Lucas Letters, USAMHI; Fuller, *Personal Recollections of the War of 1861,* 20.

12. The idea that unit and comrade provided a primary motivation for Union soldiers in battle is a debated point. This analysis agrees with the arguments advanced in McPherson, *For Cause and Comrades,* and Hess, *The Union Soldier in Battle.* By contrast, Linderman, in *Embattled Courage,* argues that the ideal of courage motivated soldiers. During the early war years, soldiers believed that the

good and the brave would not be harmed in battle.

13. Henry Lyon to Brother and Friends, June 2, 1862, in *"Desolating This Fair Country,"* 111; Herbert Willand, diary entry, June 1, 1862, Willand diary, NHSL.

14. Oliver Wendell Holmes to Mother, June 2, 1862, in *Touched with Fire,* 51; Francis Adams Donaldson, *Inside the Army of the Potomac,* 88–89.

15. Brigadier General Samuel Heintzelman to Major General George McClellan, May 31, 1862, *O.R.,* vol. 51, pt. 1, 646.

16. Report of Brigadier General Edwin Sumner, June 9, 1862; Report of Brigadier General Israel Richardson, June 6, 1862, *O.R.,* vol. 11, pt. 1, 763, 766; Herbert Willand, diary entry, June 1, 1862, Willand Diary, NHSL.

17. Samuel Foster Haven to Father, June 6, 1862, Haven Family Papers, AAS; Warren Osgood to Brother, June 8, 1862, Stephen Osgood Papers, Duke; Report of General Joseph Johnston, June 24, 1862, *O.R.,* vol. 11, pt. 1, 935.

18. Erasmus Keyes to Abraham Lincoln, August 25, 1862, *O.R.,* vol. 11, no. 3, 382–83; Report of Brigadier General Samuel Heintzelman, June 7, 1862, *O.R.,* vol. 11, no. 1, 815–16; Sears, *To the Gates of Richmond,* 145, 149.

19. Walker, *History of the Second Army Corps,* 55. The reinforcements assigned to the army in June 1862 are discussed in Sears, *To The Gates of Richmond,* 156–57. The manpower figures listed above are taken from Abstract from the Return of the Army of the Potomac, June 20, 1862, *O.R.,* vol. 11, pt. 3, 238.

20. Osborne, *A History of the Twenty-Ninth Regiment of Massachusetts Volunteer Infantry,* 142, 170.

21. Major General George McClellan, Special Orders, No. 168, June 2, 1862, *O.R.,* vol. 11, pt. 3, 210–11; Walker, *History of the Second Army Corps,* 55; Naisawald, *Cannon Blasts,* 42.

22. Report of Brigadier General Edwin Sumner, June 9, 1862; Report of Lieutenant Edmund Kirby, n.d., *O.R.*, vol. 11, pt. 1, 763, 795–96; Naisawald, *Grape and Canister*, 76. The Confederate quotation is taken from Sears, *To the Gates of Richmond*, 137.

23. McClellan's repositioning of the army after the Battle of Fair Oaks and his plans to renew his offensive toward Richmond are described in Sears, *McClellan*, 204. The position of the Second Corps during this time is described in Walker, *History of the Second Army Corps*, 54. The picket firing is described in Augustus Ayling, diary entry, June 17, 1862, in *A Yankee at Arms*, 41; and Chapin, *A Brief History of the Thirty-Fourth Regiment N.Y.S.V.*, 46.

24. Jonathan Stowe, diary entry, June 25, 1862, Stowe Diaries, CWTIC, USAMHI; Charles Benson, diary entry, June 16, 1862, in *The Civil War Diaries of Charles E. Benson*, 81. The Second Corps suffered 1,561 men sick and wounded in late June; see Walker, *History of the Second Army Corps*, 197.

25. For concerns over the cleanliness of the water around the encampments of the Second Corps, see Holcombe, *History of the First Regiment Minnesota Volunteer Infantry*, 135; and Fuller, *Personal Recollections of the War of 1861*, 21. Holcombe writes, "The surface water came through swamps and marshes wherein dead men and dead horses lay, putrid and horrible, and where there was always miasma and malaria." Fuller writes, "As our camp was in the Chickahominy swamp, the water generally was bad, and soon made itself felt in the health of the men. Hot coffee was served to the men as they stood in line, and later, rations of whiskey were issued to dilute the water with."

26. Child, *A History of the Fifth Regiment New Hampshire Volunteers*, 91;

Samuel Hoffman to Brother, June 16, 1862, Hoffman Letters, CL.

27. Sears, *To the Gates of Richmond*, 200–209. For description of the ensuing Seven Days Battles, see Burton, *Extraordinary Circumstances*.

28. Charles Benson, diary entry, June 26, 1862, in *The Civil War Diaries of Charles E. Benson*, 83; Augustus Ayling, diary entries, June 26 and 27, 1862, in *A Yankee at Arms*, 44–45.

29. Walker, *History of the Second Army Corps*, 62; Miller, "Serving under McClellan on the Peninsula in '62," 25.

30. Frank Young, diary entry, June 29, 1862, Young Diary, CWMC, USAMHI; William Scandlin, diary entry, June 28, 1862, Scandlin Papers, AAS; Wert, *The Sword of Lincoln*, 108.

31. Report of Brigadier General Edwin Sumner, July 4, 1862, *O.R.*, vol. 11, pt. 2, 52; Sears, *To the Gates of Richmond*, 267, 274.

32. Wright, *No More Gallant a Deed*, 150–51; Bloomer, "How the 1st Minn. Lost Its Colors."

33. Conyngham, *The Irish Brigade*, 197–98; William Burns, diary entry, June 29, 1862, Burns Diary, USAMHI.

34. Unidentified soldier, 64th New York, Civil War reminiscences, IU. For descriptions of Sumner's reluctance to retreat after the fighting at Savage's Station, see Franklin, "Rear-Guard Fighting during the Change of Base," 375–76; and Sears, *To the Gates of Richmond*, 275–76.

35. Walker, *History of the Second Army Corps*, 72–76; Sears, *To the Gates of Richmond*, 283–307.

36. Chapin, *A Brief History of the Thirty-Fourth Regiment N.Y.S.V.*, 49; Francis Barlow to Mother, July 4, 1862, Barlow Papers, MHS.

37. Report of Brigadier General Edwin Sumner, July 4, 1862, *O.R.*, vol. 11, pt. 2, 51–52; Osborne, *A History of the Twenty-Ninth Regiment, Massachusetts Volunteer Infantry*, 165. For the shortages of food and

water, see Fuller, *Personal Recollections of the War of 1861*, 38; and Oliver Wendell Holmes to Parents, July 5, 1862, in *Touched with Fire*, 59.

38. Report of Brigadier General Edwin Sumner, July 4, 1862, *O.R.*, vol. 11, pt. 2, 52; Franklin, "Rear-Guard Fighting during the Change of Base," 381; Conyngham, *The Irish Brigade and Its Campaigns*, 216.

39. Federal casualty returns during the Seven Days Battles are taken from Organization of Troops and Return of Casualties, June 25–July 2, 1862, *O.R.*, vol. 11, pt. 2, 24–37. For description of the fighting at Malvern Hill, see Sears, *To the Gates of Richmond*, 308–36. For the role of the Second Corps, see Walker, *History of the Second Army Corps*, 82–84.

40. Dyer, *A Compendium of the War of the Rebellion*, vol. 1, 191. The manpower return of Kimball's brigade and the rest of the Federal forces is taken from Number of Men Composing the Army of the Potomac, July 20, 1862, *O.R.*, vol. 11, pt. 3, 329.

41. Organization of Troops and Return of Casualties, June 25–July 2, 1862, *O.R.*, vol. 11, pt. 2, 37; Welcher, *The Union Army*, 315. During the Seven Days Battles, the Sixth Corps suffered 296 killed; 1,472 wounded; 1,110 missing (2,878 total casualties).

42. A description of the meeting between Lincoln and the five corps commanders is found in Sears, *McClellan*, 229.

43. For description of the fighting at Kernstown, see Ecelbarger, *"We Are In for It!"* For soldiers' pride in their role in the campaign, see Houghton, "In the Valley."

44. Samuel Maguire to Wife, August 4, 1862, Maguire Letters, WRHS; Edgar Newcomb to Sister, July 4, 1862, in *A Memorial Sketch of Lieut. Edgar M. Newcomb*, 75. Also see Lucian Bonaparte Alexander to Uncle Will, July 16, 1862, Alexander Letters, PSA.

45. Charles Eager to Wife, August 26, 1862, Eager Letters, Leigh Collection, USAMHI; Jonathan Stowe to Friends at Home, July 11, 1862, Stowe Diaries, CWTIC, USAMHI; Benjamin Chase to Father, July 28, 1862, 5th New Hampshire regimental file, ANMP.

46. Francis Barlow to Mother, July 4, 1862, Barlow Papers, MHS; Henry Ropes to Father, July 5, 1862, Ropes Letters, BPL; Richard Turner to Little Sister Sara, July 26, 1862, Turner Papers, NYSLA.

47. George Batchelder to Mother, July 8, 1862, Hinks Papers, BU; Josiah Favill, diary entry, July 24, 1862, in *Diary of a Young Officer*, 163.

48. Taaffe, *Commanding the Army of the Potomac*, 28–29. For examples of the opinions held by the Fifth Corps, see Slater, "Malvern"; and, also by Slater, "At Gaines's Mill."

49. Roland Bowen to Friend Guild, August 9, 1862, in *From Ball's Bluff to Gettysburg*, 120; Augustus Van Dyke, diary entries, August 2–5, 1862, Van Dyke Collection, IHS.

50. Rosentreter, "Samuel Hodgman's Civil War," 35; William Landon to *Vincennes (Indiana) Sun*, July 18, 1862, transcribed at: http://members.evansville.net/~tlconner/.

51. Waitt, *History of the Nineteenth Regiment, Massachusetts Volunteer Infantry*, 114–15; Fuller, *Personal Recollections of the War of 1861*, 46.

52. George Beidelman to Father, August 12, 1862, in *The Civil War Writings of George Washington Beidelman*, 78; Edward Ehlers, diary entry, July 19, 1862, Ehlers Diary, CWMC, USAMHI; Division Circular, July 19, 1862, 2d Army Corps Records, RG 393, NA.

53. Henry Lyons, diary entry, July 20, 1862, in *"Desolating This Fair Country,"* 131; Waitt, *History of the Nineteenth Regiment, Massachusetts Volunteer Infantry*, 110.

54. Chapin, *A Brief History of the Thirty-Fourth Regiment N.Y.S.V.*, 56; George Beidelman to Father, August 17, 1862, in *The Civil War Letters of George Washington Beidelman*, 80; Wert, *The Sword of Lincoln*, 132–33.

55. William Stone, diary entry, August 22, 1862, 19th Massachusetts regimental file, ANMP.

56. Livermore, *Days and Events*, 109; Sawyer, *A Military History of the 8th Regiment Ohio Vol. Inf'y*, 64; Henry Gerrish, *Letter to Lyman* 23. Gerrish also writes that the Second Corps on August 30 "arrived about five in the morning opposite Washington, and here we were given to understand we were going to rest for a whole week." The best study of the Second Bull Run Campaign is Hennessy, *Return to Bull Run*.

57. Sears, *McClellan*, 250–54; John Hay diary entry, in *Lincoln and the Civil War in the Diaries and Letters of John Hay*, 47.

58. William Stone, diary entry, September 1, 1862, 19th Massachusetts regimental file, ANMP; Child, *A History of the Fifth Regiment New Hampshire Volunteers*, 132; Fuller, *Personal Recollections of the War of 1861*, 54 and 57; Kepler, *History of the . . . Fourth Regiment Ohio Volunteer Infantry*, 81.

59. Adams, *Reminiscences of the Nineteenth Massachusetts Regiment*, 42; Galwey, *The Valiant Hours*, 29; Sawyer, *A Military History of the 8th Regiment Ohio Vol. Inf'y*, 65.

60. Francis Barlow to Mother, September 6, 1862, Barlow Papers, MHS; Charles Hamlin to Sister, August 29, 1862, Hamlin Letters, NYSLA; William Stone, diary entry, September 4, 1862, 19th Massachusetts regimental file, ANMP.

61. The manpower figures of the Army of Northern Virginia are taken from Sears, *Landscape Turned Red*, 76. For a critical assessment of the strategic reasoning behind Lee's decision to invade Maryland, see Krick, "The Army of Northern Virginia in September 1862," 35–55. Standard studies of the Antietam Campaign and its wartime significance include: Jamieson, *Death in September;* McPherson, *Crossroads of Freedom;* Murfin, *The Gleam of Bayonets;* Priest, *Antietam;* and Sears, *Landscape Turned Red*. For a series of interpretive essays, see Gallagher, ed., *The Antietam Campaign*. A detailed study of the battle is found in Luvaas and Nelson, eds., *The U.S. Army War College Guide to the Battle of Antietam*. For a veteran's perspective, see Palfrey, *The Antietam and Fredericksburg*.

62. Lincoln's decision to appoint McClellan the commander of the both the Army of the Potomac and the Army of Virginia is examined in Donald, *Lincoln*, 371–72; and Williams, *Lincoln and His Generals*, 159–64. McClellan's reorganization of the Army of the Potomac is discussed in Sears, *McClellan*, 265–67; and Welcher, *The Union Army*, 255–56. The manpower figures of the Union forces are taken from Report of Major General George McClellan, August 4, 1863, *O.R.*, vol. 19, pt. 1, 67; and Report of Brigadier General S. Williams, September 11, 1862, *O.R.*, vol. 11, pt. 3, 380.

63. Sears, *McClellan*, 266; Welcher, *The Union Army*, 345–46 and 361–62. The manpower figures of the Second Corps are taken from Abstract from the Return of the Army of the Potomac, August 20, 1862, *O.R.*, vol. 11, pt. 3, 380.

64. Sears, *McClellan*, 266, 319. The reinforcement of the Second Corps is described in Walker, *History of the Second Army Corps*, 97–98; and Welcher, *The Union Army*, 315. The recruitment of nine-month soldiers is discussed in McPherson, *Battle Cry of Freedom*, 492–93. The experience of the regiments raised during 1862 and assigned to the Army of the Potomac is detailed in Hartwig, "Who Would Not Be a Soldier."

65. The manpower of the Second Corps is taken from Report of Major General George McClellan, August 4, 1863, *O.R.,* vol. 19, pt. 1, 67.

66. Richard Oakford to Wife, August 31, 1862, Oakford Papers, PHMC; William Reed, diary entry, August 29, 1862, Reed Diary, PHS; Goddard, *Regimental Reminiscences of the War of the Rebellion,* 7; Hitchcock, *War from the Inside,* 19–20.

67. Sumner organized the Third Division on paper on September 10, but he only brought the three brigades of the division together for the first time six days later. See Walker, *History of the Second Army Corps,* 97–98; and Welcher, *The Union Army,* 315.

68. Luvaas and Nelson, introduction to *The U.S. Army War College Guide to the Battle of Antietam,* xvi–xvii. The manpower strengths of the green regiments assigned to the Second Corps and the rest of the Army of the Potomac are listed in Hartwig, "Who Would Not Be a Soldier," 164. The manpower strengths of the divisions of the Second Corps and the rest of the Army of the Potomac are listed in Priest, *Antietam,* 332–43.

69. For a brief description of French's life and military career, see Warner, *Generals in Blue,* 161–62.

70. Charles Hamlin to Sister, November 12, 1862, Hamlin Letters, NYSLA; Unidentified soldier, 64th New York, Civil War reminiscences, IU; David Rice, diary entry, September 12, 1862, Rice Collection, LC.

71. William Child to Wife, September 16, 1862, 5th New Hampshire regimental file, ANMP; Ephraim Brown, diary entry, September 16, 1862, 64th New York regimental file, ANMP. McClellan's deployment of the army around Sharpsburg and Antietam Creek is described in Sears, *McClellan,* 300–301.

72. Gerrish, *Letter to Lyman,* 30; James Maycock, diary entry, September 1862,

Maycock Diary, Dawson Flinchbaugh Collection, USAMHI.

73. Report of Major General Edwin Sumner, October 1, 1862; and Report of Brigadier General William French, September 20, 1862, *O.R.,* vol. 19, pt. 1, 276, 323–24. Neither Sumner nor French is clear why the two divisions separated on the march toward the West Woods. Sumner writes only that French's division, along with Richardson's division, "maintained a furious and successful fight from the time they entered the battle till the end of it." French writes he formed his troops "continuous with Sedgwick's, and immediately moved to the front." When the fighting in the West Woods started, French received orders from Sumner "to press the enemy with all my force." Also see Sumner, "The Antietam Campaign," 10–11. Samuel Sumner was the son of Edwin Sumner, and served as his father's aide-de-camp during the Maryland Campaign. The younger Sumner writes that somehow in the advance toward the West Woods, French's division veered "too far to the left, and not in position to connect with Sedgwick."

74. Report of Major General Edwin Sumner, October 1, 1862, *O.R.,* vol. 11, pt. 1, 275–76; Aldrich, *The History of Battery A, First Regiment Rhode Island Light Artillery,* 137–39.

75. Walter Eames to Wife, September 25, 1862, Eames Letters, USAMHI; Jonathan Peabody to Son, October 27, 1862, 59th New York regimental file, ANMP; Banes, *History of the Philadelphia Brigade,* 113; Wright, *No More Gallant a Deed,* 200.

76. Howard, *Autobiography,* 296; Return of Casualties, *O.R.,* vol. 19, pt. 1, 192–93.

77. Andrew Ford, diary entry, October 8, 1862, 15th Massachusetts regimental file, ANMP; Edward Walker to Friend Knight, October 5, 1862, Walker Letters, Leigh Collection, USAMHI; Joseph

Johnson to Parents, September 20, 1862, Johnson Letters, NYHS; Return of Casualties, *O.R.,* vol. 19, pt. 1, 192–93; Priest, *Antietam,* 335–36.

78. Wilson, *Under the Old Flag,* vol. 1, 112–14; Report of Major General George McClellan, October 15, 1862, *O.R.,* vol. 11, pt. 1, 66.

79. Marsena Rudolph Patrick, diary entry, September 18, 1862, in *Inside Lincoln's Army,* 151; Edwin Sumner testimony, February 18, 1863, *CCW,* vol. 1, 368.

80. Washburn, *A Complete Military History and Record of the 108th Regiment N.Y. Vols.,* 24, 107; Spangler, *My Little War Experience,* 31; Murfin, *Gleam of Bayonets,* 246.

81. Report of Brigadier General Nathan Kimball, September 18, 1862; Report of Colonel Dwight Morris, September 19, 1862, *O.R.,* vol. 19, pt. 1, 326–28; 332–33.

82. Fiske, *Mr. Dunn Browne's Experiences in the Army,* 38; Report of Colonel John Andrews, September 18, 1862, *O.R.,* vol. 19, pt. 1, 337; Hitchcock, *War from the Inside,* 57–58; Goddard, *Regimental Reminiscences of the War of the Rebellion,* 10. Not all green soldiers found themselves rattled by the experience of battle. For examples, see Francis Pierce to Edward Chapin, September 15, 1862, in "Civil War Letters of Francis Edwin Pierce of the 108th New York Volunteer Infantry," 154; and, John Weiser to Mother, October 13, 1862, Weiser Letters, CWMC, USAMHI.

83. The experience of the 16th Connecticut is detailed in Gordon, "'All Who Went into That Battle Were Heroes,'" 169–91.

84. Galwey, *The Valiant Hours,* 42–43; Hitchcock, *War from the Inside,* 61–62; Sears, *Landscape Turned Red,* 265–68.

85. Edward Cross, diary entry, September 17, 1862, in *The Civil War Writings of Edward E. Cross,* 45–46; Cole, *Under Five Commanders,* 83–84.

86. Charles Hale, "The Story of My Personal Experience at the Battle of Antietam," PHS; Ephraim Brown, diary entry, September 17, 1862, 64th New York regimental file, ANMP.

87. Fuller, *Personal Recollections of the War of 1861,* 59; Nelson Miles to Brother, September 24, 1862, Miles Papers, USAMHI. For description of the Federal breakthrough into the Sunken Road, see Report of Colonel Francis Barlow, September 22, 1862, *O.R.,* vol. 19, pt. 1, 289.

88. The numbers of men engaged and casualties in the First Division are taken from Return of Casualties, *O.R.,* vol. 19, pt. 1, 191–92; and Priest, *Antietam,* 334–35. The losses in the Irish Brigade are taken from Conyngham, *The Irish Brigade,* 305.

89. Edward Cross, diary entry, September 17, 1862, in *Civil War Writings of Edward E. Cross,* 50; Conyngham, *The Irish Brigade,* 306; McPherson, *Crossroads of Freedom,* 124.

90. Frederick, *The Story of a Regiment,* 90; Cole, *Under Five Commanders,* 19; Walker, *History of the Second Army Corps,* 115.

91. Stephen Martin, diary entry, September 18, 1862, Martin Diary, vol. 278, FSNMP; Chapin, *A Brief History of the Thirty-Fourth Regiment N.Y.S.V.,* 69; Joseph Johnson to S. Hastings Grant, September 20, 1862, Johnson Letters, NYHS; Adams, *Reminiscences of the Nineteenth Massachusetts Regiment,* 45; William Child to Wife, September 25, 1862, 5th New Hampshire regimental file, ANMP.

92. Report of Major General George McClellan, October 15, 1862; Return of Casualties, *O.R.,* vol. 19, pt. 1, 69, 189–200. The First Corps, Fifth Corps, Sixth Corps, Ninth Corps, and Twelfth Corps lost a combined 7,590 men killed, wounded, and missing.

93. George Beidelman to Father, September 19, 1862, in *The Civil War Letters of George Washington Beidelman,* 103; Joseph

Johnson to Parents, September 20, 1862, Johnson Letters, NYHS.

94. Ephraim Brown, diary entry, September 21, 1862, 64th New York regimental file, ANMP; Albert Manley to Wife, September 20, 1862, 20th Massachusetts regimental file, ANMP; Edward Cross to Henry Kent, September 20, 1862, in *Civil War Writings of Edward E. Cross*, 120; Samuel Maguire to Wife, September 17, 1862, Maguire Letters, WRHS.

95. Joseph Johnson to Parents, September 20, 1862, Johnson Letters, NYHS. Also see Report of Colonel Joshua Owen, September 21, 1862, *O.R.*, vol. 11, pt. 1, 319.

96. Nelson Miles to Brother, September 24, 1862, Miles Papers, USAMHI; William White to Mother, September 21, 1862, 69th Pennsylvania regimental file, ANMP.

97. Aldrich, *The History of Battery A, First Regiment Rhode Island Light Artillery*, 142; Sawyer, *A Military History of the 8th Regiment Ohio Vol. Inf'y*, 81, Galwey, *The Valiant Hours*, 45.

98. Joseph Johnson to Dear Friend, October 1, 1862, Johnson Letters, NYHS.

99. Sears, *Landscape Turned Red*, 330–35, 387–92.

100. Joseph Johnson to Friend, October 2, 1862, Johnson Letters, NYHS; McPherson, *Crossroads of Freedom*, 138–41. The statement regarding soldiers making little comment regarding the Emancipation Proclamation is made with some caution. Johnson writes, "The President's proclamation is discussed all over camp and many a hope and prediction may be heard in relation to the result."

101. William Landon to *Vincennes (Indiana) Sun*, October 6, 1862, transcribed at: http://members.evansville.net/~tlconner/. Landon writes that "The 'Wooly Horse' is 'booked' for a race on the first of January next, I see. I hope 'twill prove a d-d short one, and break the neck of both the horse and the rided [*sic*]."

102. George Beidelman to Father, September 26, 1862, in *The Civil War Letters of George Washington Beidelman*, 109; William Smith to Mother, November 14, 1862, Smith Letters, USAMHI; Elijah Cavins to Ann, November 27, 1862, Cavins Collection, IHS.

103. Unidentified soldier letter, September 23, 1862, 53rd Pennsylvania regimental file, ANMP; Albert Manley to Wife, September 23, 1862, 20th Massachusetts regimental file, ANMP.

104. Cowtan, *Services of the Tenth New York*, 152; Kepler, *History of the . . . Fourth Ohio Volunteer Infantry*, 84. The arrival of the paymaster is described in Chapin, *A Brief History of the Thirty-Fourth Regiment N.Y.S.V.*, 72.

105. Major General George McClellan, Special Orders, No. 274, October 7, 1862; George McClellan to Henry Halleck, October 25, 1862, *O.R.*, vol. 19, pt. 2, 400, 483–84; Walker, *History of the Second Army Corps*, 128; Warner, *Generals in Blue*, 95–96; Sears, *McClellan*, 335–36.

106. George Beidelman to Father, October 15, 1862, in *The Civil War Letters of George Washington Beidelman*, 127.

107. The standard biographies of Hancock are Jordan, *Winfield Scott Hancock*; and Tucker, *Hancock the Superb*. Also see Denison, *Winfield* and *Hancock "The Superb"*; Forney, *Life and Military Career of Winfield Scott Hancock*; Goodrich, *The Life of Winfield Scott Hancock*; and Jamieson, *Winfield Scott Hancock*. A biography written by Hancock's adjutant in the Second Corps is Walker, *General Hancock*. Also see Walker's "Hancock in the War of the Rebellion." For much-sanitized excerpts from some of Hancock's writings, edited by Hancock's wife, see Almira Hancock, *Reminiscences of Winfield Scott Hancock*.

108. Fuller, *Personal Recollections of the War of 1861*, 84; Theodore Lyman to Wife, May 20, 1864, in *With Grant and*

Meade from the Wilderness to Appomattox, 107; John H. W. Stuckenberg, diary entry, November 12, 1862, in *I'm Surrounded by Methodists*, 30–31. Stuckenberg disapprovingly noted that Hancock "is addicted to one very unmanly unsoldierly vice—profanity."

109. Studies of the life and career of Howard include Carpenter, *Sword and Olive Branch*; McFeely, *Yankee Stepfather*; and Weland, *O. O. Howard*. For Howard's perspective, see Howard, *Autobiography*.

110. Herbert Willand, diary entry, February 3–7, 1862, Willand Diary, NHSL; William White to unidentified recipient, October 5, 1862, 69th Pennsylvania regimental file, ANMP; J. Franklin Dyer, diary entry, November 8, 1862, in *The Journal of a Civil War Surgeon*, 46. Not all soldiers disapproved of Howard. Dyer writes that Howard "is one of our best generals, I think, though not a great man yet, and the men have the greatest confidence in him. I don't know of one of our generals that I like better as a man than General Howard."

111. Dyer, *A Compendium of the War of the Rebellion*, 296–312.

112. Abstract from Tri-monthly Return of the Army of the Potomac, October 11, 1862, *O.R.*, vol. 19, pt. 2, 410. Excluding the Second Corps, the manpower strengths of the five corps of the Army of the Potomac were as follows: First Corps, 14,673 men; Fifth Corps, 18,077 men; Sixth Corps, 25,056 men; Ninth Corps, 13,727 men; and Twelfth Corps, 14,223 men.

113. Cowtan, *Services of the Tenth New York Volunteers*, 149; *Reunions of the Nineteenth Maine Regiment Association*, 8.

114. Mulholland, *The Story of the 116th Regiment Pennsylvania Volunteers*, 13; Peter Welsh to Margaret Welsh, November 30, 1862, in *Irish Green and Union Blue*, 33; Ryan, *Campaigning with the Irish Brigade*, 71. Mulholland writes that the "brigade to which the Regiment had been assigned

was a celebrated one, renowned for hard fighting and famous fun."

115. Captain Schmitt to Paul Revere, October 30, 1862, Revere Family Papers, MHS; Adams, *Reminiscences of the Nineteenth Massachusetts Regiment*, 47.

116. Chapin, *A Brief History of the Thirty-Fourth Regiment N.Y.S.V.*, 72–73; Waitt, *History of the Nineteenth Regiment, Massachusetts Volunteer Infantry*, 152–53.

117. David Beem to Wife, October 19, 1862, Beem Papers, IHS; John Lehman to Family, October 9, 1862, Lehman Family Papers, CL; John Weiser to Parents, September 23, 1862, Weiser Letters, CWMC, USAMHI.

118. Linderman, *Embattled Courage*. Linderman argues that the death and destruction of the Civil War caused soldiers to very quickly become disillusioned in their initial idea of courage. Soldiers went to war in 1861 and 1862 believing that the brave and the Godly would survive battle and disease.

119. William White to unidentified recipient, October 14, 1862, 69th Pennsylvania regimental file, ANMP; Walter Eames to Wife, September 25, 1862, Eames Letters, USAMHI; Henry Boyd, diary entry, September 18, 1862, in Washburn, *A Complete Military History and Record of the 108th Regiment N.Y. Vols.*, 107; Amory Allen to Parents, September 20, 1862, Allen Letters, ISL.

3. DEFEAT

1. Wert, *Sword of Lincoln*, 179–83. The standard and most recent biography of Burnside is Marvel, *Burnside*.

2. William Myers to Parents, November 20, 1862, Myers Letters, CWMC, USAMHI; Henry Law to Mother, November 25, 1862, 106th Pennsylvania regimental file, GNMP; Ephraim Brown, diary entry, November 10, 1862, 64th New York regimental file, ANMP.

3. The coming and going of the Third Corps and the Twelfth Corps is detailed in Welcher, *The Union Army*, 346–47, 458, 466–67.

4. Major General Ambrose Burnside, General Orders, No. 184, November 14, 1862, *O.R.*, vol. 19, pt. 2, 583–84; Marvel, *Burnside*, 147; Walker, *History of the Second Army Corps*, 136.

5. For a discussion of the professional relationship between Burnside and each of his three top-ranking subordinates, see Marvel, "The Making of a Myth," 3–4.

6. The general deployment of the Army of the Potomac around Warrenton is detailed in Welcher, *The Union Army*, 258. The manpower strengths of the Army of the Potomac are taken from Abstract from Tri-monthly Return of the Army of the Potomac, November 10, 1862, *O.R.*, vol. 19, pt. 2, 569. The above manpower figures must be used with some caution, because they are from November 10, four days before Burnside organized grand divisions, and because the Third Corps had yet to reach Warrenton. To determine the number of men present for duty in the Third Corps, the total number of men present for duty in the Army of the Potomac at Warrenton in mid-November (92,782) was subtracted from the total number of men present for duty in the Army of the Potomac at the start of the Fredericksburg Campaign in late November (110,000), giving a likely strength for the Third Corps at 17,218 men present for duty. Given these cautions, the manpower totals for November 10 are the best available, because, for the last time until the Battle of Fredericksburg on December 13, the manpower totals of the First Corps, Second Corps, Fifth Corps, Sixth Corps, and Ninth Corps are listed.

7. Taaffe, *Commanding the Army of the Potomac*, 62–65; Wert, *The Sword of Lincoln*, 185–86.

8. Recent studies of the Fredericksburg Campaign are O'Reilly, *The Fredericksburg Campaign*; and Rable, *Fredericksburg! Fredericksburg!* Also see, Henderson, *The Campaign of Fredericksburg*; Stackpole, *The Fredericksburg Campaign*; and Whan, *Fiasco at Fredericksburg*. A series of interpretive essays is found in Gallagher, ed., *The Fredericksburg Campaign*. For the Fredericksburg Campaign in context with other campaigns, see Cullen, *The Battles of Fredericksburg, Chancellorsville, the Wilderness, and Spotsylvania Court House*; Luvaas and Nelson, *The U.S. Army War College Guide to the Battles of Chancellorsville and Fredericksburg*; Palfrey, *The Antietam and Fredericksburg*; and Sutherland, *Fredericksburg and Chancellorsville*.

9. J. E. Hodgkins, diary entry, November 21, 1862, in *The Civil War Diary of Lieut. J. E. Hodgkins*, 13; George Beidelman to Father, November 18, 1862, in *The Civil War Letters of George Washington Beidelman*, 147; Lemuel Jeffries, diary entry, November 15, 1862, in "'The Excitement Had Begun!'" 270.

10. Edwin Sumner testimony, December 19, 1862, *CCW*, pt. 1, 656–60; Mulholland, "At Fredericksburg, December 13, 1862."

11. Report of Major General Ambrose Burnside, *O.R.*, vol. 21, 87–88; Edwin Sumner testimony, December 19, 1862, *CCW*, vol. 1, 657; Howard, *Autobiography*, 316–18; Marvel, *Burnside*, 166–67; Walker, *History of the Second Army Corps*, 141.

12. Edwin Sumner testimony, December 19, 1862, *CCW*, vol. 1, 656–60.

13. Unidentified enlisted soldier letter, in Cowtan, *Services of the Tenth New York Volunteers*, 159; Oliver Hopkinson to Lizzie Hopkinson, November 24, 1862, Hopkinson Letters, PHS.

14. Miles Peabody to Brother George, December 1, 1862, Peabody Letters, CWMC, USAMHI; Edward Bassett

letter, November 23, 1862, in *From Bull Run to Bristow Station*, 23; Sutherland, *Fredericksburg and Chancellorsville*, 29–30.

15. The plan of attack is drawn from Burnside's verbal and written comments to his subordinates in early December. For description of the proposed Federal attack, see Sutherland, *Fredericksburg and Chancellorsville*, 30–32; and Marvel, *Burnside*, 170, 175. For the orders issued to the Right Grand Division, see Ambrose Burnside to Edwin Sumner, December 11, 1862, *O.R.*, vol. 21, 106. Despite these orders, Burnside continued to tinker with his plans until the morning of December 13. In a revised plan of attack, Burnside wanted Franklin's men to capture a military road running behind the Confederate right flank. Burnside hoped that the threat to the military road would force Lee to transfer troops from his left flank. With Confederate troops in transition from left to right, Sumner would send forward the Second Corps to storm Marye's Heights. Burnside poorly communicated his revised plan of attack to his subordinates, leading to a confusion of purpose throughout the battle. For the new plan of attack, see Sutherland, *Fredericksburg and Chancellorsville*, 43, 45, 51–52; and Marvel, *Burnside*, 178–83, 187–88. For the revised orders issued to the Right Grand Division, see Ambrose Burnside to Edwin Sumner, December 13, 1862, *O.R.*, vol. 21, 90.

16. The account of the meetings between Burnside and Sumner and the other high-ranking officers of the Right Grand Division is taken from Couch, "Sumner's 'Right Grand Division,'" 107–108. Couch was writing well after the magnitude of the Federal defeat at Fredericksburg was known, so his account must be taken with some caution. For a more balanced recounting of the same meetings, see Marvel, "The Making of a Myth," 6–7.

17. Corby, *Memoirs of Chaplain Life*, 131.

18. The regiments sent to the army while awaiting the attack at Fredericksburg are detailed in Welcher, *The Union Army*, 260–61. The Ninth Corps received the 15th Connecticut, 8th Michigan, 13th New Hampshire, and 25th New Jersey, while the First Corps received the 94th New York.

19. Sheldon, *The "Twenty-Seventh*," 13; Borton, *Awhile with the Blue*, 12; S. P. Conrad to L. M. Strickler, November 17, 1862, Conrad Letters, CWMC, USAMHI.

20. Sheldon, *The "Twenty-Seventh*," 21; Walker, *History of the Second Army Corps*, 143–44.

21. Rable, *Fredericksburg! Fredericksburg!* 156–64; O'Reilly, *The Fredericksburg Campaign*, 76–78.

22. Report of Colonel Norman Hall, December 17, 1862, *O.R.*, vol. 21, 282–84; Weymouth, "The Crossing of the Rappahannock by the 19th Massachusetts," 121; Adams, *Reminiscences of the Nineteenth Massachusetts Regiment*, 50; J. E. Hodgkins, diary entry, December 11, 1862, in *The Civil War Diary of Lieut. J. E. Hodgkins*, 16.

23. Henry Ropes to John Codman Ropes, December 18, 1862, Ropes Letters, BPL; Waitt, *History of the Nineteenth Regiment, Massachusetts Volunteer Infantry*, 171. The casualty figures are taken from Report of Brigadier General Oliver O. Howard, December 19, 1862, *O.R.*, vol. 21, 263.

24. Report of Colonel Norman Hall, December 17, 1862, in *O.R.*, vol. 21, 288; Oliver Wendell Holmes, *Touched with Fire*, 90–91; Report of Brigadier General Oliver O. Howard, December 19, 1862, in *O.R.*, vol. 21, 266. Ambrose Burnside quotation taken from O'Reilly, *The Fredericksburg Campaign*, 79.

25. Church, "The Crossing at Fredericksburg"; Cafferty, "The

Crossing at Fredericksburg"; Du Bois, "Fredericksburg."

26. Chapin, *A Brief History of the Thirty-Fourth Regiment N.Y.S.V.*, 80; Mulholland, *The Story of the 116th Regiment Pennsylvania Volunteers*, 35–36.

27. Charles Davis to Father, December 1862, Davis Folder, BRU; Oliver Palmer to Wife, December 16, 1862, Palmer Papers, NC; Roland Bowen to Mother, December 20, 1863, in *From Ball's Bluff to Gettysburg*, 142; E. A. Walker to Friend Knight, January 24, 1863, Walker Letters, Leigh Collection, USAMHI.

28. Page, *History of the Fourteenth Regiment, Connecticut Volunteer Infantry*, 80. For a discussion of the Union destruction in Fredericksburg as "directed severity," see Grimsley, *The Hard Hand of War*, 108–109. Also see Rable, *Fredericksburg! Fredericksburg!* 177–84; and Blair, "Barbarians at Fredericksburg's Gate," 142–70.

29. *Minnesota in the Civil and Indian Wars*, vol. 1, 29; Report of Major General Darius Couch, January 1863, *O.R.*, vol. 21, 222.

30. McCarter, *My Life in the Irish Brigade*, 157; Frank Plympton letter, December 16, 1862, vol. 74, FSNMP; Henry Abbott, *Fallen Leaves*, 156; Stuckenberg, diary entry, in *I'm Surrounded by Methodists*, 38.

31. Roland Bowen to Mother, December 20, 1862, in *From Ball's Bluff to Gettysburg*, 142; *Reunions of the Nineteenth Maine Regiment Association*, 8.

32. Cowtan, *Services of the Tenth New York Volunteers*, 169; Sheldon, *The "Twenty-Seventh,"* 30; John Lehman to Parents, December 15, 1862, Lehman Family Papers, CL; Report of Major General Darius Couch, January 1863, *O.R.*, vol. 21, 222.

33. The ground crossed by the Second Corps is described in Walker, *History of the Second Army Corps*, 162–64; and

Rable, *Fredericksburg! Fredericksburg!* 219–20.

34. Kepler, *History of the . . . Fourth Regiment Ohio Volunteer Infantry*, 94; Sawyer, *A Military History of the 8th Regiment Ohio Vol. Inf'y*, 95; Longstreet, "The Battle of Fredericksburg," 78.

35. Kepler, *History of the . . . Fourth Regiment Ohio Volunteer Infantry*, 95; Cory, "A Private's Recollections of Fredericksburg," 137.

36. Sheldon, *The "Twenty-Seventh,"* 28; Hitchcock, *War from the Inside*, 121; Page, *History of the Fourteenth Regiment, Connecticut Volunteer Infantry*, 84; Borton, *Awhile with the Blue*, 42.

37. David Beem to Mahala Beem, December 14, 1862, Beem Papers, IHS; John Weiser to Parents, December 17, 1862, Weiser Papers, CWMC, USAMHI.

38. Fuller, *Personal Recollections of the War of 1861*, 78; McCarter, *My Life in the Irish Brigade*, 165.

39. Cowtan, *Services of the Tenth New York Volunteers*, 170; Mulholland, *The Story of the 116th Regiment Pennsylvania Volunteers*, 43.

40. George Hopper to J. Hopper, December 21, 1862, Hopper Letters, USAMHI; Page, *History of the Fourteenth Regiment, Connecticut Volunteer Infantry*, 88.

41. Levi Fritz, "The Battle of Fredericksburg," December 15, 1862, volume 74, FSNMP; Josiah Favill, diary entry, December 13, 1862, in *Diary of a Young Officer*, 211–12; John McCrillis letter in Child, *A History of the Fifth Regiment New Hampshire Volunteers*, 156.

42. Couch, "Sumner's 'Right Grand Division,'" 113; Report of Major General Darius Couch, January 1863, *O.R.*, vol. 21, 223.

43. Walker, *History of the Second Army Corps*, 177; Rhodes, *History of Battery B, First Rhode Island Light Artillery*, 141.

44. O'Reilly, *The Fredericksburg Campaign*, 501–502.

45. Report of Brigadier General Winfield S. Hancock, December 25, 1862, *O.R.*, vol. 21, 228. Hancock's claims later were disputed by soldiers of the Fifth Corps and Ninth Corps, who also had attacked against the stone wall. For description of the controversy, see Reardon, "The Forlorn Hope," 103–106.

46. Couch, "Sumner's 'Right Grand Division,'" 117; Edwin Sumner testimony, December 19, 1862, *CCW*, vol. 1, 658.

47. Andrew Humphreys to Daniel Butterfield, December 13, 1862; Report of Brigadier General Andrew Humphreys, December 16, 1862, *O.R.*, vol. 21, 74, 430–34; Walker, *History of the Second Army Corps*, 181–87.

48. The number of men present for duty in each Union corps is uncertain, since returns are listed only by Grand Division. The numbers cited above are taken from Stackpole, *The Fredericksburg Campaign*. Stackpole lists the Second Corps as fielding 15,838 men present for duty at the battle. Casualty figures for the Second Corps and the rest of the Army of the Potomac are taken from Return of Casualties in the Union Forces, December 13, 1862, *O.R.*, vol. 21, 129–42.

49. Report of Brigadier General Winfield S. Hancock, December 25, 1862, *O.R.*, vol. 21, 228–29; Walker, *History of the Second Army Corps*, 190–93.

50. Report of Brigadier General Winfield S. Hancock, December 25, 1862, *O.R.*, vol. 21, 228–29; Conyngham, *The Irish Brigade*, 349; T. Groves, diary entry, December 17, 1862, in Child, *A History of the Fifth Regiment New Hampshire Volunteers*, 150; Edward Cross, private journal, in *Civil War Writings of Edward E. Cross*, 59.

51. Darius Couch to Lt. Col. Taylor, December 13, 1862, Sumner Family Papers, LC; E. L. Stratton, diary entry, December 19, 1862, in Haines, *History of*

the *Men of Co. F*, 31. The Second Corps listed 13,689 men absent from duty in late December 1862. See Walker, *History of the Second Army Corps*, 196.

52. James Mitchell to Mother, December 21, 1862, Mitchell Letters, USAMHI; Rodney Ramsey to Father, December 24, 1862, vol. 252, FSNMP; Darius Couch, journal entry, December 13, 1862, Couch Journal, Old Colony Historical Society; Isaac Taylor, diary entry, December 14, 1862, in "Campaigning with the First Minnesota," 237.

53. Galwey, *The Valiant Hours*, 65; Kepler, *History of the … Fourth Regiment Ohio Volunteer Infantry*, 98–99; Charles Davis, diary entry, December 1862, Davis Folder, BRU.

54. Adams, *Reminiscences of the Nineteenth Massachusetts Regiment*, 54; Galwey, *The Valiant Hours*, 66; Walker, *History of the Second Army Corps*, 187–88.

55. William Plumer to Mother, December 15, 1862, vol. 280, FSNMP; Wright, *No More Gallant a Deed*, 247.

56. Abraham Lincoln, "Congratulations to the Army of the Potomac," December 22, 1862, in *The Collected Works of Abraham Lincoln*, vol. 6, 13.

57. E. A. Walker to Friend Knight, January 24, 1863, Walker Letters, Leigh Collection, USAMHI; Charles Eager to Wife, December 14, 1862, Eager Letters, Leigh Collection, USAMHI; Joseph Elliott, diary entry, December 16, 1862, Elliott Diary, CWMC, USAMHI; Rodney Ramsey to Father, December 24, 1862, vol. 252, FSNMP.

58. Augustus Wallen to Friend Samuel, December 22, 1862, Bond Letters, PHS; Hamlet Richardson to Cousins Grace and Mary, January 19, 1863, Richardson Letters, LC; Edward Cotter to John Cotter, January 23, 1863, Cotter Letters, CWMC, USAMHI; Isaac Hillyer to Wife, December 20, 1862, vol. 33, FSNMP;

Oliver Palmer to Wife, December 16, 1862, Palmer Papers, NC.

59. Winfield Scott Hancock, special orders 544, December 16, 1862, 2d Army Corps Records, RG 393, NA; O'Reilly, *The Fredericksburg Campaign*, 458–60.

60. William Teall to wife, December 18, 1862, Teall Letters, TSLA; P. C. Campbell, diary entry, December 17, 1862, vol. 276, FSNMP. Teall writes that "Col. Brooks came to our room last night and told me he had buried 620 during the day and thought there would be 400 more today." Campbell writes that "they buried over 1,100 dead they had been stript to the _____ of all clothing."

61. Ryan, *Campaigning with the Irish Brigade*, 83; A. Stokes Jones to Sister, December 28, 1862, vol. 44, FSNMP; Kepler, *History of the . . . Fourth Regiment Ohio Volunteer Infantry*, 99–100.

62. Page, *History of the Fourteenth Regiment, Connecticut Volunteer Infantry*, 107; Charles Hamlin to Father, January 21, 1863, Hamlin Letters, NYSLA; William Teall to Wife, January 24, 1862, Teall Letters, TSLA; Stephen Martin, diary entry, January 17, 1862, vol. 278, FSNMP; Stewart, *History of the One Hundred and Fortieth Regiment Pennsylvania Volunteers*, 30–31.

63. Isaac Plumb, "Record of Life and Service," January 1, 1863, CWMC, USAMHI; James Fay to Aunt Martha, February 2, 1863, vol. 146, FSNMP. Some soldiers of the Second Corps gave at least tepid support to the Emancipation Proclamation. Captain Isaac Plumb wrote, "Our northern traitors tell us we are fighting for the Negro, those traitors would sooner see the country disrupted and lost than have the institution of slavery die. I have some regard for the conscientious rebels of the South, they are sincere and prove by their sacrifices their sincerity." Private James Fay took pragmatic view, writing that "I don't like to fight for [the] niggar I

come to fight for the Union. But it cant be helped now."

64. Reaction to the Emancipation Proclamation throughout the army is discussed in Rable, *Fredericksburg! Fredericksburg!* 373–78; and Sutherland, *Fredericksburg and Chancellorsville*, 85–86. For reaction throughout the Union army in general, see McPherson, *For Cause and Comrades*, 121–28.

65. John McClure to Sister, January 2, 1863, in *Hoosier Farm Boy in Lincoln's Army*, 35–36; Peter Welsh to Margaret Welsh, February 1863, in *Irish Green and Union Blue*, 62.

66. William A. Smith to Sister, February 11, 1863, Smith Letters, Leigh Collection, USAMHI; Miles Peabody to Brother and Sister, February 14, 1863, Peabody Letters, CWMC, USAMHI.

67. William Jackson letter, early January 1863, vol. 275, FSNMP; George Seaman, diary entry, January 1, 1863, vol. 274, FSNMP.

68. Page, *History of the Fourteenth Regiment, Connecticut Volunteer Infantry*, 71; Lauren Hotchkiss to Sister, November 16, 1862, Hotchkiss Letters, CHS; Joseph Law to Wife, January 28, 1863, Law Family Papers, CWMC, USAMHI.

69. William Burns, diary entry, January 1, 1863, Burns Diary, CWMC, USAMHI; John McClure to Sister, January 2, 1863, in *Hoosier Farm Boy in Lincoln's Army*, 35.

70. William Jackson to Brothers, November 26, 1862, vol. 275, FSNMP; Unidentified Soldier, 19th Massachusetts, letter, December 4, 1862, FSNMP; Charles Hamlin to Parents, January 18, 1863, Hamlin Letters, NYSLA.

71. Chapin, *A Brief History of the Thirty-Fourth Regiment N.Y.S.V.*, 86; Sergeant Powelson reminiscences, in Stewart, *History of the One Hundred and Fortieth Regiment Pennsylvania Volunteers*, 36–37.

72. Edwin Sumner testimony, December 19, 1862, *CCW*, vol. 1, 660.

73. John Newton testimony, *CCW*, vol. 1, 730–31. For description of Burnside's failed offensive, see Rable, *Fredericksburg! Fredericksburg!* 409–19; and Sutherland, *Fredericksburg and Chancellorsville*, 89–91.

74. Walker, *History of the Second Army Corps*, 199, 209–10.

75. The commanding officers of the regiments of the Second Corps are taken from Organization of the Army of the Potomac, January 31, 1863, *O.R.*, vol. 25, pt. 2, 17–18.

76. Richard Thompson to Sister, January 4, 1863, in *While My Country Is in Danger*, 39; Arch Jones to Mary, January 18, 1863, vol. 275, FSNMP; Jeremiah Rohrer, diary entry, March 24, 1863, Rohrer Collection, PHMC; Goddard, *14th C.V. Regimental Reminiscences of the War of the Rebellion*, 12.

77. For the arrival of the Eleventh Corps and Twelfth Corps and the departure of the Ninth Corps, see Welcher, *The Union Army*, 261–62. For the inspection of the Army of the Potomac, see Bigelow, *Chancellorsville*, 490–91. Bigelow ranks the seven corps of the army, in order of instruction and discipline, as follows: Eleventh Corps, Fifth Corps, Third Corps, Sixth Corps, Twelfth Corps, First Corps, Second Corps.

78. George Macy, Extract of Inspection Report, February 13, 1863, 2d Army Corps Records, RG 393, NA; A. F. Devereux, Extract of Inspection Report, February 13, 1863, 2d Army Corps Records, RG 393, NA; William French, Special Order, January 14, 1863, 2d Army Corps Records, RG 393, NA.

79. Miles Peabody to Brother and Sister, February 14, 1863, Peabody Letters, CWMC, USAMHI; Mathew Marvin to Parents, January 18, 1863, Marvin Papers, MNHS.

80. William French to Darius Couch, February 6, 1863; Joseph Hooker to Lorenzo Thomas, February 13, 1863, *O.R.*,

vol. 25, pt. 2, 72–73; Bigelow, *The Campaign of Chancellorsville*, 36. Bigelow estimates that about 9 percent of the soldiers of the Second Corps and about 10 percent of soldiers throughout the rest of the army deserted during the winter of 1862–63.

81. Henry Ropes to John Ropes, January 21, 1863, Ropes Letters, BPL. For a contrasting view, see Charles Eager to Wife, January 27, 1863, Leigh Collection, USAMHI. Eager asked, "Have you heard the reports of the 15th becoming disloyal and cheer[ing] for Jeff Davis and any quantity of other reports? It is all humbug. . . . It is a sham and the men feel indignant enough about it. We have gone through [too] much for the past year and a half and gained a reputation thereby to have our dish upset."

82. The numbers of men sick are taken from Bigelow, *Chancellorsville*, 493.

83. *Reunions of the Nineteenth Maine Regiment Association*, 9. The manpower of the Second Corps and the rest of the army is taken from Abstract from Consolidated Morning Report, February 10, 1863, *O.R.*, vol. 25, pt. 2, 65–66.

84. Augustus Wallen to Friend Samuel, December 22, 1862, Samuel Maker Correspondence, PHS.

4. PINNACLE

1. The best biography of Hooker remains Hebert, *Fighting Joe Hooker*.

2. Kepler, *History of the . . . Fourth Regiment Ohio Volunteer Infantry*, 104. For praise of Hooker's reforms, see Henry Bassett letter, April 6, 1863, in *From Bull Run to Bristow Station*, 26; Smith, *The History of the Nineteenth Regiment of Maine Volunteer Infantry*, 39; and John Stuckenberg, diary entry, April 14, 1863, in *I'm Surrounded by Methodists*, 57. For a dissenting view, see Joe Moody to Family, March 3, 1863, Moody Letters, Leigh Collection, USAMHI. Moody writes that Hooker "is quite a pompous looking

fellow, by the way dressed to death. Burnside suited my views of the real gen. for he was dressed no better than many of us its not the coat that makes the man." The administrative reforms of Hooker and their beneficial effects on the morale of the army are discussed in Hebert, *Fighting Joe Hooker*, 171–84; and Wert, *The Sword of Lincoln*, 225–27.

3. Corby, *Memoirs of Chaplain Life*, 142. For detailed description of the various activities at the St. Patrick's Day celebration, see Conyngham, *The Irish Brigade and Its Campaigns*, 372–87; and Mulholland, *The Story of the 116th Regiment Pennsylvania Volunteers*, 77–83.

4. Samuel Fiske letter, in *Mr. Dunn Browne's Experiences*, 129–31; Allen Landis to Father, March 20, 1863, Landis Family Papers, LC; Elijah Cavins to Wife, April 1, 1863, Cavins Collection, IHS. Reaction of Union soldiers to the perceived threat to the Union war effort by the political successes of the Peace Democrats is discussed in Sutherland, *Fredericksburg and Chancellorsville*, 105–106; and Hennessy, "'We Shall Make Richmond Howl,'" 5.

5. Major General Joseph Hooker, Circular, Headquarters Army of the Potomac, March 21, 1863, *O.R.*, vol. 25, pt. 2, 152. For discussion of Hooker's decision to issue corps badges, see Hennessy, "'We Shall Make Richmond Howl,'" 11.

6. Stewart, *History of the One Hundred and Fortieth Regiment Pennsylvania Volunteers*, 45–46. The claim continues through today. See Sears, *Chancellorsville*, 72. Sears claims that the Second Corps received the trefoil badge "for its resemblance to the shamrock badge beloved by the many Irishmen in the corps."

7. Wright, *No More Gallant a Deed*, 252; Waitt, *History of the Nineteenth Regiment, Massachusetts Volunteer Infantry*, 211; Charles Mills to Mother, October 19, 1864, in *Through Blood and Fire*, 204; Wert, *The Sword of Lincoln*, 226.

8. General Orders, No. 20, War Department, Adjt. Gen.'s Office, January 25, 1863, *O.R.*, vol. 25, pt. 2, 3; Walker, *History of the Second Army Corps*, 200–201.

9. Major General Edwin Sumner, General Orders, No. 1, January 26, 1863, *O.R.*, vol. 25, pt. 2, 6.

10. Charles Hamlin to Parents, January 18, 1863, Hamlin Letters, NYSLA; Josiah Favill, diary entry, February 1863, in *Diary of a Young Army Officer*, 220; Frederick, *The Story of a Regiment*, 140; Edward Bassett letter, n.d., in *From Bull Run to Bristow Station*, 25.

11. Hennessy, "'We Shall Make Richmond Howl,'" 3–4 and 16; Taaffe, *Commanding the Army of the Potomac*, 80, 87.

12. The regimental commanders of the Second Corps on May 1, 1863, are taken from Organization of the Army of the Potomac, May 1–6, 1863, *O.R.*, vol. 25, pt. 1, 159–60.

13. William French to John MacGregor, February 19, 1863, 2d Army Corps Records, RG 393, NA; Major General Joseph Hooker, General Orders, Numbers 27, March 14, 1863, *O.R.*, vol. 25, pt. 1, 159–60. French complained after the first inspection that in the 132nd Pennsylvania "one hundred and twelve enlisted men are without arms and most were lost at the battle of Fredericksburg and up to this time have never been replaced. The men have no knapsacks." In a far cry from the improvement made by the Second Corps, only a handful of the nineteen regiments throughout the rest of the army that had failed the first inspection passed the second inspection.

14. James Walker, diary entry, March 21, 1863, Walker Diary, PHS. For description of the same ceremony, see James Beaver reminiscence in Muffly, *The Story of Our Regiment*, 77.

15. Isaac Taylor, diary entry, April 25, 1863, in "Campaigning with the First Minnesota," 344; Walker, *History of the*

Second Army Corps, 310. Walker lists the numbers of men under arrest for the first four months of 1863 as: January, 111 men; February, 144 men; March, 161 men; and April, 81 men.

16. Isaac Plumb letter, April 12, 1863, "Record of Life and Service," CWMC, USAMHI; William Smith to Mother, April 9, 1863, Smith Letters, USAMHI; William Houghton to Father, April 13, 1863, Houghton Collection, IHS; Joseph Graham to Aunt, April 18, 1863, Graham Letters, CWMC, USAMHI.

17. The recollections of Gibbon are found in his *Personal Recollections*. Discussion of the transfer of Howard is found in Howard, *Autobiography*, 348–49. Howard pushed Hooker for a corps command, offended that Sickles, a general junior in rank, had received command of the Third Corps earlier in the spring.

18. The story of the Iron Brigade is found in Nolan, *The Iron Brigade*; and Wert, *A Brotherhood of Valor*.

19. Smith, *History of the Nineteenth Regiment of Maine Volunteer Infantry*, 77; Theodore Lyman to Wife, May 18, 1864, in *Meade's Headquarters*, 107; J. Franklin Dyer, diary entry, April 23, 1863, in *The Journal of a Civil War Surgeon*, 72.

20. Joseph Snider to Wife, April 19, 1862, vol. 327, FSNMP; Warner, *Generals in Blue*, 73, 225; Walker, *History of the Second Army Corps*, 206.

21. Report of Brigadier General Winfield Scott Hancock, December 25, 1862, *O.R.*, vol. 21, pt. 1, 229. Hancock glowed that Brooke had performed the "highest service to his country, and added to the laurels he and his regiment had already won on many fields."

22. The organization of the army is listed in Organization of the Army of the Potomac, May 1–6, 1863, *O.R.*, vol. 25, pt. 1, 156–70. Brigadier General James Wadsworth's division (First Corps) also listed four brigades.

23. The exception was Colonel John MacGregor of the 4th New York, who, as senior-ranking regimental commander, assumed command of the Third Brigade, Third Division, during the winter of 1862–63.

24. Major General William French and Brigadier Generals John Caldwell, Thomas Meagher, Alfred Sully, and Joshua Owen all had commanded divisions or brigades in the Second Corps since the summer of 1862. Major Generals Darius Couch and Winfield Scott Hancock, Brigadier General John Gibbon, and Colonel Samuel Carroll all had led divisions and brigades before coming to the Second Corps.

25. The data on the leadership experience of the army in the spring of 1863 are taken from Hennessy, "'We Shall Make Richmond Howl,'" 15–16. Hooker's order to disband Burnside's Grand Division is found in Major General Joseph Hooker, General Orders, Hdqrs. Army of the Potomac, No. 6, February 5, 1863, *O.R.* vol. 25, pt. 2, 51. The shortage of leadership in the army on the eve of the Chancellorsville Campaign is discussed in Sears, *Chancellorsville*, 63–64.

26. To be fair to Hooker, the Second Corps, if not among the favored, likely stood well above the Eleventh Corps and Twelfth Corps. The two Federal corps had served in the now disbanded Army of Virginia during the Second Bull Run Campaign, and had yet to shake the perceived taint of their association. For a description of the standing of the Eleventh Corps and Twelfth Corps in the Army of the Potomac, see Hennessy, "'We Shall Make Richmond Howl,'" 23–26.

27. Couch, "Sumner's 'Right Grand Division,'" 119. Couch claimed that when Hooker "was placed in command of the army, many of us were very much surprised; I think the superior officers did not regard him competent for the task. He

had fine qualities as an officer, but not the weight of character to take charge of that army."

28. Hennessy, "'We Shall Make Richmond Howl,'" 21–23. Hennessy claims the "Sixth Corps had to this point in the war done relatively little fighting." The attempts by Hooker to make the Army of the Potomac more mobile, including the creation of the Light Division, are described in Sears, *Chancellorsville*, 104–107.

29. Hooker's pride in the Third Corps is described in Hebert, *Fighting Joe Hooker*, 175. The politics behind Hooker's promotion of Sickles is discussed in Sears, *Chancellorsville*, 64–66. An excellent recent biography of Sickles is found in Keneally, *American Scoundrel*.

30. The standard study of the Chancellorsville Campaign is Bigelow, *The Campaign of Chancellorsville*. For studies of the campaign and battle other than those previously cited, see Dodge, *The Campaign of Chancellorsville*; Doubleday, *Chancellorsville and Gettysburg*; Furgurson, *Chancellorsville 1863*; Stackpole, *Chancellorsville*. Hooker's plan of maneuver is described in Sutherland, *Fredericksburg and Chancellorsville*, 131–33; and Sears, *Chancellorsville*, 136–41.

31. Lemuel Jeffries, diary entry, April 30, 1863, in "The Excitement Had Begun," 272; T. Grove, diary entry, May 1, 1863, in Child, *A History of the Fifth Regiment New Hampshire Volunteers*, 176.

32. Warren Pearsons to Daniel Pearsons, May 30, 1863, vol. 283, FSNMP; Report of Colonel Orlando Morris, May 8, 1863, *O.R.*, vol. 25, pt. 1, 331–32; Josiah Favill, diary entry, early May 1863, in *Diary of a Young Army Officer*, 234–35.

33. Sheldon, *The "Twenty-Seventh,"* 51–55; Jones, "How the 145th Pa. Got Captured."

34. For Hancock's description of the fighting on the late morning of May 3,

see Report of Major General Winfield S. Hancock, May 19, 1863, *O.R.*, vol. 25, pt. 1, 313–14. For a description of the role of the First Division throughout the Chancellorsville Campaign, see Reardon, "The Valiant Rearguard," 143–75. Quotation in Almira Hancock, *Reminiscences of Winfield Scott Hancock*, 94.

35. Conyngham, *The Irish Brigade and Its Campaigns*, 400; Benjamin Powelson to Friend Annie, May 20, 1863, Powelson Letters, Leigh Collection, USAMHI.

36. "Maj. L. J. Sacriste"; Mulholland, *The Story of the 116th Regiment Pennsylvania Volunteers*, 100–107. For another perspective, see Stewart, *History of the One Hundred and Fortieth Regiment Pennsylvania Volunteers*, 70–71.

37. Henry Crofoot to Perry Smith, May 10, 1863, Crofoot Letters, CWTIC, USAMHI. Some men blamed Hooker's words rather than actions for the Federal defeat. Hooker reportedly declared after the army had occupied Chancellorsville on April 30 that "God Almighty could not prevent me from winning a victory tomorrow." The boast bothered many, including the normally rough-spoken Hancock. The exasperated First Division commander later asked, "Pray, could we expect a victory after that?" Hooker's boast is described in Sears, *Chancellorsville*, 191–92; Hancock's response is described in Almira Hancock, *Reminiscences of Winfield Scott Hancock*, 92.

38. Willis Babcock to Brother, May 21, 1863, Willoughby Babcock Papers, MNHS; Henry Abbott to Father, May 5, 1863, in *Fallen Leaves*, 176. The rout of the Eleventh Corps has generated a considerable body of literature, mostly critical of Howard and his men. For a blow-by-blow account of the fighting, see Bigelow, *Chancellorsville*, 295–328. For another perspective, see Howard, "The Eleventh Corps at Chancellorsville," 189–202.

Also see Keller, *Chancellorsville and the Germans.*

39. William Houghton to Father, May 8, 1863, Houghton Collection, IHS. Also see Joseph Johnson to S. Hastings Grant, May 26, 1863, Johnson Letters, NYHS; Joseph Moody to Family, May 13, 1863, Moody Letters, Leigh Collection, USAMHI; Martin Sigman, diary entry, vol. 320, FSNMP.

40. The operations of the Second Corps during the Chancellorsville Campaign are detailed in Report of Major General Darius Couch, May 20, 1863, *O.R.,* vol. 25, pt. 1, 306–307; and Walker, *History of the Second Army Corps,* 215–49. The casualties suffered by the Army of the Potomac are taken from Return of Casualties in Union Forces, Battle of Chancellorsville, *O.R.,* vol. 25, pt. 1, 174–85, 188–91.

41. Welcher, *The Union Army,* 265; Sears, *Gettysburg,* 29–30. Welcher lists fifty-five two-year and nine-month regiments leaving the army. Sears lists the Fifth Corps as the hardest hit, with the loss of thirteen short-term regiments. The two-year regiments that left the Second Corps were the 4th New York, 7th New York, 10th New York, and 34th New York. Among the 718 soldiers of the 10th New York in the spring of 1863, 240 soldiers had enlisted for a three-year term of service, and were formed into a battalion. The numbers of men in the regiment are taken from Darius Couch to S. Williams, March 29, 1863, 2d Army Corps Records, RG 393, NA. The nine-month regiments that left the Second Corps were the 24th New Jersey, 28th New Jersey, 127th Pennsylvania, 130th Pennsylvania, and 132nd Pennsylvania. The 27th Connecticut was also a nine-month regiment, with a muster-out date in midsummer 1863.

42. For details of the threatened mutiny of the 34th New York, see Gibbon, *Personal Recollections,* 112–16. Gibbon, the Second Division commander, was so angered over the affair that he relieved Sully, the brigade commander, for failure "to enforce discipline in his command." Sully was reinstated by a court of inquiry in mid-May, but soon after he was transferred to Minnesota and replaced by Brigadier General William Harrow, the former colonel of the 14th Indiana. The findings of the court of inquiry are detailed in Report of Brigadier General John Gibbon, May 7, 1863, *O.R.,* vol. 25, pt. 1, 351–52. A brief biography of Harrow is found in Warner, *Generals in Blue,* 210–11. For the perspective of soldiers in the 34th New York, see Chapin, *A Brief History of the Thirty-Fourth Regiment N.Y.S.V.,* 89–91.

43. Benjamin Appleby to Wife, February 14, 1862, Appleby Letters, RU; Sears, *Chancellorsville,* 103.

44. The reorganization of the Second Corps and the rest of the Army of the Potomac following the Chancellorsville Campaign is detailed in Welcher, *The Union Army,* 265–67.

45. Coddington, *The Gettysburg Campaign,* 39–40. Coddington writes that with the reorganization of many divisions and brigades, some "groups which had been together for months, if not years, disappeared and became matters of history. The bonds of friendship between individuals and the efficient cooperation of units created through close association were destroyed, not as a result of combat but through a lack of planning in raising the army."

46. The manpower figures are taken from Abstract from Tri-monthly Return of the Army of the Potomac, April 30, 1863, *O.R.,* vol. 25, pt. 3, 320; and Abstract from Tri-monthly Return of the Army of the Potomac, May 31, 1863, *O.R.,* vol. 25, pt. 2, 574. The number of regiments is taken from Organization of the Army of the Potomac, May 31, 1863, *O.R.,* vol. 25, pt. 2, 575–86. The average manpower strength

in regiments outside the Second Corps was 415 men present for duty.

47. The manpower of the 63rd New York and 69th New York is taken from Winfield Scott Hancock to J. W. Potter, May 9, 1863, 2d Army Corps Records, RG 393, NA. The manpower strength of the Irish Brigade is taken from Busey and Martin, *Regimental Strengths at Gettysburg*, 36. The consolidation of the Irish Brigade and Meagher's subsequent resignation is described in Conyngham, *The Irish Brigade*, 405–14.

48. The Hooker-Couch feud is discussed in Sears, *Chancellorsville*, 434–38.

49. Report of Major General Darius Couch, May 20, 1863, *O.R.*, vol. 25, pt. 1, 307–308; Edwin Stanton to Winfield Scott Hancock, August 5, 1863, Winfield Scott Hancock Papers of MOLLUS, USAMHI.

50. The friendship between Stanton and Hancock is described in more detail in Jordan, *Winfield Scott Hancock,* 75. Hancock did occasionally allow politics to color his view of the Union war effort. Hancock heard rumors that he might be asked to replace Hooker in command of the Army of the Potomac in late May. Hancock made known his unwillingness to accept the position, declaring to his wife, "I do not belong to that class of general whom the Republicans care to bolster up. I should be sacrificed." See Almira Hancock, *Reminiscences of Winfield Scott Hancock*, 94–95. For the intrigue behind the search for a possible replacement for Hooker, see Sears, *Gettysburg*, 18–26.

51. Walker, *History of the Second Army Corps*, 252–53; Van Naisawald, *Grape and Canister*, 329–30; Epstein, "The Creation and Evolution of the Army Corps," 35–37.

52. Walker, *History of the Second Army Corps*, 207–208, 533–34.

53. The Gettysburg Campaign remains among one of the most studied of the war. A standard account is Coddington, *The Gettysburg Campaign*. The best of the most

recent studies include: Sears, *Gettysburg;* and Woodworth, *Beneath a Northern Sky.* For a compilation of essays on each of the three days of the ensuing Battle of Gettysburg, see Gallagher, ed., *Three Days at Gettysburg.* For a bibliography of the many studies of the battle through the early 1980s, see Richard A. Sauers, *The Gettysburg Campaign.*

54. Chauncey Harris to Father, June 19, 1863, in Washburn, *A Complete Military History and Record of the 108th Regiment N.Y. Vols.,* 51; Coddington, *The Gettysburg Campaign,* 72; Mulholland, *The Gettysburg Campaign,* 4. Mulholland claims that the Second Corps covered over two hundred miles in marching from Fredericksburg to, eventually, Gettysburg.

55. George Finch to Dear Folks at Home, June 28, 1863, 145th Pennsylvania regimental file, GNMP; Warren Pearsons to Mother, June 21, 1863, vol. 283, FSNMP; Lauren Hotchkiss to Sister, June 2, 1863, Watson Hitchcock Papers, CHS. The hot weather experienced during June 1863 is described as a "heat wave" in Coddington, *The Gettysburg Campaign,* 72.

56. Walker, *History of the Second Army Corps,* 259–60; Busey and Martin, *Regimental Strengths at Gettysburg,* 31. Busey and Martin list the number of regiments and manpower strength of each division of the Second Corps on June 30 as: First Division—eighteen regiments and 4,006 men; Second Division—thirteen regiments and 4,389 men; and Third Division—thirteen regiments and 4,390 men.

57. The manpower of Hays's brigade is taken from Busey and Martin, *Regimental Strengths at Gettysburg,* 44. The reinforcements received are discussed in Wert, *Sword of Lincoln,* 265. The manpower of the Federal army is taken from Abstract from Return of the Army of the Potomac, June 30, 1863, *O.R.,* vol. 27, pt. 1, 151.

58. Walker, *History of the Second Army Corps,* 260. For the Union defense of

Harpers Ferry in the fall of 1862, see the relevant sections of Sears, *Landscape Turned Red*.

59. John H. W. Stuckenberg, diary entry, June 29, 1863, in *I'm Surrounded by Methodists*, 71; Isaac Taylor, diary entry, June 19, 1863, in "Campaigning with the First Minnesota," 356; Page, *History of the Fourteenth Regiment, Connecticut Volunteer Infantry*, 132.

60. Wert, *The Sword of Lincoln*, 265.

61. Warner, *Generals in Blue*, 223–24; Walker, *History of the Second Army Corps*, 260–61. Walker provides no insight regarding the departure of French beyond noting that he received transfer to Harpers Ferry. French might have resented that he missed out from command of the Second Corps in favor of Hancock. French might have requested transfer earlier, unhappy with serving in the Second Corps while still under Couch. French's division received poor marks in an inspection held in late May. French railed in response, "My command drills twice a day and I will challenge a comparison in brigade or division drill with any division in the army, regular or volunteer. It is remarkable that such a charge involving a division commander should emanate from Corps Headquarters without inspection from these Head Quarters and as the reputation of my command have been compromised by the Corps Commander and also my own. I desire to place on record my positive denial of the charges so far as it involves the entire division and request that some competent officer may be detailed who knows enough about drill to express a reliable opinion on the subject." William French to J. Schultz, May 30, 1863, 2d Army Corps Records, RG 393, NA.

62. Warner, *Generals in Blue*, 544–45; Walker, *History of the Second Army Corps*, 260; Banes, *History of the Philadelphia Brigade*, 173; Stewart, *Pickett's Charge*, 74–75.

Why Gibbon ordered the arrest of Owen is unclear. Walker and Banes both note only that the change occurred. Stewart engages in ethnic stereotype. He writes that "what was Owen's offense is uncertain; being Irish, he may have taken a drop too much at the wrong time." Insight might be gained from J. Franklin Dyer, diary entry, June 28, 1863, in *The Journal of a Civil War Surgeon*, 90. Dyer, a surgeon in the Second Division, wrote that "Owen is now under arrest for irregular conduct. He had a very good brigade, but his discipline has been so loose that they have become notorious stragglers." Also see Gottfried, *Stopping Pickett*, 151. Gottfried speculates that Owen might have suffered arrest from taking to drink and that other unspecified "lapses in discipline" failed to help his cause.

63. Sears, *Gettysburg*, 119–23. The best biography of Meade is Cleaves, *Meade of Gettysburg*. Also see Meade and Meade, *The Life and Letters of George Gordon Meade*.

64. George Finch to Wife, June 28, 1863, 145th Pennsylvania regimental file, GNMP; Galwey, *The Valiant Hours*, 96; Robert Penn Smith to Isaac Wistar, July 29, 1863, Wistar Papers, Wistar Institute.

65. Taaffe, *Commanding the Army of the Potomac*, 113–16; Sears, *Gettysburg*, 185–89, 240–44. For a description of the fighting in and around Gettysburg on July 1, see Pfanz, *Gettysburg—The First Day*.

66. Henry Hunt, "The First Day at Gettysburg," 283. For a concise account of the Hancock-Howard controversy, which otherwise consumed much ink and many years, see Jordan, *Hancock*, 82–84. Also see Wert, *The Sword of Lincoln*, 281–82.

67. Fuller, *Personal Recollections of the War of 1861*, 92; Lemuel Jeffries, diary entry, July 2, 1863, in "The Excitement Had Begun!" 274; Unidentified soldier letter, July 2, 1863, in Smith, *The History of the Nineteenth Regiment of Maine*

Volunteer Infantry, 388; Josiah Favill, diary
entry, July 2, 1863, in *Diary of a Young
Army Officer,* 244.

68. Sears, *Gettysburg,* 249–52; Taaffe,
Commanding the Army of the Potomac,
117–18.

69. Hancock quotation taken from
Foote, *The Civil War,* vol. 2, 486; Haskell,
Haskell of Gettysburg, 120. For description
of the fighting throughout the second day
of the battle, see Pfanz, *Gettysburg: The
Second Day.*

70. The experiences of soldiers in
Caldwell's division on July 2, 1863, are
examined in both Hartwig, "'No Troops
on the Field Had Done Better,'" 136–71;
and Campbell, "Caldwell Clears the
Wheatfield," 47–77.

71. Hale, "With Colonel Cross at the
Wheatfield," 34; Stewart, *History of the
One Hundred and Fortieth Regiment Pennsylvania Volunteers,* 97–98; Walker, *History of the Second Army Corps,* 543.

72. St. Clair Mulholland speech at
Gettysburg, September 11, 1889, in Mulholland, *The Story of the 116th Regiment
Pennsylvania Volunteers,* 407–408. Also
see Corby, *Memoirs of Chaplain Life,*
184–86. Corby writes, "In performing
this ceremony I faced the army. My eye
covered thousands of officers and men. I
noticed that *all,* Catholic and non-Cath-
olic, officers and private soldiers showed
a profound respect, wishing at this fatal
crisis to receive every benefit of divine
grace that could be imparted through the
instrumentality of the Church ministry.
Even Maj.-Gen. Hancock removed his
hat, and, as far as compatible with the
situation, bowed in reverential devotion."

73. Stewart, *History of the One Hundred
and Fortieth Regiment Pennsylvania Volunteers,* 104; Report of Major Peter Nelson,
August 3, 1863, *O.R.,* vol. 27, pt. 1, 398;
Sheldon, *The "Twenty-Seventh,"* 77; Statement of William P. Wilson, in *The Batchelder Papers,* vol. 2, 1196; Unidentified

soldier, 64th New York, Civil War reminiscences, IU; Mulholland, *The Gettysburg
Campaign,* 9–10; Almond Clark, "The
27th Connecticut at Gettysburg," CHS.

74. George Whipple, memoir, 19–20,
64th New York regimental file, GNMP;
John Brooke to Francis Walker, Novem-
ber 14, 1885, and March 18, 1886; in *The
Batchelder Papers,* vol. 2, 1141, 1234;
Stewart, *History of the One Hundred
and Fortieth Regiment Pennsylvania
Volunteers,* 104.

75. Report of Major Peter Nelson,
August 3, 1863, *O.R.,* vol. 27, pt. 1, 398.

76. Eight divisions in the Army of
the Potomac served from the Peninsula
through Gettysburg. Three of these divisions had a higher percentage of regiments that had served together continuously than Caldwell's division. One of
these divisions was Gibbon's Second Division. The other two were Humphreys's
Third Corps division and Brigadier
General Samuel Crawford's Fifth Corps
division.

77. Report of Brigadier General John
Caldwell, September 5, 1863; Report of
Lieutenant James Smith, August 5, 1863,
O.R., vol. 27, pt. 1, 381, 389.

78. George Bullock to Friend Miles,
July 24, 1863, 61st New York regimental
file, GNMP; Unidentified soldier, 64th
New York, Civil War reminiscences, IU;
Stephen Allen Osborne, "Reminiscence
of the Civil War," 145th Pennsylvania
regimental file, GNMP.

79. Return of Casualties in the Union
Forces, *O.R.,* vol. 27, pt. 1, 175; Statement
of Charles Morgan, in *The Batchelder
Papers,* vol. 3, 1355–56; Busey and Martin,
Regimental Strengths at Gettysburg, 31.
Busey and Martin estimate that 3,320 sol-
diers of the First Division went into action
at the Wheatfield.

80. Report of Major General George
Sykes, *O.R.,* vol. 27, pt. 1, 592. Ayres quotation taken from Sears, *Gettysburg,* 302.

81. Statement of Charles Morgan, in *The Batchelder Papers,* vol. 3, 1355–56; Walker, *History of the Second Army Corps,* 404.

82. Report of Major General Winfield S. Hancock, 1863, *O.R.,* vol. 27, pt. 1, 370.

83. Gibbon, *Personal Recollections,* 137.

84. Campbell, "'Remember Harper's Ferry,'" 64–73; Simons, *The One Hundred and Twenty-Fifth New York State Volunteers,* 110–13; Jordan, *Winfield Scott Hancock,* 92–93; Sears, *Gettysburg,* 318–19.

85. Failing, "Gen. Alex. Hays at Gettysburg"; Report of Brigadier General Alexander Hays, July 8, 1863, *O.R.,* vol. 27, pt. 1, 453.

86. Statement of William Colvill, June 9, 1866, in *The Batchelder Papers,* vol. 1, 257; Report of Major General Winfield Scott Hancock, 1863, *O.R.,* vol. 27, pt. 1, 371; Walker, *History of the Second Army Corps,* 283. The charge of the 1st Minnesota on July 2 is well detailed in Lochren, "The First Minnesota at Gettysburg," 48–51; and Moe, *The Last Full Measure,* 264–74. The percentage of losses in the regiment is taken from Sears, *Gettysburg,* 268. For a discussion of the number of casualties suffered, see Meinhard, "The First Minnesota at Gettysburg," 83.

87. Report of Major General Winfield Scott Hancock, 1863, *O.R.,* vol. 27, pt. 1, 372; Kepler, *History of the ... Fourth Regiment Ohio Volunteer Infantry,* 129.

88. Statement of Elijah H. C. Cavins, in *The Batchelder Papers,* vol. 2, 976–77; Walker, *History of the Second Army Corps,* 286–87. Soldiers of the 8th Ohio were posted on picket duty before Cemetery Ridge and remained behind from the rest of the brigade fighting on the Union right. For the fighting on the Union right on the evening of July 2, see Sears, *Gettysburg,* 325–41. For fighting on the Union right throughout the battle, see Pfanz, *Gettysburg—Culp's Hill and Cemetery Hill.*

89. Jordan, *Winfield Scott Hancock,* 94; Fishel, *The Secret War for the Union,* 526–30; Longstreet quotation taken from Sears, *Gettysburg,* 346.

90. Gibbon, *Personal Recollections,* 145. For recent and thorough studies of Pickett's Charge and its postwar remembrance, see Hess, *Pickett's Charge;* and Reardon, *Pickett's Charge In History and Memory.*

91. William Clough to Mrs. Elijah Hayden, July 22, 1862, 8th Ohio regimental file, GNMP; N. Eldred, "Only a Boy: A First Hand Account of the Civil War," 111th New York regimental file, GNMP; Cyril Tyler to Father, July 7, 1863, Tyler Papers, Duke.

92. Walker, *General Hancock,* 97; "Hancock's Heroism at Gettysburg."

93. William Clough to Mrs. Elijah Hayden, July 22, 1863, 8th Ohio regimental file, GNMP Thompson, "A Scrap of Gettysburg," 102; William Burns, diary entry, July 3, 1863, 71st Pennsylvania regimental file, GNMP; Chauncey Harris to Father, July 4, 1863, in Washburn, *A Complete Military History and Record of the 108th Regiment N.Y. Vols.,* 52.

94. Alexander McNeil to David Porter, August 16, 1863, CWTIC, USAMHI; Calvin Haynes to Wife, July 19, 1863, Haynes Letters, NYSLA.

95. Henry Abbott to Josiah Gardner Abbott, July 6, 1863, in *Fallen Leaves,* 188; Stevens, *Souvenir of Excursion to Battlefields of the Society of the Fourteenth Connecticut Regiment,* 32.

96. Cyril Tyler to Father, July 7, 1863, Tyler Papers, Duke; George Bowen, diary entry, July 13, 1863, CWMC, USAMHI; Seville, *History of the First Regiment Delaware Volunteers,* 81; Gottfried, *Stopping Pickett,* 172–73.

97. Frederick W. Oesterle, "Incidents Connected with the Civil War," 9, CWTIC, USAMHI; Francis Heath to John Batchelder, October 12, 1889, 19th

Maine regimental file, GNMP. Also see Adams, "The Nineteenth Maine at Gettysburg," 262.

98. Haskell, *The Battle of Gettysburg*, 66; Page, *History of the Fourteenth Regiment, Connecticut Volunteer Infantry*, 156; Waitt, *History of the Nineteenth Regiment, Massachusetts Volunteer Infantry*, 250.

99. Haines, *History of the Men of Co. F*, 41; Jacob Betchel to Connie, July 6, 1863, 59th New York regimental file, GNMP; Charles Nash letter, July 29, 1863, in Smith, *The History of the Nineteenth Regiment of Maine Volunteer Infantry*, 100.

100. Stephen Martin, diary entry, July 4, 1863, vol. 278, FSNMP; Child, "From Fredericksburg to Gettysburg," 188; Robert Penn Smith to Isaac Wistar, July 29, 1863, Wistar Papers, Wistar Institute.

101. Winfield Scott Hancock to George Meade, July 3, 1863, *O.R.*, vol. 27, pt. 1, 366; Holcombe, *History of the First Regiment Minnesota Volunteer Infantry*, 372.

102. Banes, *History of the Philadelphia Brigade*, 192; Daniel Zackman, diary entry, July 4, 1863, Zackman Diary, Western Historical Manuscripts Collection, University of Missouri.

103. The casualty returns are taken from Return of Casualties in the Union Forces, Battle of Gettysburg, July 1–3, 1863, *O.R.*, vol. 27, pt. 1, 173–87.

104. Walker, *History of the Second Army Corps*, 299–300.

105. The casualties of the Second Corps are taken from Return of Casualties in the Union Forces, Battle of Gettysburg, July 1–3, 1863, in *O.R.*, vol. 27, pt. 1, 173–87. The numbers of men engaged in each regiment are taken from Busey and Martin, *Regimental Losses at Gettysburg*, 33–44.

106. Stephen Martin, diary entry, July 5, 1863, vol. 278, FSNMP; George Bullock to Friend Miles, July 24, 1863, 61st New York regimental file, GNMP; Ammi Williams to Henry Williams, July 10, 1863, 8th Ohio regimental file, GNMP.

107. Albert Davis to Mother, July 4, 1863, Davis Letters, Bentley Library, University of Michigan; Lauren Hotchkiss to Brother and Sister, July 7, 1863, Watson Hitchcock Papers, CHS; Allen Landis to Parents, July 12, 1863, Landis Family Papers, LC. The maneuvers following the fighting at Gettysburg are well discussed in Brown, *Retreat from Gettysburg*.

108. John Lehman to Father, September 5, 1863, Lehman Family Papers, CL; Cyrus Bacon letter, July 6, 1863, "The Daily Register of Dr. Cyrus Bacon, Jr.," 378; James Mitchell to Mother, September 16, 1863, James Mitchell Letters, USAMHI.

109. Taaffe, *Commanding the Army of the Potomac*, 120–21; Sears, *Gettysburg*, 486–90. For a discussion of whether Meade should have attacked, see Greene, "From Gettysburg to Falling Waters," 161–94.

110. Lemuel Jeffries, diary entry, July 14, 1863, in "The Excitement Had Begun!" 275; Fiske, *Mr. Dunn Browne's Experiences*, 122–23.

111. Augustus Van Dyke to Father, July 12, 1863, Van Dyke Collection, IHS; Charles Edward Davis to Father, September 24, 1863, Davis Folder, BRU; Alexander McNeil to David Porter, August 16, 1863, McNeil Letter, CWTIC, USAMHI; RH Rea to Cousin, July 8, 1863, 7th New York regimental file, GNMP.

112. J. Franklin Dyer to Maria, July 21, 1863, in *The Journal of a Civil War Surgeon*, xxii; John Reid letter, *National Tribune*, January 22, 1885.

113. William Plumer to Emily Plumer, July 4, 1863, vol. 280, FSNMP; Chauncey Harris to Father, July 4, 1863, in Washburn, *A Complete Military History and Record of the 108th Regiment N.Y. Vols.*, 52; Robert Penn Smith to Isaac Wistar, July 29, 1863, Wistar Papers, Wistar Institute; Report of Colonel Norman Hall, July 14, 1863, *O.R.*, vol. 27, pt. 1, 441.

114. George Washington Beidelman to Father, July 4, 1863, in *The Civil War*

Letters of George Washington Beidelman, 178; John Hirst, diary entry, summer 1863, in Page, History of the Fourteenth Regiment, Connecticut Volunteer Infantry, 186.

115. Nelson Miles to Aunt, July 19, 1863, Miles Papers, USAMHI; J. Franklin Dyer, diary entry, September 28, 1863, in The Journal of a Civil War Surgeon, 118.

116. Albert Emmell to Aunt, July 17, 1863, 12th New Jersey regimental file, GNMP; Edward Walker to Friend Knight, July 29, 1863, Walker Letters, Leigh Collection, USAMHI. For a similar account, but by Richard Thompson of the 12th New Jersey, see Thompson, "A Scrap of Gettysburg," 109. Thompson has a Confederate prisoner stating, "When we saw that old Clover-Leaf unfurled, we knew what kind of green militia we had to contend with." For another recounting, see Waitt, History of the Nineteenth Regiment, Massachusetts Volunteer Infantry, 244.

5. REBUILDING

1. Lemuel Jeffries, diary entry, July 16, 1863, in "The Excitement Had Begun!" 275; George Bullock to Friend Miles, July 24, 1863, 61st New York regimental file, GNMP. The marches of the Second Corps in the immediate aftermath of the Gettysburg Campaign are detailed in Walker, History of the Second Army Corps, 309–10.

2. Charles Nash letter, July 29, 1863, in Smith, History of the Nineteenth Regiment of Maine Volunteer Infantry, 100. The manpower figures are taken from Walker, History of the Second Army Corps, 310. Walker lists the Second Corps with 11,163 men absent on July 31.

3. Wert, The Sword of Lincoln, 310–11.

4. J. E. Hodgkins, diary entry, August 27, 1863, in The Civil War Diary of Lieut. J. E. Hodgkins, 50; Cowtan, Services of the Tenth New York Volunteers, 215.

5. Charles Benson to Father, July 21, 1863, vol. 326, FSNMP; Joseph Graham to Aunt, August 7, 1863, Graham Letters,

CWMC, USAMHI. For negative comment regarding rations received, see Edward Cotter to Parents, August 20, 1863, Cotter Letters, CWMC, USAMHI. Cotter wrote, "You will find the hard tack as bad as Henry said. To day I broke three hard tack into a tin cup of coffee and I skimed 15 worms off it and they would average from half an inch to an inch long and besides the most of them are full of little bugs but then it [is] nothing after you get use to it."

6. Allen Landis to Parents, August 27, 1863, Landis Family Papers, LC; Nelson Miles to Brother, August 4, 1863, Nelson Miles Papers, USAMHI; Edward Cross to Murat Halstead, June 1, 1863, in Stand Firm and Fire Low, 141; Joseph Graham to Aunt, August 1, 1863, CWMC, USAMHI.

7. Richard Thompson to Brother and Sister, October 15, 1863, in While My Country Is in Danger, 91; Isaac Plumb, November 25, 1863, "Record of Life and Service," CWMC, USAMHI.

8. The best study of the draft riots in New York City is Bernstein, The New York City Draft Riots.

9. Elijah Cavins to Ann Cavins, July 16, 1863, Cavins Collection, IHS; Alexander McNeil to David Porters, August 16, 1863, McNeil Letter, CWTIC, USAMHI; Peter Welsh to Wife, July 17, 1863, in Irish Green and Union Blue, 108. Criticism of the Irish American community is detailed in Bruce, The Harp and The Eagle, 182–83.

10. Wert, Sword of Lincoln, 311.

11. Walker, History of the Second Army Corps, 312–13; Kepler, History of the . . . Fourth Regiment Ohio Volunteer Infantry, 140–41; Galwey, The Valiant Hours, 135–38.

12. Josiah Favill, diary entry, January 8, 1864, in Diary of a Young Officer, 274. For a contrasting view of Warren, see James Beaver letter, late summer 1863, in Muffly, The Story of Our Regiment, 97. Beaver writes that Warren "is said to be

an accomplished officer and has been for
some time on the staff of the commander
of the Army." A good biography of Warren
is Jordan, "Happiness Is Not My Companion." Also see Taylor, Gouverneur Kemble
Warren.

13. George G. Meade to Margaret
Meade, July 18, 1863, in The Life and Letters of George Gordon Meade, vol. 2, 136.
For a description of the Union high command in the late summer and fall of 1863,
see Taaffe, Commanding the Army of the
Potomac, 123–28.

14. John Caldwell to Francis Walker,
October 28, 1863, 2d Army Corps
Records, RG 393, NA; James Beaver remi-
niscence, in Muffly, The Story of Our Regi-
ment, 103. Manpower returns are taken
from Abstract from the Tri-monthly
Return of the Army of the Potomac,
August 10, 1863, O.R., vol. 29, pt. 1, 28; and
December 1863, O.R., vol. 29, pt. 2, 598.

15. Nelson Miles to Aunt, August 26,
1863, Miles Papers, USAMHI; Augustus
Van Dyke to Angie, October 3, 1863, Van
Dyke Collection, IHS; Rhodes, History of
Battery B, First Rhode Island, 236–37; Peter
Welsh to Mary Welsh, August 16, 1863, in
Irish Green and Union Blue, 121; William
Hays, Corps Circular, August 15, 1863, 2d
Army Corps Records, RG 393, NA.

16. John Hirst reminiscence, in Page,
History of the Fourteenth Regiment Connecticut Volunteer Infantry, 186; Fiske, Mr.
Dunn Browne's Experiences, 286; Gouverneur Warren, General Order 30, October
31, 1863, 2d Army Corps Records, RG 393,
NA.

17. J. Franklin Dyer, diary entry,
August 16, 1863, in The Journal of a Civil
War Surgeon, 111; Edward Bassett letter,
September 9, 1863, in From Bull Run to
Bristow Station, 31; William Potter to
Wife, August 21, 1863, in One Surgeon's
Private War, 80; Henry Abbott to Fletcher
Abbott, September 6, 1863, in Fallen
Leaves, 213.

18. Augustus Van Dyke to Brother,
December 28, 1863, Van Dyke Collec-
tion, IHS; James Beaver reminiscence,
in Muffly, The Story of Our Regiment, 97;
Waitt, History of the Nineteenth Regiment,
Massachusetts Volunteer Infantry, 260.

19. Franklin Haskell, letter, October
9, 1863, in Haskell of Gettysburg, 207;
George Hegeman, diary entries, October
12 and 13, 1863, in Hegeman, "The Diary
of a Union Soldier in Confederate Pris-
ons," 238. The best study of the plans and
maneuvers of the Union and Confederate
armies in northern Virginia in the late
summer and fall of 1863 is Henderson, The
Road to Bristoe Station.

20. Report of Major General Gouverneur Warren, October 25, 1863, O.R., vol.
29, pt. 1, 239; Walker, History of the Second
Army Corps, 331–38.

21. Amory Allen to Wife, November
1, 1863, Allen Letters, ISL; James Rea
to Wife, October 21, 1863, Rea Letters,
CWMC, USAMHI.

22. Haines, History of the Men of Co. F,
48; Report of Major General Gouverneur
Warren, October 25, 1863, O.R., vol. 29, pt.
1, 240–42; Walker, History of the Second
Army Corps, 341–47.

23. Aldrich, The History of Battery A,
First Regiment Rhode Island Light Artillery,
250–51; Simons, A Regimental History, 157;
Edward Bassett to Parents, October 16,
1863, in From Bull Run to Bristow Station,
108; Walker, History of the Second Army
Corps, 355–58.

24. Report of Lieutenant General
Ambrose Hill, October 26, 1863; Report
of Major General Henry Heth; Report
of General Robert E. Lee, November 21,
1863, O.R., vol. 29, pt. 1, 427, 428, 432.

25. Waitt, History of the Nineteenth
Regiment, Massachusetts Volunteer Infantry, 272; Sawyer, A Military History of the
8th Regiment Ohio Vol. Inf'y, 146; Cowtan,
Services of the Tenth New York Volunteers,
224; Galwey, The Valiant Hours, 159.

Casualty figures are taken from Report of Major General Gouverneur Warren, October 25, 1863, *O.R.* vol. 29, pt. 1, 235, 248–50.

26. Major General George Meade, General Orders, No. 96, October 15, 1863, *O.R.*, vol. 29, pt. 1, 250.

27. Richard Thompson to Brother and Sister, October 15, 1863, in *While My Country Is in Danger*, 91; Augustus Van Dyke to Brother, November 6, 1863, Van Dyke Collection, IHS; Edward Bassett to Parents, October 16, 1863, in *From Bull Run to Bristow Station*, 109; Waitt, *History of the Nineteenth Regiment, Massachusetts Volunteer Infantry*, 271. Waitt recounts Confederate prisoners cursing "those damned white clubs again" when brought into the Union lines. Morale throughout the rest of the Army of the Potomac in the aftermath of the Bristoe Campaign is discussed in Wert, *The Sword of Lincoln*, 317.

28. Report of Lieutenant Colonel Ansel Wass, October 15, 1863, *O.R.*, vol. 29, pt. 1, 283–84; Smith, *History of the Nineteenth Regiment of Maine Volunteer Infantry*, 111; Report of Major Henry Abbott, October 17, 1863, *O.R.*, vol. 29, pt. 1, 286; William Wyman to R. D. Parker, March 22, 1899, Parker Collection, NYHS.

29. Wert, *Sword of Lincoln*, 311, 318–19.

30. Report of Major General Gouverneur Warren, October 25, 1863, *O.R.*, vol. 29, pt. 1, 24; Walker, *History of the Second Army Corps*, 343, 348.

31. Gouverneur Warren testimony, March 9, 1864, *CCW*, vol. 1, 381; Taaffe, *Commanding the Army of the Potomac*, 148.

32. William Trisler to Wife, October 28, 1863, Trisler Collection, IHS; Wright, *No More Gallant a Deed*, 377.

33. Charles Benson to Sister, November 22, 1863, vol. 326, FSNMP; Charles Davis to Father, December 3, 1863, Charles Davis Folder, BRU.

34. Report of Major General George Meade, December 2, 1863; Report of Major General Gouverneur Warren, December 3, 1863, *O.R.*, vol. 29, pt. 1, 11–12, 696–97; Wert, *Sword of Lincoln*, 320; Charles Davis to Father, December 3, 1863, Davis Folder, BRU. The best treatment of the Mine Run Campaign is Graham and Skoch, *Mine Run*. For the participation of the Second Corps, see Walker, *History of the Second Army Corps*, 365–91.

35. Report of Major General Gouverneur Warren, December 3, 1863, *O.R.*, vol. 29, pt. 1, 698; E. B. Tyler reminiscences, in Page, *History of the Fourteenth Regiment, Connecticut Volunteer Infantry*, 204; McDermott, *A Brief History of the 69th Regiment Pennsylvania Volunteers*, 36–37; Seville, *History of the First Regiment Delaware Volunteers*, 101.

36. William Fogler reminiscence, in Smith, *The History of the Nineteenth Regiment of Maine Volunteer Infantry*, 118–19; Kepler, *History of the . . . Fourth Regiment Ohio Volunteer Infantry*, 150.

37. John Hirst reminiscence, in Page, *History of the Fourteenth Regiment, Connecticut Volunteer Infantry*, 201–202; Holcombe, *History of the First Regiment Minnesota Volunteer Infantry*, 415; Galwey, *The Valiant Hours*, 175.

38. James Stratton to Father, December 4, 1863, in *Proceedings of the First Annual Reunion . . . of the Twelfth Regiment New Jersey Volunteers*, 44; Edward Walker, diary entry, November 30, 1863, Walker Letters, Leigh Collection, USAMHI; Murphey, *Four Years in the War*, 144.

39. J. E. Hodgkins, diary entry, December 1, 1863, in *The Civil War Diary of Lieut. J. E. Hodgkins*, 64; Report of Colonel Hiram Brown, December 4, 1863, *O.R.*, vol. 29, pt. 1, 720–21; Samuel Dean to Parents, December 4, 1863, Dean Letters, vol. 185, FSNMP; William Fogler reminiscence, in Smith, *The History of the*

Nineteenth Regiment of Maine Volunteer Infantry, 120–21.

40. Edwin Stanton to George Meade, January 6, 1864; Adjutant General's Office, Special Orders, No. 16, January 12, 1864, *O.R.*, vol. 33, 357, 373; Freed, *The Life and Public Services of Winfield Scott Hancock*, 63–64; Jordan, *Winfield Scott Hancock*, 104–105.

41. John Caldwell to S. Williams, January 30, 1864, 2d Army Corps Records, RG 393, NA; Gouverneur Warren to S. Williams, February 8, 1864, 2d Army Corps Records, RG 393, NA; Winfield Scott Hancock, corps circular, April 3, 1864, 2d Army Corps Records, RG 393, NA.

42. Charles Wainwright, diary entry, March 20, 1864, in *A Diary of Battle*, 332; Winfield Scott Hancock to S. Williams, April 6, 1864, 2d Army Corps Records, RG 393, NA.

43. Mulholland, *The Story of the 116th Regiment Pennsylvania Volunteers*, 160, 176–77; William Smith to Father and Mother, April 13, 1864, Smith Letters, Leigh Collection, USAMHI; Recruits Received for This Command This Morning, April 20, 1864, 2d Army Corps Records, RG 393, NA; Adams, *Reminiscences of the Nineteenth Massachusetts Regiment*, 82.

44. The various incentives utilized to attempt to convince the volunteers of 1861 to reenlist are detailed in E. D. Townsend, General Orders, Adjt. General's Office, June 25, 1863, *O.R.*, ser. III, vol. 5, 415–16.

45. Winfield Scott Hancock to S. Williams, April 18, 1864, 2d Army Corps Records, RG 393, NA; Major General George Meade to Major T. M. Vincent, March 31, 1864, *O.R.*, vol. 33, 776. Hancock lists 114 officers and 2,962 men as reenlisting; and 377 officers and 4,239 men as not reenlisting.

46. Charles Davis, diary entry, September 24, 1863, Davis Folder, BRU; Wright, *No More Gallant a Deed*, 420; David

Beem to Sister, January 19, 1864, Beem Papers, IHS.

47. John McClure to Sister Mary, February 8, 1864, in *Hoosier Farm Boy in Lincoln's Army*, 49. The role of the Second Corps at Morton's Ford is detailed in Walker, *History of the Second Corps*, 394–97.

48. Gouverneur Warren to S. Williams, January 15, 1864, 2d Army Corps Records, RG 393, NA; John Caldwell to S. Williams, January 27, 1864, 2d Army Corps Records, RG 393, NA; Winfield Scott Hancock to S. Williams, April 18, 1864, 2d Army Corps Records, RG 393, NA. Recruiting officers listed the number of reenlisted veterans at 2,377 men on January 15; 2,401 men on January 27; and 2,576 men on April 18.

49. Horace Hill, diary entries, February 6 and 7, 1864, vol. 217, FSNMP; Cowtan, *Services of the Tenth New York Volunteers*, 238.

50. Josiah Favill, diary entry, January 1, 1864, in *Diary of a Young Army Officer*, 273–74; Elijah Cavins to Wife, October 11, 1863, Cavins Papers, IHS; James Mitchell to Father, February 23, 1864, Mitchell Papers, USAMHI.

51. William Smith to Mother, winter 1863, Smith Letters, USAMHI; Winfield Scott Hancock to S. Williams, December 30, 1863, 2d Army Corps Records, RG 393, NA.

52. James Walker, diary entry, January 1, 1864, Walker Diary, PHS; Amory Allen to Wife, Allen Letters, ISL; Samuel Maguire to Wife, October 5, 1862, Maguire Letters, WRHS; James Rea to Wife, March 16 and 20, 1864, Rea Letters, CWMC, USAMHI.

53. The text of the reorganization order is taken from Major General George G. Meade, General Orders, No. 10, Hdqrs. Army of the Potomac, March 24, 1864, *O.R.*, vol. 33, 722–23. Manpower returns are taken from Abstract from Tri-monthly

Return of the Army of the Potomac, April 30, 1864, *O.R.*, vol. 36, pt. 1, 198.

54. Meade's reasons for reorganizing the Army of the Potomac are detailed in Hennessy, "'I Dread the Spring,'" 82–93.

55. Walker, *History of the Second Army Corps*, 380 and 405; Report of Major General Gouverneur Warren, December 3, 1863, *O.R.*, vol. 29, pt. 1, 698. Warren wrote that during the Mine Run Campaign "all under my command behaved in the most praiseworthy manner."

56. Lyman, *Meade's Headquarters, 1863–1865*, 189.

57. Green, "From the Wilderness to Spotsylvania," 248–57. The Battle of Williamsburg is described in Sears, *To the Gates of Richmond*, 71–75.

58. Rhea, *The Battle of the Wilderness*, 38–40.

59. Major General George G. Meade, General Orders, No. 10, Hdqrs. Army of the Potomac, March 24, 1864, *O.R.*, vol. 33, 722–23. The reorganized Army of the Potomac is listed in Organization of Forces Operating against Richmond, May 5, 1864, *O.R.*, vol. 36, pt. 1, 106–19.

60. Winfield S. Hancock to J. W. Potter, May 7 and May 9, 1863, 2d Army Corps Records, RG 393. On May 7, Hancock requested that the "69th, 88th, and 63rd Regiment NY Vols. be consolidated into one regiment bearing the number 69th or 88th as may be thought best. The 2d Brigade known as the Irish Brigade is reduced to a very small number, having four times as many officers as necessary. I recommend that this organization be broken up and that the Regiments be transferred to other brigades of this division." Two days later, Hancock dropped mention of the Irish Brigade. He unsuccessfully requested that "the men and a portion of the officers" of the 116th Pennsylvania be combined into the 53rd Pennsylvania.

61. Ward, *History of the One Hundred and Sixth Regiment Pennsylvania Volunteers*, 194; Banes, *History of the Philadelphia Brigade*, 214–15.

62. Lieutenant Colonel Francis Walker, General Orders, No. 12, March 30, 1864; Abstract from the Tri-monthly Return of the Army of the Potomac, April 30, 1864, *O.R.*, vol. 33, 772, 1036; Report of Captain Benjamin Fisher, July 21, 1864, *O.R.*, vol. 36, pt. 1, 281–82.

63. Letter of Unidentified Soldier of the 19th Maine, March 30, 1864, in *Reunions of the Nineteenth Maine Regiment Association*, 85.

64. Studies of Grant are numerous. The best of the most recent books include: McFeely, *Grant*; Perret, *Ulysses S. Grant*; Simpson, *Ulysses S. Grant*; and Smith, *Grant*. For Grant's perspective, see his *Personal Memoirs of U.S. Grant*.

65. Dyer, diary entry, April 22, 1864, in *The Journal of a Civil War Surgeon*, 144–45; Allen Landis to Brother, April 27, 1864, Landis Family Papers, LC; George Whipple, unpublished memoir, 64th New York regimental file, GNMP; Unidentified soldier, 64th New York, Civil War reminiscences, IU.

66. Timothy Bateman, diary entry, January 1, 1864, Bateman Diary, CWMC, USAMHI; Robertson, *Personal Recollections of the War*, 82–83; T. Grove Smith to Mother, April 18, 1864, Smith Collection, USAMHI; Isaac Hadden to Friends, April 27, 1864, Hadden Letters, NYHS.

67. Elijah Cavins to Wife, March 6, 1864, Cavins Collection, IHS; Stewart, *History of the One Hundred and Fortieth Regiment Pennsylvania Volunteers*, 169; Banes, *History of the Philadelphia Brigade*, 212.

68. Timothy Bateman, diary entry, February 24, 1864, Bateman Diary, CWMC, USAMHI; Uriah Parmelee letter, March 5, 1864, Parmelee Papers, Duke; Josiah Favill, diary entries, January–February

1864, in *Diary of a Young Officer*, 276–78; Banes, *History of the Philadelphia Brigade*, 213; Stewart, *History of the One Hundred and Fortieth Regiment Pennsylvania Volunteers*, 169.

69. Page, *History of the Fourteenth Regiment, Connecticut Volunteer Infantry*, 231; James Beaver reminiscence, in Muffly, *The Story of Our Regiment*, 110; Amos Stewart, diary entry, March 23, 1864, vol. 198, FSNMP; Joseph Graham to Brother, March 24, 1864, Graham Letters, CWMC, USAMHI.

70. Charles Nash to Father, March 30, 1864, in Smith, *The History of the Nineteenth Regiment of Maine Volunteer Infantry*, 132; Joseph Graham to Aunt, February 25, 1864, Graham Letters, CWMC, USAMHI; Horace Hill, diary entry, January 24, 1864, vol. 217, FSNMP; Robert McAllister to Ellen McAllister, March 31, 1864, in *The Civil War Letters of General Robert McAllister*, 401.

71. Billings, *The History of the Tenth Massachusetts Battery of Light Artillery*, 146; William Smith to Mother, late April 1864, Smith Letters, USAMHI; Walker, *History of the Second Army Corps*, 405; Winfield Scott Hancock, General Order 17, April 23, 1864, 2d Army Corps Records, RG 393, NA.

6. CARNAGE

1. Report of Lieutenant General Ulysses S. Grant, July 22, 1865, *O.R.*, vol. 36, pt. 1, 12–13; Ulysses S. Grant to George Meade, April 9, 1864, *O.R.*, vol. 33, pt. 1, 828; Isaac Plumb, "Record of Life and Services," CWMC, USAMHI.

2. Hays, *Under the Red Patch*, 225–26; Floyd, *History of the Fortieth (Mozart) Regiment, New York Volunteers*, 215; Unidentified soldier, 15th Massachusetts, to Friend David, April 27, 1864, Misc. Manuscripts, LC; Benjamin Draper, diary entry, May 4, 1864, vol. 47, FSNMP.

3. Almira Hancock, *Reminiscences*, 101; Winfield Scott Hancock to S. Williams, May 1, 1864, *O.R.*, vol. 36, pt. 2, 320; Walker, *General Hancock*, 148–49; John Haley, diary entry, May 12, 1864, in *The Rebel Yell and the Yankee Hurrah*, 157; Banes, *History of the Philadelphia Brigade*, 219. Banes argues that Hancock inspired soldiers through his reputation for battlefield bravery, regardless of his physical appearance. He writes "There are some officers whose appearance on the battle-field, or at the head of a column, imparts hope and secures the admiration of those serving under them. Hancock not only possessed this influence, but had the prestige that came from past success and that inspired anticipations of brilliant achievements in the future."

4. Brief description of the strengths and weaknesses of the Union high command on the eve of the Overland Campaign is found in Rhea, *The Battle of the Wilderness*, 37–41.

5. Theodore Lyman to Wife, May 20, 1864, in *Meade's Headquarters*, 107; Charles Hamlin to Sister Louise, May 2, 1864, Hamlin Letters, NYSLA; Isaac Plumb, "Record of Life and Services," CWMC, USAMHI; William Potter to Wife, April 5, 1864, in *One Surgeon's Private War*, 97; Walker, *History of the Second Army Corps*, 404. For a description of the life and career of Barlow, see Warner, *Generals in Blue*, 34.

6. The life and career of Birney is detailed in Warner, *Generals in Blue*, 347–48. For a very dated biography of Birney, see Davis, *Life of David Bell Birney*. Description of Birney on May 3, 1863 is in Bigelow, *Chancellorsville*, 361. The Meade-Sickles controversy is detailed in Taaffe, *Commanding the Army of the Potomac*, 135–37. The involvement of Hancock in the squabble is discussed in Jordan, *Winfield Scott Hancock*, 108.

7. George Meade to Edwin Stanton, April 30, 1864, *O.R.*, vol. 33, 1025; Walker, *History of the Second Army Corps*, 403. For a brief description of the life and career of Mott, see Warner, *Generals in Blue*, 347–48.

8. Francis Barlow to Henry Wilson, November 28, 1863, Barlow Papers, MHS. For discussion of Miles and his life and Civil War service, see Amchan, *The Most Famous Soldier in America*; and DeMontravel, *A Hero to His Fighting Men*. Miles's autobiography is found in *Serving the Republic*.

9. Organization of the Army of the Potomac, April 30, 1864, *O.R.*, vol. 33, 1037–44; Walker, *History of the Second Army Corps*, 404; Ansell White to Mother, October 21, 1863, White Letters, Leigh Collection, USAMHI.

10. Winfield Scott Hancock to S. Williams, April 9, 1864, 2d Army Corps Records, RG 393, NA. Hancock proposed to increase the number of orderlies under the command of each brigadier commander from three men to five men. He explained that "with commands of this size" three orderlies were too few, "especially on those occasions when time is of great importance."

11. Charles Hamlin to Sister Louise, January 12, 1864, Hamlin Letters, NYSLA; David Beem to Wife, January 17, 1864, Beem Papers, IHS.

12. William Hawley letter, in Page, *History of the Fourteenth Regiment, Connecticut Volunteer Infantry*, 224–25; Levander Sawtelle to Parents, February 12, 1864, Sawtelle Letters, CWMC, USAMHI; Charles Pollard to Mother, March 21, 1864, Pollard Letters, CHS.

13. Major General John Newton, General Orders, No. 9, March 25, 1864, *O.R.*, vol. 33, 735; Robertson, "From the Wilderness to Spotsylvania," 82.

14. Green, "From the Wilderness to Spotsylvania," 91; Hays, *Under the Red Patch*, 222; Arner, *The Mutiny at Brandy Station*, 44; Floyd, *History of the Mozart Regiment*, 214.

15. Henry Abbott to Francis Walker, March 25, 1864; Winfield Scott Hancock to Seth Williams, March 26, 1864, *O.R.*, vol. 33, 743, 744.

16. Abstract from Tri-monthly Return of the Army of the Potomac, April 30, 1864, *O.R.*, vol. 36, pt. 1, 198; Page, *History of the Fourteenth Regiment, Connecticut Volunteer Infantry*, 230; Albert Van Derveer, unpublished memoir, Van Derveer Papers, Albany Institute of History and Art; A. Doughaby to D. H. Houston, April 7, 1864, 2d Army Corps Records, RG 393, NA.

17. Cole, *Under Five Commanders*, 210; Bruce, *The Twentieth Regiment of Massachusetts Volunteer Infantry*, 329–30.

18. David Beem to Wife, January 19, 1864, IHS; Charles Hamlin to Sister, February 1, 1864, Hamlin Letters, NYSLA; John McClure to Sister Mary, February 8, 1864, in *Hoosier Farm Boy in Lincoln's Army*, 49.

19. John Gibbon to Winfield S. Hancock, May 2, 1864; Major General George Meade, General Orders, No. 23, Headquarters, Army of the Potomac, May 2, 1864, *O.R.*, vol. 36, pt. 2, 331, 336.

20. The muster-out dates of the regiments organized in 1861 in the Fifth Corps and Sixth Corps are listed in Dyer, *A Compendium of the War of the Rebellion*, vol. 3, 300–13.

21. Floyd, *History of the Fortieth (Mozart) Regiment, New York Volunteers*, 216; Robertson, *Personal Recollections of the War*, 88–89; Page, *History of the Fourteenth Regiment, Connecticut Volunteer Infantry*, 233–34; Cudworth, *History of the First Regiment Massachusetts Infantry*, 456; Walker, *History of the Second Army Corps*, 407–408.

22. Unidentified soldier, 64th New York, Civil War reminiscences, IU;

Marbaker, *History of the Eleventh New Jersey Volunteers*, 161; Stewart, *History of the One Hundred and Fortieth Regiment Pennsylvania Volunteers*, 176–77; Bloodgood, *Personal Reminiscences of the War*, 231–32; J. P. Coburn letter, in Craft, *History of the One Hundred Forty-First Regiment, Pennsylvania Volunteers*, 176.

23. Billings, *The History of the Tenth Massachusetts Battery*, 154–55; Kirk, *Heavy Guns and Light*, 185; Sawyer, *A Military History of the 8th Regiment Ohio Vol. Inf'y*, 160; Rhea, *Battle of the Wilderness*, 193–200; Grimsley, *And Keep Moving On*, 41–43.

24. Walker, *History of the Second Corps*, 411–12; Rhea, *Battle of the Wilderness*, 187–90; Grimsley, *And Keep Moving On*, 41–42; Smith, *The History of the Nineteenth Regiment of Maine Volunteer Infantry*, 135.

25. Green, "From the Wilderness to Spotsylvania," 92–93; Cudworth, *History of the First Regiment Massachusetts Infantry*, 459–60; Report of Lieutenant Colonel John Shoonover, n.d.; Report of Lieutenant Colonel Michael Burns, August 9, 1864; Report of Colonel Robert McAllister, August 11, 1864, *O.R.*, vol. 36, pt. 1, 488, 492–93, 503–504.

26. Report of Major General Winfield Scott Hancock, February 1865; Report of Major General John Gibbon, November 7, 1864, *O.R.*, vol. 36, pt. 1, 322, 430; Page, *History of the Fourteenth Regiment, Connecticut Volunteer Infantry*, 234; Robertson, *Personal Recollections of the War*, 91.

27. Cudworth, *History of the First Regiment Massachusetts Infantry*, 459; Marbaker, *History of the Eleventh New Jersey Volunteers*, 162; Bloodgood, *Reminiscences of the War*, 234–35; Rhea, *Battle of the Wilderness*, 149–84.

28. Marbaker, *History of the Eleventh New Jersey Volunteers*, 166; King, *History of the Ninety-Third Regiment, New York*

Volunteer Infantry, 303; Banes, *History of the Philadelphia Brigade*, 227; Wicklein, "The Incomplete Civil War Memoir," vol. 232, FSNMP.

29. George Meade to Winfield Scott Hancock, May 5, 1864, *O.R.*, vol. 36, pt. 2, 412; Galwey, *The Valiant Hours*, 197; Rhea, *The Battle of the Wilderness*, 283–95; Walker, *History of the Second Army Corps*, 421–22.

30. Report of Major General Winfield Scott Hancock, February 1865, *O.R.*, vol. 36, pt. 1, 320; Gibbon, *Personal Recollections*, 386–411. For a discussion of the Hancock-Gibbon quarrel, see Jordan, *Winfield Scott Hancock*, 120–21.

31. Winfield S. Hancock to Andrew Humphreys, May 6, 1864, *O.R.*, vol. 36, pt. 2, 440–41; Rhea, *The Battle of the Wilderness*, 295–316; Jordan, *Winfield Scott Hancock*, 123.

32. Galwey, *The Valiant Hours*, 199–200; Weygant, *History of the One Hundred and Twenty-Fourth Regiment N.Y.S.V.*, 293–94; Webb, "Through the Wilderness," 160–61.

33. Sorrel, *Recollections of a Confederate Staff Officer*, 243; Wert, *General James Longstreet*, 386–89; Taylor, *General Lee*, 236–37; Alexander, *Fighting for the Confederacy*, 360.

34. Theodore Lyman, diary entry, May 6, 1864, in *Meade's Army*, 138–39; Report of Major General Winfield Scott Hancock, February 1865, *O.R.*, vol. 36, pt. 1, 323; Mertz, "No Turning Back," 19.

35. William Wyman to R. D. Parker, March 22, 1899, Parker Collection, NYHS; Brockway, "Across the Rapidan"; Walker, *History of the Second Army Corps*, 433.

36. Report of Major General Winfield S. Hancock, February 1865; Report of Brigadier General Samuel S. Carroll, September 9, 1864, *O.R.*, vol. 36, pt. 1, 323–24, 447; Cudworth, *History of the First Regiment Massachusetts Infantry*, 464; Smith,

History of the Nineteenth Regiment of Maine Infantry, 138; Walker, *History of the Second Army Corps,* 432–33.

37. W. C. Sloan to J. W. Sloan, May 9, 1864, in Muffly, *The Story of Our Regiment,* 813; Joseph Graham to Aunt Ellen, May 6, 1864, Graham Letters, CWMC, USAMHI; Alexander, *Fighting for the Confederacy,* 363.

38. Report of Lieutenant Colonel Otho Binkley, September 7, 1864; Report of Colonel John Horn, September 14, 1864, *O.R.,* vol. 36, no. 1, 737, 742; Theodore Lyman quotation taken from Rhea, *The Battle of the Wilderness,* 429. Also see Theodore Lyman, diary entry, May 6, 1864, in *Meade's Army,* 140. The Confederate flank attack and its prospects for achieving any greater battlefield success is detailed in Rhea, *The Battle of the Wilderness,* 416–30; and Grimsley, *And Keep Moving On,* 54–58.

39. Isaac Plumb, "Record of Life and Services," CWMC, USAMHI; Connor, "In the Wilderness," 229; Nathanial Stanton, diary entry, May 7, 1864, Leigh Collection, USAMHI; Grimsley, *And Keep Moving On,* 58–59.

40. Grimsley, *And Keep Moving On,* 72–80; Wert, *The Sword of Lincoln,* 348–50. Studies of the ensuing fighting around Spotsylvania Court House include: Cannan, *Bloody Angle;* Matter, *If It Takes All Summer;* and Rhea, *The Battles for Spotsylvania Court House and the Road to Yellow Tavern.* For series of interpretive essays, see Gallagher, ed., *The Spotsylvania Campaign.*

41. Report of Major General Winfield S. Hancock, February 1865, *O.R.,* vol. 36, pt. 1, 332; Walker, *History of the Second Army Corps,* 446–56. Barlow's men left behind a cannon wedged between two trees, the first artillery piece lost in battle by the Second Corps. Hancock cared little about the loss of the gun. Instead he praised the survivors for displaying

"such coolness and steadiness as is rarely exhibited in the presence of dangers so appalling."

42. Banes, *History of the Philadelphia Brigade,* 243–44; Smith, *The History of the Nineteenth Regiment of Maine Volunteer Infantry,* 151; Adams, *Reminiscences of the Nineteenth Massachusetts Regiment,* 89; Marbaker, *History of the Eleventh New Jersey Volunteers,* 169.

43. Robert McAllister to Ellen and Family, May 11, 1864, in *The Civil War Letters of General Robert McAllister,* 417.

44. Theodore Lyman to Wife, May 10, 1864, in *Meade's Headquarters,* 110; Walker, *History of the Second Army Corps,* 467.

45. Martin, *History of the Fifty-Seventh Regiment, Pennsylvania Veteran Volunteer Infantry,* 115; Hays, *Under the Red Patch,* 237; Kepler, *History of the . . . Fourth Regiment Ohio Volunteer Infantry,* 169; Haines, *History of the Men of Co. F,* 59; Kirk, *Heavy Guns and Light,* 204.

46. Jackson, "The Bloody Angle," 258–59; King, *History of the Ninety-Third Regiment, New York Volunteer Infantry,* 297–98; John Haley, diary entry, May 12, 1864, in *The Rebel Yell and The Yankee Hurrah,* 155; Walker, *History of the Second Army Corps,* 408–409.

47. Pennsylvanian quotation taken from Lash, *"Duty Well Done,"* 392; Isaac Plumb, letter, May 16, 1864, "Record of Life and Services," CWMC, USAMHI; J. E. Hodgkins, diary entry, May 12, 1864, in *The Civil War Diary of Lieut. J. E. Hodgkins,* 85.

48. Barlow, "The Capture of the Salient," 246–49; Houghton, *The Campaigns of the Seventeenth Maine,* 177; Stewart, *History of the One Hundred and Fortieth Regiment Pennsylvania Volunteers,* 196; John Dillon letter, March 27, 1895, vol. 356, FSNMP.

49. Black, "Reminiscences of the Bloody Angle," 425; Miner, "Spot-

sylvania"; Matter, *If It Takes All Summer*, 189. Miner believed that the Union cheering alerted the Confederate defenders that the attack was coming. Would that soldiers of the Second Corps had waited to cheer until actually crossing into the Confederate defensive lines, "we should not have lost as many men as we did."

50. Green, "From the Wilderness to Spotsylvania," 98–99; Isaac Hadden to Kate, May 15, 1864, Hadden Letters, NYHS; Nelson Miles to Francis Barlow, January 6, 1879, in "Capture of the Salient," 260–62; Haines, *History of the Men of Co. F*, 60.

51. Francis Harris, diary entry, May 12, 1864, Harris Diary, vol. 352, FSNMP; Jackson, "The Bloody Angle," 261; Josiah Favill, diary entry, May 11, 1864, in *The Diary of a Young Officer*, 297.

52. Barlow, "Capture of the Salient," 254–55; Winfield Scott Hancock testimony, March 22, 1865, *CCW*, vol. 3, 409; Rhea, *The Battles for Spotsylvania Court House*, 261–63.

53. Barlow, "Capture of the Salient," 253–54; James Beaver, diary entry, May 12, 1864, in Muffly, *The Story of Our Regiment*, 122; Benjamin Peck letter, May 12, 1864, in Craft, *History of the One Hundred Forty-First Regiment, Pennsylvania Volunteers*, 193; F. M. Thrasher reminiscence, in Washburn, *A Complete Military History and Record of the 108 N.Y. Vols.*, 72–73; Ward, *History of the One Hundred and Sixth Regiment Pennsylvania Volunteers*, 206; Rhea, *The Battles for Spotsylvania Court House*, 250–52, 255–59.

54. Black, "Reminiscences of the Bloody Angle," 432; Muffly, *The Story of Our Regiment*, 261–63; J. Franklin Dyer, diary entry, May 12, 1864, in *The Journal of a Civil War Surgeon*, 152; Mulholland, *The Story of the 116th Regiment Pennsylvania Volunteers*, 210; King, *History of the*

Ninety-Third Regiment, New York Volunteer Infantry, 299.

55. Galwey, *The Valiant Hours*, 210; A. B. Ramsey to R. D. Parker, November 28, 1899, Parker Collection, NYHS; Rhea, *The Battles for Spotsylvania Court House*, 306–307.

56. William Hewitt reminiscence, in Craft, *History of the One Hundred Forty-First Regiment, Pennsylvania Volunteers* 195; John Shoovner reminiscence, in Marbaker, *History of the Eleventh New Jersey Volunteers*, 175; Robertson, *Personal Recollections of the War*, 106.

57. Unidentified officer letter, May 13, 1864, in Craft, *History of the One Hundred Forty-First Regiment, Pennsylvania Volunteers* 195; Scott, *History of the One Hundred and Fifth Regiment of Pennsylvania Volunteers*, 103.

58. J. E. Hodgkins, diary entry, May 14, 1864, in *The Civil War Diary of Lieut. J. E. Hodgkins*, 86; Lobb letter, May 13, 1864, in Craft, *History of the One Hundred Forty-First Regiment, Pennsylvania Volunteers* 196; A. B. Stanton to Wife, May 17, 1864, file 39, PNMP; Green, "From the Wilderness to Spotsylvania," 103; Kepler, *History of the . . . Fourth Regiment Ohio Volunteer Infantry*, 172; Floyd, *History of the Fortieth (Mozart) Regiment, New York Volunteers*, 219; Bloodgood, *Personal Reminiscences*, 255; Houghton, *The Campaigns of the Seventeenth Maine*, 180.

59. Guy Watkins letter, May 16, 1864, in Craft, *History of the One Hundred Forty-First Regiment, Pennsylvania Volunteers*, 200; Joseph Graham to James Lee, May 19, 1864, Graham Letters, CWMC, USAMHI.

60. A. B. Stanton to Wife, May 17, 1864, file 39, PNMP; Guy Watkins letter, May 16, 1864, in Craft, *History of the One Hundred Forty-First Regiment, Pennsylvania Volunteers*, 200; Floyd, *History of the Fortieth (Mozart) Regiment, New York Volunteers*, 219.

61. Seville, *History of the First Regiment Delaware Volunteers,* 109; Bloodgood, *Personal Reminiscences,* 259; Benjamin Draper, diary entry, May 13, 1864, vol. 47, FSNMP.

62. Unidentified soldier, Carroll's brigade, "Reminiscences of Spotsylvania"; Cowtan, *Services of the Tenth New York Volunteers,* 211; Conyngham, *The Irish Brigade and Its Campaigns,* 450; Mulholland, *The Story of the 116th Regiment Pennsylvania Volunteers,* 223; Walker, "General Gibbon in the Second Corps," 310; Walker, *History of the Second Army Corps,* 480, 484–86.

63. Return of Casualties in the Union Forces, Battle of the Wilderness, May 5–7, 1864; Return of Casualties in the Union Forces, Battle of Spotsylvania Court-House, May 8–21, O.R., vol. 36, pt. 1, 119–33, 136–49; Report of Major General Winfield S. Hancock, February 1865, O.R., vol. 36, pt. 1, 337; Walker, *History of the Second Army Corps,* 481. The Fifth Corps suffered 9,612 casualties, the Sixth Corps 9,077 casualties, and the Ninth Corps 4,786 casualties.

64. Banes, *History of the Philadelphia Brigade,* 249. Banes writes that at Spotsylvania the "effect of the victory . . . more than compensated for the losses sustained, and the entire army received a new impulse from the success of the Second Corps."

65. William Smith to Mother, May 11, 1864, Smith Letters, USAMHI; William Trisler to Wife, May 15, 1864, Trisler Collection, IHS; Isaac Hadden to Brother, May 24, 1864, Hadden Letters, NYHS; Guy Watkins letter, May 13, 1864, in Craft, *History of the One Hundred Forty-First Regiment, Pennsylvania Volunteers,* 195.

66. Ulysses Grant to Edwin Stanton, May 13, 1864, in *The Papers of Ulysses S. Grant,* vol. 10, 434; Taaffe, *Commanding the Army of the Potomac,* 161–62. Grant

also recommended Meade for promotion in the Regular Army.

67. Augustus Brown, diary entry, May 18, 1864, in Brown, *The Diary of a Line Officer,* 48; Virginian quotation taken from Rhea, *The Battles for Spotsylvania Court House,* 252; Report of Lieutenant General Richard Ewell, March 20, 1865, O.R., vol. 36, pt. 1, 1072.

68. Ulysses Grant to Edwin Stanton, May 13, 1864, in *The Papers of Ulysses S. Grant,* vol. 10, 434; Taaffe, *Commanding the Army of the Potomac,* 163–64. Also see, Matter, "The Federal High Command at Spotsylvania," 29–60.

69. Field Return of the Army of the Potomac for June 1, 1864, O.R., vol. 36, pt. 1, 209; Walker, *History of the Second Army Corps,* 483; Catton, *A Stillness at Appomattox,* 47–48; Wert, *The Sword of Lincoln,* 356. For a brief history of the military service of the Corcoran Legion before assigned to the Second Corps, see Conyngham, *The Irish Brigade,* 460–66.

70. Walter Gilman, "Life in Virginia or Thirty-Four Days in Grant's Army in the Field," Leigh Collection, USAMHI; Walker, *History of the Second Army Corps,* 486–89.

71. Ulysses Grant to Henry Halleck, May 10, 1864; Henry Halleck to Ulysses Grant, May 16, 1864, O.R., vol. 36, pt. 2, 595, 810.

72. Hays, *Under the Red Patch,* 245–47; Billings, *The History of the Tenth Massachusetts Battery of Light Artillery,* 183; Cowtan, *Services of the Tenth New York Volunteers,* 274–75; Marbaker, *History of the Eleventh New Jersey Volunteers,* 183. The operations of the Army of the Potomac around the North Anna River are explored in Miller, *"Even to Hell Itself"*; and Rhea, *To the North Anna River.*

73. Grimsley, *And Keep Moving On,* 148–60; Wert, *Sword of Lincoln,* 360–61. For a description of the role played by the Second Corps in the maneuvers and

fighting around the North Anna River and Totopotomoy Creek, see Walker, *History of the Second Army Corps*, 491–504.

74. Fisk, *Hard Marching Every Day*, 225; Haines, *History of the Fifteenth Regiment New Jersey Volunteers*, 183. For a discussion of attitudes toward Grant during the Overland Campaign, see Reardon, "A Hard Road to Travel." Reardon argues that many soldiers understood that Grant was attempting to apply continuous pressure on the Confederate army. The high cost in casualties, however, prompted many other soldiers to voice "serious criticisms of their new commander." Also see Wert, *The Sword of Lincoln*, 357. Wert argues that despite the bloodshed, Grant remained popular among soldiers.

75. James Rea to Wife, May 25, 1864, Rea Letters, CWMC, USAMHI; William Smith to Mother, May 30, 1864, Smith Letters, USAMHI; Daniel Godkin to Wife, May 31, 1864, Godkin Letters, Leigh Collection, USAMHI. For frustration with the army's high command, see Crotty, *Four Years Campaigning in the Army of the Potomac*, 134. A former soldier in the 3rd Michigan, Crotty rails against Grant for losing "so many men in such a short time."

76. Ford, *The Story of the Fifteenth Massachusetts Volunteer Infantry*, 330; Herbert Willand, diary entry, June 1, 1864, Willand Diary, NHSL; Timothy Bateman, diary entry, June 1, 1864, Bateman Diary, CWMC, USAMHI; Simons, *The One Hundred Twenty-Fifth New York State Volunteers*, 212; John Hirst letter, in Page, *History of the Fourteenth Regiment, Connecticut Volunteer Infantry*, 262. For description of the wear on the rest of the Army of the Potomac, see Reardon, "A Hard Road to Travel."

77. Guy Watkins letter, May 30, 1864, in Craft, *History of the One Hundred Forty-First Regiment, Pennsylvania Volunteers*,

207; Mulholland, *The Story of the 116th Regiment Pennsylvania Volunteers*, 253.

78. John Brooke, circular, May 30, 1864, 2d Army Corps Records, RG 393, NA; David Birney, circular, May 7, 1864, 2d Army Corps Records, RG 393, NA; J. Franklin Dyer, diary entry, May 31, 1864, in *The Journal of a Civil War Surgeon*, 164. Dyer writes that "There are hundreds of men straggling in the woods—'coffee boilers' who drop out on the march when they get a chance. They steal whenever they can and never fight."

79. Gibbon, *Personal Recollections*, 233–34; Galwey, *Valiant Hours*, 219; Robertson, *Personal Recollections of the War*, 111; David Birney, circular, May 7, 1864, 2d Army Corps Records, RG 393, NA; Theodore Lyman to Wife, May 23, 1864, in *With Grant and Meade*, 117; Rhea, *To the North Anna River*, 189–90. Commenting on increasing foraging by Union soldiers, Lyman writes, "Some of the generals, particularly Birney and Barlow, have punished pillagers in a way they will not forget."

80. Adams, *Reminiscences of the Nineteenth Massachusetts Regiment*, 94; Banes, *History of the Philadelphia Brigade*, 259; Grimsley, *And Keep Moving On*, 136.

81. James Beaver, diary entry, June 2, 1864, in Muffly, *The Story of Our Regiment*, 129; Jones, "From the North Anna to Cold Harbor," 153–54; Billings, *The History of the Tenth Massachusetts Battery of Light Artillery*, 197; Wert, *Sword of Lincoln*, 361–62. Recent studies on the maneuvers and fighting around Cold Harbor include: Furgurson, *Not War but Murder*; Maney, *Marching to Cold Harbor*; and Rhea, *Cold Harbor*.

82. Report of Major General Winfield S. Hancock, February 1865, *O.R.*, vol. 36, pt. 1, 344; Ulysses S. Grant to George G. Meade, June 2, 1864, *O.R.*, vol. 36, pt. 3, 478; Theodore Lyman to Wife, June 12, 1864, in *With Grant and Meade*, 140;

Kepler, *History of the ... Fourth Regiment Ohio Volunteer Infantry*, 178; Winfield S. Hancock to Andrew Humphreys, June 2, 1864, *O.R.*, vol. 36, pt. 3, 481; Walker, *History of the Second Army Corps*, 506. Hancock in his June 2 report wrote that on the march to Cold Harbor, "there was a good deal of straggling, owing to extreme fatigue of the men and the dusty roads."

83. Circular, Headquarters Second Corps, June 2, 1864, *O.R.*, vol. 36, pt. 3, 483; Rhea, *Cold Harbor*, 307-11.

84. Haines, *History of the Men of Co. F*, 66; David Birney to George Gross, late May 1864; Birney Papers, USAMHI; J. Franklin Dyer, diary entry, May 30, 1864, in *The Journal of a Civil War Surgeon*, 161; Martin, *History of the Fifty-Seventh Regiment, Pennsylvania Veteran Volunteer Infantry*, 119; Cowtan, *Services of the Tenth New York Volunteers*, 279-80.

85. Ulysses Grant to Henry Halleck, May 26, 1864, *O.R.*, vol. 36, pt. 3, 206-207; Rhea, *Cold Harbor*, 312-17.

86. Report of Brigadier General John Brooke, November 1, 1865, *O.R.*, vol. 36, pt. 1, 414; Walker, *History of the Second Army Corps*, 509-12; Walker, "General Gibbon," 310; Wilkenson, *Recollections of a Private Soldier*, 131; James Maginnis letter, July 29, 1864, and Eli Nichols letter, June 5, 1864, in Rhea, *Cold Harbor*, 332-33; DuBois, "Cold Harbor Salient," 277-78.

87. Waitt, *History of the Nineteenth Regiment, Massachusetts Volunteer Infantry*, 318; McDermott, *A Brief History of the 69th Regiment Pennsylvania Volunteers*, 43; Seville, *History of the First Regiment Delaware Volunteers*, 113; Report of Major George Scott, August 9, 1864; Report of Captain Nelson Penfield, August 8, 1864; Report of Captain F. Weaver, August 9, 1864, *O.R.*, vol. 36, pt. 1, 381, 405, 429.

88. Page, *History of the Fourteenth Regiment, Connecticut Volunteer Infantry*, 264; Kepler, *History of the ... Fourth Regiment Ohio Volunteer Infantry*, 179-80.

89. Winfield Scott Hancock to George Meade, June 3, 1864; George Meade to Ulysses Grant, June 3, 1864; Ulysses Grant to George Meade, June 3, 1864, *O.R.*, vol. 36, pt. 3, 525, 530-31; Grimsley, *And Keep Moving On*, 216.

90. Grant, *Personal Memoirs*, 272; Ulysses Grant to George Meade, June 3, 1864, *O.R.*, vol. 36, pt. 3, 526; Rhea, *Cold Harbor*, 374-75.

91. Swinton, *Campaigns of the Army of the Potomac*, 487; Rhea, *Cold Harbor*, 376-77; Grimsley, *And Keep Moving On*, 217-18. Swinton was a newspaper reporter who accompanied the Army of the Potomac. He writes that after Meade's orders to again attack circulated through the army, "no man stirred, and the immobile lines pronounced a verdict, silent, yet emphatic, against further slaughter."

92. Wilkenson, *Recollections of a Private Soldier*, 135; George Bowen, diary entry, CWMC, USAMHI. Regarding Meade's order for a new round of Union attacks, Wilkenson writes, "I heard the order given, and I saw it disobeyed." Bowen's diary entry is dated June 3, 1864. However, the section on Cold Harbor is written as a typed memorandum, composed well into the postwar era.

93. Justus Livingston, diary entry, June 3, 1864, Livingston Diary, RU; Haines, *History of the Men of Co. F*, 67; Martin Sigman, diary entry, early June 1864, vol. 320, FSNMP; Walker, *History of the Second Army Corps*, 516. Also see Walker, *General Hancock*, 224.

94. Daniel Chisholm, diary entry, June 5, 1864, in *The Civil War Notebook of Daniel Chisholm*, 21; Walker, *History of the Second Army Corps*, 516-17; Rhea, *Cold Harbor*, 382-84.

95. Robert McAllister to Wife, June 4, 1864, in *The Civil War Letters of General Robert McAllister*, 432; Kepler, *History of the ... Fourth Regiment Ohio Volunteer Infantry*, 180; Hays, *Under the Red Patch*,

250–51; Scott, *History of the One Hundred and Fifth Regiment of Pennsylvania Volunteers*, 110.

96. Return of Casualties, Cold Harbor, Bethesda Church, etc., June 2–15, 1864, *O.R.*, vol. 36, pt. 1, 166–80; Herbert Willand, diary entry, June 5, 1864, NHSL. Also see Winfield Scott Hancock to Adjutant General of the Army, September 16, 1867, Brooke Papers, PHS. Hancock believed that the turning point in the Union assault came with the severe wounding of Colonel John Brooke, a brigade commander in the First Division. Brooke fell soon after the 7th New York Heavy Artillery had captured a line of Confederate entrenchments. Hancock lamented that the wounding of Brooke was a "severe loss to us" because, had he remained unscathed, he might "by his presence have retained his troops in the enemy's works, and held the ground until they could have been supported."

97. Corcoran Legion private quotation, in Baltz, *The Battle of Cold Harbor*, 142; Henry Swan to Abbie, June 4, 1864, *Civil War Times Illustrated* 9 (1972): 43; Rhea, *Cold Harbor*, 386–87.

98. Report of Major General Winfield Scott Hancock, February 1865, *O.R.*, vol. 36, pt. 1, 345–46; Morgan quotation taken from Walker, *History of the Second Army Corps*, 522.

99. Bartlett, *History of the Twelfth Regiment, New Hampshire Volunteers*, 204. For a discussion of whether the Army of the Potomac actually suffered a "Cold Harbor" syndrome, see Rhea, *Cold Harbor*, 267–68. Rhea makes the cogent point that many veteran soldiers were skittish about assaulting Confederate defensive works, even before going into battle on June 3.

100. Friend Sam to Vaname Family, June 10, 1864, Stone Collection, USAMHI. "Friend Sam," an unidentified soldier in the 14th Indiana, fumed, "I like not the way he [Grant] butchers up men and gains

nothing." The Confederate defensive works are mentioned in Baltz, *The Battle of Cold Harbor*, 209.

101. Winfield S. Hancock to Seth Williams, June 5, 1864, *O.R.*, vol. 36, pt. 3, 603; Grimsley, *And Keep Moving On*, 220.

102. Wilkenson, *Recollections of a Private Soldier*, 139; Adams, *Reminiscences of the Nineteenth Massachusetts Regiment*, 100; Walker, *History of the Second Army Corps*, 518–19.

103. Muffly, *The Story of Our Regiment*, 266; Banes, *History of the Philadelphia Brigade*, 274; Joseph Law to Wife, June 11, 1864, Law Family Papers, CWMC, USAMHI; Walker, *History of the Second Army Corps*, 520. Walker writes that the lines of the Second Corps were "nearest to the enemy" of any in the Army of the Potomac.

104. Leonard Ferguson, diary entries, June 4 and 5, 1864, in "The Civil War Diaries of Leonard C. Ferguson," 209; Amos Yeakel, diary entry, June 12, 1864, 145th Pennsylvania unpublished history, file 20, PNMP; David Megraw to Eliza Wentz, June 5, 1864, Megraw Letter, vol. 322, FSNMP; J. E. Hodgkins, diary entry, June 5, 1864, in *The Civil War Diary of Lieut. J. E. Hodgkins*, 92.

105. Page, *History of the Fourteenth Regiment, Connecticut Volunteer Infantry*, 268; Houghton, *The Campaigns of the Seventeenth Maine*, 198; Marbaker, *History of the Eleventh New Jersey Volunteers*, 190–91; McDermott, *A Brief History of the 69th Regiment Pennsylvania Volunteers*, 44; Haines, *History of the Men of Co. F.*, 69; Charles Hamlin to Sister, June 10, 1864, Hamlin Letters, NYSLA; Bloodgood, *Personal Reminiscences*, 279.

106. George Salmon, diary entry, June 12, 1864, 145th Pennsylvania unpublished history, file 20, PNMP; Walker, *History of the Second Army Corps*, 520–21.

7. VICTORY

1. Ulysses S. Grant to Henry Halleck, June 5, 1864, *O.R.*, vol. 36, pt. 3, 598–99; Report of Major General Winfield S. Hancock, September 21, 1865, *O.R.*, vol. 40, pt. 1, 303; Walker, *History of the Second Army Corps*, 525–26; Amos Yeakel, diary entry, June 14, 1864, 145th Pennsylvania unpublished history, file 20, PNMP.

2. Charles Dana to Edwin Stanton, June 15, 1864, *O.R.*, vol. 40, pt. 1, 19–20; Howe, *Wasted Valor*, 28–29. Studies that explore the ensuing Union siege of Petersburg in its entirety are few. Two of the more recent studies are: Horn, *The Petersburg Campaign*; and Trudeau, *The Last Citadel*. For description of the initial Union attacks upon Petersburg, see Howe, *Wasted Valor*.

3. Report of Major General Winfield Scott Hancock, September 21, 1865, *O.R.*, vol. 40, pt. 1, 303–304; J. Franklin Dyer to Wife, June 14, 1864, in *The Journal of a Civil War Surgeon*, 168; Cowtan, *Services of the Tenth New York Volunteers*, 292; Walker, *History of the Second Army Corps*, 526–32.

4. William F. Smith to Winfield S. Hancock, June 15, 1864; Ulysses S. Grant to John Gibbon, June 15, 1864, *O.R.*, vol. 40, pt. 2, 59, 63; Report of Major General Winfield Scott Hancock, September 21, 1865, *O.R.*, vol. 40, pt. 1, 304. Hancock wrote in his report that the "messages from Lieutenant-General Grant and from General Smith, which I received between 5 and 6 p.m. on the 15th, were the first and only intimations I had that Petersburg was to be attacked that day. Up to that hour I had not been notified from any source that I was expected to assist General Smith in assaulting that city."

5. Report of Major General Winfield Scott Hancock, September 21, 1865, *O.R.*, vol. 40, pt. 1, 305; Walker, *History of the Second Army Corps*, 533–34; Howe, *Wasted Valor*, 35–36.

6. Theodore Lyman to Wife, June 15, 1864, in *Meade's Headquarters*, 162; "How We Failed to Take Petersburgh"; Jordan, *Winfield Scott Hancock*, 145. Smith also was active in defending his action before Petersburg in both his autobiography, *From Chattanooga to Petersburg under Generals Grant and Butler*, and "The Movement against Petersburg, June, 1864."

7. Winfield Scott Hancock to Seth Williams, June 26, 1864, *O.R.*, vol. 40, pt. 1, 313–15.

8. Winfield Scott Hancock to Francis Barlow, June 26, 1864, *O.R.*, vol. 40, pt. 2, 436–44.

9. Marbaker, *History of the Eleventh New Jersey Volunteers*, 193; Page, *History of the Fourteenth Regiment, Connecticut Volunteer Infantry*, 286; Howe, *Wasted Valor*, 26–27.

10. Stephen Osborne letter, June 15, 1864, 145th Pennsylvania unpublished history, file 20, PNMP; Herbert Willand, diary entry, June 16, 1864, Willand Diary, NHSL.

11. Mulholland, *The Story of the 116th Regiment Pennsylvania Volunteers*, 268–69; Howe, *Wasted Valor*, 57; Humphreys, *Virginia Campaign*, 215–16; Catton, *A Stillness at Appomattox*, 194–96.

12. Bradley, *A Soldier-Boys Letters*, 41; Burr, *James Addams Beaver*, 159–61; Simons, *The One Hundred and Twenty-Fifth New York State Volunteers*, 222; Report of Major George Scott, August 9, 1864; Report of Captain Nelson Penfield, August 8, 1864; Report of Captain James Patten, August 7, 1864, *O.R.*, vol. 40, pt. 1, 342, 352, 358; Stephen Osborne letter, June 16, 1864, 145th Pennsylvania unpublished history, file 20, PNMP.

13. Winfield Scott Hancock to S. Williams, June 22, 1864, 2d Army Corps Records, RG 393, NA; David Birney to S. Williams, June 21, 1864, *O.R.*, vol. 40, pt. 2, 277; Walker, *History of the Second*

Army Corps, 535–37. Birney reported the Second Corps at 21,190 men present for duty.

14. Francis Barlow to Francis Walker, June 17, 1864, *O.R.,* vol. 40, pt. 2, 123; David Birney to George Meade, June 18, 1864, *O.R.,* vol. 40, pt. 1, 168; Jordan, *Winfield Scott Hancock,* 147–48.

15. Smith, *The History of the Nineteenth Regiment of Maine Volunteer Infantry,* 203–204; Cornelius Moore to Sister Ad, July 1, 1864, in *Cornie,* 189; William Brady to Captain Baker, June 20, 1864, File 39, PNMP; William Potter, diary entry, June 20, 1864, in *One Surgeon's Private War,* 109.

16. Winfield Scott Hancock to Seth Williams, June 16, 1864, *O.R.,* vol. 40, pt. 2, 91; Report of Captain James Fleming, *O.R.,* vol. 40, pt. 1, 334; George Hopper to J. Hopper, July 2, 1864, Hopper Letters, USAMHI; Guy Watkins letter, June 17, 1864, in Craft, *History of the One Hundred Forty-First Regiment, Pennsylvania Volunteers,* 215.

17. Howe, *Wasted Valor,* 106–18; Walker, *History of the Second Army Corps,* 539–41.

18. Robert McAllister to Wife, June 19, 1864, in *The Civil War Letters of General Robert McAllister,* 443–44; Robert Goldthwaite Carter, *Four Brothers in Blue,* 441; Report of Lieutenant Colonel William Neeper, August 10, 1864; Report of Captain Thomas Thompson, August 8, 1864, *O.R.,* vol. 40 pt. 1, 404, 418; Howe, *Wasted Valor,* 119–20.

19. William Brady to Captain Baker, June 20, 1864, file 39, PNMP; Houghton, *The Campaigns of the Seventeenth Maine,* 205; George Bowen, diary entry, June 18, 1864, Bowen Diary, CWMC, USAMHI; Cowtan, *Services of the Tenth New York Volunteers,* 298; Roe, *History of the First Regiment of Heavy Artillery, Massachusetts Volunteers,* 173–75.

20. Quotation taken from Catton, *A Stillness at Appomattox,* 198; Fox,

Regimental Losses, 451. During the fighting on June 18, the 1st Maine Heavy Artillery suffered the highest numerical losses by any Federal regiment in one battle in the war.

21. Gaff, *On Many a Bloody Field,* 363; Roebling, *Wash Roebling's War,* 27; Return of Casualties in the Union Forces, June 15–30, 1864, *O.R.,* vol. 40, no. 1, 218–38.

22. Billings, *The History of the Tenth Massachusetts Battery of Light Artillery,* 228; Nelson Miles to Brother, June 22, 1864, Miles Papers, USAMHI; Wert, *Sword of Lincoln,* 375–76; Humphreys, *The Virginia Campaign,* 198.

23. Report of Major General David Birney, June 26, 1864; Report by Lieutenant Colonel Charles Morgan, June 25, 1864, *O.R.,* vol. 40, pt. 1, 326, 328; Walker, *History of the Second Army Corps,* 544–45.

24. Hays, *Under the Red Patch,* 257–58; Scott, *History of the One Hundred and Fifth Regiment Pennsylvania Volunteers,* 113; Mulholland, *The Story of the 116th Regiment Pennsylvania Volunteers,* 276; Brigade commander quotation taken from Trudeau, *The Last Citadel,* 75.

25. Allen Landis to Father, July 2, 1864, Landis Family Papers, LC; Ulysses S. Grant to Henry W. Halleck, June 24, 1864, *O.R.,* vol. 40, pt. 1, 13–14; Walker, *History of the Second Army Corps,* 545–46.

26. David Birney to George Gross, July 14, 1864, Birney Letters, USAMHI; Francis Barlow to Edward Barlow, July 24, 1864, Barlow Papers, MHS; John Gibbon to Francis Walker, July 7, 1864, *O.R.,* vol. 40, pt. 2, 65.

27. R. Briggs to Mr. Andrews, June 22, 1864, 11th New York Battery newspaper clipping, file 39, PNMP; Haley, diary entry, June 22, 1864, in *Rebel Yell and Yankee Hurrah,* 175.

28. Richard Thompson to Sister Hann, June 26, 1864, in *While My Country Is in Danger,* 111.

29. Major General Winfield Scott Hancock, General Orders No. 22, June 27, 1864, O.R., vol. 40, pt. 2, 468; Report of Brigadier General Francis Barlow, June 25, 1864; Report of Major General John Gibbon, O.R., vol. 40, pt. 1, 330; 368; George Armes letter, June 21, 1864, in *Ups and Downs of an Army Officer*, 104.

30. Winfield Scott Hancock to Seth Williams, July 4, 1864, 2d Army Corps Records, RG 393, NA; George Dauchy, "The Battle Of Reams Station," file 39, PNMP; Unidentified soldier, 64th New York, Civil War reminiscences, IU; Walker, *History of the Second Army Corps*, 197, 548–49. Walker lists 27,045 men absent from duty on June 30, 1864. The high previous to the start of the campaigns of 1864 had been 13,869 men absent from duty on December 31, 1862.

31. Bloodgood, *Personal Reminiscences of the War*, 289; Abstract from Tri-monthly Return, June 30, 1864, O.R., vol. 40, pt. 1, 177.

32. Major General Winfield Scott Hancock, General Orders, No. 22, June 27, 1864, O.R., vol. 40, pt. 2, 468; Daniel Chisholm, diary entry, June 26, 1864, in *The Civil War Notebook of Daniel Chisholm*, 26; Conyngham, *The Irish Brigade*, 467.

33. Organization of the Army of the Potomac, June 30, 1864, O.R., vol. 40, pt. 1, 542–51; Wert, *A Brotherhood of Valor*, 305.

34. J. Franklin Dyer, diary entry, July 8, 1864, in *The Journal of a Civil War Surgeon*, 179; R. Briggs to Mr. Andrews, July 8, 1864, 11th New York Battery newspaper clipping, file 39, PNMP; Timothy Bateman, diary entry, July 7 and 11, 1864, Bateman Diary, CWMC, USAMHI; Richard Thompson to Sister Hann, August 3, 1864, in *While My Country Is in Danger*, 117; Cole, *Under Five Commanders*, 223.

35. Herbert Willand, diary entry, July 5, 1864, Willand Diary, NHSL; David Cone to Wife, July 23, 1864, in "Civil War Letters of David Cone," 206–207; J. Franklin Dyer, diary entry, July 4, 1864, in *The Journal of a Civil War Surgeon*, 178; Smith, *The History of the Nineteenth Regiment of Maine Volunteer Infantry*, 224; Joseph Law to Wife, July 31, 1864, Law Family Papers, CWMC, USAMHI; Edward Cotter to Parents, August 25, 1864, Cotter Letters, CWMC, USAMHI.

36. Cyrus Comstock, diary entry, July 27, 1864, in *The Diary of Cyrus Comstock*, 284. The best description of the Union operation around Deep Bottom is Suderow, "Glory Denied," 17–30.

37. Jordan, *Winfield Scott Hancock*, 155; Meade, *Life and Letters*, vol. 2, 218–19.

38. Hays, *Under the Red Patch*, 264; Trudeau, *The Last Citadel*, 99–127.

39. Robert McAllister to Ellen McAllister, July 31, 1864, in *The Civil War Letters of General Robert McAllister*, 471; Herbert Willand, diary entry, July 30, 1864, Willand Diary, NHSL; William Myers to Family, August 14, 1864, Myers Letters, CWMC, USAMHI.

40. Joseph Atkins letter, August 30, 1864, in Craft, *History of the One Hundred Forty-First Regiment, Pennsylvania Volunteers*, 224; Cowtan, *Services of the Tenth New York Volunteers*, 308; Billings, *The History of the Tenth Massachusetts Battery of Light Artillery*, 235; Ansell White to Family, July 14, 1864, White Letters, Leigh Collection, USAMHI; Walker, *History of the Second Army Corps*, 568–69. For criticism of the northern home front, see Charles Hamlin to Sister Dora, July 14, 1864, Hamlin Letters, NYSLA; and, Francis Barlow to Edward, July 15, 1864, Barlow Letters, MHS.

41. Haines, *History of the Men of Co. F*, 73. For an overview of the second Union offensive around Deep Bottom, see Suderow, "'Nothing but a Miracle Could Save Us,'" 12–32.

42. Report of Brigadier General Francis Barlow, n.d.; Report of Major George

Hogg, August 17, 1864 *O.R.*, vol. 42, pt. 1, 248, 267; Smith, *The History of the Nineteenth Regiment of Maine Volunteer Infantry*, 226; Suderow, "'Nothing but a Miracle Could Save Us,'" 18.

43. Report of Major General Winfield S. Hancock, November 12, 1864, *O.R.*, vol. 42, pt. 1, 267; George Bowen, diary entry, August 21, 1864, Bowen Diary, CWMC, USAMHI; Kirk, *Heavy Guns and Light*, 332; Elias Marston reminiscence, in Child, *A History of the Fifth Regiment New Hampshire Volunteers*, 287.

44. Marbaker, *History of the Eleventh New Jersey Volunteers*, 206; Muffly, *The Story of Our Regiment*, 275; Elias Marston reminiscence, in Child, *A History of the Fifth Regiment New Hampshire Volunteers*, 287; Simons, *The One Hundred Twenty-Fifth New York State Volunteers*, 197; Page, *History of the Fourteenth Regiment, Connecticut Volunteer Infantry*, 302.

45. Report of Major General Winfield S. Hancock, November 12, 1864, *O.R.*, vol. 42, pt. 1, 228; Waitt, *History of the Nineteenth Regiment, Massachusetts Volunteer Infantry*, 347; Child, *A History of the Fifth Regiment New Hampshire Volunteers*, 278; J. Franklin Dyer, diary entry, August 25, 1864, in *The Journal of a Civil War Surgeon*, 193; Levi Jewett reminiscence, in Page, *History of the Fourteenth Regiment, Connecticut Volunteer Infantry*, 295. A detailed description of the fighting at Ream's Station is found in Horn, *The Destruction of the Weldon Railroad*, 122–40; 154–76.

46. The Consolidated Brigade fielded the 7th New York (five companies); 39th New York (six companies); 52nd New York (six companies); 57th New York; 63rd New York (six companies); 69th New York (six companies); 88th New York (five companies); 111th New York; 125th New York; and 126th New York.

47. Unidentified soldier, 64th New York, Civil War reminiscences, IU; Billings, *The History of the Tenth*

Massachusetts Battery of Light Artillery, 253; Simons, *The One-Hundred Twenty Fifth New York State Volunteers*, 243; Return of Casualties in the Union Forces, Ream's Station, Va., *O.R.*, vol. 42, pt. 1, 129–30; Walker, *History of the Second Army Corps*, 600.

48. George Meade to Winfield S. Hancock, August 25, 1864, *O.R.*, vol. 42, pt. 2, 486.

49. Cowtan, *Services of the Tenth New York Volunteers*, 314; Haines, *History of the Men of Co. F*, 81; Nelson Miles to Brother, September 12, 1864, Miles Papers, USAMHI; Joseph Muffly reminiscence, in *The Story of Our Regiment*, 278. Some men gave nothing and greatly inflated Confederate numbers and losses at Ream's Station. Rumors circulated regarding the "heavy numbers of the enemy," perhaps as many as five times the totals fielded by the Second Corps.

50. Report of Major General Winfield Scott Hancock, *O.R.*, vol. 42, pt. 1, 223–25; Winfield Scott Hancock to Alexander Webb, August 30, 1864, in Jordan, *Winfield Scott Hancock*, 163; Horn, *The Destruction of the Weldon Railroad*, 171.

51. Andrew Humphreys to Winfield Scott Hancock, August 24, 1864, and August 25, 1864, *O.R.*, vol. 42, pt. 2, 449, 481; Walker, *General Hancock*, 261; "Hancock Attacked at Ream's Station."

52. Report of Brigadier General Nelson Miles, August 30, 1864, *O.R.*, vol. 42, pt. 1, 253; Walker, *History of the Second Army Corps*, 605.

53. Herbert Willand, diary entry, August 24, 1864, Willand Diary, NHSL; William Potter, August 28, 1864, in *One Surgeon's Private War*, 120.

54. Stedman, "Battle of Ream's Station," 116; Horn, *The Destruction of the Weldon Railroad*, 171.

55. Gibbon, *Personal Recollections*, 259–62.

56. Major General John Gibbon, General Orders, No. 63, August 30, 1864, *O.R.*, vol. 42, pt. 2, 595; Walker, "General Gibbon in the Second Corps," 314–15.

57. John Gibbon to Winfield S. Hancock, September 3, 1864, *O.R.*, vol. 42, pt. 2, 595.

58. Ibid.; Winfield S. Hancock to George Meade, n.d.; Major General George Meade, General Orders, No. 37, Headquarters Army of the Potomac, September 23, 1864; Ulysses S. Grant, Special Orders, No. 87, Headquarters Armies of the United States, September 4, 1864, *O.R.*, vol. 42, pt. 2, 595, 691, 981; Horn, *The Destruction of the Weldon Railroad*, 173.

59. Aubrey, *The Thirty-Sixth Wisconsin Volunteer Infantry*, 132.

60. De Trobriand, *Four Years with the Army of the Potomac*, 658–59.

61. Walker, *History of the Second Army Corps*, 606–608; 613–39.

62. Winfield Scott Hancock to Seth Williams, September 24, 1864, 2d Army Corps Records, RG 393, NA; Houghton, *The Campaigns of the Seventeenth Maine*, 226; Amory Allen to Wife, September 19, 1864, Allen Letters, ISL; Bartholomew Perkins to Mother, October 22, 1864, Perkins Letters, CHS.

63. Child, *A History of the Fifth Regiment New Hampshire Volunteers*, 285; George Arnd, diary entry, August 20, 1864, file 20, PNMP; Charles Field letter, September 19, 1864, Hattie Burleigh Papers, USAMHI; Herbert Willand, diary entry, October 10, 1864, Willand Diary, NHSL; James Rea to Wife, September 27, 1864, Rea Letters, CWMC, USAMHI.

64. Edwin Stanton to Ulysses Grant, October 25, 1864; Ulysses Grant to Edwin Stanton, October 25, 1864, *O.R.*, vol. 42, pt. 3, 337; Jordan, *Winfield Scott Hancock*, 169–70.

65. Major General Winfield Scott Hancock, "Soldiers of the Second Corps," General Orders No. 44, November 26,

1864, *O.R.*, vol. 42, pt. 3, 713–14; Livermore, *Days and Events*, 410; Billings, *History of the Tenth Massachusetts Battery of Light Artillery*, 298.

66. Amory Allen to Wife, September 27, 1864, Allen Letters, ISL; John Haley, diary entry, September 25, 1864, in *The Rebel Yell and The Yankee Hurrah*, 202.

67. Timothy Bateman, diary entry, August 20, 1864, Bateman Diary, CWMC, USAMHI; Charles Field letter, September 19, 1864, Hattie Burleigh Papers, USAMHI. Standard studies of the maneuvers and fighting in the Shenandoah Valley in 1864 are Brice, *Conquest of a Valley*; and Wert, *From Winchester to Cedar Creek*. Other studies include: Heatwole, *The Burning*; Lepa, *The Shenandoah Valley Campaign of 1864*. For a series of interpretive essays, see Gallagher, ed., *Struggle for the Shenandoah*.

68. Hays, *Under the Red Patch*, 275–76; Child, *A History of the Fifth Regiment New Hampshire Volunteers*, 283. Studies of the Atlanta Campaign are numerous. The best recent studies include: Castel, *Decision in the West*; Coffey, *John Bell Hood and the Struggle for Atlanta*; Davis, *Atlanta Will Fall*; McDonough, *War So Terrible*; and McMurry, *Atlanta 1864*.

69. Cornelius Moore to Sister Ad, July 7, 1864, in *Cornie*, 192; James Mitchell to Parents, February 23, 1864, Mitchell Papers, USAMHI.

70. Welcher, *The Union Army*, 504–507. For examples of black soldiers going into battle around Petersburg, see Glatthaar, *Forged in Battle*, 150–51.

71. Timothy Bateman, diary entry, June 30, 1864, Bateman Diary, CWMC, USAMHI; J. Franklin Dyer, diary entry, June 19, 1864, in *The Journal of a Civil War Surgeon*, 174; William Brady to Captain Baker, June 20, 1864, file 39, PNMP; Charles Hamlin to Sister, June 17, 1864, Hamlin Letters, NYSLA; Ryan, *Campaigning with the Irish Brigade*, 112–13;

Charles Merrick to Wife, June 15, 1864, Merrick Papers, WRHS.

72. Winfield S. Hancock to George Meade, November 8 and 9, 1864, *O.R.*, vol. 42, pt. 2, 560, 574; Meade, *Life and Letters*, vol. 2, 239; Charles Mills to Mother, November 12, 1864, in *Through Blood and Fire*, 225–26. Meade calculated Lincoln carrying 13,500 of the 20,000 votes cast by soldiers. For discussion of soldiers' vote throughout the Union army, see Benton, *Voting in the Field*. More recent perspective is found in Waugh, *Reelecting Lincoln*.

73. Winfield S. Hancock to George Meade, November 8 and 9, 1864, *O.R.*, vol. 42, pt. 2, 560; Smith, *The History of the Nineteenth Regiment of Maine Volunteer Infantry*, 225.

74. Ansell White to Wife, November 14, 1864, White Letters, Leigh Collection, USAMHI; Daniel Chisholm, diary entry, October 11, 1864, in *The Civil War Notebook of Daniel Chisholm*, 43; Amory Allen to Wife, November 26, 1864, Allen Letters, ISL.

75. Charles Hamlin to Sister Louise, October 19, 1864, Hamlin Letters, NYSLA; Edward Cotter to Parents, November 15, 1864, Cotter Letters, CWMC, USAMHI; Nelson Miles to Brother, November 9, 1864, Miles Papers, USAMHI; Charles Field to Hattie, June 23, 1864, Hattie Burleigh Papers, USAMHI.

76. For a brief summary of the life and career of Humphreys, see Warner, *Generals in Blue*, 239–41. The standard biography of Humphreys, written by his son, is Henry H. Humphreys, *Andrew Atkinson Humphreys: A Biography*.

77. Livermore, *Days and Events*, 414; Dana, *Recollections of the Civil War*, 192; Smith, *The History of the Nineteenth Regiment of Maine Volunteer Infantry*, 257; de Trobriand, *Four Years with the Army of the Potomac*, 688. For discussion of Humphreys's attention to the welfare of the

troops while serving as chief of staff, see Hennessy, "'I Dread the Spring,'" 72–73.

78. Abstract from Tri-monthly Return of Armies Operating against Richmond, March 31, 1865, *O.R.*, vol. 46, pt. 1, 62; Marbaker, *History of the Eleventh New Jersey Volunteers*, 228; Cowtan, *Services of the Tenth New York Volunteers*, 330–31.

79. Andrew Humphreys to Nelson Miles, December 3, 1864, 2d Army Corps Records, RG 393, NA; Andrew Humphreys to Seth Williams, December 9, 1864, 2d Army Corps Records, RG 393, NA; Nelson Miles to Uncle, October 21, 1864, Miles Papers, USAMHI. Humphreys writes that several replacement soldiers "attempted to desert to the enemy"; Miles writes that "many" newly arriving soldiers "desert to the enemy."

80. Walker, *History of the Second Army Corps*, 557–58, 650; Gibbon, *Personal Recollections*, 273–78.

81. Organization of the Union Forces Operating against Richmond, March 31, 1865, *O.R.*, vol. 46, pt. 1, 564–80.

82. Walker, *History of the Second Army Corps*, 641–42, 646–49; Wert, *Sword of Lincoln*, 394.

83. D. S. Hopkins, "Reminiscences," PMHC; Andrew Humphreys, Corps Circular, December 16, 1865, 2d Army Corps Records, RG 393, NA; Nelson Stowe, diary entry, March 1, 1865, Stowe Diary, CHS; Page, *History of the Fourteenth Regiment, Connecticut Volunteer Infantry*, 323.

84. Billings, *The History of the Tenth Massachusetts Battery of Light Artillery*, 308; Houghton, *The Campaigns of the Seventeenth Maine*, 255–56; Cowtan, *Services of the Tenth New York Volunteers*, 335; Conyngham, *The Irish Brigade and Its Campaigns*, 514; Stewart, *History of the One Hundred and Fortieth Regiment Pennsylvania Volunteers*, 245; Child, *A History of the Fifth Regiment New Hampshire Volunteers*, 291.

85. Scott, *History of the One Hundred and Fifth Regiment of Pennsylvania Volunteers*, 125; Charles Mills to Mother, November 16, 1864, in *Through Blood and Fire*, 229; Livermore, *Days and Events*, 395; Marbaker, *History of the Eleventh New Jersey Volunteers*, 246–47.

86. Billings, *The History of the Tenth Massachusetts Battery of Light Artillery*, 309; Cowtan, *Services of the Tenth New York Volunteers*, 339–40; George Bowen, diary entry, March 19, 1865, Bowen Diary, CWMC, USAMHI; J. E. Hodgkins, diary entry, March 26, 1865, in *The Civil War Diary of Lieut. J. E. Hodgkins*, 127; Trudeau, *The Last Citadel*, 337–51; Catton, *A Stillness at Appomattox*, 335–38.

87. Bloodgood, *Personal Reminiscences of the War*, 310–11; Wert, *Sword of Lincoln*, 399–400; Walker, *History of the Second Army Corps*, 657–64. Studies of the fighting at Five Forks and the subsequent Appomattox Campaign include: Calkins, *The Appomattox Campaign*; Hendrickson, *The Road to Appomattox*; and Marvel, *Lee's Last Retreat*.

88. Martin, *History of the Fifty-Seventh Regiment, Pennsylvania Veteran Volunteer Infantry*, 152–53; Seville, *History of the First Regiment Delaware Volunteers*, 137; Edward Hamilton, diary entry, April 2, 1865, in "A Union Chaplain's Diary," 6.

89. Frederick Oesterle, "Incidents Connected with the Civil War," CWTI, USAMHI; Report of Major John McHyde, April 10, 1865, O.R., vol. 46, pt. 1, 738; Kirk, *Heavy Guns and Light*, 386–87; Miles, *Serving the Republic*, 85. For a description of the fighting at Sutherland Station see Walker, *History of the Second Army Corps*, 670–72; and Trudeau, *The Last Citadel*, 394–97.

90. John Hirst letter, April 14, 1865, in Page, *History of the Fourteenth Regiment, Connecticut Volunteer Infantry*, 334; Clifford Stickney to Brother, April 13, 1865, Stickney Papers, NC; Walker, *History of*

the Second Army Corps, 675–80; Edward Hamilton, diary entry, April 8, 1865, in "A Union Chaplain's Diary," 8; Smith, *The History of the Nineteenth Regiment of Maine Volunteer Infantry*, 299; Thomas Grove to Mother, April 14, 1865, William Smith Letters, USAMHI. Firsthand account of the action at High Bridge is found in Spaulding, "Nineteenth Maine at High Bridge."

91. George Bowen, diary entry, April 9, 1865, CWMC, USAMHI; Waitt, *History of the Nineteenth Regiment, Massachusetts Volunteer Infantry*, 363; Nelson Stowe, diary entry, April 9, 1865, Stowe Diary, CHS; Haines, *History of the Men of Co. F*, 89; Page, *History of the Fourteenth Regiment, Connecticut Volunteer Infantry*, 335.

92. Ansell White to Wife, April 12, 1865, White Letters, Leigh Collection, USAMHI; Robert Morehead, diary entry, April 9, 1865, Morehead Diary, CWMC, USAMHI; William Baker, diary entry, April 9, 1865, Baker Diary, CWMC, USAMHI.

93. Major General Andrew Humphreys, Officers and Soldiers of the Second Army Corps, April 10, 1865, O.R., vol. 46, pt. 1, 686–87; James Mitchell to Parents, April 17, 1865, Mitchell Papers, USAMHI.

94. Charles Whittier, July 1, 1865, 2d Army Corps Records, RG 393, NA; Walker, *History of the Second Army Corps*, 690–92.

8. MEMORIES

1. Cornelius Moore to Sister, February 15, 1864, in *Cornie*, 164. The history of the regiment is published in the same title, 205–11; Minutes of the Fifteenth Regiment Association, First Annual Meeting, AAS.

2. The interpretation that Union veterans wanted to make their stories known agrees with Hess, *The Union Soldier in Battle*, 159–60. For a contrasting

view, see Linderman, *Embattled Courage,*
266–74. Linderman argues that veterans entered into an extended period of
"hibernation," either unwilling or unable
to come to grips with their role in the war.
On the transition of Civil War soldiers
to peacetime in general, see Logue, *To
Appomattox and Beyond.*

3. Page, *History of the Fourteenth Regi-
ment, Connecticut Volunteer Infantry,* 350;
Washburn, *A Complete Military History
and Record of the 108th N.Y. Vols.,* 344;
Haines, *History of the Men of Co. F,* 100;
William Potter, 1875 reunion speech, in
*Proceedings of the First [-Sixth] Annual
Reunion of the Society of the Twelfth Regi-
ment New Jersey Volunteers,* 8; *Twenty-
Fifth Anniversary of the . . . Tenth Regi-
ment of New York Volunteer Infantry,* 16;
*Reunions of the Nineteenth Maine Regiment
Association,* 46.

4. Murphey, *Four Years in the War,*
147–48, 199–200; Conyngham, *The Irish
Brigade,* 5–6, 8.

5. Stevens, "Preface," *Three Years in the
Sixth Corps,* iii–xii.

6. Charles Morgan to Francis Walker,
July 10, 1867, and November 4, 1867,
General Walker Correspondence, Win-
field Scott Hancock Papers of MOLLUS,
USAMHI.

7. The following corps also met with
the Society of the Army of the Potomac:
First Corps, Third Corps, Fifth Corps,
Sixth Corps, Ninth Corps, Eleventh
Corps, and Twelfth Corps. Stories of
Union veterans' organizations are few.
For a political history of the Grand Army
of the Republic, the largest national orga-
nization for Union veterans, see Dearing,
Veterans in Politics. For a social history of
the GAR, see McConnell, *Glorious Con-
tentment.* For a historiographical essay,
see Foster, "Veterans' Organizations and
Memories of the War," 586–600.

8. Society of the Army of the Potomac,
Thirteenth Annual Re-Union at Detroit,

Michigan, . . . 1882, 82. The Society of the
Army of the Potomac did not meet in
1875. For a listing of the Constitution of
the Society of the Army of the Potomac,
see, Society of the Army of the Potomac,
*26th Annual Re-Union at New London,
Connecticut, . . . 1895,* 72–73.

9. Charles Troutman to Richard
Thompson, February 6, 1886, in *While
My Country Is in Danger,* 175–76; Society
of the Army of the Potomac, *Thirteenth
Annual Re-Union at Detroit, . . . 1882,* 82;
Society of the Army of the Potomac,
*Sixteenth Annual Re-Union at Baltimore,
Maryland, . . . 1885,* 91.

10. Society of the Army of the Potomac,
*Thirteenth Annual Re-Union at Detroit,
. . . 1882,* 13, 82; Society of the Army of the
Potomac, *28th Annual Re-Union at Troy,
New York, . . . 1897,* 92; Society of the Army
of the Potomac, *34th Annual Reunion at
Boston, Massachusetts, . . . 1903,* 80.

11. Society of the Army of the Potomac,
*Thirteenth Annual Re-Union at Detroit, . . .
1882,* 83. The current and past presidents
of the Society of the Army of the Potomac
are listed at the end of each reunion
pamphlet.

12. Daniel Dougherty speech, June 23,
1880, in Jordan, *Winfield Scott Hancock,*
275–76; W. Corcoran to Winfield Scott
Hancock, June 28, 1880, Hancock Papers
of MOLLUS, USAMHI.

13. Mulholland, *The Gettysburg Cam-
paign,* 15–16, 8; "General Hancock at His
Home," newspaper clipping, Hancock
Presidential Scrapbook, Hancock Papers
of MOLLUS, USAMHI; Jordan, *Winfield
Scott Hancock,* 179–80, 219.

14. McCarter, *My Life In the Irish Brigade,* 87; Elijah Cavins, 1880 campaign
speech, Cavins Papers, IHS; Jordan,
Winfield Scott Hancock, 304–305.

15. Thelan, "Memory and American
History," 1117–29. Union veterans were
not alone in remembering the past to
address a perceived wrong. Thelan argues

that memories form when something in the present "triggers an association" to the past. Confederate veterans also argued over the interpretation of the past. See, Levin, "'Is Not the Glory Enough to Give Us All a Share?'" 227–48; and Reardon, *Pickett's Charge in History and Memory.*

16. Deacon, "The Third Corps"; "The Jersey Brigade"; "Old Battlefields."

17. Troutman, "Second Corps"; David Newcomb letter, *National Tribune*, March 5, 1885; Aldrich, "The Old Second Corps."

18. Grant, "Review of Major-General Barlow's Paper on the Capture of the Salient at Spotsylvania," 263–71. Grant was replying to a paper recently presented by Francis Barlow. Barlow had criticized Grant and his men for jumbling the Union lines after the capture of the Bloody Angle. See, Francis Barlow, "Capture of the Salient," 245–62. The Civil War in memory is an increasingly fruitful area of scholarship. A standard work in the field is Foster, *Ghosts of the Confederacy.* For more recent studies, see Blair, *Cities of the Dead;* Cimprich, *Fort Pillow;* Fahs and Waugh, eds., *The Memory of the Civil War in American Culture;* Neff, *Honoring the Civil War Dead;* Rubin, *A Shattered Nation;* and Smith, *This Great Battlefield of Shiloh.*

19. Driver, "The Capture of the Salient at Spotsylvania," 273–85.

20. Merrick, "Regiments Which Lost Most Men"; Samuel Blummer letter, *National Tribune*, April 9, 1885; Smith, "The 5th N.H."

21. Munroe, *A Life of Francis Amasa Walker,* 102; Walker, *History of the Second Army Corps,* 3.

22. John Billings to Francis Walker, October 15, 1881, General Walker Correspondence, Winfield Scott Hancock Papers of MOLLUS, USAMHI; W. G. Mitchell to Francis Walker, in Munroe, *A Life of Francis Amasa Walker,* 262–63.

23. Charles Morgan to Francis Walker, July 10, 1867, General Walker Correspondence, Winfield Scott Hancock Papers of MOLLUS, USAMHI; Society of the Army of the Potomac, *Thirteenth Annual Re-Union at Detroit, . . . 1882,* 82; Francis Walker to Alfred Marshall, November 29, 1886, in Munroe, *A Life of Francis Amasa Walker,* 263–64.

24. James Brady to Francis Walker, January 2–3, 1885, General Walker Correspondence, Winfield Scott Hancock Papers of MOLLUS, USAMHI; T. F. Brown to Francis Walker, December 2, 1885, General Walker Correspondence, Winfield Scott Hancock Papers of MOLLUS, USAMHI.

25. Society of the Army of the Potomac, *16th Annual Re-Union at Baltimore, . . . 1885,* 92; Blight, *Race and Reunion,* 174–81; Walker, *History of the Second Army Corps,* v. Walker never quotes from Heth when describing the fighting at either Bristoe Station or Mine Run. For examples of Walker using quotations from Confederate battle reports at Fredericksburg, see 164–65, 169, 170, and 186.

26. Walker, "Ream's Station," 267–305.

27. Heth, *The Memoirs of Henry Heth,* 206.

28. Munroe, *A Life of Francis Amasa Walker,* 264–65; Walker, *History of the Second Army Corps,* v–vi, 102, 107.

29. Nelson Miles to Francis Walker, October 28, 1886, General Walker Correspondence, Winfield Scott Hancock Papers of MOLLUS, USAMHI; Walker, *History of the Second Army Corps,* xi–xii.

30. Humphreys, *Major General Andrew Atkinson Humphreys,* 12; Walker, *History of the Second Army Corps,* 185–87.

31. Munroe, *A Life of Francis Amasa Walker,* 263–64.

32. Francis Barlow, Resolutions of the Society of the Second Army Corps, June 21, 1887, in Munroe, *A Life of Francis Amasa Walker,* 265; Robert Nugent to Francis

Walker, September 3, 1884, General Walker Correspondence, Winfield Scott Hancock Papers of MOLLUS, USAMHI.

33. Frederick Locke to Francis Walker, April 1, 1887, General Walker Correspondence, Winfield Scott Hancock Papers of MOLLUS, USAMHI.

34. Earle, *History of the Excursion of the Fifteenth Massachusetts Regiment*, 4; *One Hundred and Thirtieth Regiment Pennsylvania Volunteer Infantry*, 5–6; Goddard, *Souvenir of Excursion to Battlefields of the Society of the Fourteenth Connecticut Regiment*, 5.

35. Earle, *History of the Excursion of the Fifteenth Massachusetts Regiment*, 12; Stevens, *Souvenir of Excursion to Battlefields by the Society of the Fourteenth Connecticut Regiment*, 5–6, 44–45; "Attention 108th New York Volunteers," in Washburn, *A Complete Military History and Record of the 108th N.Y. Vols.*, 408–409.

36. Charles Devens speech, in *History of the Excursion of the Fifteenth Massachusetts Regiment*, 15; Reilly, *A Brief History of the 69th Regiment Pennsylvania Volunteers*, 52; John C. Hilton and D. B. McCreary, 145th Pennsylvania, 1889 speeches, in *Pennsylvania at Gettysburg*, vol. 2, 689, 692; Edward Spangler speech, in *One Hundred and Thirtieth Regiment Pennsylvania Volunteer Infantry*, 51–52.

37. W. W. Wiltbank, 72nd Pennsylvania, 1891 speech, in *Pennsylvania at Gettysburg*, vol. 1, 388; Charles Devens, 1886 speech, in *History of the Excursion of the Fifteenth Massachusetts Regiment*, 22–23; John E. Reilly, 1889 speech, in *Pennsylvania at Gettysburg*, vol. 1, 379.

38. A. S. Shallenberger, 140th Pennsylvania, 1889 speech, in *Pennsylvania at Gettysburg*, vol. 2, 674–75; S. M. Whistler speech, in *One Hundred and Thirtieth Regiment Pennsylvania Volunteer Infantry*, 23–24.

39. William Glenny, 64th New York, 1890 speech, in *New York at Gettysburg*,

vol. 2, 521. For competing claims about the farthest advance into the Wheatfield, see D. B. McCreary, 145th Pennsylvania, 1889 speech, in *Pennsylvania at Gettysburg*, vol. 2, 692; and Almond Clark, "The 27th Connecticut at Gettysburg," CHS.

40. Banes, *History of the Philadelphia Brigade*, 180; *Reply of the Philadelphia Brigade Association to the Foolish and Absurd Narrative of Lieutenant Frank A. Haskell*, 8–10; Harry Wilson, 81st Pennsylvania, 1889 speech, in *Pennsylvania at Gettysburg*, vol. 1, 411.

41. William Helmbold to Charles Weiss, July 23, 1890, in Smith, *A Brief Account of the Services Rendered by the Second Regiment Delaware Volunteers*, 10–13.

42. Thompson, "A Scrap of Gettysburg," 97; Scott, "Pickett's Charge As Seen from the Front Line," 7; Page, *History of the Fourteenth Regiment, Connecticut Volunteer Infantry*, 151; *Reunions of the Nineteenth Maine*, 13.

43. L. H. Fassett, 64th New York, 1890 speech, *New York at Gettysburg*, vol. 2, 527; Wilson, *Disaster, Struggle, Triumph*, 85.

44. De Peyster, "An Ideal Soldier"; Daniel Sickles, 1893 speech; James Tanner, 40th New York, 1888 speech, *New York at Gettysburg*, vol. 1, 239, 290. Sickles reinforced the importance of the fighting done by the Third Corps in his speech, declaring, "There is a day and an hour in the life of every nation when its fate hangs on the issue of a battle; such a day and hour—thirty years ago—was the crisis of the battle of Gettysburg on the afternoon of the 2d day of July, 1863."

45. "Gettysburg after Twenty Years"; "Address of J. H. Stine"; Stewart, "Gettysburg"; "Fifth Corps at Gettysburg"; "25 Years After."

46. R. H. Foster, 148th Pennsylvania, 1889 speech, in *Pennsylvania at Gettysburg*, vol. 2, 720; William W. Kerr, 72nd Pennsylvania, 1889 speech, in *Pennsylvania at*

Gettysburg, vol. 1, 389; Samuel G. Adams, 66th New York, 1889 speech, *New York at Gettysburg*, vol. 1, 553; Harry Wilson, 81st Pennsylvania, 1889 speech, in *Pennsylvania at Gettysburg*, vol. 1, 412.

47. Clinton MacDougall, 111th New York, 1891 speech, in *New York at Gettysburg*, vol. 3, 801; Washburn, *A Complete Military History and Record of the 108th N.Y. Vols.*, 48; Sherman D. Richardson, 108th New York, "The Clover Leaf," in *New York at Gettysburg*, vol. 3, 787–88; *One Hundred and Thirtieth Regiment Pennsylvania Volunteer Infantry*, 46, 27.

48. "Grand Army Matters"; "Saving the Nation"; Ropes, "A Reminiscence of Gettysburg."

49. Cardwell, "The Battle of Five Forks," 117; R. M. Stribling, "Gen. James Dearing," 216; James Poindexter, "General Armistead's Portrait Represented," 149–50; George T. Rogers, "Retaking Railroad at Reams Station," 580–81.

50. John C. Hilton, 145th Pennsylvania, 1889 speech, in *Pennsylvania at Gettysburg*, vol. 2, 691; Martin McMahon, 42nd New York, 1891 speech, in *New York at Gettysburg*, vol. 1, 320; Unidentified speaker, 82nd New York, 1890 speech, in *New York at Gettysburg*, vol. 2, 665–66; George E. Vickers, 106th Pennsylvania, "Gettysburg," in *Pennsylvania at Gettysburg*, vol. 2, 550–55.

51. "Gen. W. S. Hancock"; Charles, "Gen. Hancock"; Walker, "General Hancock," 51, 60, 65–66.

52. Frazier, *Reunion of the Blue and Gray*, 86, 113; "Echoes from Gettysburg," 429; Champ Clark, 1913 address, in *Fiftieth Anniversary of the Battle of Gettysburg*, 137.

53. "Pennsylvania Monument in Virginia," 115.

54. R. H. Foster, 148th Pennsylvania, 1889 speech, in *Pennsylvania at Gettysburg*, vol. 2, 712; Harry Wilson, 81st Pennsylvania, 1889 speech, in *Pennsylvania at Gettysburg*, vol. 1, 413. The use of eyewitness

history to shape popular assumptions about the past is detailed in Kammen, *Mystic Chords of Memory.*

55. James O'Reilly, 69th Pennsylvania, 1889 speech, in *Pennsylvania at Gettysburg*, vol. 1, 376; Joseph Kay, 10th New York, 1889 speech, in *New York at Gettysburg*, vol. 1, 276; William Glenny, 64th New York, 1890 speech, in *New York at Gettysburg*, vol. 2, 523–24; Ely Parker, 42nd New York, 1891 speech, in *New York at Gettysburg*, vol. 1, 324. Parker served on Grant's staff throughout much of the war.

56. The move toward national reconciliation at the expense of the wartime contributions made by African Americans is detailed in Blight, *Race and Reunion.* For the postwar experience of black Union veterans in the postwar era, see Shaffer, *After the Glory.*

57. Stewart, *History of the One Hundred and Fortieth Regiment Pennsylvania Volunteers*, iii; "Dedication," *History of the 127th Pennsylvania Regiment Pennsylvania Volunteers*, n.p.; Roback, *The Veteran Volunteers of Herkimer and Otsego Counties in the War of the Rebellion*, 166; Muffly, *The Story of Our Regiment*, 13–14. The standard study of the Civil War in literature is Wilson, *Patriotic Gore.*

58. Smith, *The History of the Nineteenth Regiment of Maine Volunteer Infantry*, x, 33, 39, 133; Searles and Taylor, "Forward," in *History of the First Regiment Minnesota Volunteer Infantry*, n.p.; Waitt, *History of the Nineteenth Regiment, Massachusetts Volunteer Infantry*, iv.

59. Marbaker, *History of the Eleventh New Jersey Volunteers*, 160; Chapin, *A Brief History of the Thirty-Fourth Regiment N.Y.S.V.*, 52; Unidentified Soldier, 64th New York, Civil War reminiscences, IU.

60. Washburn, *A Complete Military History and Record of the 108th Regiment N.Y. Vols.*, 5; George Whipple, unpublished memoir, 64th New York

regimental file, GNMP; Wright, *No More Gallant a Deed*, 6.

61. Page, *History of the Fourteenth Regiment, Connecticut Volunteer Infantry*, 38; Simons, *The One Hundred and Twenty-Fifth New York State Volunteers*, 85–86; Stewart, *History of the One Hundred and Fortieth Regiment Pennsylvania Volunteers*, v; Waitt, *History of the Nineteenth Regiment, Massachusetts Volunteer Infantry*, 311–12.

62. Kirk, *Heavy Guns and Light*, 374–75; Adams, *Reminiscences of the Nineteenth Massachusetts Regiment*, 70; Banes, *History of the Philadelphia Brigade*, 69; Scott, *History of the One Hundred and Fifth Regiment of Pennsylvania Volunteers*, 113.

63. Charles Cowtan, "Recollections," 19, Cowtan Papers, NYPL; F. M. Thrasher reminiscence, in Washburn, *A Complete Military History and Record of the 108th Regiment N.Y. Vols.*, 68; George Whipple, unpublished memoir, 64th New York regimental file, GNMP; Waitt, *History of the Nineteenth Regiment, Massachusetts*

Volunteer Infantry, 62; Marbaker, *History of the Eleventh New Jersey Volunteers*, 183.

64. Stevens, *Souvenir of Excursion to Battlefields by the Society of the Fourteenth Connecticut Regiment*, 19; Child, *A History of the Fifth Regiment New Hampshire Volunteers*, 83; Haines, *History of the Men of Co. F*, 42; Wright, *No More Gallant a Deed*, 239; Fuller, *Personal Recollections of the War of 1861*, 18–19, 79.

65. Hays, *The 130th Regiment, Pennsylvania Volunteers in the Maryland Campaign and the Battle of Antietam*, 12–13; Child, "From Fredericksburg to Gettysburg," 159; Thompson, "A Scrap of Gettysburg," 109; Lochren, "The First Minnesota at Gettysburg," 47.

66. Haines, *History of the Men of Co. F*, 98, 132; John Brooke speech, in The Society of the Army of the Potomac, *Report of the Thirty-Third Annual Re-Union at Gettysburg, . . . 1902*, 49–50; The Society of the Army of the Potomac, *Report of the Twenty-Ninth Annual Re-Union at Niagara Falls . . . 1898*, 62.

BIBLIOGRAPHY

MANUSCRIPTS

Albany Institute of History and Art,
Albany, New York
Albert Van Derveer Papers

American Antiquarian Society,
Worcester, Massachusetts
Haven Family Papers
  Samuel Haven Letters
Minutes of the Fifteenth Regiment
  Association, First Annual Meeting
William Scandlin Papers

Antietam National Military Park,
Maryland
Ephraim Brown Diary
Benjamin Chase Letters
William Child Letters
Jeremiah Danforth Letters
Andrew Ford Diary
Albert Manley Letters
Jonathan Peabody Letters
William Stone Diary
James Turrill Letters
Unidentified Soldier, 53rd Pennsylvania
William White Letters

Boston Public Library, Massachusetts
Henry Ropes Letters
Twentieth Massachusetts Regimental
  Association Collection

Boston University, Department of
Special Collections, Mugar Memorial
Library, Boston, Massachusetts
Military Historical Society of
  Massachusetts Collection
  Edward Hinks Papers

Brown University, Special Collections,
John Hay Library, Providence, Rhode
Island
Civil War Collection
  Charles Davis Folder

Connecticut Historical Society, New
Haven
Almond Clark, "The 27th Connecticut at
  Gettysburg"
Watson Hitchcock Papers
  Lauren Hotchkiss Letters
Bartholomew Perkins Letters
Charles Pollard Letters
Nelson Stowe Diary

Cornell University, Department of
Manuscripts and Archives, Kroch
Library, Ithaca, New York
John Ostrander Papers

Duke University, Special Collections,
Perkins Library, Durham, North
Carolina
Stephen Osgood Papers
Uriah Parmelee Papers

Cyril Tyler Papers

Emory University, Special Collections, Woodruff Library, Atlanta, Georgia
Joseph Dimock Family Papers

Fredericksburg and Spotsylvania National Military Park, Fredericksburg, Virginia
Charles Benson Letters
P. C. Campbell Diary
John Dillon Letter
Benjamin Draper Diary
James Fay Letters
Levi Fritz, "The Battle of Fredericksburg"
Chalkly Garrett Letters
Francis Harris Diary
Isaac Hillyer Letters
William Jackson Letter
Arch Jones Letters
A. Stokes Jones Letters
Stephen Martin Diary
David Megraw Letter
Warren Pearsons Letters
William Plumer Letters
Frank Plympton Letter
Rodney Ramsey Letters
George Seaman Diary
Martin Sigman Diary
Joseph Snider Letters
Unidentified Soldier, 19th Massachusetts, Letter
Unidentified Soldier, 64th New York, Letter
Joseph Wicklein, "The Incomplete Civil War Memoir"
Isaac Wistar Journal
Samuel Zook Letters

Gettysburg National Military Park, Pennsylvania
Jacob Betchel Letters
George Bullock Letters
William Clough Letter
N. Eldred, "Only a Boy: A First Hand Account of the Civil War"
Albert Emmell Letters

George Finch Letters
Francis Heath Letter
Henry Law Letters
Stephen A. Osborne, "Reminiscence of the Civil War"
R. H. Rea Letter
Robert Penn Smith Letters
George Whipple Unpublished Memoir
Ammi Williams Letter

Indiana Historical Society, Indianapolis
David Beem Papers
Elijah H. C. Cavins Collection
William Houghton Collection
William Trisler Letters
Augustus Van Dyke Collection

Indiana State Library, Indianapolis
Amory Allen Letters

Indiana University, Lilly Library, Bloomington
Civil War Reminiscences of a Soldier in Co. C, 64th New York, 1861–1864

Library of Congress, Manuscript Division, Washington, D.C.
Allen Landis Family Papers
David Rice Collection
Hamlet Richardson Letters
Edwin V. Sumner Family Papers
Miscellaneous Manuscripts
    Unidentified Soldier, 15th Massachusetts, Letter

Massachusetts Historical Society, Boston
Francis C. Barlow Papers
Crowninshield-Magnus Papers
    Casper Crowninshield Diary
Henry Lyman Patten Papers
Sumner Paine Papers
Paul Revere Family Papers

Massachusetts Institute of Technology, Archives, Boston
Francis A. Walker Papers

Minnesota Historical Society, St. Paul
Mathew Marvin Papers

National Archives, Washington, D.C.
Record Group 393
2d Army Corps Records, 1862–65

Navarro College, Pearce Collections,
Corsicana, Tex.
Pearce Civil War Collection
Oliver H. Palmer Papers

New Hampshire State Library, Concord
Herbert Willand Diary

New-York Historical Society, New York
Thomas Dolan Collection
Israel B. Richardson Letter
Gabriel Grant Letters
Isaac Hadden Letters
Penny Family Papers
Alfred Penny Letters
Joseph Johnson Letters
R. D. Parker Collection

New York Public Library, New York
Charles Cowtan Papers

New York State Library and Archives,
Albany
Charles Hamlin Letters
Calvin Haynes Letters
Richard Turner Papers

Ohio Historical Society, Columbus
Samuel Sexton Papers
Peter Weidner Papers

Old Colony Historical Society, Taunton,
Massachusetts
Darius Couch Journal

Pennsylvania Historical Society,
Philadelphia
John Brooke Papers
Charles Hale, "The Story of My Personal
Experiences at the Battle of Antietam"

Oliver Hopkinson Letters
Samuel S. Maker Correspondence
Augustus Bond Wallen Letters
William Reed Diary
James Walker Diary

Pennsylvania Historical and Museum
Commission, Harrisburg
Hiram Alleman Collection
Lucian Bonaparte Alexander Letters
D. S. Hopkins, "Reminiscences"
Richard Oakford Papers
Jeremiah Rohrer Collection

Petersburg National Military Park,
Virginia
George Arnd Diary
William Brady Letter
George Dauchy, "The Battle of Reams
Station," newspaper clipping
11th New York Battery, newspaper
clipping
A. B. Stanton Letters
145th Pennsylvania unpublished history

Rutgers University, Special Collections,
Archibald S. Alexander Library, New
Brunswick, New Jersey
Benjamin Appleby Letters
Justus Livingston Diary

Tennessee State Library and Archives,
Nashville
William Teall Letters

United States Army Military History
Institute, Carlisle, Pennsylvania
David B. Birney Papers
Hattie Burleigh Papers
Martin Connolly Letters
Charles Field Letters
William Burns Diary
Walter A. Eames Letters
Winfield Scott Hancock Papers of
MOLLUS
George Hopper Letters
Charles Johnson Papers

W. H. Lucas Letters
Nelson Miles Papers
James Mitchell Letters
Alfred Wheeler Letters

Civil War Miscellaneous Collection
Timothy Bateman Diary
George Bowen Diary
Arnold Daines Letters
S. P. Conrad Letters
Edward Cotter Letters
Joseph Elliott Diary
Joseph Graham Letters
Joseph Law Family Papers
William Myers Letters
Miles Peabody Letters
Isaac Plumb, "Record of Life and Service"
Jacob Pyewell Letters
James Rea Letters
Levander Sawtelle Letters
John Weiser Letters
Alfred Wheeler Papers
Frank Young Diary

Civil War Times Illustrated Collection
Henry Crofoot Letters
Alexander McNeil Letters
Frederick W. Oesterle, "Incidents
    Connected with the Civil War"
Jonathan Stowe Diary
Dawson Flinchbaugh Collection
    James Maycock Diary

Leigh Collection
Charles Eager Letters
Walter Gilman, "Life in Virginia or
    Thirty-Four Days in Grant's Army in
    the Field"
Daniel Godkin Letters
John Hays, "Account of the Battle of
    Antietam"
Joseph Moody Letters
William F. Smith Letters
Nathanial Stanton Diary
Edward A. Walker Letters
Ansell White Letters

University of Michigan, Bentley
Library, Michigan Historical
Collections, Ann Arbor
Albert Davis Letters

University of Michigan, William L.
Clements Library, Ann Arbor
John Lehman Family Papers
Samuel Hoffman Letters
Kent Family Correspondence
    Daniel Kent Letters

University of Missouri, Ellis Library,
Columbia, Missouri
Western Historical Manuscripts
    Collection
    Daniel Zackman Diary

Western Reserve Historical Society,
Cleveland, Ohio
Charles Merrick Papers
Samuel Maguire Letters

Wistar Institute, Archive, Philadelphia,
Pennsylvania
Isaac Wistar Papers

PRINTED PRIMARY SOURCES

Books, Government
Publications, and Pamphlets
Abbott, Henry L. *Fallen Leaves: The Civil
    War Letters of Major Henry Livermore
    Abbott*. Ed. Robert Garth Scott. Kent,
    Ohio: Kent State University Press, 1991.
Adams, John G. B. *Reminiscences of the
    Nineteenth Massachusetts Regiment*.
    Boston: Wright and Potter Printing,
    1899.
Aldrich, Thomas M. *The History of Bat-
    tery A, First Regiment Rhode Island
    Light Artillery in the War to Preserve
    the Union, 1861–1865*. Providence, R.I.:
    Snow and Farnham, 1904.
Alexander, Edward P. *Fighting for the
    Confederacy: The Personal Recollections
    of General Edward Porter Alexander*.

Ed. Gary W. Gallagher. Chapel Hill: University of North Carolina Press, 1989.

Ames, Nelson. *History of Battery G, First Regiment New York Light Artillery.* Marshalltown, Iowa: Marshall Printing, 1900.

Armes, Augustus. *Ups and Downs of an Army Officer.* Washington, D.C.: n.p., 1900.

Aubery, James Madison. *The Thirty-Sixth Wisconsin Volunteer Infantry.* Milwaukee: Evening Wisconsin, 1900.

Ayling, Augustus D. *A Yankee at Arms: The Diary of Lieutenant Augustus D. Ayling, 29th Massachusetts Volunteers.* Ed. Charles F. Herberger. Knoxville: University of Tennessee Press, 1989.

Banes, Charles. *History of the Philadelphia Brigade: Sixty-Ninth, Seventy-First, Seventy-Second, and One Hundred and Sixth Pennsylvania Volunteers.* Philadelphia: J. B. Lippincott, 1876.

Bartlett, Asa W. *History of the Twelfth Regiment, New Hampshire Volunteers, in the War of the Rebellion.* Concord, N.H.: Ira C. Evans, 1897.

Bassett, Edward. *From Bull Run to Bristow Station.* Ed. M. H. Bassett. St. Paul, Minn.: North Central Publishing, 1962.

The Batchelder Papers: Gettysburg in Their Own Words. 3 vols. Ed. David L. and Audrey J. Ladd. Dayton, Ohio: Morningside, 1994.

Beidelman, George. *The Civil War Letters of George Washington Beidelman.* Ed. Catherine Vanderslice. New York: Vantage Press, 1978.

Benson, Charles. *The Civil War Diaries of Charles E. Benson.* Ed. Richard H. Benson. Decorah, Iowa: Anundsen Publishing, 1991.

Billings, John D. *The History of the Tenth Massachusetts Battery of Light Artillery in the War of the Rebellion.* Boston: Arakelyan Press, 1881.

Bloodgood, John D. *Personal Reminiscences of the War.* New York: Hunt and Eaton, 1893.

Borton, Benjamin. *Awhile with the Blue; Or, Memories of War Days, the True Story of a Private.* Passaic, N.J.: William Taylor, 1898.

Bowen, Ronald. *From Ball's Bluff to Gettysburg... And Beyond.* Ed. Gregory A. Coco. Gettysburg, Pa.: Thomas Publications, 1994.

Bradley, Leverett. *A Soldier-Boys Letters.* N.p; n.d.

Brown, Augustus C. *The Diary of a Line Officer.* New York: N.p., 1906.

Bruce, George A. *The Twentieth Regiment of Massachusetts Volunteer Infantry, 1861–1865.* Boston: Houghton Mifflin, 1906.

Buell, Augustus C. *"The Cannoneer": Recollections of Service in the Army of the Potomac by "A Detached Volunteer" in the Regular Artillery.* Washington, D.C.: National Tribune, 1890.

Carter, Robert Goldthwaite. *Four Brothers in Blue; Or, Sunshine and Shadows of the War of the Rebellion: A Story of the Great Civil War from Bull Run to Appomattox.* Reprint, Austin: University of Texas Press, 1978.

Cavanagh, Michael. *Memoirs of Gen. Thomas Francis Meagher.* Worcester, Mass.: Messenger Press, 1892.

Cavins, Elijah Henry Clay. *The Civil War Letters of Col. Elijah H. C. Cavins, 14th Indiana.* Compiled by Barbara A. Smith. Owensboro, Ky.: Cook-McDowell Publications, 1981.

Chapin, Louis N. *A Brief History of the Thirty-Fourth Regiment N.Y.S.V.* Albany, N.Y.: n.p., 1903.

Child, William A. *A History of the Fifth Regiment New Hampshire Volunteers in the American Civil War, 1861–1865.* Bristol, N.H.: R. W. Musgrove, 1893.

Chisholm, Daniel. *The Civil War Notebook of Daniel Chisholm: A Chronicle of*

Daily Life in the Union Army, 1864–1865. Ed. W. Springer Menge and J. August Shimrak. New York: Orion Books, 1989.

Cole, Jacob H. *Under Five Commanders: Or, a Boy's Experiences with the Army of the Potomac.* Paterson, N.J.: New Print, 1906.

Comstock, Cyrus. *The Diary of Cyrus Comstock.* Ed. Merlin Sumner. Dayton, Ohio: Morningside, 1984.

Contant, George W. *"Each Bee Was a Bullet": Corporal Thomas Geer and Color Sergeant Judson Hicks, Company A, 111th New York Infantry, at the Battles of Harpers Ferry and Gettysburg.* Dover, Del.: Grand Army Historic Publications, 1998.

Conyngham, David P. *The Irish Brigade and Its Campaigns.* Ed. Lawrence Frederick Kohl. New York: Fordham University Press, 1994.

Corby, William. *Memoirs of Chaplain Life: Three Years with the Irish Brigade in the Army of the Potomac.* Ed. Lawrence Frederick Kohl. New York: Fordham University Press, 2002.

Cowtan, Charles W. *Services of the Tenth New York Volunteers (National Zouaves) in the War of the Rebellion.* New York: C. H. Ludwig, 1882.

Craft, David. *History of the One Hundred Forty-First Regiment, Pennsylvania Volunteers, 1862–1865.* Towanda, Pa.: Reporter-Journal Printing, 1885.

Cross, Edward. *Stand Firm and Fire Low: The Civil War Writings of Colonel Edward Cross.* Ed. Walter Holden, William E. Ross, and Elizabeth Slomba. Hanover, N.H.: University Press of New England, 2003.

Crotty, D. G. *Four Years Campaigning in the Army of the Potomac.* Grand Rapids, Mich.: Dygert Brothers, 1874.

Cudworth, Warren. *History of the First Regiment Massachusetts Infantry.* Boston: Walker, Fuller, 1866.

Dana, Charles A. *Recollections of the Civil War with the Leaders at Washington and in the Field in the Sixties.* New York: D. Appleton, 1899.

De Trobriand, Regis. *Four Years with the Army of the Potomac.* Reprint, Gaithersburg, Md.: Ron R. Van Sickles Military Books, 1988.

Donaldson, Francis Adams. *Inside the Army of the Potomac: The Civil War Experience of Captain Francis Adams Donaldson.* Ed. J. Gregory Acken. Mechanicsburg, Pa.: Stackpole Books, 1998.

Dyer, J. Franklin. *The Journal of a Civil War Surgeon.* Ed. Michael B. Chesson. Lincoln: University of Nebraska Press, 2003.

Earle, David M. *History of the Excursion of the Fifteenth Massachusetts Regiments and Its Friends to the Battle-fields of Gettysburg, Pa., Antietam, Md., Ball's Bluff, Virginia, and Washington, D.C., May 31–June 12, 1886.* Worcester: Press of Charles Hamilton, 1886.

Favill, Josiah M. *The Diary of a Young Officer Serving with the Armies of the United States during the War of the Rebellion.* Chicago: R. R. Donnelley and Sons, 1909.

Fifth Annual Report of the Chief of the Bureau of Military Statistics. Albany, N.Y.: C. Van Benthuysen, 1868.

Fisk, Wilbur. *Hard Marching Every Day: The Civil War Letters of Private Wilbur Fisk, 1861–1865.* Ed. Emil and Ruth Rosenblatt. Lawrence: University Press of Kansas, 1992.

Fiske, Samuel W. *Mr. Dunn Browne's Experiences in the Army: The Civil War Letters of Samuel Fiske.* Ed. Stephen W. Sears. New York: Fordham University Press, 1998.

Floyd, Frederick Clark. *History of the Fortieth (Mozart) Regiment, New York Volunteers.* Boston: F. H. Gibson, 1909.

Ford, Andrew E. *The Story of the Fifteenth Massachusetts Volunteer Infantry in the Civil War, 1861–1864.* Clinton, Mass.: W. J. Coulter, 1898.

Fourth Annual Report of the Bureau of Military Statistics. Albany, N.Y.: C. Van Benthuysen, 1867.

Fox, William F. *New York at Gettysburg.* 3 vols. Albany, N.Y.: J. B. Lyon, 1900.

Frazier, John W. *Reunions of the Blue and Gray. Philadelphia Brigade and Pickett's Division, July 2, 3,4, 1887, and Sept. 15, 16, 17, 1906.* Philadelphia: Ware Brothers, 1906.

Frederick, Gilbert. *The Story of a Regiment: Being a Record of the Military Services of the Fifty-Seventh Volunteer Infantry in the War of the Rebellion, 1861–1865.* Chicago: Fifty-Seventh Veteran's Association, 1895.

Fuller, Charles. *Personal Recollections of the War of 1861.* Sherburne, N.Y.: News Job Printing House, 1906.

Galwey, Thomas F. *The Valiant Hours: Narrative of "Captain Brevet," an Irish-American in the Army of the Potomac.* Ed. W. S. Nye. Harrisburg, Pa.: Stackpole, 1961.

Gerrish, Henry. *Letter to Lyman: The Personal Letter of a Civil War Soldier to His Grandson, Walter Lyman Medding, Recounting His Wartime Experiences.* Ed. Walter S. Medding. Springfield, Va.: Genealogical Books in Print, 1978.

Gibbon, John. *Personal Recollections of the Civil War.* New York: G. P. Putnam's Sons, 1928.

Goddard, Henry P. *Regimental Reminiscences of the War of the Rebellion.* Middletown, Conn.: C. W. Church, 1877.

Graham Family. *Aunt and the Soldier Boys from Cross Creek Village, Pennsylvania, 1856–1866, and to Honor Them a Set of Genealogical Charts as an Appendix.* Compiled by Janice Bartlett Reeder

McFadden. Santa Cruz, Calif.: Moore's Graphic Arts, 1970.

Grant, Ulysses S. *Personal Memoirs of U. S. Grant.* Reprint, New York: Penguin Books, 1999.

———. *The Papers of Ulysses S. Grant.* 31 vols. Ed. John Y. Simon. Carbondale: Southern Illinois University Press, 1967–2009.

Haines, Alanson A. *History of the Fifteenth Regiment New Jersey Volunteers.* New York: Jenkins and Thomas, 1883.

Haines, William. *History of the Men of Co. F, with Descriptions of the Marches and Battles of the 12th New Jersey Vols.* Mickleton, N.J.: C. S. Magrath, 1897.

Haley, John. *The Rebel Yell and the Yankee Hurrah: The Civil War Journal of a Maine Volunteer.* Ed. Ruth L. Silliker. Camden, Maine: Down East Books, 1985.

Hancock, Almira Russell. *Reminiscences of Winfield Scott Hancock.* New York: C. L. Webster, 1887.

Hanford, P. A. *The Young Captain: A Memorial to Capt. Richard C. Derby, Fifteenth Reg. Mass. Volunteers, Who Fell at Antietam.* Boston: Degen, Estes, 1865.

Haskell, Frank A. *The Battle of Gettysburg.* Boston: Mudge Press, 1908.

———. *Haskell of Gettysburg: His Life and Civil War Papers.* Ed. Frank L. Byrne and Thomas Weaver. Madison: State Historical Society of Wisconsin, 1970.

Hay, John. *Lincoln and the Civil War in the Diaries and Letters of John Hay.* Ed. Tyler Dennett. New York: Dodd, Mead, 1939.

Hays, Gilbert. *Under the Red Patch: The Story of the Sixty-Third Regiment Pennsylvania Volunteers, 1861–1864.* Pittsburgh: Market Review Publishers, 1908.

Hays, John. *The 130th Regiment, Pennsylvania Volunteers in the Maryland Campaign and the Battle of Antietam: An Address Delivered June 7, 1894, before*

Capt. Cowell Post 201 G.A.R. Carlisle, Pa.: Herald Print, 1894.

Heth, Henry. *The Memoirs of Henry Heth.* Ed. James L. Morrison. Westport, Conn.: Greenwood Press, 1974.

History of the First N.H. Battery, during the War of the Rebellion: Together with the By Laws of Platoon A, First N.H. Light Artillery. Manchester, New Hampshire: T. H. Tuson, 1878.

History of the 127th Regiment Pennsylvania Volunteers, Familiarly Known as the "Dauphin County Regiment." Lebanon, Pa.: Press of Report Pub., 1902.

Hitchcock, Frederick L. *War from the Inside; Or, Personal Experiences, Impressions, and Reminiscences of One of the "Boys" in the War of the Rebellion.* Philadelphia: J. B. Lippincott, 1904.

Hodgkins, J. E. *The Civil War Diary of Lieut. J. E. Hodgkins, 19th Massachusetts Volunteers, from August 11, 1862 to June 3, 1865.* Ed. Kenneth C. Turino. Camden, Maine: Picton Press, 1994.

Holcombe, Return I. *History of the First Regiment Minnesota Volunteer Infantry, 1861–1864.* Stillwater, Minn.: Easton and Masterman, 1916.

Holmes, Oliver Wendell, Jr. *Speeches.* Boston: Little, Brown, 1918.

———. *Touched with Fire: Civil War Letters and Diary of Oliver Wendell Holmes, Jr., 1861–1864.* Ed. Mark de Wolfe Howe. Cambridge, Mass.: Harvard University Press, 1946.

Houghton, Edwin B. *The Campaigns of the Seventeenth Maine.* Portland, Maine: Short and Loring, 1866.

Howard, Oliver Otis. *Autobiography of Oliver Otis Howard, Major General, United States Army.* 2 vols. New York: Baker and Taylor, 1907.

Hyde, Thomas W. *Following the Greek Cross; Or, Memories of the Sixth Army Corps.* Boston: Houghton Mifflin, 1894.

Irwin, Richard B. *History of the Nineteenth Army Corps.* New York: G. P. Putnam's Sons, 1893.

Kepler, William. *History of the Three Months' and Three Years' Service from April 16th, 1861, to June 22d, 1864, of the Fourth Regiment Ohio Volunteer Infantry in the War for the Union.* Cleveland, Ohio: Leader Printing, 1886.

King, David. *History of the Ninety-Third Regiment, New York Volunteer Infantry, 1861–1865.* Milwaukee, Wis.: Swain and Tate, 1895.

Kirk, Hyland Clare. *Heavy Guns and Light: A History of the 4th New York Heavy Artillery.* New York: C. T. Dillingham, 1890.

Lee, Henry T. *The Last Campaign of the Army of the Potomac, from a "Mud Crusher's" Point of View.* San Francisco: Co-operative Printing, 1893.

Lincoln, Abraham. *The Collected Works of Abraham Lincoln.* 9 vols. Ed. Roy P. Basler. New Brunswick, N.J.: Rutgers University Press, 1954.

Livermore, Thomas L. *Days and Events, 1860–1866.* New York: Houghton Mifflin, 1920.

Lockwood, James D. *Life and Adventures of a Drummer-Boy; Or, Seven Years a Soldier.* Albany: J. Skinner, 1893.

Lyman, Theodore. *Meade's Army: The Private Notebooks of Lt. Col. Theodore Lyman.* Ed. David W. Lowe. Kent, Ohio: Kent State University Press, 2007.

———. *Meade's Headquarters, 1863–1865: Letters of Colonel Theodore Lyman from the Wilderness to Appomattox.* Ed. George R. Agassiz. Reprint, Salem, N.H.: Ayer, 1987.

Lyon, Henry C. *"Desolating This Fair Country": The Civil War Diary and Letters of Lt. Henry C. Lyon, 34th New York.* Ed. Emily N. Radigan. Jefferson, N.C.: McFarland, 1999.

Marbaker, Thomas D. *History of the Eleventh New Jersey Volunteers from Its Organization to Appomattox.* Trenton, N.J.: MacCrellish and Quigley, 1898.

Martin, James M. *History of the Fifty-Seventh Regiment, Pennsylvania Veteran Volunteer Infantry; First Brigade, First Division, Third Corps, and Second Brigade, Third Division, Second Corps, Army of the Potomac.* Meadville, Pa.: McCoy and Calvin, n.d.

McAllister, Robert. *The Civil War Letters of General Robert McAllister.* Ed. James I. Robertson, Jr. New Brunswick, N.J.: Rutgers University Press, 1965.

McCarter, William. *My Life in the Irish Brigade: The Civil War Memoirs of Private William McCarter, 116th Pennsylvania Infantry.* Ed. Kevin E. O'Brien. Campbell, Calif.: Savas Publishing, 1996.

McClellan, George B. *The Civil War Papers of George B. McClellan: Selected Correspondence, 1860–1865.* Ed. Stephen W. Sears. New York: Ticknor and Fields, 1989.

———. *McClellan's Own Story: The War for the Union, the Soldiers Who Fought It, the Civilians Who Directed It, and His Relations to It and Them.* New York: Charles L. Webster, 1887.

McClure, John. *Hoosier Farmboy in Lincoln's Army: The Civil War Letters of Pvt. John R. McClure.* Ed. Nancy Baxter. Indianapolis: Guild Press of Indiana, 1992.

Meade, George G., and George G. Meade, Jr. *The Life and Letters of George Gordon Meade, Major General United States Army.* Ed. George G. Meade III. 2 vols. New York: Charles Scribner's Sons, 1913.

Miles, Nelson A. *Serving the Republic: Memoirs of the Civil and Military Life of Nelson A. Miles, United States Army.* New York: Harper and Brothers, 1911.

Mills, Charles J. *Through Blood and Fire: The Civil War Letters of Major Charles J. Mills 1862–1865.* Ed. Gregory A. Coco. Gettysburg, Pa.: Gregory A. Coco, 1982.

Moore, Cornelius L. *Cornie: The Civil War Letters of Lt. Cornelius L. Moore.* Ed. Gilbert C. Moore. N.p.: n.p., 1989.

Muffly, J. W. *The Story of Our Regiment: A History of the 148th Pennsylvania Vols.* Des Moines, Iowa: Kenyon Printing, 1904.

Mulholland, St. Clair A. *The Gettysburg Campaign: The Story of the Second Corps on the March and in Battle.* Philadelphia: McLaughlin Brothers, 1880.

———. *The Story of the 116th Regiment Pennsylvania Volunteers in the War of the Rebellion.* Ed. Lawrence Frederick Kohl. New York: Fordham University Press, 1996.

Murphey, Thomas G. *Four Years in the War: The History of the First Regiment of Delaware Veteran Volunteers (Infantry), . . . From Its Organization in 1861, to the Close of the War in 1865.* Philadelphia: J. S. Claxton, 1866.

Names and Records of All the Members Who Served in the First N.H. Battery of Light Artillery during the Late Rebellion. Manchester, N.H.: Budget Job Print, 1891.

Newcomb, Edgar M. *A Memorial Sketch of Lieut. Edgar M. Newcomb of the Nineteenth Mass. Vols.* Ed. Albert B. Weymouth. Malden, Mass.: Alvin G. Brown, 1883.

Nicholson, John P., and Lewis E. Beitler, eds. *Pennsylvania at Gettysburg.* 2 vols. Harrisburg, Pa.: E. K. Meyers, 1914.

O'Mara, Daniel A. *Proceedings of the Associated Survivors of the Fifty-Ninth Reg't, N.Y. Vet. Vols. First Annual Re-Union and Dedication of Monument at Gettysburg, Pa., July 3d, 1889.* New York: Wm. Finley, Printer, 1889.

One Hundred and Thirtieth Regiment Pennsylvania Volunteer Infantry: Ceremonies and Addresses at Dedication of Monument at Bloody Lane, Antietam Battlefield, September 17, 1904. N.p.: n.p., 1904.

Osborne, William H. A History of the Twenty-Ninth Regiment of Massachusetts Volunteer Infantry, in the Late War of the Rebellion. Boston: Albert J. Wright, 1877.

Page, Charles D. History of the Fourteenth Regiment, Connecticut Volunteer Infantry. Meriden, Conn.: Horton Printing, 1906.

Patrick, Marsena Rudolph. Inside Lincoln's Army: The Diary of Marsena Rudolph Patrick, Provost Marshal General, Army of the Potomac. Ed. David S. Sparks. New York: Thomas Yoseloff, 1964.

Perry, John Gardner. Letters from a Surgeon of the Civil War. Compiled by Martha Derby Perry. Boston: Little, Brown, 1906.

Potter, William W. One Surgeon's Private War: Doctor William W. Potter of the 57th New York. Ed. John Michael Priest. Shippensburg, Pa.: White Mane Publishing, 1996.

Powell, William H. The Fifth Army Corps (Army of the Potomac): A Record of Operations during the Civil War in the United States of America, 1861–1865. New York: G. P. Putnam's Sons, 1896.

Powelson, Benjamin F. History of Company K of the 140th Regiment Pennsylvania Volunteers, 1862–65. Steubenville, Ohio: Carnahan Printing, 1906.

Proceedings of the First [-Sixth] Annual Reunion of the Society of the Twelfth Regiment New Jersey Volunteers. Society of the Twelfth Regiment New Jersey Volunteers, 1875.

Reply of the Philadelphia Brigade Association to the Foolish and Absurd Narrative of Lieutenant Frank Haskell, which appears to be Endorsed by the MOLLUS

Commandery of Massachusetts and the Wisconsin History Commission. Philadelphia: n.p., 1910.

Report of Seventh Annual Reunion of the 64th N.Y. Regimental Association at Salamanca, New York, August 21 and 22, 1895. New York: Randolph Publishing, 1895.

Report of the Joint Committee on the Conduct of the War. 3 pts. Washington, D.C.: Government Printing Office, 1865.

Reunions of the Nineteenth Maine Regiment Association. Augusta, Maine: Press of Sprague, Owen and Nash, 1878.

Rhodes, John H. The Gettysburg Gun. Providence, R.I.: The Society, 1892.

———. The History of Battery B, First Regiment Rhode Island Light Artillery, in the War to Preserve the Union, 1861–1865. Providence, R.I.: Snow and Farnham, 1894.

Roback, Henry. The Veteran Volunteers of Herkimer and Otsego Counties in the War of the Rebellion. Utica, N.Y.: Press of L. C. Childs, 1888.

Robertson, Robert Stoddart. Personal Recollections of the War: A Record of Service with the Ninety-Third New York Vol. Infantry and the First Brigade, First Division, Second Corps, Army of the Potomac. Milwaukee, Wis.: Swain and Tate, 1895.

Roe, Alfred S. History of the First Regiment of Heavy Artillery, Massachusetts Volunteers, . . . 1862–1865. Worcester, Mass.: Regimental Association, 1917.

Roebling, Washington A. Wash Roebling's War: Being a Selection from the Unpublished Civil War Letters of Washington Augustus Roebling. Ed. Earl Schenck Miers. Newark, Del.: Curtis Paper, 1961.

Ryan, John. Campaigning with the Irish Brigade: Pvt. John Ryan, 28th Massachusetts. Ed. Sandy Barnard. Terre Haute, Ind.: AST Press, 2001.

Sawyer, Franklin. *A Military History of the 8th Regiment Ohio Vol. Inf'y: Its Battles, Marches and Army Movements.* Ed. George A. Groot. Cleveland, Ohio: Fairbanks, 1881.

Scott, Kate M. *History of the One Hundred and Fifth Regiment of Pennsylvania Volunteers: A Complete History of the Organization, Marches, Battles, Toils, and Dangers Participated in by the Regiment from the Beginning to the Close of the War.* Philadelphia: New-World Publishing, 1877.

Sedgwick, John. *Correspondence of John Sedgwick, Major General.* 2 vols. Ed. Henry D. Sedgwick. New York: De Vinne Press, 1902–1903.

Seville, William P. *History of the First Regiment Delaware Volunteers, from the Commencement of the "Three Months' Service" to the Final Muster-Out at the Close of the Rebellion.* Wilmington: Historical Society of Delaware, 1884.

Shaw, Horace H. *The First Maine Heavy Artillery, 1861–1865: A History of Its Part and Place in the War for the Union.* Portland, Maine: n.p., 1903.

Sheldon, Winthrop Dudley. *The "Twenty-Seventh": A Regimental History.* New Haven, Conn.: Morris and Benham, 1866.

Simons, Ezra D. *A Regimental History: The One Hundred Twenty-Fifth New York State Volunteers.* New York: E. D. Simons, 1888.

Slater, Thomas Ogden. *Incidents of Personal Experience.* New York: Knickerbocker Press, 1916.

Small, Abner R. *The Road to Richmond: The Civil War Memoirs of Major Abner R. Small of the Sixteenth Maine Volunteers.* Ed. Harold Adams Small. Reprint, New York: Fordham University Press, 2000.

Smith, John Day. *The History of the Nineteenth Regiment of Maine Volunteer Infantry, 1862–1865.* Minneapolis, Minn.: Great Western Printing, 1909.

Smith, Robert G. *A Brief Account of the Services Rendered by the Second Regiment Delaware Volunteers in the War of the Rebellion.* Wilmington: Historical Society of Delaware, 1909.

Smith, William F. *From Chattanooga to Petersburg under General Grant and Butler: A Contribution to the History of the War, and a Personal Vindication.* Boston: Houghton Mifflin, 1893.

Society of the Army of the Potomac. *Report of the . . . Annual Re-union [1870–1919].* New York: Macgowan and Slipper, 1870–1919.

Sorrel, G. Moxley. *Recollections of a Confederate Staff Officer.* New York: Neale Publishing, 1905.

Souvenir of Excursion to Antietam and Dedication of Monuments of the 8th, 11th, 14th, and 16th Regiments of Connecticut Volunteers. N.p.: n.p., 1894.

Spangler, Edward W. *My Little War Experience, with Historical Sketches and Memorabilia.* New York: Daily Publishing, 1904.

Stevens, George T. *Three Years in the Sixth Corps: A Concise Narrative of Events in the Army of the Potomac, from 1861 to the Close of the Rebellion, April 1865.* Albany, N.Y.: S. R. Gray, 1866.

Stevens, Henry S. *Souvenir of Excursion to Battlefields of the Society of the Fourteenth Connecticut Regiment.* Washington: Gibson Bros., 1893.

Stewart, Robert Laird. *History of the One Hundred and Fortieth Regiment Pennsylvania Volunteers.* Philadelphia: Franklin Bindery, 1912.

Straight, Charles T. *Battery B, First R.I. Light Artillery, August 13, 1861–June 12, 1865.* Central Falls, R.I.: E. L. Freeman, 1907.

Stuckenberg, John H. W. *I'm Surrounded by Methodists: Diary of John H. W. Stuckenberg, Chaplain of the 145th*

Pennsylvania Volunteer Infantry. Ed. David T. Hedrick and Gordon Barry Davis, Jr. Gettysburg, Pa.: Thomas Publications, 1995.

Taylor, Walter H. General Lee: His Campaigns in Virginia, 1861–1865. New York: Press of Braunworth, 1906.

Thompson, Richard S. While My Country Is in Danger: The Life and Letters of Lieutenant Colonel Richard S. Thompson, Twelfth New Jersey Volunteers. Ed. Gerry H. Poriss and Ralph G. Poriss. Hamilton, N.Y.: Edmonston Publishing, 1994.

Tivy, Joseph A. Souvenir of the Seventh. Detroit: n.p., n.d.

Twenty-fifth Anniversary of the Muster into the Service of the United States of the Tenth Regiment of New York Volunteer Infantry (National Zouaves). New York: Charles H. Ludwig, 1886.

United States Bureau of the Census. Historical Statistics of the United States: Colonial Times to 1970. 2 vols. Washington, D.C.: Government Printing Office, 1975.

United States War Department. The War of the Rebellion: A Compilation of the Official Records of the Union and Confederate Armies. 128 vols. Washington, D.C.: Government Printing Office, 1880–1901.

Waitt, Ernest L. History of the Nineteenth Regiment Massachusetts Volunteer Infantry, 1861–1865. Salem, Mass.: Salem Press, 1906.

Walker, Francis A. History of the Second Army Corps in the Army of the Potomac. New York: Charles Scribner's Sons, 1887.

Ward, Joseph J. C. History of the One Hundred and Sixth Regiment Pennsylvania Volunteers, 2d Brigade, 2d Division, 2d Corps, 1861–1865. Philadelphia: Grant, Faires and Rodgers, 1883.

Washburn, George H. A Complete Military History and Record of the 108th Regiment N.Y. Vols., from 1862 to 1894. Rochester, N.Y.: E. R. Andrews, 1894.

Webb, Alexander S. An Address Delivered at Gettysburg, August 27, 1883. Philadelphia: Porter and Coates, 1883.

Welsh, Peter. Irish Green and Union Blue: The Civil War Letters of Peter Welsh. Ed. Lawrence Frederick Kohl and Margaret Cosse Richard. New York: Fordham University Press, 1986.

Weygant, Charles H. History of the One Hundred and Twenty-Fourth Regiment N.Y.S.V. Newburgh, N.Y.: Journal Print House, 1877.

Wilkeson, Frank. Recollections of a Private Soldier in the Army of the Potomac. New York: G. P. Putnam's Sons, 1898.

Wilson, James H. Under the Old Flag: Recollections of Military Operations in the War for the Union, the Spanish War and the Boxer Rebellion, etc. Vol. 1. Reprint, Greenwood Press, 1971.

Wistar, Isaac J. Autobiography of Isaac Jones Wistar, 1827–1905. Philadelphia: Wistar Institute of Anatomy and Biology, 1937.

Woodbury, Augustus. Major General Ambrose Burnside and the Ninth Army Corps: A Narrative of Campaigns in North Carolina, Maryland, Virginia, Ohio, Kentucky, Mississippi, and Tennessee, during the War for the Preservation of the Republic. Providence, R.I.: S. S. Rider and Brother, 1867.

Wright, James A. No More Gallant A Deed: A Civil War Memoir of the First Minnesota Volunteers. Ed. Steven J. Keillor. St. Paul: Minnesota Historical Society Press, 2001.

Articles

Adams, John G. B. "Sunshine and Shadows of Army Life." In Civil War Papers Read before the Commandery of the State of Massachusetts, Military Order of the Loyal Legion of the United States,

2:447–63. Reprint, Wilmington, N.C.: Broadfoot Publishing, 1993.

Adams, Silas. "The Nineteenth Maine at Gettysburg." In *War Papers Read before the Commandery of the State of Maine, Military Order of the Loyal Legion of the United States,* 4:250–63. Portland, Maine: Lefavor-Tower, 1915.

"Address of J. H. Stine." *National Tribune.* August 30, 1888.

Aldrich, S. H. "The Old Second Corps." *National Tribune.* November 15, 1885.

Bacon, Cyrus, Jr. "The Daily Register of Dr. Cyrus Bacon, Jr.: Care of the Wounded at the Battle of Gettysburg." Ed. Frank Whitehouse, Jr. *Michigan Academician* 8 (1976): 373–86.

Barlow, Francis C. "The Capture of the Salient, May 12, 1864." In *Papers of the Military Historical Society of Massachusetts,* 4:245–62. Boston: Military Historical Society of Massachusetts, 1905.

Bartlett, William Francis. "Debacle at Ball's Bluff." Ed. Jon M. Nielson. *Civil War Times Illustrated* 14 (January 1976): 24–36.

Black, John D. "Reminiscences of the Bloody Angle." In *Glimpses of the Nation's Struggle: Papers Read before the Commandery of the State of Minnesota, Military Order of the Loyal Legion of the United States, 1892–1897,* 4:420–36. St. Paul: H. L. Collins, 1898.

Bloomer, Samuel. "How the 1st Minn. Lost Its Colors." *National Tribune.* August 13, 1885.

———. Letter. *National Tribune.* April 9, 1885.

Brooke, John R. "Patriotism." In *Personal Recollections of the War of the Rebellion, Addresses Delivered before the Commandery of the State of New York, Military Order of the Loyal Legion of the United States,* 3:247–51. New York: G. P. Putnam's Sons, 1907.

Bowen, George A. "Boys, Your Work Is Done." Ed. Edward G. Longacre. *New Jersey History* 45 (Summer 1977): 101–109.

Brockway, Charles. "Across the Rapidan: Pushing into the Wilderness." *National Tribune.* March 4, 1882.

Cafferty, E. M. "The Crossing at Fredericksburg." *National Tribune.* May 17, 1888.

Cardwell, David. "The Battle of Five Forks." *Confederate Veteran* 22 (March 1914): 117–20.

Carlin, W. P. "'Before the War': What the Regular Army Found to Do 30 Years Ago." *National Tribune.* January 29, 1885.

Caukin, Gavin B. "From Cold Harbor to Petersburg with the Second Army Corps." In *Military Order of the Loyal Legion of the United States; Commandery of the State of Oregon,* 4:8–24. Portland, Ore.: Schwab Bros., 1896.

Charles, Emily Thornton. "Gen. Hancock: An Hour with Him in His Home." *National Tribune.* April 22, 1886.

Child, Benjamin H. "From Fredericksburg to Gettysburg." In *Personal Narratives of Events in the War of the Rebellion, Being Papers Read before the Rhode Island Soldiers and Sailors Historical Society,* 7:159–90. Providence: Rhode Island Soldiers and Sailors Historical Society, 1894–99.

Church, W. J. "The Crossing at Fredericksburg." *National Tribune.* April 12, 1888.

Coffin, Gorham. "Civil War Letters of Gorham Coffin." Ed. Herbert A. Wisbey, Jr. *Essex Institute Historical Collections* 93 (January 1957): 58–92.

Cone, David. "Civil War Letters of David Cone." *North Dakota Historical Quarterly* 8 (1941): 191–218.

Connor, Selden. "In the Wilderness." In *War Papers Read before the*

Commandery of the State of Maine, Military Order of the Loyal Legion of the United States, 4:200–229. Portland, Maine: Lefavor-Tower, 1915.

Cory, Eugene A. "A Private's Recollections of Fredericksburg." In *Personal Narratives of Events in the Rebellion, Being Papers Read before the Rhode Island Soldiers and Sailors Historical Society,* 4:117–42. Providence: Rhode Island Soldiers and Sailors Historical Society, 1883–85.

Couch, Darius N. "Sumner's 'Right Grand Division.'" In *B&L* 3:105–20.

Cox, Jacob D. "McClellan in West Virginia." In *B&L* 1:126–48.

Dauchy, George K. "The Battle of Ream's Station." In *Military Essays and Recollections: Papers Read before the Commandery of the State of Illinois, Military Order of the Loyal Legion of the United States,* 3:125–40. Chicago: Dial, 1899.

Deacon, William. "The Third Corps: Why Do Historians Seem to Agree in Ignoring It?" *National Tribune.* November 13, 1884.

De Peyster, J. Watts. "An Ideal Soldier: A Tribute to Maj. Gen. Daniel E. Sickles." *National Tribune.* July 26, 1888.

Devereaux, Arthur Forrester. "Some Account of Pickett's Charge at Gettysburg." *Magazine of American History* 17 (January 1887): 13–19.

Driver, William R. "The Capture of the Salient at Spotsylvania, May 12, 1864." In *Papers of the Military Historical Society of Massachusetts,* 4:275–85. Boston: Military Historical Society of Massachusetts, 1905.

DuBois, A. "Cold Harbor Salient." *Southern Historical Society Papers* 30 (1902): 276–79.

Du Bois, D. F. "Fredericksburg." *National Tribune.* May 24, 1888.

"Echoes from Gettysburg." *Confederate Veteran* 21 (September 1913): 429.

Failing, Myron. "Gen. Alex. Hays at Gettysburg." *National Tribune.* October 15, 1885.

Ferguson, Leonard. "The Civil War Diaries of Leonard C. Ferguson." Ed. William A. Hunter. *Pennsylvania History* 14 (1947): 196–224; 289–313.

"Fifth Corps at Gettysburg." *National Tribune.* October 18, 1888.

Franklin, William. "Rear-Guard Fighting during the Change of Base." In *B&L* 2:366–82.

Galwey, Thomas F. "At the Battle of Antietam with the Eighth Ohio Infantry." In *Personal Recollections of the War of the Rebellion, Addresses Delivered before the Commandery of the State of New York, Military Order of the Loyal Legion of the United States,* 3:70–85. New York: G. P. Putnam's Sons, 1907.

"Gen. W. S. Hancock: His Sudden Death on Governor's Island." *National Tribune.* February 18, 1886.

"Gettysburg after Twenty Years: Visit of the First Corps to the Battlefield." *National Tribune.* May 14, 1885.

Gorham, Coffin. "Civil War Letters of Gorham Coffin." Ed. Herbert A. Wisbey, Jr. *Essex Institute Historical Collections* 93 (January 1957): 58–92.

"Grand Army Matters: The Pennsylvania Veterans' Grand Reunions at Gettysburg." *National Tribune.* July 29, 1882.

Grant, Lewis A. "Review of Major-General Barlow's Paper on the Capture of the Salient at Spotsylvania, May 12, 1864." In *Papers of the Military Historical Society of Massachusetts,* 4:265–71. Boston: Military Historical Society of Massachusetts, 1905.

Green, William H. "From the Wilderness to Spotsylvania." In *War Papers Read before the Commandery of the State of Maine, Military Order of the Loyal Legion of the United States,* 2:91–104. Portland: Lefavor-Tower, 1902.

Hale, Charles A. "With Colonel Cross at the Wheatfield." *Civil War Times Illustrated* 13 (August 1974): 30–38.

Hallock, W. I. Letter. *American Tribune.* August 24, 1893.

Hamilton, Edward John. "A Union Chaplain's Diary." Ed. Chase C. Mooney. *Proceedings of the New Jersey Historical Society* 75 (January 1957): 1–17.

"Hancock Attacked at Ream's Station." *New York Times.* August 28, 1864.

"Hancock's Heroism at Gettysburg." *National Tribune.* November 8, 1886.

Hegeman, George. "The Diary of a Union Soldier in Confederate Prison." Ed. James J. Heslin. *New York Historical Society Quarterly* 41 (July 1957): 233–78.

Hodgman, Samuel. "Samuel Hodgman's Civil War." Ed. Roger L. Rosentreter. *Michigan History* 64 (November/ December 1980): 31–38.

Houghton, William. "In the Valley: The Fighting Done by Shield's Division." *National Tribune.* May 30, 1889.

"How We Failed to Take Petersburgh." *New York Times.* June 23, 1864.

Howard, Oliver O. "The Eleventh Corps at Chancellorsville." In *B&L* 3:189–202.

Hunt, Henry. "The First Day at Gettysburg." In *B&L* 3:255–84.

Jackson, Edward C. "The Bloody Angle." In *Civil War Sketches and Incidents, Papers Read By Companions of the State of Nebraska, Military Order of the Loyal Legion of the United States,* 1:258–62. Omaha: Commandery of the State of Nebraska, 1902.

Jeffries, Lemuel. "'The Excitement Had Begun!': The Civil War Diary of Lemuel Jeffries, 1862–1863." Ed. Jason H. Silverman. *Manuscripts* 30 (Fall 1978): 265–78.

"The Jersey Brigade." *National Tribune.* December 31, 1885.

Jones, F. C. "How the 145th Pa. Got Captured." *National Tribune.* October 8, 1885.

Jones, John S. "From North Anna to Cold Harbor." In *Sketches of War History 1861–1865: Papers Read before the Ohio Commandery of the Military Order of the Loyal Legion of the United States,* 4:147–58. Cincinnati, Ohio: R. Clark, 1888.

Lochren, William. "The First Minnesota at Gettysburg." In *Glimpses of the Nation's Struggle: Papers Read before the Minnesota Commandery of the Military Order of the Loyal Legion of the United States, 1889–1892,* 3:42–56. St. Paul: D. D. Merrill, 1893.

Lockley, Fred. "Letters of Fred Lockley, Union Soldier, 1864–65." Ed. John E. Pomfret. *Huntington Library Quarterly* 16 (1952/53): 75–112.

Longstreet, James. "The Battle of Fredericksburg." In *B&L* 3:70–85.

"Maj. L. J. Sacriste: He Is Given a Medal of Honor for Gallantry." *National Tribune.* April 25, 1889.

Merrick, C. H. "Regiments Which Lost Most Men." *National Tribune.* January 7, 1886.

Miles, Nelson A. "An Address Delivered at the Stated Meeting of May 1, 1918." In *War Papers Being Papers Read before the Commandery of the District of Columbia, Military Order of the Loyal Legion of the United States,* 4:501–505. Reprint, Wilmington, N.C.: Broadfoot Publishing, 1993.

Miller, James. "Serving under McClellan on the Peninsula in '62." *Civil War Times Illustrated* 8 (June 1969): 24–30.

Miner, Joseph. "Spotsylvania: The Way in Which the Rebels Were Surprised." *National Tribune.* March 18, 1886.

Mulholland, St. Clair A. "At Fredericksburg, December 13, 1862." *National Tribune.* October 8, 1881.

Neill, Edward D. "Incidents of the Battles of Fair Oaks and Malvern Hill." In *Glimpses of the Nation's Struggle: A Series of Papers Read before the*

Minnesota Commandery of the Military Order of the Loyal Legion of the United States, 1887–1889, 3:454–79. St. Paul, Minn.: St. Paul Book and Stationary, 1893.

Newcomb, David. Letter. *National Tribune*. March 5, 1885.

"Old Battlefields: Visits of the Sixth Corps Boys to Their Virginia Camps." *National Tribune*. May 21, 1885.

"Pennsylvania Monument in Virginia." *Confederate Veteran* 17 (March 1909): 115.

Pierce, Francis E. "I have with the reg't been through a terrible battle." *Civil War Times Illustrated* 1 (December 1962): 6–9, 28–32.

———. "Civil War Letters of Francis Edwin Pierce of the 108th New York Volunteer Infantry." Ed. Blake McKelvey. *Rochester Historical Society Publications* 22 (1944): 150–73.

Poindexter, James. "General Armistead's Portrait Represented." *Southern Historical Society Papers* 40 (January 1909): 144–51.

Reid, John. Letter. *National Tribune*. January 22, 1885.

Robertson, Robert Stoddart. "From Spotsylvania Onward." In *War Papers Read before the Indiana Commandery Military Order of the Loyal Legion of the United States*, 344–58. Reprint, Wilmington, N.C.: Broadfoot Publishing, 1993.

———. "From the Wilderness to Spotsylvania." In *Sketches of War History, 1861–1865: Papers Read before the Ohio Commandery of the Military Order of the Loyal Legion of the United States*, 1:252–92. Cincinnati: Robert Clarke, 1894.

Rogers, George T. "Retaking Railroad at Reams Station." *Confederate Veteran* 5 (November 1897): 580–81.

Ropes, E. H. "A Reminiscence of Gettysburg—Gen. Webb's Brigade." *National Tribune*. March 1879.

"Saving the Nation: Pickett's Great Charge." *National Tribune*. May 21, 1885.

Scott, Winfield. "Pickett's Charge as Seen from the Front Line." In *Civil War Papers of the California Commandery of the Military Order of the Loyal Legion of the United States*, 6:1–15. Reprint, Wilmington, N.C.: Broadfoot Publishing, 1995.

Searles, J. N. "The First Minnesota Volunteer Infantry." In *Glimpses of the Nation's Struggle: A Series of Papers Read before the Minnesota Commandery of the Military Order of the Loyal Legion of the United States, 1887–1899*, 2:80–113. Ed. Edward D. Neill. St. Paul, Minn.: St. Paul Book and Stationary, 1890.

Slater, J. S. "At Gaines's Mill: Episodes and Incidents of the Battle." *National Tribune*. September 17, 1881.

———. "Malvern: The End of the Seven Days." *National Tribune*. September 10, 1881.

Smith, E. W. "The 5th N.H." *National Tribune*. February 18, 1886.

Smith, William F. "The Movement Against Petersburg, June 1864." In *Papers of the Military Historical Society of Massachusetts*, 5:75–115. Boston: Military Historical Society of Massachusetts, 1905.

Spaulding, Joseph W. "Nineteenth Maine at High Bridge." In *War Papers Read before the Commandery of the State of Maine, Military Order of the Loyal Legion of the United States*, 4:294–306. Portland, Maine: Lefavor-Tower, 1915.

Spencer, William. "How I Felt in Battle and Prison." In *War Papers Read before the Commandery of the State of Maine, Military Order of the Loyal Legion of the United States*, 2:122–49. Portland, Maine: Lefavor-Tower, 1902.

Stedman, Charles M. "The Battle of Ream's Station." *Southern Historical Society Papers* 19 (January 1891): 116.

Steward, A. D. "Gettysburg: A Defense of Meade, Howard, and the Eleventh Corps." *National Tribune.* August 30, 1888.

Stowe, Jonathan P. "Life with the 15th Mass." *Civil War Times Illustrated* 11 (August 1972): 4–11, 48–54.

Stribling, R. M. "Gen. James Dearing." *Confederate Veteran* 9 (May 1901): 550.

Sumner, Samuel. "The Antietam Campaign." In *Papers of the Military Historical Society of Massachusetts*, 14: 7–18. Boston: Military Historical Society of Massachusetts, 1918.

Thompson, Richard S. "A Scrap of Gettysburg." In *Military Essays and Recollections: Papers Read before the Commandery of the State of Illinois, Military Order of the Loyal Legion of the United States*, 3:97–109. Chicago: Dial, 1899.

Taylor, Isaac L. "Campaigning with the First Minnesota: A Civil War Diary." Ed. Hazel C. Wolf. *Minnesota History* 25 (March, June, September, December 1944): 11–39, 117–52, 224–57, 342–61.

Teall, William W. ". . . Ringside Seat at Fredericksburg." *Civil War Times Illustrated* 4 (May 1965): 17–34.

Troutman, Charles. "Second Corps: All the Wearers of the Clover Leaf Wanted to Join the Club." *National Tribune.* July 9, 1885.

"25 Years After: Friend and Foe Tenting on the Old Camp Ground." *National Tribune.* July 12, 1888.

Unidentified Soldier, Carroll's Brigade. "Reminiscences of Spotsylvania." *National Tribune.* April 15, 1882.

Van Ness, W. W. "Gen. Sumner: How Col. Van Ness Meets the Famous Corps Commander." *National Tribune.* April 25, 1889.

Walker, Francis A. "The Expedition to the Boydton Plank Road, October, 1864." In *Papers of the Military Historical Society of Massachusetts*, 5:321–50.

Boston: Military Historical Society of Massachusetts, 1906.

———. "General Gibbon in the Second Corps." In *Personal Recollections of the War of the Rebellion: Addresses Delivered before the Commandery of the State of New York, Military Order of the Loyal Legion of the United States*, 2:290–315. New York: G. P. Putnam's Sons, 1907.

———. "General Hancock." In *Critical Sketches of Some of the Federal and Confederate Commanders*, 51–67. Ed. Theodore F. Dwight. Boston: Houghton, Mifflin, 1895.

———. "Hancock in the War of the Rebellion." In *Personal Recollections of the War of the Rebellion: Addresses Delivered before the New York Commandery of the Loyal Legion of the United States, 1883–1891*, 349–64. Ed. James Grant Wilson and Titus Munson Coan. New York: New York Commandery, 1891.

———. "Ream's Station." In *Papers of the Military Historical Society of Massachusetts*, 5:269–305. Boston: Military Historical Society of Massachusetts, 1906.

Webb, Alexander. "Through the Wilderness." In *B&L* 4:160.

Weymouth, H. G. O. "The Crossing of the Rappahannock by the 19th Massachusetts." In *B&L* 3:121.

Wilson, James H. "General Humphreys." In *Critical Sketches of Some of the Federal and Confederate Commanders*, 71–96. Ed. Theodore F. Dwight. Boston: Houghton, Mifflin, 1895.

Websites

William Landon Letters to *Vincennes (Indiana) Sun*. Transcribed at: http://www.members.evansville .net/~tlconner/ (December 17, 2009). Last viewed on February 26, 2010.

SECONDARY SOURCES

Amchan, Arthur J. *The Most Famous Soldier in America: A Biography of Lt. Gen. Nelson A. Miles, 1839–1925.* Alexandria, Va.: Amchan Publications, 1989.

Anbinder, Tyler. *Nativism and Slavery: The Northern Know Nothings and the Politics of the 1850s.* New York: Oxford University Press, 1992.

Arner, Frederick B. *The Mutiny at Brandy Station, The Last Battle of the Hooker Brigade: A Controversial Army Reorganization, Courts Martial, and the Bloody Days That Followed.* Kensington, Md.: Bates and Blood Press, 1993.

Athearn, Robert G. *Thomas Francis Meagher: An Irish Revolutionary in America.* Boulder: University of Colorado Press, 1949.

Ballard, Ted. *Battle of Ball's Bluff.* Washington, D.C.: Center of Military History, 2001.

Baltz, Louis J., III. *The Battle of Cold Harbor, May 27–June 13, 1864.* 2nd ed. Lynchburg, Va.: H. A. Howard, 1994.

Barton, Michael. *Goodmen: The Character of Civil War Soldiers.* University Park: Pennsylvania State University Press, 1981.

Bates, Samuel P. *History of Pennsylvania Volunteers, 1861–5.* Reprint, Wilmington, N.C.: Broadfoot Publishing, 1993.

Beatie, Russel H. *The Army of the Potomac: Birth of Command, November 1860–September 1861.* New York: Da Capo Press, 2002.

Benton, Josiah H. *Voting in the Field: A Forgotten Chapter of the Civil War.* Boston: privately printed, 1915.

Bernstein, Iver. *The New York City Draft Riots: Their Significance for American Society and Politics in the Age of the Civil War.* New York: Oxford University Press, 1990.

Bigelow, John, Jr. *The Campaign of Chancellorsville: A Strategic and Tactical Study.* New Haven, Conn.: Yale University Press, 1910.

Blair, William A. "Barbarians at Fredericksburg's Gate: The Impact of the Union Army on Civilians." In *The Fredericksburg Campaign: Decision on the Rappahannock,* ed. Gary W. Gallagher, 142–70. Chapel Hill: University of North Carolina Press, 1995.

———. *Cities of the Dead: Contesting the Memory of the Civil War in the South, 1865–1914.* Chapel Hill: University of North Carolina Press, 2004.

Blight, David. *Beyond the Battlefield: Race, Memory, and the American Civil War.* Amherst: University of Massachusetts Press, 2002.

———. *Race and Reunion: The Civil War in American Memory.* Cambridge, Mass.: Harvard University Press, 2001.

Brice, Marshall M. *Conquest of a Valley.* Charlottesville: University Press of Virginia, 1965.

Brooks, Victor. *The Fredericksburg Campaign: October 1862–January 1863.* Conshohocken, Pa.: Combined Publishing, 2000.

Brown, Kent Masterson. *Retreat from Gettysburg: Lee, Logistics and the Pennsylvania Campaign.* Chapel Hill: University of North Carolina Press, 2005.

Bruce, Susannah Ural. *The Harp and the Eagle: Irish-American Volunteers and the Union Army, 1861–1865.* New York: New York University Press, 2006.

Burr, Frank A. *Life and Achievements of James Addams Beaver: Early Life, Military Services and Public Career.* Philadelphia: Ferguson Bros., 1882.

Burrows, Edwin G., and Mike Wallace. *Gotham: A History of New York City to 1898.* New York: Oxford University Press, 1999.

Burton, Brian K. *Extraordinary Circumstances: The Seven Days Battles.* Bloomington: Indiana University Press, 2001.

Burton, William L. *Melting Pot Soldiers: The Union's Ethnic Regiments.* New York: Fordham University Press, 1998.

Busey, John W., and David G. Martin. *Regimental Strengths at Gettysburg.* Baltimore: Gateway Press, 1982.

Calkins, Chris. *The Appomattox Campaign: March 29–April 9, 1865.* Conshohocken, Pa.: Combined Books, 1997.

Campbell, Eric. "Caldwell Clears the Wheatfield." *Gettysburg Magazine* 7 (1990): 47–77.

———. "'Remember Harper's Ferry': The Degradation, Humiliation, and Redemption of Col. George L. Willard's Brigade." *Gettysburg Magazine* 7 (1992): 64–73.

Cannan, John. *Bloody Angle: Hancock's Assault on the Mule Shoe Salient, May 12, 1864.* Cambridge, Mass.: Da Capo Press, 2002.

Carpenter, John A. *Sword and Olive Branch: Oliver Otis Howard.* New York: Fordham University Press, 1999.

Castel, Albert E. *Decision in the West: The Atlanta Campaign of 1864.* Lawrence: University Press of Kansas, 1992.

Catton, Bruce. *Glory Road.* Garden City, N.Y.: Doubleday, 1952.

———. *Grant Takes Command.* Boston: Little, Brown, 1969.

———. *Mr. Lincoln's Army.* Garden City, N.Y.: Doubleday, 1951.

———. *A Stillness at Appomattox.* Garden City, N.Y.: Doubleday, 1953.

Chalfant, William Y. *Cheyennes and Horse Soldiers: The 1857 Expedition and the Battle of Solomon's Fork.* Norman: University of Oklahoma Press, 1989.

Christ, Elwood W. *The Struggle for the Bliss Farm at Gettysburg, July 2nd and 3rd, 1863.* Baltimore: Butternut and Blue, 1993.

Cimprich, John. *Fort Pillow: A Civil War Massacre and Public Memory.* Baton

Rouge: Louisiana State University, 2005.

Clark, Charles B. "Baltimore and the Attack on the Sixth Massachusetts Regiment, April 19, 1861." *Maryland Historical Magazine* 56 (March 1961): 39–71.

Cleaves, Freeman. *Meade of Gettysburg.* Norman: University of Oklahoma Press, 1960.

Coddington, Edwin B. *The Gettysburg Campaign: A Study in Command.* New York: Charles Scribner's Sons, 1968.

Coffey, David. *John Bell Hood and the Struggle for Atlanta.* Abilene, Tex.: McWhiney Foundation Press, 1998.

Coffin, Howard. *Nine Months to Gettysburg: Stannard's Vermonters and the Repulse of Pickett's Charge.* Woodstock, Vt.: Countryman Press, 1997.

Cooling, Benjamin F. *Forts Henry and Donelson: The Key to the Confederate Heartland.* Knoxville: University of Tennessee Press, 1987.

Cowley, Robert, ed. *With My Face to the Enemy: Perspectives on the Civil War.* New York: G. P. Putnam's Sons, 2001.

Cullen, Joseph P. *The Battles of Fredericksburg, Chancellorsville, the Wilderness, and Spotsylvania Court House, Where a Hundred Thousand Fell.* Washington, D.C.: U.S. Department of the Interior, National Park Service, 1966.

Daniel, Larry. *Days of Glory: The Army of the Cumberland, 1861–1865.* Baton Rouge: Louisiana State University Press, 2004.

Davis, Oliver W. *Life of David Bell Birney, Major-General United States Volunteers.* Philadelphia: King and Baird, 1867.

Davis, Stephen. *Atlanta Will Fall: Sherman, Joe Johnston, and the Yankee Heavy Battalions.* Wilmington, Del.: Scholarly Resources, 2001.

Davis, William C. *Battle at Bull Run: A History of the First Major Campaign of the Civil War.* Garden City, N.Y.: Doubleday, 1977.

Dean, Eric T. *Shook over Hell: Post-Traumatic Stress, Vietnam, and the Civil War.* Cambridge, Mass.: Harvard University Press, 1997.

Dearing, Mary R. *Veterans in Politics: The Story of the GAR.* Baton Rouge: Louisiana State University Press, 1952.

DeMontravel, Peter R. *A Hero to His Fighting Men: Nelson A. Miles, 1839–1925.* Kent, Ohio: Kent State University Press, 1998.

Denison, Charles W. *Hancock "The Superb": The Early Life and Public Career of Winfield S. Hancock, Major-General U.S.A.* Philadelphia: H. W. Kelley, 1880.

———. *Winfield: The Lawyer's Son, and How He Became a Major General.* Philadelphia: Ashmead and Evans, 1865.

Dodge, Theodore A. *The Campaign of Chancellorsville.* Boston: J. R. Osgood, 1881.

Donald, David Herbert. *Lincoln.* New York: Simon and Schuster, 1995.

Doubleday, Abner. *Chancellorsville and Gettysburg.* Reprint, New York: Da Capo Press, 1994.

Dreese, Michael A. *The 151st Pennsylvania Volunteers at Gettysburg: Like Ripe Apples in a Storm.* Jefferson, N.C.: McFarland, 2000.

Dubbs, Carol Kettenburg. *Defend This Old Town: Williamsburg during the Civil War.* Baton Rouge: Louisiana State University Press, 2002.

Dusinberre, William. *Civil War Issues in Philadelphia, 1856–65.* Philadelphia: University of Pennsylvania Press, 1965.

Dyer, Frederick H. *A Compendium of the War of the Rebellion: From Official Records of the Union and Confederate Armies, Reports of the Adjutant Generals of the Several States, the Army Registers, and Other Reliable Documents and Sources.* 3 vols. Des Moines, Iowa: Dyer Publishing, 1908.

Ecelbarger, Gary L. *"We Are In for It!" The First Battle of Kernstown, March 23, 1862.* Shippensburg, Pa.: White Mane Books, 1997.

Engle, Stephen D. *Yankee Dutchman: The Life of Franz Sigel.* Fayetteville: University of Arkansas Press, 1993.

Epstein, Robert M. *Napoleon's Last Victory and the Emergence of Modern War.* Lawrence: University Press of Kansas, 1994.

———. "The Creation and Evolution of the Army Corps in the American Civil War." *Journal of Military History* 55 (January 1991): 21–46.

———. "Patterns of Change and Continuity in Nineteenth-Century Warfare." *Journal of Military History* 56, no. 3 (July 1992): 375–88.

Fahs, Alice, and Joan Waugh, eds. *The Memory of the Civil War in American Culture.* Chapel Hill: University of North Carolina Press, 2004.

Fiftieth Anniversary of the Battle of Gettysburg, Report of the Pennsylvania Commission, December 13, 1913. Revised edition, April 1915. Harrisburg, Pa.: William Stanley Ray, 1915.

Fishel, Edwin C. *The Secret War for the Union: The Untold Story of Military Intelligence in the Civil War.* Boston: Houghton Mifflin, 1996.

Foner, Eric. *Free Soil, Free Labor, Free Men: The Ideology of the Republican Party before the Civil War.* New York: Oxford University Press, 1970.

Foote, Shelby. *The Civil War: A Narrative.* 3 vols. New York: Random House, 1958–74.

Forney, John W. *Life and Military Career of Winfield Scott Hancock.* Philadelphia: Hubbard Bros., 1880.

Foster, Gaines M. *Ghosts of the Confederacy: Defeat, the Lost Cause, and the*

Emergence of a New South. New York: Oxford University Press, 1987.

———. "Veterans' Organizations and Memories of the War." In *The American Civil War: A Handbook of Literature and Research*, ed. Steven E. Woodworth, 586–602. Westport, Conn.: Greenwood Press, 1996.

Fox, William F. *Regimental Losses in the American Civil War, 1861–1865*. Albany, N.Y.: Albany Publishing, 1889.

Frank, Joseph Allan, and George A. Reaves. *"Seeing the Elephant": Raw Recruits at the Battle of Shiloh*. Westport, Conn.: Greenwood Press, 1989.

Furgurson, Ernest B. *Chancellorsville 1863: The Souls of the Brave*. New York: Knopf, 1992.

———. *Not War but Murder: Cold Harbor, 1864*. New York: Knopf, 2000.

Gaff, Alan D. *On Many a Bloody Field: Four Years in the Iron Brigade*. Bloomington: Indiana University Press, 1996.

Gallagher, Gary W., ed. *Antietam: Essays on the 1862 Maryland Campaign*. Kent, Ohio: Kent State University Press, 1989.

———. *The Antietam Campaign*. Chapel Hill: University of North Carolina Press, 1999.

———. *Chancellorsville: The Battle and Its Aftermath*. Chapel Hill: University of North Carolina Press, 1996.

———. *The Fredericksburg Campaign: Decision on the Rappahannock*. Chapel Hill: University of North Carolina Press, 1995.

———. *The Richmond Campaign of 1862: The Peninsula and the Seven Days*. Chapel Hill: University of North Carolina Press, 2000.

———. *The Second Day at Gettysburg: Essays on Confederate and Union Leadership*. Kent, Ohio: Kent State University Press, 1993.

———. *The Spotsylvania Campaign*. Chapel Hill: University of North Carolina Press, 1998.

———. *Struggle for the Shenandoah: Essays on the 1864 Valley Campaign*. Kent, Ohio: Kent State University Press, 1991.

———. *The Third Day at Gettysburg and Beyond*. Chapel Hill: University of North Carolina Press, 1994.

———. *Three Days at Gettysburg: Essays on Confederate and Union Leadership*. Kent, Ohio: Kent State University Press, 1999.

———. *The Wilderness Campaign*. Chapel Hill: University of North Carolina Press, 1997.

Gallman, J. Matthew. *Mastering Wartime: A Social History of Philadelphia during the Civil War*. New York: Cambridge University Press, 1990.

Geary, James W. *We Need Men: The Union Draft in the Civil War*. Dekalb: Northern Illinois University Press, 1991.

Gibbs, Joseph. *Three Years in the Bloody Eleventh: The Campaigns of a Pennsylvania Reserve Regiment*. University Park: Pennsylvania State University Press, 2002.

Gienapp, William E. *The Origins of the Republican Party, 1852–56*. New York: Oxford University Press, 1987.

Glatthaar, Joseph T. *Forged in Battle: The Civil War Alliance of Black Soldiers and White Officers*. New York: Free Press, 1990.

———. *The March to the Sea and Beyond: Sherman's Troops in the Savannah and Carolinas Campaigns*. Baton Rouge: Louisiana State University Press, 1985.

Goodrich, Frederick E. *The Life of Winfield Scott Hancock, Major General, U.S.A.* Boston: B. B. Russell, 1886.

Goss, Thomas J. *The War within the Union High Command: Politics and*

Generalship during the Civil War. Lawrence: University Press of Kansas, 2003.

Gottfried, Bradley M. *Stopping Pickett: The History of the Philadelphia Brigade.* Shippensburg, Pa.: White Mane Books, 1999.

Green, A. Wilson. "From Gettysburg to Falling Waters: Meade's Pursuit of Lee." In *The Third Day at Gettysburg and Beyond,* ed. Gary W. Gallagher, 161–201. Chapel Hill: University of North Carolina Press, 1994.

Griffith, Paddy. *Rally Once Again: Battle Tactics of the Civil War.* New Haven, Conn.: Yale University Press, 1989.

Grimsley, Mark. *The Hard Hand of War: Union Military Policy toward Southern Civilians, 1861–1865.* Cambridge: Cambridge University Press, 1995.

———. *And Keep Moving On: The Virginia Campaign, May–June 1864.* Lincoln: University of Nebraska Press, 2002.

Hagerman, Edward. *The American Civil War and the Origins of Modern Warfare: Ideas, Organization, and Field Command.* Bloomington: Indiana University Press, 1988.

Hagerty, Edward J. *Collis' Zouaves: The 114th Pennsylvania Volunteers in the Civil War.* Baton Rouge: Louisiana State University Press, 1997.

Hartwig, D. Scott. "It Struck Horror to Us All." *Gettysburg Magazine* 4 (1991): 89–100.

———. "'No Troops on the Field Had Done Better': John C. Caldwell's Division in the Wheatfield, July 2, 1863." In *The Second Day at Gettysburg: Essays on Confederate and Union Leadership,* ed. Gary W. Gallagher, 203–30. Kent, Ohio: Kent State University Press, 1993.

———. "Who Would Not Be a Soldier: The Volunteers of '62 in the Maryland Campaign." In *The Antietam Campaign,* ed. Gary W. Gallagher, 143–68. Chapel

Hill: University of North Carolina Press, 1999.

Hassler, Warren W., Jr. *General George B. McClellan: Shield of the Union.* Baton Rouge: Louisiana State University Press, 1957.

Hattaway, Herman M. "The Civil War Armies: Creation, Mobilization, and Development." In *On the Road to Total War: The American Civil War and The German Wars of Unification, 1861–1871,* ed. Stig Foster and Jorg Nagler, 173–98. New York: Cambridge University Press, 1997.

Hattaway, Herman M., and Archer Jones. *How the North Won: A Military History of the Civil War.* Urbana: University of Illinois Press, 1983.

Heatwole, John L. *The Burning: Sheridan in the Shenandoah Valley.* Charlottesville, Va.: Rockbridge Publishing, 1998.

Hebert, Walter H. *Fighting Joe Hooker.* Indianapolis: Bobbs-Merrill, 1944.

Henderson, G. F. R. *The Campaign of Fredericksburg, Nov.–Dec. 1862.* London: K. Paul, Trench, 1886.

Henderson, William D. *The Road to Bristoe Station: Campaigning with Lee and Meade, August 1–October 20, 1863.* Lynchburg, Va.: H. E. Howard, 1987.

Hendrickson, Robert. *The Road to Appomattox.* New York: J. Wiley, 1998.

Hennessy, John. *The First Battle of Manassas: An End to Innocence July 18–21, 1861.* Lynchburg, Va.: H. E. Howard, 1989.

———. *Return to Bull Run: The Campaign and Battle of Second Manassas.* New York: Simon and Schuster, 1993.

———. "'We Shall Make Richmond Howl': The Army of the Potomac on the Eve of Chancellorsville." In *Chancellorsville: The Battle and Its Aftermath,* ed. Gary W. Gallagher, 1–35. Chapel Hill: University of North Carolina Press, 1996.

Herbert, Walter H. *Fighting Joe Hooker.* Indianapolis: Bobbs-Merrill, 1944.

Herdegen, Lance J. *The Men Stood Like Iron: How the Iron Brigade Won Its Name*. Bloomington: Indiana University Press, 1997.

Hess, Earl J. *Pickett's Charge: The Last Attack at Gettysburg*. Chapel Hill: University of North Carolina Press, 2001.

———. *The Union Soldier in Battle: Enduring the Ordeal of Combat*. Lawrence: University Press of Kansas, 1997.

Heth, Henry. *The Memoirs of Henry Heth*. Ed. James L. Morrison. Westport, Conn.: Greenwood Press, 1974.

Horn, John. *The Petersburg Campaign, June 1864–April 1865*. Conshohocken, Pa.: Combined Books, 1993.

Howe, Thomas J. *Wasted Valor: The Petersburg Campaign, June 15–18, 1864*. Lynchburg, Va.: H. E. Howard, 1988.

Humphreys, Andrew A. *The Virginia Campaign of 1864 and 1865: The Army of the Potomac and the Army of the James*. New York: Charles Scribner's Sons, 1903.

Humphreys, Henry H. *Andrew Atkinson Humphreys: A Biography*. Philadelphia: John C. Winston, 1924.

Huston, James L. *The Panic of 1857 and the Coming of the Civil War*. Baton Rouge: Louisiana State University Press, 1987.

Ignatiev, Noel. *How the Irish Became White*. New York: Routledge, 1995.

Jago, Frederick. *12th New Jersey Volunteers, 1862–1865*. Pennsawken, N.J.: Gloucester County Historical Society, 1967.

Jamieson, Perry D. *Death in September: The Antietam Campaign*. Fort Worth, Tex.: Ryan Place Publishers, 1995.

———. *Winfield Scott Hancock: Gettysburg Hero*. Abilene, Tex.: McWhiney Foundation Press, McMurray University, 2003.

Jones, Wilbur D., Jr. *Giants in the Cornfield: The 27th Indiana Infantry*. Shippensburg, Pa.: White Mane, 1997.

Jordan, David M. *"Happiness Is Not My Companion": The Life of General G. K. Warren*. Bloomington: Indiana University Press, 2001.

———. *Winfield Scott Hancock: A Soldier's Life*. Bloomington: Indiana University Press, 1988.

Kammen, Michael. *Mystic Cores of Memory: The Transformation of Tradition in American Culture*. New York: Knopf, 1993.

Keating, Robert. *Carnival of Blood: The Civil War Ordeal of the Seventh New York Heavy Artillery*. Baltimore: Butternut and Blue, 1998.

Keller, Christian B. *Chancellorsville and the Germans: Nativism, Ethnicity, and Civil War Memory*. New York: Fordham University Press, 2007.

Keneally, Thomas. *American Scoundrel: The Life of the Notorious Civil War General Dan Sickles*. New York: Doubleday, 2002.

Kenny, Kevin. *The American Irish: A History*. New York: Longman, 2000.

Kreidberg, Marvin A., and Merton G. Henry. *History of Military Mobilization in the United States Army, 1775–1945*. Reprint, Westport, Conn.: Greenwood Press, 1975.

Krick, Robert K. "The Army of Northern Virginia in September 1862: Its Circumstances, Its Operations, and Why It Should Not Have Been at Sharpsburg." In *Antietam: Essays on the 1862 Maryland Campaign*, ed. Gary W. Gallagher, 35–55. Kent, Ohio: Kent State University Press, 1989.

Lash, Gary G. *"Duty Well Done": The History of Edward Baker's California Regiment (71st Pennsylvania Infantry)*. Baltimore: Butternut and Blue, 2001.

Lepa, Jack H. *The Shenandoah Valley Campaign of 1864*. Jefferson, N.C.: McFarland, 2003.

Levin, Kevin M. "'Is Not the Glory Enough to Give Us All a Share?': An Analysis of Competing Memories of the Battle of the Crater." In *The View from the Ground: Experiences of Civil War Soldiers,* ed. Aaron Sheehan-Dean, 227–48. Lexington: University Press of Kentucky, 2007.

Levine, Bruce. *Half Slave and Half Free: The Roots of the Civil War.* New York: Hill and Wang, 1992.

Linderman, Gerald. *Embattled Courage: The Experience of Combat in the American Civil War.* New York: Free Press, 1987.

Logue, Larry M. *To Appomattox and Beyond: The Civil War Soldier in War and Peace.* Chicago: Ivan Dee, 1996.

Lonn, Ella. *Foreigners in the Union Army and Navy.* Baton Rouge: Louisiana State University Press, 1951.

Lord, Francis A. *They Fought for the Union.* Harrisburg, Pa.: Stackpole, 1960.

Luvaas, Jay, and Harold W. Nelson, eds. *The U.S. Army War College Guide to the Battle of Antietam: The Maryland Campaign of 1862.* Carlisle, Pa.: South Mountain Press, 1987.

———. *The U.S. Army War College Guide to the Battles of Chancellorsville and Fredericksburg.* Carlisle, Pa.: South Mountain Press, 1987.

Macneal, Douglas. *"The Centre County Regiment": Story of the 148th Regiment Pennsylvania Volunteers.* State College, Pa.: Centre County Historical Society, 2000.

Maney, R. Wayne. *Marching to Cold Harbor: Victory and Failure, 1864.* Shippensburg, Pa.: White Mane Publishing, 1995.

Manning, Chandra. *What This Cruel War Was Over: Soldiers, Slavery, and the Civil War.* New York: Alfred A. Knopf, 2007.

Marvel, William. *Burnside.* Chapel Hill: University of North Carolina Press, 1991.

———. *Lee's Last Retreat: The Flight to Appomattox.* Chapel Hill: University of North Carolina Press, 2002.

———. "The Making of a Myth: Ambrose E. Burnside and the Union High Command at Fredericksburg." In *The Fredericksburg Campaign: Decision on the Rappahannock,* ed. Gary W. Gallagher, 1–25. Chapel Hill: University of North Carolina Press, 1995.

———. *Mr. Lincoln Goes to War.* New York: Houghton Mifflin, 2006.

Matter, William D. "The Federal High Command at Spotsylvania." In *The Spotsylvania Campaign,* ed. Gary W. Gallagher, 29–60. Chapel Hill: University of North Carolina Press, 1998.

———. *If It Takes All Summer: The Battle of Spotsylvania.* Chapel Hill: University of North Carolina Press, 1988.

McConnell, Stuart. *Glorious Contentment: The Grand Army of the Republic, 1865–1900.* Chapel Hill: University of North Carolina Press, 1992.

McDonough, James L. *War So Terrible: Sherman and Atlanta.* New York: Norton, 1987.

McFeely, William S. *Grant: A Biography.* New York: Norton, 1991.

———. *Yankee Stepfather: General O. O. Howard and the Freedmen.* New York: W. W. Norton, 1994.

McMurry, Richard M. *Atlanta 1864: Last Chance for the Confederacy.* Lincoln: University of Nebraska Press, 2000.

McPherson, James M. *Battle Cry of Freedom: The Civil War Era.* New York: Oxford University Press, 1988.

———. *Crossroads of Freedom: Antietam.* New York: Oxford University Press, 2002.

———. *For Cause and Comrades: Why Men Fought in the Civil War.* New York: Oxford University Press, 1997.

———. *What They Fought For.* Baton Rouge: Louisiana State University Press, 1994.

McPherson, James M., and William J. Cooper, Jr., eds. *Writing the Civil*

War: The Quest to Understand. Columbia: University of South Carolina Press, 1998.

McWhiney, Grady, and Perry D. Jamieson. *Attack and Die: Civil War Military Tactics and the Southern Heritage.* Tuscaloosa: University of Alabama Press, 1982.

McWhiney, Grady. *Battle in the Wilderness: Grant Meets Lee.* Fort Worth, Tex.: Ryan Place Publishers, 1995.

Meinhard, Robert W. "The First Minnesota at Gettysburg." *Gettysburg Magazine* 5 (July 1991): 79–88.

Mertz, Gregory A. "No Turning Back: The Battle of the Wilderness, Part II— The Fighting on May 6, 1864." *Blue and Gray Magazine* 12 (June 1995): 8–20, 48–50.

Michigan in the War. Compiled by Jno. Robertson. Lansing, Mich.: W. S. George, 1882.

Miller, J. Michael. *"Even to Hell Itself": The North Anna Campaign, May 21–26, 1864.* Lynchburg, Va.: H. E. Howard, 1989.

Miller, Richard F. *Harvard's Civil War: A History of the Twentieth Massachusetts Volunteer Infantry.* Hanover, N.H.: University Press of New England, 2005.

Miller, William J. *The Peninsula Campaign of 1862: Yorktown to the Seven Days.* Campbell, Calif.: Savas Woodbury, 1995.

———. *The Training of an Army: Camp Curtin and the North's Civil War.* Shippensburg, Pa.: White Mane Publishing, 1990.

Minnesota in the Civil and Indian Wars, 1861–1865. 2 vols. St. Paul, Minn.: Pioneer Press, 1890–93.

Mitchell, Reid. *Civil War Soldiers: Their Expectations and Their Experiences.* New York: Viking, 1988.

———. *The Vacant Chair: The Northern Soldier Leaves Home.* New York: Oxford University Press, 1993.

Moe, Richard. *The Last Full Measure: The Life and Death of the First Minnesota Volunteers.* New York: Henry Holt, 1993.

Mullis, Tony. *Peacekeeping on the Plains: Army Operations in Bleeding Kansas.* Columbia: University of Missouri Press, 2004.

Munroe, James Phinney. *A Life of Francis Amasa Walker.* New York: H. Holt, 1923.

Murfin, James V. *The Gleam of Bayonets: The Battle of Antietam and the Maryland Campaign of 1862.* New York: T. Yoseloff, 1965.

Myers, Irvin G. *We Might as Well Die Here: The 53d Pennsylvania Veteran Volunteer Infantry.* Shippensburg, Pa.: White Mane, 2004.

Myers, William Storr. *General George Brinton McClellan: A Study in Personality.* New York: D. Appleton-Century, 1934.

Naisawald, L. VanLoan. *Cannon Blasts: Civil War Artillery in the Eastern Armies.* Shippensburg, Pa.: White Mane, 2004.

———. *Grape and Canister: The Story of the Field Artillery of the Army of the Potomac, 1861–1865.* Mechanicsburg, Pa.: Stackpole, 1999.

Nash, Gary B. *The Urban Crucible: Social Change, Political Consciousness, and the Origins of the American Revolution.* Cambridge, Mass.: Harvard University Press, 1979.

Neff, John R. *Honoring the Civil War Dead: Commemoration and the Problem of Reconciliation.* Lawrence: University Press of Kansas, 2005.

Newton, Steven H. *The Battle of Seven Pines, May 31–June 1, 1862.* Lynchburg, Va.: H. E. Howard, 1993.

———. *Joseph E. Johnston and the Defense of Richmond.* Lawrence: University Press of Kansas, 1998.

Nolan, Alan T. *The Iron Brigade: A Military History*. New York: Macmillan, 1961.

O'Beirne, Kevin M. "Into the Valley of the Shadow of Death: The Corcoran Legion at Cold Harbor." *North and South* 3 (2000): 68–81.

O'Reilly, Francis A. *The Fredericksburg Campaign: Winter War on the Rappahannock*. Baton Rouge: Louisiana State University Press, 2003.

Overmyer, Jack K. *A Stupendous Effort: The 87th Indiana in the War of the Rebellion*. Bloomington: Indiana University Press, 1997.

Palfrey, Francis W. *The Antietam and Fredericksburg*. Reprint, New York: Da Capo Press, 1996.

Parsons, Phillip W. *The Union Sixth Army Corps in the Chancellorsville Campaign: A Study of the Engagements of Second Fredericksburg, Salem Church, and Banks's Ford, May 3–4, 1863*. Jefferson, N.C.: McFarland, 2006.

Patch, Joseph Dorst. *The Battle of Ball's Bluff*. Ed. Fitzhugh Turner. Leesburg, Va.: Potomac Press, 1958.

Perret, Geoffrey. *Ulysses S. Grant: Soldier and President*. New York: Random House, 1997.

Peskin, Allan. *Winfield Scott and the Profession of Arms*. Kent, Ohio: Kent State University Press, 2003.

Pfanz, Harry W. *Gettysburg—Culp's Hill and Cemetery Hill*. Chapel Hill: University of North Carolina Press, 1993.

———. *Gettysburg: The First Day*. Chapel Hill: University of North Carolina Press, 2001.

———. *Gettysburg: The Second Day*. Chapel Hill: University of North Carolina Press, 1987.

Phisterer, Frederick. *New York in the War of the Rebellion*. 6 vols. Albany: J. B. Lyon, State Printers, 1912.

Potter, David. *The Impending Crisis, 1848–1861*. New York: Harper and Row, 1976.

Pride, Mike, and Mark Travis. *My Brave Boys: To War with Colonel Cross and the Fighting Fifth*. Hanover, N.H.: University Press of New England, 2001.

Priest, John M. *Antietam: The Soldiers' Battle*. Shippensburg, Pa.: White Mane Publishing, 1989.

———. *Before Antietam: The Battle for South Mountain*. Shippensburg, Pa.: White Mane Publishing, 1992.

———. *Nowhere to Run: The Wilderness, May 4th and 5th, 1864*. Shippensburg, Pa.: White Mane Publishing, 1995.

———. *Victory without Triumph: The Wilderness, May 6th and 7th, 1864*. Shippensburg, Pa.: White Mane Publishing, 1996.

Prokopowicz, Gerald J. *All for the Regiment: The Army of the Ohio, 1861–1862*. Chapel Hill: University of North Carolina Press, 2001.

Rable, George C. *Fredericksburg! Fredericksburg!* Chapel Hill: University of North Carolina Press, 2002.

Rafuse, Ethan S. *McClellan's War: The Failure of Moderation in the Struggle for the Union*. Bloomington: Indiana University Press, 2005.

———. *A Single Grand Victory: The First Campaign and Battle of Manassas*. Wilmington, Del.: Scholarly Resources Books, 2002.

Raus, Edmund J., Jr. *A Generation on the March: The Union Army at Gettysburg*. Lynchburg, Va.: H. E. Howard, 1987.

Reardon, Carol. "The Forlorn Hope: Brig. Gen. Andrew A. Humphreys's Pennsylvania Division at Fredericksburg." In *The Fredericksburg Campaign: Decision on the Rappahannock*, ed. Gary W. Gallagher, 80–112. Chapel Hill: University of North Carolina Press, 1995.

———. "The Impact of Continuous Operations on the Army of the Potomac and the Army of Northern Virginia in May 1864." In *The Spotsylvania Campaign,* ed. Gary W. Gallagher, 170–202. Chapel Hill: University of North Carolina Press, 1998.

———. *Pickett's Charge in History and Memory.* Chapel Hill: University of North Carolina Press, 1997.

———. "The Valiant Rearguard: Hancock's Division at Chancellorsville." In *Chancellorsville: The Battle and Its Aftermath,* ed. Gary W. Gallagher, 143–75. Chapel Hill: University of North Carolina Press, 1996.

Rhea, Gordon. *The Battles for Spotsylvania Court House and the Road to Yellow Tavern, May 7–12, 1864.* Baton Rouge: Louisiana State University Press, 1997.

———. *The Battle of the Wilderness, May 5–6, 1864.* Baton Rouge: Louisiana State University Press, 1994.

———. *Cold Harbor: Grant and Lee, May 26–June 3, 1864.* Baton Rouge: Louisiana State University Press, 2002.

———. *To the North Anna River: Grant and Lee, May 13–25, 1864.* Baton Rouge: Louisiana State University Press, 2000.

Robertson, James I. *Soldiers Blue and Gray.* Columbia: University of South Carolina Press, 1988.

Rosentreter, Roger L. "Samuel Hodgman's Civil War." *Michigan History* 64 (November/December 1980): 34–38.

Rubin, Anne S. *A Shattered Nation: The Rise and Fall of the Confederacy, 1861–1868.* Chapel Hill: University of North Carolina Press, 2005.

Sauers, Richard A. *The Gettysburg Campaign, June 3–August 1, 1863: A Comprehensive, Selectively Annotated Bibliography.* Westport, Conn.: Greenwood Press, 1982.

———. "Laurels for Burnside: The Invasion of North Carolina, January–July 1862." *Blue and Gray* (May 1988): 8–20, 44–62.

Scott, Robert G. *Into the Wilderness with the Army of the Potomac.* Bloomington: Indiana University Press, 1985.

Sears, Stephen W. *Chancellorsville.* New York: Houghton Mifflin, 1996.

———. *Controversies and Commanders: Dispatches from the Army of the Potomac.* Boston: Houghton Mifflin, 1999.

———. *George B. McClellan: The Young Napoleon.* New York: Ticknor and Fields, 1988.

———. *Gettysburg.* Boston: Houghton Mifflin, 2003.

———. *Landscape Turned Red: The Battle of Antietam.* New Haven, Conn.: Ticknor and Fields, 1983.

———. *To the Gates of Richmond: The Peninsula Campaign.* New York: Houghton Mifflin, 1992.

Severo, Richard, and Lewis Milford. *The Wages of War: When America's Soldiers Came Home—From Valley Forge to Vietnam.* New York: Simon and Schuster, 1989.

Sewell, Richard. *Ballots for Freedom: Antislavery Politics in the United States, 1837–1860.* New York: Oxford University Press, 1976.

Shaffer, Donald R. *After the Glory: The Struggles of Black Civil War Veterans.* Lawrence: University Press of Kansas, 2004.

Shannon, Fred. A. *The Organization and Administration of the Union Army, 1861–1865.* 2 vols. Cleveland: Arthur H. Clark, 1928.

Simpson, Brooks D. *Ulysses S. Grant: Triumph over Adversity, 1822–1865.* Boston: Houghton Mifflin, 2000.

Skoch, George F. *Mine Run: A Campaign of Lost Opportunities, October 21, 1863–May 1, 1864.* Lynchburg, Va.: H. E. Howard, 1987.

Smith, Jean Edward. *Grant.* New York: Simon and Schuster, 2001.

Smith, Timothy. *This Great Battlefield of Shiloh: History, Memory, and the Establishment of a Civil War National Military Park*. Knoxville: University of Tennessee Press, 2004.

Spann, Edward K. *Gotham at War: New York City, 1860–1865*. Wilmington, Del.: Scholarly Resources, 2002.

Stackpole, Edward J. *Chancellorsville: Lee's Greatest Battle*. Harrisburg, Pa.: Stackpole, 1958.

——. *The Fredericksburg Campaign: Drama on the Rappahannock*. Harrisburg, Pa.: Stackpole Books, 1957.

——. *From Cedar Mountain to Antietam, August–September 1862*. Harrisburg, Pa.: Stackpole, 1952.

Stampp, Kenneth. *America in 1857: A Nation on the Brink*. New York: Oxford University Press, 1990.

Starr, Stephen Z. *The Union Cavalry in the Civil War*. 3 vols. Baton Rouge: Louisiana State University Press, 1979–85.

Steere, Edward. *The Wilderness Campaign*. Harrisburg, Pa.: Stackpole, 1960.

Stewart, George R. *Pickett's Charge: A Microhistory of the Final Attack at Gettysburg, July 3, 1863*. Boston: Houghton Mifflin, 1959.

Suderow, Bryce A. "Glory Denied: The First Battle of Deep Bottom, July 27–29, 1864." *North and South* 3, no. 7 (September 2000): 17–30.

——. "'Nothing but a Miracle Could Save Us': Second Battle of Deep Bottom, Virginia, August 14–20, 1864." *North and South* 4, no. 2 (January 2001): 12–32.

Sutherland, Daniel E. *Fredericksburg and Chancellorsville: The Dare Mark Campaign*. Lincoln: University of Nebraska Press, 1998.

Swinton, William. *Campaigns of the Army of the Potomac: A Critical History of Operations in Virginia, Maryland, and Pennsylvania, from the Commencement to the Close of the War, 1861–5*. New York: Charles Scribner's Sons, 1882.

Taaffe, Stephen R. *Commanding the Army of the Potomac*. Lawrence: University Press of Kansas, 2006.

Tap, Bruce. *Over Lincoln's Shoulder: The Committee on the Conduct of the War*. Lawrence: University Press of Kansas, 1998.

Taylor, Emerson G. *Gouverneur Kemble Warren*. Boston: Houghton Mifflin, 1932.

Thelan, David. "Memory and American History." *Journal of American History* 75 (March 1989): 1117–29.

Townshend, David G. *The Seventh Michigan Volunteer Infantry: The Gallant Men and Flag in the Civil War, 1861 to 1865*. Fort Lauderdale, Fla.: Southeast Publications, 1994.

Trudeau, Noah Andre. *The Last Citadel: Petersburg, Virginia, June 1864–April 1865*. Baton Rouge: Louisiana State University Press, 1991.

Tucker, Glenn. *Hancock the Superb*. Indianapolis: Bobbs-Merrill, 1960.

Walker, Francis A. *General Hancock*. New York: D. Appleton, 1894.

Wallace, Mike. *Gotham: A History of New York City to 1898*. New York: Oxford University Press, 1999.

Warner, Ezra J. *Generals in Blue: Lives of Union Commanders*. Baton Rouge: Louisiana State University Press, 1964.

Waugh, John C. *Reelecting Lincoln: The Battle for the 1864 Presidency*. New York: Crown, 1997.

Webb, Alexander S. *The Peninsula: McClellan's Campaign of 1862*. New York: Charles Scribner's Sons, 1881.

Wecter, Dixon. *When Johnny Comes Marching Home*. Cambridge, Mass.: Houghton Mifflin, 1944.

Weigley, Russell F. "The Border City in the Civil War, 1854–1865." *Philadelphia: A 300-Year History*. Ed. Russell

F. Weigley, 363–416. New York: W. W. Norton, 1982.

———. *A Great Civil War: A Military and Political History, 1861–1865*. Bloomington: Indiana University Press, 2000.

Weland, Gerald. *O. O. Howard, Union General*. Jefferson, N.C.: McFarland, 1995.

Welcher, Frank J. *The Union Army*. 2 vols. Bloomington: Indiana University Press, 1989.

Welsh, Jack D. *Medical Histories of Union Generals*. Kent, Ohio: Kent State University Press, 1996.

Wert, Jeffry D. *A Brotherhood of Valor: The Common Soldiers of the Stonewall Brigade, C.S.A., and the Iron Brigade, U.S.A.* New York: Simon and Schuster, 1999.

———. *From Winchester to Cedar Creek: The Shenandoah Campaign of 1864*. New York: Simon and Schuster, 1989.

———. *General James Longstreet: The Confederacy's Most Controversial Soldier*. New York: Simon and Schuster, 1993.

———. *The Sword of Lincoln: The Army of the Potomac*. New York: Simon and Schuster, 2005.

Whan, Vorin E. *Fiasco at Fredericksburg*. University Park: Pennsylvania State University Press, 1961.

Wiley, Bell I. *The Life of Billy Yank: The Common Soldier of the Union*. Indianapolis: Bobbs-Merrill, 1952.

———. *The Life of Johnny Reb: The Common Soldier of the Confederacy*. Indianapolis: Bobbs-Merrill, 1943.

Williams, T. Harry. *Lincoln and His Generals*. New York: Alfred A. Knopf, 1952.

———. *Lincoln and the Radicals*. Madison: University of Wisconsin Press, 1941.

Wilson, Edmund. *Patriotic Gore: Studies of Literature in the American Civil War*. New York: Oxford University Press, 1962.

Winslow, Richard Elliott, III. *General John Sedgwick: The Story of a Union Corps Commander*. Novato, Calif.: Presidio Press, 1982.

Wolff, Gerald W. *The Kansas-Nebraska Bill: Party, Section, and the Coming of the Civil War*. New York: Revisionist Press, 1977.

Woodworth, Steven. *Beneath a Northern Sky: A Short History of the Gettysburg Campaign*. Wilmington, Del.: SR Books, 2003.

———. *Nothing but Victory: The Army of the Tennessee, 1861–1865*. New York: Alfred A. Knopf, 2005.

———. *While God Is Marching On: The Religious World of Civil War Soldiers*. Lawrence: University Press of Kansas, 2001.

INDEX

LAWRENCE A. KREISER, JR., is Associate Professor of History at Stillman College, a historically black college located in Tuscaloosa, Alabama. He is co-author of *The Civil War and Reconstruction* and *Voices of Civil War America: Contemporary Accounts of Daily Life*.